C. L. Ballard

United States Tax Reform in the 21st Century

Tax reform debates in the United States have for some time been dominated by the issue of fundamental tax reform – whether the existing corporate and individual income tax system should be replaced with some form of a national consumption tax. This book contains essays by a group of internationally recognized tax experts who describe the current state of the art in economic thinking on the question of whether fundamental tax reform is preferable to continued incremental reform of the existing income tax. The ten chapters in the volume were originally commissioned by the James A. Baker III Institute for Public Policy at Rice University, Houston, Texas. The collection covers a wide range of tax policy issues related to consumption tax reforms, including their economic effects, distributional consequences, effects on administrative and compliance costs, transitional issues, the political aspects of fundamental tax reform, and international experience with consumption taxes. The book will serve as a comprehensive guide to the ongoing tax reform debate to tax policy makers, scholars, and the general electorate.

George R. Zodrow is Professor of Economics at Rice University; he chaired the Department of Economics in 1995–2000. He served as a staff economist at the U.S. Treasury Office of Tax Analysis in 1984–85 and participated in the preparation of "Treasury I," the precursor to the Tax Reform Act of 1986. Professor Zodrow's articles on taxation have appeared in leading journals such as the *Journal of Public Economics*, *National Tax Journal*, *International Tax and Public Finance*, *Tax Law Review*, the *Journal of Economic Perspectives*, and the *Journal of Economic Literature*, and he has written numerous book chapters on taxation. He is the author of *State Sales and Income Taxes: An Economic Analysis* and coauthor of *The Taxation of Income from Business and Capital in Colombia*, and he is currently working on a variety of issues related to consumption taxation, the incidence of the property tax, and the taxation of electronic commerce. Professor Zodrow has also served as a consultant on tax reform issues to the World Bank and the Agency for International Development, and he has been involved in taxation projects in numerous countries, including Bolivia, China, Colombia, Egypt, Mexico, Russia, and Venezuela.

Peter Mieszkowski has been the Cline Professor of Economics at Rice University since 1981; he previously held faculty positions at Yale University (1962–71), Queen's University, Ontario (1971–74), and the University of Houston (1974–81). He has served as associate editor of the *Journal of Public Economics* and the *Journal of Urban Economics*, and he is currently an associate editor of *Public Finance Quarterly*. A book of his selected essays was recently published under the title *Taxes, Public Goods and Urban Economics*. Professor Mieszkowski's current research interests deal with the measurement of the relative skill intensities of different industries and the effects of international trade on the relative wages of skilled and unskilled workers. He is also working on the efficiency of wage subsidies as an instrument of income maintenance and on the design of a hybrid indirect consumption tax. He has served as a consultant to various public agencies including the U.S. Treasury, Housing and Urban Development Department, the World Bank, and the Polish Finance Ministry.

United States Tax Reform in the 21st Century

Edited by

GEORGE R. ZODROW

Rice University

PETER MIESZKOWSKI

Rice University

PUBLISHED BY THE PRESS SYNDICATE OF THE UNIVERSITY OF CAMBRIDGE
The Pitt Building, Trumpington Street, Cambridge, United Kingdom

CAMBRIDGE UNIVERSITY PRESS
The Edinburgh Building, Cambridge CB2 2RU, UK
40 West 20th Street, New York, NY 10011-4211, USA
477 Williamstown Road, Port Melbourne, VIC 3207, Australia
Ruiz de Alarcón 13, 28014 Madrid, Spain
Dock House, The Waterfront, Cape Town 8001, South Africa

http://www.cambridge.org

© George R. Zodrow and Peter Mieszkowski 2002

First published 2002

Printed in the United States of America

Typeface   Times New Roman 10/12 pt.   *System* QuarkXPress [BTS]

A catalog record for this book is available from the British Library.

Library of Congress Cataloging in Publication data
United States tax reform in the 21st century / edited by George R. Zodrow,
Peter Mieszkowski.
    p.   cm.
  Includes bibliographical references and index.
  ISBN 0-521-80383-7
  1. Taxation – United States.   2. Income tax – United States.   3. Spendings tax
– United States.   I. Zodrow, George R.   II. Mieszkowski, Peter M.
HJ2381 .U575 2002
336.2′00973 – dc21   2001037348

ISBN   0 521 80383 7   hardback

With special thanks to our mentors, colleagues, and friends,

Charlie McLure
and
Richard Musgrave

Contents

Contributors

Charles L. Ballard
Michigan State University

Joe Barnes
Rice University

Sijbren Cnossen
Erasmus University Rotterdam

William G. Gale
The Brookings Institution

Malcolm Gillis
Rice University

Jane G. Gravelle
Congressional Research Service

Janet Holtzblatt
U.S. Department of the Treasury

R. Glenn Hubbard
Columbia University

Dale W. Jorgenson
Harvard University

Peter Mieszkowski
Rice University

ix

Michael G. Palumbo
University of Houston

Peter J. Wilcoxen
University of Texas at Austin

George R. Zodrow
Rice University

Preface

Tax reform debates in the United States have for some time been dominated by the question of whether the existing corporate and individual income tax system should be replaced with some form of a national consumption tax. Although opinion is far from unanimous, a wide variety of individuals in the academic, business, and government communities has long advocated such a reform, and Congress has recently been inundated with a host of consumption-based tax reform proposals. Nevertheless, the likelihood of passage of such "fundamental tax reform" currently does not seem particularly high. Thus a natural question is why the enactment of a consumption-based tax does not appear to be a viable tax reform option for the new millennium, despite the fact that the virtues of consumption taxation have been actively promoted, at least in some circles, for more than twenty-five years.

This critical issue is addressed in this volume, which contains essays by a group of internationally recognized tax experts who describe the current state of the art in economic thinking on the issue of whether fundamental tax reform is preferable to continued incremental reform of the existing income tax. The ten essays were commissioned by the James A. Baker III Institute for Public Policy at Rice University and were initially presented at a conference on Tax Reform for the Millennium held on November 5–6, 1998, at the Baker Institute on the campus of Rice University in Houston. The volume covers a wide range of tax policy issues and can serve as a comprehensive guide to the ongoing tax reform debate to both tax policy makers and the general electorate, as well as to the many individuals in academia, the business world, and the political arena who are following – and, in many cases, affecting the course of – this critical and highly publicized debate.

This volume and the conference that preceded it would not have been possible without the sponsorship of the Baker Institute for Public Policy at Rice. We especially would like to thank Baker Institute Director

Edward Djerejian and Associate Director Ric Stoll for their support of both the conference and this volume, as well as longtime Rice University benefactors Gordon and Mary Cain for their generous financial support of the tax policy conference. Finally, we would like to thank John Diamond and Craig Johnson for help with a wide variety of tasks associated with the conference and the volume, and especially Elisabeth Gugl, whose cheerful yet painstaking editorial assistance was absolutely critical to the preparation of the book.

Chapter 1

Introduction: The Fundamental Question in Fundamental Tax Reform

George R. Zodrow and Peter Mieszkowski

Should the United States adopt a "fundamental tax reform" in the form of replacing its current personal and corporate income tax system with some form of consumption-based taxation? This question has been the central issue of debates on tax reform for the past twenty-five years. The discussion was kindled by a seminal article by Andrews (1974), who extolled the administrative advantages of taxation based on consumption rather than income. Shortly thereafter, the U.S. Treasury (1977) issued its much-cited report *Blueprints for Basic Tax Reform*, which described in detail the merits of consumption taxes relative to income taxes and discussed alternative methods of implementing consumption taxation; similar studies favorable to consumption-based taxes were published contemporaneously in Great Britain (Institute for Fiscal Studies, 1978), Australia (Matthews Committee, 1975), and Sweden (Lodin, 1978). These contributions were followed by the influential flat tax proposal developed by Hall and Rabushka (1983, [1985] 1995) and related studies in the U.S. and elsewhere, including Aaron and Galper (1985), Bradford (1986), McLure et al. (1990), R. Hall (1995), Weidenbaum (1996), McLure and Zodrow (1996a), and Seidman (1997).[1] All of these studies argue that consumption-based tax systems are inherently superior to a tax system based on income in terms of the three standard criteria public finance economists use to evaluate alternative tax systems – efficiency, equity, and simplicity.[2]

Scholarly interest in fundamental tax reform has been accompanied by heightened political interest in replacing the income tax with a consumption tax. Indeed, in the United States, Washington has been inun-

---

[1] For recent discussions of the relative merits of economic effects of consumption tax reforms, see the articles in the volumes edited by Boskin (1996) and Aaron and Gale (1996).

[2] For a summary of these arguments, see Zodrow and McLure (1991).

1

dated in recent years with proposals for consumption-based tax reforms. Early proposals included the "Business Activities Tax" supported by Senators Danforth and Boren, a subtraction-method value-added tax (VAT) proposed by Representative Gibbons, and the "Unlimited Saving Allowance" (USA) Tax advocated by Senators Nunn and Domenici. More recently, attention has focused on the Hall-Rabushka flat tax as well as proposals for a national retail sales tax (NRST). In particular, versions of the flat tax have been proposed by Representative Armey and Senator Shelby and by Senator Specter, and Representatives Schaefer and Tauzin have introduced a proposal for an NRST, which is similar to a plan developed by the lobbying group Americans for Fair Taxation. Nevertheless, despite considerable interest and support among many (although by no means all) academic and business economists as well as some governmental officials, a direct consumption tax has never been adopted in an industrialized country. Moreover, the chances of passage of such a reform in the United States currently do not seem to be great, and no other country is particularly close to enacting a consumption-based direct tax system.[3]

The essays in this volume examine in considerable detail the relative merits of the current income tax and various proposals for fundamental tax reform, including the flat tax and the NRST, as well as reform of the existing income tax system. The authors attempt to identify both issues on which a consensus has developed as well as areas in which there is still considerable dispute. Many provide surveys of the existing literature, focusing in particular on what we have learned in the years since the Armey-Shelby flat tax was initially introduced in July 1995. More specifically, they provide a comprehensive examination of the fundamental question of tax reform – why the enactment of a consumption-based tax does not currently appear to be a viable tax reform option in the United States or elsewhere. In our view, this state of affairs exists primarily because the case for a consumption tax reform is still perceived to be rather tenuous in many quarters – especially in the political arena – despite the claims of the many advocates of fundamental tax reform. Questions can be raised in at least five important areas:

---

[3] It should be noted, however, that the United States has significantly hampered efforts at the enactment of consumption-based tax reforms in several other countries, as it has clearly indicated that it would deny foreign tax credits for U.S.-based multinationals for a foreign business cash flow tax, a key element of virtually all consumption tax reform proposals. The prospect of enacting a tax that would not be creditable in the United States has dissuaded several countries from pursuing consumption tax reforms. For further discussion, including a detailed exposition of the case for creditability of the cash flow tax, see McLure and Zodrow (1998).

1. Would significant economic benefits follow replacement of the current income tax with a consumption tax?
2. Are the distributional implications of most consumption tax reform proposals unfavorable?
3. Would considerable gains in administrative and compliance simplicity be obtained with a consumption tax reform, especially relative to alternative reforms of the current income tax system?
4. Even if a consumption tax reform generated sizable long-run gains, would the transitional costs associated with such a sweeping reform of the existing tax structure be prohibitively large?
5. Would the enactment of fundamental tax reform pose a formidable political problem far greater than that associated with large-scale incremental changes of the current income tax system?

Each of these five issues is addressed by one or more of the contributions in this volume. Together they provide an insightful and provocative perspective on the problems that have thus far prevented the implementation of fundamental tax reform in the United States.

THE ECONOMIC EFFECTS OF FUNDAMENTAL TAX REFORM

Various well-known economic simulation models have suggested that the economic gains from a consumption tax reform might be very large, with long-run increases in GDP on the order of 10 percent, coupled with smaller but still quite significant gains in economic welfare. Many observers, however, argue that economic effects of this magnitude require tax-induced responses in saving and labor supply that are far beyond those found in the empirical literature. Moreover, these models do not adequately consider all of the complicating features of the current tax system, including some of the details of the tax treatment of different types of capital income and a variety of difficult issues in the complex area of international taxation. Four of the chapters in the volume address these critical issues.

Behavioral Effects

In a far-ranging contribution to the volume, Jane Gravelle surveys various attempts – including some of her own – to model the effects of implementing consumption and income tax reforms. In particular, Gravelle considers two general types of dynamic models of tax reform – life-cycle overlapping generations models and models that assume infinitely lived representative individuals. The range of results obtained by such models is large, with some versions of both types predicting that adoption of a consumption tax will lead to sizable changes in output in both the short and long runs, while other versions predict more modest changes. Gravelle discusses the differences in model specification and parameter value choices that lead to such variance. In examining the effects of a change from a 20 percent income tax to either a flat consumption tax or a flat wage tax, for example, Engen, Gravelle, and Smetters (1997) show that models without a large labor supply elasticity cannot yield large output changes in the short run, as the size of the capital stock must change slowly over time, even with large saving responses. Gravelle also notes that although many models are characterized by large labor supply elasticities, the sources of these large elasticities are somewhat surprising. Specifically, in addition to responding to increases in after-tax wages, individuals increase their labor supply in response to a reform-induced increase in the after-tax return to capital; that is, individuals work more because the return to working and then saving the earnings has increased. She argues that there is no empirical evidence to support such a labor supply response to changes in the after-tax rate of return. In addition, she notes that labor supply is more elastic in these models if the initial amount of leisure is large relative to time spent at work, although this variable is typically set arbitrarily. Finally, Gravelle observes that labor supply increases in some models reflect a significant increase in hours worked on the part of the retired, which she argues is implausible. For all of these reasons, she concludes that models that predict large increases in labor supply in response to a consumption tax reform should be viewed with considerable skepticism.

Gravelle then draws on the simulation experiments of Engen et al. to argue that savings responses are also implausibly large in both the life-cycle and especially the infinite horizon dynamic models, which typically have implied savings elasticities in the neighborhood of 3 to 4. She argues that such large responses are also inconsistent with existing empirical evidence and thus significantly overstate the extent to which savings and investment would respond to the implementation of a consumption tax. For example, she notes that Engen et al. show that reduced form growth models that incorporate the savings elasticities found in the empirical literature find savings responses roughly one-tenth of those predicted by many of the life-cycle or infinite horizon models, with similar reductions in predicted output changes in the first four to five years following reform.[4] Finally, Gravelle stresses that most models used to analyze con-

---

[4] Gravelle also identifies and discusses other differences among the various models that give rise to differences in their predictions about the effects of fundamental tax reform. Such factors include differences in assumptions about the degree of foresight possessed by individuals and firms, the modeling of uncertainty, bequest motives, the modeling of the existing tax system, the number of production sectors included in the model, transition provisions, and the extent to which the model is assumed to be open to capital flows.

sumption tax reforms neglect adjustment costs, including those associated with wage, price, and employment changes such as those that would
occur in response to the dramatic changes in the locus of tax collections
implied by many consumption tax reforms, especially the VAT and the
NRST.

Gravelle concludes that the enactment of fundamental tax reform is
a questionable tax policy, as the costs of short-run disruptions could be
significant and the magnitudes of the benefits are unclear, especially if
one focuses on welfare gains rather than simply increases in output.
Moreover, she argues that much of the efficiency gains that might be
obtained with a consumption tax reform could also be achieved with
reform of the existing income tax system, which would involve fewer
short-run disruptions and more certain benefits. Accordingly, she concludes that incremental reform of the income tax system is preferable to
fundamental tax reform.

The Jorgenson-Wilcoxen Infinite-Horizon Model

The most widely cited version of the infinite-horizon modeling approach
discussed by Gravelle is the computer simulation model constructed by
Dale Jorgenson and Peter Wilcoxen (1997, and in Norland and Ninassi,
1998). In their contribution to this volume, Jorgenson and Wilcoxen
utilize the model to analyze the effects of enacting fundamental tax
reform and conclude that the enactment of a consumption tax reform
might result in huge macroeconomic gains in the U.S. economy. They
examine the effects of replacing all federal, state, and local income taxes
with either a flat tax (which includes a standard deduction and personal
exemptions) or a comprehensive retail sales tax with no exemptions or
tax rebates whatsoever. Their complex model includes a highly disaggregated representation of both the production and consumption sectors
of the economy, and includes a detailed description of the effects of the
tax system on firm and individual decisions. Consumer behavior is
modeled assuming infinitely lived individuals, rather than the more
common life-cycle approach.[5] In addition, the Jorgenson-Wilcoxen
model differs from other models in the literature in that many of the
essential production and consumption parameter values are estimated
econometrically from many years of data, rather than taken from the
econometric literature in the construction of a single "calibrated benchmark" equilibrium. Jorgensen and Wilcoxen also assume a relatively high
value of 1 for the intertemporal elasticity of substitution in their model,

[5] Their model can thus not be used to analyze the intergenerational redistributive effects
of reform.

which, as described by Gravelle, tends to result in large savings responses, especially because consumers in their model are infinitely lived.

The effects of enacting a consumption tax reform in the Jorgenson-Wilcoxen model are most striking in the case of the pure flat-rate national retail sales tax (with no exemptions or tax rebates). Domestic output (GDP) increases by 13 percent in the short run and by 9 percent in the long run. This increase is attributable primarily to a surge in investment that is initially nearly 80 percent and declines in the long run to roughly 16.5 percent, as well as an increase in labor supply that initially approaches 30 percent and eventually declines to roughly 15 percent. As stressed by Gravelle, such huge reform-induced responses, although typical of infinite-horizon models, are difficult to reconcile with the much lower responsiveness of labor supply and savings that characterizes the empirical literature.

By comparison, the enactment of the flat tax (with a standard deduction and personal exemptions) gives rise to dramatically smaller economic effects in the Jorgenson-Wilcoxen model. Under the flat tax, domestic output (GDP) increases by only 0.6 percent in the short run and by 1.3 percent in the long run, with investment actually declining in both the short and long runs (although consumption increases) and labor supply increasing relatively modestly – by 2 percent initially and by 5 percent in the long run. They stress that these dramatic differences between the two tax plans arise because (1) the tax rate is significantly higher under the flat tax (25 percent) than under the retail sales tax (15.7 percent), because the personal exemptions and standard deductions of the flat tax must be financed; and (2), in their highly disaggregated model of the production side of the economy, the relative price of investment goods falls much more in the case of the retail sales tax than under the flat tax. The latter effect is important enough in their model that investment falls under the flat tax, even though that reform (like the retail sales tax) implies that the marginal effective tax rate on investment goods falls to zero. As noted by Gravelle, the negative effect of the flat tax on investment is quite surprising, given that Jorgenson and Wilcoxen assume a relatively high intertemporal elasticity of substitution and infinitely lived consumers – factors that typically give rise to large increases in saving in response to a consumption tax reform, as in fact occurs in their simulation of the effects of the retail sales tax.

The Taxation of Capital Income under Income and Consumption Taxes

Most of the models reviewed by Gravelle, including the work of Jorgenson and Wilcoxen, share two common features: they assume perfectly competitive markets and ignore risk and uncertainty. In this context, consumption taxes differ dramatically from income taxes in that the former exempt all capital income from taxation, whereas full taxation of capital income is an essential element of an (ideal) income tax. In his contribution to the volume, Glenn Hubbard argues that this interpretation of the relative effects of income and consumption taxes is highly misleading once one considers (1) market imperfections that give rise to inframarginal returns to saving and investment, and (2) returns to risk taking in models characterized by risk and uncertainty.

Hubbard's novel perspective stresses that the primary difference between a proportional income tax and a proportional consumption tax is that capital is depreciated under the former and immediately expensed under the latter. He notes that expensing is sufficiently generous to exempt only the riskless rate of return to saving and investment. By comparison, inframarginal returns generated by innovative ideas, managerial skills, or market power, as well as the expected and unexpected returns to risk taking, are taxed similarly under consumption and income taxation. Thus, the differences between the two taxes are not as great as sometimes claimed, which implies that many of the economic gains that a consumption tax reform offers could also be attained with suitable reforms of the income tax. Moreover, Hubbard's insight has important implications for the distributional effects of fundamental tax reform. He notes that the holdings of assets likely to generate inframarginal returns are concentrated among the wealthy. As a result, distributional analyses that simply assume that all capital income is exempt under a consumption tax may significantly overstate the extent to which such a reform will reduce the progressivity of the tax system, because inframarginal returns will be taxed under both tax systems.

Hubbard also notes that the life-cycle models of savings that are typically used to analyze the effects of fundamental tax reform do not do a good job in explaining the size of the aggregate capital stock. In particular, these models cannot explain the high rate of savings of high-income or high-net-worth individuals. He argues that these high savings rates are related to the entrepreneurial activities of such individuals. In particular, he argues that actual or potential entrepreneurs tend to save a disproportionately large fraction of their income, in response to the prospect of very high rates of return ("instant wealth") to their entrepreneurial investments and because the cost of external finance is relatively high for entrepreneurial ventures. Such saving is not likely to be very responsive to reform-induced changes in after-tax normal returns to capital, which in turn implies that aggregate savings may be much less responsive to the enactment of a consumption tax than predicted by the life-cycle model. By comparison, Hubbard notes that entrepreneurial saving is more likely to be stimulated by increased cash flow than by increased rates of return, which in turn implies that tax rate reductions, especially at the high end of the income distribution, are the most effective tool for stimulating entrepreneurial saving. Such rate reductions (including those applied to capital gains) could of course be achieved under an income tax reform as easily as under a consumption tax reform.

International Aspects

Most of the models utilized to analyze the economic effects of fundamental tax reform either assume that the United States is a closed economy, or have a relatively primitive modeling of the international sector and the tax treatment of international trade and capital flows. In his contribution to the volume, Charles Ballard explores the international ramifications of fundamental tax reform in considerable detail, focusing on two main issues.

The first is the tax treatment of international firms under the current income tax, which is often cited as the source of the most complex provisions of the tax code. Ballard first describes many of the intricacies of international tax law, including provisions for crediting foreign taxes and the definitions of separate "baskets" or different types of foreign-source income subject to differing tax treatments. He then discusses the considerable administrative simplifications in international taxation that would arise from the adoption of consumption-based taxes like the flat tax or the NRST; both of these taxes provide for the taxation of foreign source income on a territorial basis, effectively exempting such income from tax.

The second main issue Ballard addresses is the effects of introducing capital mobility into general equilibrium simulation models of fundamental tax reform, including the extent to which labor rather than capital owners benefit from the enactment of a consumption tax. In discussing the empirical evidence on the sensitivity of foreign investment to rates of return and tax differentials, he observes that various studies have demonstrated that a country's rate of investment is highly correlated with its rate of savings, suggesting that international capital is imperfectly mobile; however, this correlation has weakened in recent years, indicating that international capital is becoming more mobile as globalization progresses. Ballard also discusses recent studies that show that foreign direct investment is responsive to taxes but not to the extent that would be implied by perfect capital mobility. He concludes that international capital is responsive to tax effects, but that the empirical evidence implies that capital is imperfectly mobile internationally and that there is a bias toward investing savings domestically.

Ballard stresses that these issues are central to the analysis of the incidence of the corporate income tax in an open economy. If capital were perfectly mobile across national borders, the brunt of the corporate profits tax in the United States would be borne by domestic labor rather than by the owners of capital. As a result, labor rather than capital would gain when the corporate tax was eliminated as part of fundamental tax reform, which in turn implies that the distributional effects of reform would be less regressive than implied by a closed-economy analysis. This effect is reinforced to the extent that domestic and foreign products are imperfect substitutes. He estimates that capital bears only between 50 and 75 percent of the burden of the corporate income tax in the short to medium run and notes that the capital share of the tax burden decreases over time if the international supply of capital declines in response to the decrease in the rate of return to saving and investing.

Finally, Ballard considers general equilibrium simulation models of fundamental tax reform. Looking first at closed-economy models, he concurs with Gravelle that many current models are characterized by unreasonably large saving and labor supply responses, and their results should be viewed with caution. He concludes that the plausible range of estimates of the aggregate welfare gain from implementing a consumption tax lies in the range of 1 to 3 percent of GDP. Ballard stresses that the effects of "opening" these models to international capital flows depend on the net effect of reform on rates of return; as long as this effect is positive, as would be expected under fundamental tax reform, then international capital flows tend to increase reform-induced welfare gains. However, because any such effects are likely to be modest, Ballard concludes that international considerations strengthen the case for fundamental tax reform but only to a moderate extent.

DISTRIBUTIONAL EFFECTS OF FUNDAMENTAL TAX REFORM

A second critical issue that has significantly hampered efforts to enact fundamental tax reform is a pervasive concern about the distributional implications of enacting a consumption tax. A few tax reform proposals have attempted to circumvent this issue by following the lead of the Tax Reform Act of 1986 in the United States and designing an individual consumption tax with a progressive rate structure that is "distributionally neutral" in the sense of replicating the burden of the current tax system across income groups.[6] But it is impossible to replace a progressive

---

[6] The USA Tax proposed by Senators Nunn and Domenici is a prominent example of this approach.

income tax and a corporate income tax that falls disproportionately on high-income groups with a flat-rate consumption tax without affecting the distribution of after-tax income. In particular, although low-income groups can be protected from any adverse effects of reform by means of exemptions or tax rebates, the tax burden on the broadly defined middle class must increase while the tax burden on the wealthy must decline under such a tax reform. This result has been confirmed by analyses in which households are classified according to either annual or lifetime income and in simulation studies that account for reform-induced gains in economic growth and efficiency. Such distributional effects are very controversial, especially at a time when income at the upper end of the income distribution is growing relatively rapidly, widening the gap between the wealthy and lower- and middle-income households. Thus, any tax reform proposal that involves a significant redistribution of tax burden from the very wealthy to middle-income families will inevitably be highly controversial.[7]

In their contribution to the volume, Peter Mieszkowski and Michael Palumbo review the existing literature on the distributional effects of fundamental tax reform, including their own current research that focuses on understanding differences in saving behavior at different income levels – with saving increasing with income, especially at very high income levels – to predict better the effects of consumption tax reforms.

Mieszkowski and Palumbo note that either a flat tax or an NRST will reduce the tax burden on upper-income groups, especially the very wealthy, at the expense of middle- (and perhaps lower-) income groups because the progressivity of the rate structure is reduced, the corporate income tax is eliminated, and the switch to a consumption rather than an income base disproportionately benefits the very wealthy.

These results depend to differing degrees, however, on three key assumptions that are typically made in such studies. First, households are generally categorized according to annual income; many consumption tax proponents argue that a lifetime income measure is more appropriate, and such an approach would reduce the apparent regressivity of taxes based on consumption. Second, these studies often assume that the corporate income tax is borne by capital owners. However, if fundamental tax reform were to increase capital flows to the United States (as

---

[7] A separate issue is the extent to which the various alternatives are perceived to be fair, even if their economic effects are quite similar. For example, under the flat tax, the explicit exemption of capital income under a system that looks much like the current income tax may create a perception of unfairness that will be exceedingly difficult to overcome in the political arena.

suggested in the chapter by Ballard), the resulting increase in wages would benefit the owners of labor rather than capital and thus act to offset the regressive impact of reform. Third, many studies allocate the tax burden of consumption taxes according to consumption; however, some observers argue that an allocation according to factor income would be more appropriate and would also reduce the apparent regressivity of taxes based on consumption.

Mieszkowski and Palumbo also make the case for allocating the burden of a consumption tax according to consumption rather than factor income. The latter approach has been used in several recent studies, primarily to capture the fact that the imposition of a consumption tax effectively applies tax to the owners of existing capital. Mieszkowski and Palumbo argue, however, that such an approach is appropriate only if individuals are subject to a strict life-cycle budget constraint. They provide evidence that this assumption is invalid, especially for the very wealthy; in particular, they describe a number of studies that demonstrate that wealth decumulation with age – an essential characteristic of the life-cycle model – does not characterize the behavior of the very wealthy. Under such circumstances, they argue that allocating tax burdens according to consumption is more accurate than allocating them according to factor income, as the latter approach will overstate the tax burden imposed on the very wealthy.

This argument is not inconsistent with Hubbard's important observation that some types of capital income – specifically economic rents and the expected and unexpected returns to risk taking – continue to be taxed under a consumption tax exactly as they are under an income tax. However, Mieszkowski and Palumbo stress that this income is taxed only when it is consumed. For a personal consumption tax, rents earned on a particular investment are reported as the cash flow income of the individual. If the individual saves all of this income, no consumption tax is paid and any tax liability on these rents is deferred until this wealth is consumed. This is in marked contrast to an income tax where economic rents are taxed as they accrue independently of whether they are consumed or saved. This point applies to all forms of consumption-based taxation.

Mieszkowski and Palumbo conclude that existing studies of the distributional effects of a consumption tax reform, including their own recent work, demonstrate that the existing income tax system is broadly proportional with respect to annual income over a large range of the income distribution, but becomes quite progressive at the highest income levels. They argue that a pure flat-rate, consumption-based tax system would have negative effects on the lowest income classes, but this effect could be eliminated with the addition of exemptions or tax rebates. In either case (and especially in the latter), however, a consumption tax would reduce taxes significantly on the very wealthy at the expense of higher tax burdens on a broadly defined middle class. On the other hand, they also stress that general equilibrium studies that account for behavioral responses in saving and labor supply are less likely to indicate reform-induced losses for the middle classes if such responses are large enough.

SIMPLICITY GAINS FROM FUNDAMENTAL TAX REFORM

A third issue is the magnitude of the simplicity and compliance cost gains that might be obtained with fundamental tax reform. Consumption tax proponents often stress that its cash flow approach to tax accounting is inherently simpler than the accrual approach that underlies the income tax. In particular, the inflation adjustment and timing issues (e.g., the measurement of depreciation, inventory accounting, calculation of capital gains, multiperiod accounting) that plague the income tax largely disappear under the consumption tax. However, inflation adjustment is a relatively minor problem in today's low-inflation environment; moreover, even consumption taxes cannot escape all timing issues, as losses (more accurately, negative cash flows) under an appropriately designed business cash flow tax must be carried forward with interest, and the determination of the appropriate interest rate would be a contentious issue, especially in an inflationary environment. In addition, many observers have noted that much of the simplicity of current consumption tax proposals could be obtained with appropriate reforms of the existing income tax.

The potential administrative and compliance cost savings that might be obtained under fundamental tax reform are subject to considerable debate, and the magnitude of such gains depends very much on the specific form of consumption tax chosen. Most observers agree that there would be substantial compliance cost savings associated with the adoption of a flat tax. For example, Slemrod (1996) estimates that the social costs of complying with this relatively simple tax would be about $35 billion, less than half of his estimate of the cost of complying with the personal and corporate tax systems of $75 billion. On the other hand, Slemrod maintains that an NRST is not administrable at a reasonable rate of compliance without an intolerable level of intrusion by the tax enforcement agency. Although this is an extreme position, there is no experience with a high-rate NRST, and the mechanisms for administrating and auditing an NRST have not been developed; thus, the compliance cost savings of the adoption of an NRST are highly uncertain. By comparison, there is a wealth of experience around the world with the value-added tax (VAT), a tax that is economically similar to, but administratively quite different from, the NRST. Thus, a closely related issue is whether a VAT is preferable to the NRST on administrative grounds, and whether the largest simplicity gains attainable under a consumption tax reform would occur with adoption of the VAT. These issues are examined in the next two chapters in the volume.

Administrative and Compliance Savings under the Flat Tax and the NRST

William Gale and Janet Holtzblatt examine the administrative and compliance issues associated with fundamental tax reform, focusing on a comparison between the existing income tax and the NRST and flat tax options. After arguing that the administrative differences between pure, flat-rate versions of the two options are relatively small, they stress that the primary differences between the current income tax and the flat tax and NRST alternatives arise because the current system has deviated from a pure flat-rate income tax. This in turn implies that many of the simplicity gains that could be attained under fundamental tax reform could also be achieved with the appropriate reforms of the existing system,[8] although considerable further gains could be achieved if reformers are successful in passing a pure consumption tax.

Gale and Holtzblatt then discuss issues related to administrative and compliance costs under the current income tax system: the aggregate costs of administering and complying with the income tax (which range from \$75–\$200 billion), the inherent difficulties in constructing such estimates, the factors that give rise to the considerable variance across estimates, the amount of tax evasion in the United States, the determinants of evasion, and the factors that appear to deter evasion. They suggest procedural, administrative, and structural reforms of the current income tax that would reduce its complexity.

To evaluate current proposals for a national retail sales tax, Gale and Holtzblatt calculate potential tax rates under the NRST under different scenarios, including alternative assumptions about the comprehensiveness of the sales tax base, the treatment of government expenditures, and the degree of evasion; they conclude that the rates required under a realistic NRST could easily be much higher than those commonly touted by proponents of this reform. After examining complexity and compliance cost issues under the NRST, they argue that, although the

[8] Ballard's chapter provides an important example of such a reform – the territorial approach to taxing foreign source income characterizes most consumption tax proposals, but could also be adopted under the current income tax system. As noted by Ballard, such a reform would eliminate many of the most complex provisions of the tax code.

sales tax would be simpler than the current tax system, especially for individuals, there are potential sources of complexity, including problems associated with business purchases of goods that can be used for both business purposes and personal consumption, and with the purchase of consumer goods from abroad. In addition, Gale and Holtzblatt argue that relatively high tax rates, coupled with the absence of withholding and income reporting requirements, would encourage evasion, which would imply even higher tax rates, and more evasion; they also suggest that the perception that the sales tax is unfair from a distributional stand-point could also fuel greater evasion.

In evaluating the flat tax, Gale and Holtzblatt argue that rates under a realistic version of the flat tax would be considerably higher than under pure versions of the plan, as the base would possibly be reduced with special exemptions and deductions, transition rules, and progressive rates. They note that the flat tax also has considerable potential for sim-plification at both the individual and firm levels. On the other hand, various problems under the current income tax would remain and certain new ones, attributable to differences in the tax treatment of certain trans-actions relative to the income tax, would be created. In particular, the tax exemption of interest income and the elimination of interest deduc-tions under the flat tax would create new and potentially important opportunities for tax avoidance and evasion.

Administrative and Compliance Issues under the VAT and the NRST

Although the debate on fundamental tax reform in the United States has focused on either direct consumption taxes or the NRST, the most widely used consumption tax in the world, especially in Europe and Latin America, is the VAT – an indirect tax that is assessed on the value added by firms at each stage of the production process and results in a final tax burden that is in principle identical to that imposed by the NRST. In his contribution to the volume, Sijbren Cnossen provides a detailed com-parison of the relative administrative and compliance costs of the NRST and the credit-invoice method VAT, which is far and away the most popular form of VAT. He concludes that if the United States is to enact a relatively high-rate indirect consumption tax, the VAT is preferable to an NRST.

Cnossen sets the stage for his discussion by describing the structural differences between these alternative taxes and demonstrating the eco-nomic equivalences between them. He notes in particular that several countries switched to the VAT after experimenting with the sales tax, primarily because it was difficult to eliminate sales taxation of business inputs and it was easier to tax services under the VAT.

The remainder of his chapter is devoted to a detailed evaluation of the two tax options. According to Cnossen, problems plague both the NRST and the VAT in defining their tax bases, including the treatment of food and other necessities, housing, health and education, financial services, and government expenditures; however, the VAT is clearly superior to the NRST in the tax treatment of producer goods and services, because it is much more effective in ensuring that "dual use" goods and services – those that can be used both as business inputs and as consumption commodities – are exempt from tax when purchased for business purposes. An implication of this point is that "border tax adjustments" – the removal of the NRST or the VAT on exports and the imposition of tax on imports – can be done more easily and accurately under the VAT.

Although the number of firms subject to tax is fewer under the NRST, Cnossen argues that the collection of tax and thus the presence of an audit trail throughout each step of the production process are important advantages of the VAT. He also notes that the marginal incentives to evade tax by underreporting sales and to divert business purchases to personal use are similar under both taxes. Nevertheless, the VAT is less susceptible to evasion for a number of reasons, most of which are related to the tax crediting process, which is an essential feature of the VAT but does not occur under the NRST. In addition, tax collection under the NRST is focused on retailers, who are generally the weakest link in the production-distribution chain from a tax collection perspective. Finally, Cnossen suggests that the administrative and compliance costs of the VAT, though not trivial, are low in comparison to those under the income tax.

TRANSITIONAL ISSUES RAISED BY THE ENACTMENT OF FUNDAMENTAL TAX REFORM

The fourth obstacle to the enactment of fundamental tax reform is a potential "show stopper," even if one is convinced that the long-run benefits of implementing a consumption tax reform would be significant. Specifically, many observers have noted that the transition costs of moving from the current income tax system to a consumption-based tax may be sufficiently large to preclude its enactment. The prospect of such a large-scale tax change raises numerous transitional issues, especially the effect of reform on the values of existing assets, including currently tax-favored assets such as owner-occupied housing, and the short-run macroeconomic effects of switching tax systems.

In his contribution to the volume, George Zodrow notes that much of the concern about the transition from an income tax to a consumption tax like the flat tax or the NRST has focused on a single issue, the potential capital levy or onetime windfall loss that such a reform might impose on the holders of existing capital assets. Under the NRST – with the conventional assumption that monetary policy is sufficiently accommodating that consumer prices increase by the amount of the tax – this loss to capital owners would be reflected in the form of reduced purchasing power of existing assets. By comparison, under the flat tax, expensing under the business tax, coupled with arbitrage across new and old assets, implies that the prices of existing assets would fall by the product of the value of the capital stock and the tax rate. Moreover, because nominal prices would remain unchanged under the flat tax, this loss would be borne entirely by equity owners.

Zodrow notes that the potential of such a windfall loss on existing capital owners would be a huge impediment to the enactment of a consumption tax reform. Other reform-induced factors, however, would also affect asset prices, most acting to offset such a windfall loss. Factors that fall into the latter group include (1) the short-run costs of adjusting the capital stock; (2) higher short-run postreform after-tax interest rates; (3) the elimination or reduction of future expected taxes on income attributable to intangible assets, assets that have received accelerated depreciation under current law, and on the future income associated with growth opportunities that are captured in current asset values; (4) any increase in asset values attributable to the elimination of the taxation of dividends at the individual level (under the "new view" of dividend taxes); and (5) the efficiency gains from reform. In addition, any declines in asset values would be smaller than predicted by conventional models to the extent that they ignore the similarities in the taxation of certain components of capital income (as stressed by Hubbard) and do not adequately capture the features of current law that provide for consumption tax treatment of certain types of investment (such as those made through tax-deferred retirement accounts). Several simulation studies suggest that such factors mitigate, and in some cases completely offset, both the tendency toward a onetime reduction in asset values and the welfare losses for the elderly owners of such assets commonly associated with a consumption tax reform.

In discussing economic, legal, and political perspectives on the transitional problems associated with tax reform, Zodrow observes that both economists and lawyers are divided on the desirability of using transition rules to protect individuals from reform-induced losses. From a political perspective, the perceived need to protect constituents from incurring such redistributions through the use of transition rules is pervasive, although one could argue that their usage has declined and become more highly targeted in recent years. According to Zodrow, some simulation studies have shown that the use of some transition rules under the flat tax and the NRST can limit or even reverse the declines in asset values that might occur.

Zodrow concludes by noting that consideration of all these factors suggests that the enactment of a consumption tax reform might not dramatically reduce the values of existing assets or impose huge generation-specific losses; in particular, the elderly might not experience large windfall losses – and, indeed, could even be net gainers – with the implementation of the flat tax or an NRST.

POLITICAL OBSTACLES TO THE ENACTMENT OF FUNDAMENTAL TAX REFORM

From a political standpoint, the enactment of fundamental tax reform is without question much more difficult than incremental income tax reform. Such a large-scale change involves significant economic, political, and ideological risks, and thus poses a formidable legislative challenge, especially because the final reform product that emerges from the political process is not likely to be as "pure" as the proposals envisaged by the advocates of fundamental tax reform. By comparison, even fairly sweeping changes of the income tax system can be packaged as incremental reforms; indeed, the proponents of income tax reform often stress that many – although not all – of the advantages of consumption tax reform proposals can also be obtained with the appropriate income tax reforms, and that such reforms are much more feasible from a political standpoint than enacting an entirely new consumption-based tax system. In addition, the case for a consumption tax reform has been complicated by the fact that there are so many alternative proposals. Criticisms of specific features of certain reform packages are often (inadvertently or intentionally) used to disparage consumption taxes generally. Moreover, although all of these proposals are economically similar, their proponents have often chosen to emphasize their differences rather than stressing their similarities, in the process providing additional ammunition to those opposed to reform. Finally, some of the reform proposals are truly sweeping in nature, as they involve huge redistributions of income, drastic reductions in the level of government expenditures, the elimination of estate and gift taxation, or a restructuring of the social security system. Adding any of these features to an already controversial proposal to change the tax base only increases the odds of opposition from powerful interest groups. Indeed, all of these factors act to dissipate general political support for the notion of fundamental tax reform – a difficult proposition to sell in the political arena in any case. These and many other political obstacles to the enactment of fundamental tax reform are addressed in the final two chapters in the volume.

A Historical and Political Perspective on the Debate

Malcolm Gillis provides a historical perspective on the long debate over the relative merits of taxation on the basis of income and consumption. He notes that the constituency for consumption-based taxation has not been confined to economists and politicians who rely primarily on market-based arguments to support their positions. Instead, proponents of consumption-based taxes have included (1) philosophers who supported taxation on the basis of what individuals took out of society (as measured by their consumption) as opposed to what they put in (as measured by their income); (2) socialists, such as the famed British advocate of expenditure taxation, economist Nicholas Kaldor; and (3) leftist and center-to-leftist governments in Europe, including all of the Scandinavian countries, which are commonly associated with expansive welfare systems rather than efficient taxes. Gillis also describes the considerable experience that has been obtained with "indirect" consumption taxes (those based on transactions, in contrast to "direct" taxes, which are assessed on individuals), including retail sales taxes in most states in the United States and the value-added tax in many countries around the world, especially in Europe and Latin America.

Gillis then turns to the political outlook for fundamental reform in the United States. He observes that the stage for consumption-based tax reform has to some extent been set by the increasing public perception of the income tax as an inherently unfair tax, as well as by numerous academic studies extolling the virtues of taxation on the basis of consumption rather than income. In addition, societal concerns over alleged violations of civil liberties by the Internal Revenue Service (IRS) have prompted interest in less intrusive forms of taxation, especially indirect taxes like the NRST or a VAT.

Nevertheless, Gillis believes that the prospects for the adoption of a consumption-based tax system in the United States are doubtful for several reasons. For example, he argues that proponents of the flat tax have oversold the advantages of its adoption, especially in terms of its simplicity and ease of administration, to the point that the public is suspicious of all of their claims. Proponents of the NRST have made the dubious claim that only their proposal will "abolish" the IRS (by using the states to collect the tax), when in fact the IRS or some similar federal agency would still be required to standardize the detailed provisions of the tax, enforce its application, and supervise its administration. In addition, the advocates of the NRST have largely ignored the states' concerns that an NRST would infringe on their tax bases, have inadequately addressed concerns about the large extent to which the bases of state retail sales taxes inappropriately include business purchases, and have not fully considered the evasion problems associated with relatively high-rate retail sales taxes. By comparison, proponents of the cash flow approach (such as the Nunn-Domenici USA Tax) have primarily reacted to widespread criticism of their detailed proposal, and have not adequately explained its considerable advantages. At the same time, supporters of the VAT have in general been strangely silent in the recent debate and have never been able to dispel the commonly held notion that the VAT is more of a "money machine" than the economically similar NRST, and thus more likely to lead to an undesirable expansion of the public sector.

In addition, Gillis stresses that the supporters of the various consumption tax proposals have remained bitterly divided, promoting their own proposals while disparaging alternative and economically similar consumption-based tax plans. For example, flat tax advocates argue without justification that any sales tax will inevitably become a complex, multirate valued-added tax. Proponents of the NRST have often focused on the supposed differences between their proposal and a single-rate VAT, when in fact the two approaches are quite similar from an economic standpoint, and the VAT has some advantages over the NRST in terms of ease of administration and enforcement. Gillis also notes that, at least in the U.S. context, the rise of electronic commerce has introduced a factor that tends to favor direct consumption taxes (the flat tax and the USA Tax) over the indirect consumption tax options (the NRST and the VAT). Specifically, much of electronic commerce currently escapes tax under the existing state sales tax system, and some current proposals would permanently exempt all e-commerce from sales taxation. If such exemptions were also applied to an NRST or a national VAT, the case for these reforms, relative to the direct consumption tax alternatives, would be weakened considerably (if similar tax preferences for e-commerce were not grafted onto the flat tax or USA Tax proposals). Finally, Gillis concludes – as do various other writers – that political opposition to fundamental tax reform will remain intense if the reform is perceived to change drastically the current distribution of after-tax income.

Political Aspects of Fundamental Tax Reform

In the final chapter of the volume, Joe Barnes focuses on the political and ideological issues raised by fundamental tax reform. Barnes begins by observing that the task facing proponents of fundamental tax reform is one of gargantuan proportions. In particular, he argues that passage of the Tax Reform Act of 1986, which was hailed as a heroic achievement and represented two and a half years of intense bipartisan effort in the face of concerted opposition, pales in comparison. However, Barnes believes that the prospects for such sweeping reform have improved markedly in recent years, primarily as a result of the confluence of three contemporary trends: the ideological ascendancy of conservatism, the political resurgence of the Republican Party, and a large and growing body of economic research that is harshly critical of the current income tax system and supportive of consumption tax alternatives. Nevertheless, he argues that certain aspects of these three trends may create large and perhaps insurmountable obstacles to reform.

On the ideological front, Barnes stresses that the two currently most popular reform options, the flat tax and the NRST, to an important degree represent a dramatic change in the extent to which tax burden increases with the ability to pay tax as measured by annual income – a change viewed as desirable by proponents of the proposals. Debates over the nature of a "fair" tax system are, of course, as old as taxation itself. Barnes traces the historical antecedents of the current debate and notes that the opposition to progressivity that characterizes the current tax reform movement is consistent with the antigovernment stance of the libertarians and the free-market tendencies of traditionalists in the conservative movement. However, he stresses that tax reforms that focus their benefits on the rich may alienate less affluent social conservatives, who may in any case be suspicious of tax reform incentives to the extent that they divert attention from their favorite causes.

In political terms, Barnes notes that the ascendancy of conservatism has clearly had a large and positive effect on the Republican Party. Moreover, Republican control of both the executive and legislative branches of government would greatly increase the prospects for fundamental tax reform. Indeed, such reform has considerable appeal to many Republican constituencies – the rich, who would receive much of the economic benefits; the self-employed, whose compliance costs would be reduced; and those opposed to big government, especially in the form of what is perceived to be a highly intrusive IRS. However, the specific provisions of the various plans – such as the elimination of long treasured deductions, greatly reduced tax burdens for the very rich, and the absence of transition rules to protect existing investments – could easily offend many other Republican stalwarts, especially among the middle class.

Finally, Barnes provides a brief history of support among economists for taxation on the basis of consumption. Recent academic research suggesting that the implementation of a consumption tax reform would generate large economic benefits has played an important role in advancing the cause of reform. At the same time, however, he (following Gravelle) notes that considerable uncertainty about these benefits remains within the profession, and that this uncertainty increases the importance of political and ideological factors in the tax reform debate.

Barnes concludes that fundamental tax reform entails significant economic, political, and ideological risks, so that its enactment may not be within reach. This is especially the case if the final product to emerge from the legislative process falls far short of the pure reforms advocated by current proponents of proposals like the flat tax and the NRST.

CONCLUSION

The chapters presented in this volume provide a wealth of information on the state of the art in current academic thinking on the relative desirability of both fundamental tax reform and more incremental reform of the existing income tax structure. In particular, they cover in great detail a wide range of issues that shed light on what we believe to be the "fundamental question" of fundamental tax reform – why the enactment of a consumption-based tax does not appear to be a viable tax reform option for the new millennium and any tax reform that might occur is much more likely to be incremental income tax reform – despite the fact that the virtues of consumption taxes have been promoted, at least in some circles, for nearly twenty-five years. Accordingly, the volume should serve as a comprehensive guide to the ongoing tax reform debate that will be helpful to both tax policy makers and the general electorate.

More specifically, however, what does a reading of the chapters in this volume tell us about the strength of the case for fundamental tax reform? On balance, our view is that the "bottom line" is that fundamental tax reform is probably desirable but that several critical issues must be resolved before one can make a reasonably convincing case that replacing the income tax with a consumption tax is desirable from an economic standpoint and feasible from a political standpoint.[9]

The first is the magnitude of the economic gains that might be obtained from implementing fundamental tax reform. Our view is that these gains are not likely to be as large as those envisioned by Jorgenson and Wilcoxen (at least in their NRST simulation) for a number of

---

[9] Of course, one critical issue is the form that the consumption tax would take. The discussion here has focused on the flat tax and the NRST, but the VAT and a cash flow approach similar to that proposed in the Nunn-Domenici plan are still contenders. Moreover, alternative plans, such as the Bradford (1986) multirate version of the flat tax and the McLure-Zodrow (1996a) proposal for a multirate flat tax with cash flow treatment of loans at the firm level, may also be considered.

reasons. In particular, some form of exempting the very poor from tax will almost assuredly be enacted and will require rate increases, which will lower efficiency gains. Moreover, as argued by Gravelle, adjustment costs will delay and transition rules will reduce the long-run gains from reform, current consumption tax treatment of many assets implies that smaller gains will be obtained from enacting reform than if the existing system were a pure income tax, and reform-induced behavioral responses will be smaller than those envisioned by the infinite-horizon, no-adjustment-cost scenario modeled by Jorgenson and Wilcoxen. However, that does not imply that significant gains in economic welfare cannot be obtained from fundamental tax reform – likely on the order of at least 1 percent of GDP and perhaps considerably more once all of the welfare-enhancing effects of reform are considered.[10] The key here is continued research efforts to model more accurately the economic effects of consumption tax reforms. In particular, despite the extremely complex nature of the computer simulation models used to evaluate the effects of tax reforms, many of these models still do not adequately consider a number of factors (such as those discussed by Gravelle) that will affect the course of the economy after the enactment of reform. Accordingly, these models must be extended to consider such factors before their simulation results can be viewed as a reliable guide to policy makers.

Second, distributional concerns about the enactment of a consumption tax must be assuaged. It seems likely that this would have to be done in two steps. The first is simply calculating as carefully as possible the distributional implications of reform, taking into account the many issues raised in this volume, including differences in saving behavior across income classes (analyzed by Mieszkowski and Palumbo), similarities in the tax treatment under income and consumption taxes of certain forms of capital income (stressed by Hubbard), the distributional implications of international capital mobility (discussed by Ballard), and the magnitude of any transitional windfall loss imposed on the owners of existing capital at the time of reform (analyzed by Zodrow); all of these factors should be considered in a framework that calculates the efficiency gains that would be obtained from reform and that views incidence from a multiyear or lifetime perspective, taking into account the importance of non-life-cycle saving stressed by Mieszkowski and Palumbo.

---

[10] Note that the short-run increases in growth rates that would accompany such an increase in GDP would arise from an efficiency-enhancing reallocation of resources in the economy, and thus should not in principle give rise to the inflationary pressures that tend to occur under demand-driven increases in the growth rate.

However, even if these factors are taken into account, a distributional analysis of flat-rate consumption tax proposals (including those with provisions designed to exempt the poor from tax) is likely to suggest that such reforms will redistribute income to the very wealthy from a broadly defined middle class. If such redistribution is deemed undesirable from a political perspective – and this seems likely to be the case, given recent increases in income disparities unrelated to tax factors – the second step would be to make structural alterations to the reform proposal designed to lessen their redistributional impact. For direct taxes such as the flat tax, the obvious candidate is a second tax rate applied only to those with relatively high incomes. A less desirable alternative – but one that would be equally feasible under any consumption tax plan – would be a wealth tax or expansion of current gift and estate taxes. Finally, differential "luxury" tax rates are possible under the indirect consumption tax options like the NRST and the VAT although, as stressed by Cnossen, the European experience with such differentiation under the VAT has been decidedly negative.

Third, the simplicity gains that could be achieved with a consumption tax reform need to be better defined and measured. As described by Gale and Holtzblatt, the magnitude of these gains is uncertain; moreover, many of the gains could also be achieved under an appropriate income tax reform. Nevertheless, we would stress that many important gains in simplicity can be obtained only under a consumption tax, especially those related to the elimination of a wide variety of timing issues (such as the determination of deductions for depreciation, inventory accounting, and the calculation of capital gains) and the need for inflation accounting.[11] Although we believe that these gains are far from trivial and provide an important rationale for reform, they need to be isolated better and measured to obtain a real feeling for the magnitude of the simplicity gains obtained from fundamental as opposed to incremental tax reform. In addition, as emphasized by Cnossen, the greatest gains in tax simplicity may in fact be possible with adoption of the valued-added tax rather than the proposals currently under active discussion in the United States. It seems clear, as suggested by Gillis, that the VAT is worthy of serious consideration in the U.S. context.

Fourth, any politically viable consumption tax reform proposal will have to provide some transition rules to minimize the disruptions associated with fundamental tax reform. The proponents of the various proposals have thus far addressed this issue only peripherally, but a fully articulated set of transition rules must be specified before the efficiency

---

[11] See McLure and Zodrow (1990) for further discussion.

and distributional (and, indeed, the short-run simplicity) properties of fundamental tax reform can be understood. As suggested by Zodrow, the goal should be protection from large windfall losses, taking into account both the tendency of a consumption tax reform to impose a onetime windfall loss on the owners of existing capital, as well as the variety of factors – such as adjustment costs, interest rate changes, and the current treatment of assets under the income tax – that act to offset this loss.

Fifth, as suggested by the wide-ranging discussions by Gillis and by Barnes, a viable consumption tax proposal must take a variety of political and ideological factors into account. In our view, the case for any particular consumption tax proposal is much more compelling if its proponents (1) structure the proposal so that the distribution of gains is broad, (2) identify the nature of these (often subtle) gains as clearly as possible, and (3) work with other advocates of consumption-based tax reforms to make the case for fundamental tax reform, rather than expending great energy on criticizing plans that are similar in spirit and general effect, if not in detail. Finally, many current reform proposals are truly sweeping in scope in that they not only change the tax base from income to consumption, but also effect a large redistribution of income, eliminate estate and gift taxes, attempt to force a large reduction in government expenditures by reducing revenues, and even change the entire nature of the Social Security system. In our view, the difficulties of enacting a reform as fundamental as changing the tax base are sufficiently great – on the order of those facing recent failed efforts at health care reform – that the likelihood of fundamental tax reform would be greatly increased with proposals that are less ambitious in scope. In particular, consumption tax proponents would be wise to follow the lead of the successful Tax Reform Act of 1986 and attempt to structure their proposals to minimize reform-induced redistributions of income, forced reductions in government spending, and reforms of the Social Security system.

Chapter 2

Behavioral Responses to a Consumption Tax

Jane G. Gravelle

A shift from the current income tax system to a consumption tax would have potentially far-reaching implications for the economy, changing the incentives for savings and investment, for work effort, and for the allocation of investment and consumption. Relative prices would change, in some cases in a dramatic way. Most plans also envision a flatter (or even completely flat) rate structure, and some would dramatically change the point of collection of revenues.

In order to consider seriously such a radical change in the tax system, it is important to understand the behavioral responses to these new tax incentives. Despite much attention to this issue, there is little consensus on these effects. The lack of consensus is not for lack of studies; policy makers can consult a wide variety of studies of the effects of fundamental tax reform. The difficulty is the dramatic variations in projected effects among the studies.

This understanding of potential behavioral responses is complicated because of the variety of behavioral effects. For example, one of the rationales for shifting to a consumption tax is to increase savings. A consumption tax, by exempting resources devoted to savings and only taxing those resources, and their earnings, in the future when converted to consumption, is the equivalent of exempting the normal return to capital income from tax (see Hubbard, Chapter 4 in this volume). Such favorable treatment of capital income should increase savings, and, therefore future output and welfare. Output and welfare may also be increased with a more efficient allocation of resources. A focus on the intermediate and longer run has characterized many dynamic studies of consumption taxation. Yet, the reallocation of investment and consumption, and the relocation of collection sources, could be disruptive to the

This chapter does not reflect the views of the Congressional Research Service or the Library of Congress.

economy in the short run, an important issue. Indeed, if such changes are too disruptive, policy makers will be reluctant to undertake them even if benefits will ultimately be realized. In addition, currently tax-favored activities would be adversely affected, igniting political opposition. The most obvious of these activities is housing, where a contraction in demand could damage the construction industry and lower housing prices. But concern about the consequences to any other tax-favored sector or activity – state and local bonds, pensions, insurance companies, health care, charity – is likely to breed potential opposition to fundamental tax reform.

In this chapter I summarize the variation in predictions of macroeconomic effects, focusing on predicted changes in output levels; explore sources of these differences, including the presence or absence of short-run disequilibrium effects; examine fundamental factors that affect the supply-driven changes in output, both in the short and long run; and focus on some specific issues, including the effects of reform on stock market prices, housing, interest rates, and the role of existing tax-favored investments and forms of consumption.

THE RANGE OF ESTIMATED EFFECTS
ON AGGREGATE OUTPUT

In early 1996 the Brookings Institution convened a seminar on fundamental tax reform. Among the papers presented were those reporting results of the tax shift on growth from three life-cycle models. Life-cycle models use a basic function for expressing preferences across time (for consumption and, in some cases, for leisure), and then estimate the response of each age cohort to a change in the tax regime. These responses are combined through a production function to produce output changes, which feed back into individual choices until an equilibrium output path is reached.

The results varied considerably. Auerbach (1996), using the Auerbach and Kotlikoff (1987) model, found shifting to a value-added tax (VAT) (without exemptions) would initially increase output by 6.8 percent, with a 9.7 percent long-run increase. (Similar results were previously reported in a simulation of a shift to a national sales tax by Kotlikoff, 1996a). Fullerton and Rogers (1996) found short- and long-run output increases of 1.4 percent and 4.5 percent, respectively. Engen and Gale (1996) present no numerical results for output but clearly found very small effects.

Later that year, the Joint Committee on Taxation (JCT) assembled nine modelers to study tax changes, adding representatives of commercial macroeconomic models and others (JCT, 1997). Models in the JCT

Table 2.1. Percentage Increases in Output from Substitution of a Broad-Based Consumption Tax for the Current Income Tax (JCT Modeling Experiment)

Model Type	Year				Long Run
	1	4	9	14	
Intertemporal: Life-cycle					
Auerbach, Kotlikoff, Smetters, and Walliser	1.2	2.4	4.0	5.0	7.5
Engen-Gale	0.8	1.4	1.8	2.1	2.4
Fullerton-Rogers (low)	1.2				1.7
Fullerton-Rogers (high)	5.8				5.8
Intertemporal: Infinite horizon					
Jorgenson-Wilcoxen	3.4	3.7	3.6	3.3	3.3
Reduced-form: Full employment					
Gravelle	0.1	0.3	0.7	1.0	3.7
Robbins	7.8	14.0	16.4	16.9	
Reduced-form: Unemployment allowed					
Coopers & Lybrand	0.2	0.7	1.2		
DRI/McGraw-Hill	−0.3	−0.8	4.7		
DRI/McGraw-Hill (VAT)	−2.3	−12.5	−4.2		
Macroeconomic Advisers	−1.8	4.2	1.4	1.3	

Source: Joint Committee on Taxation (1997).

study comprise four types: two intertemporal types (life-cycle and infinite horizon), where allocations are made with a long time horizon, and two reduced-form types (with and without full employment), which rely on labor and savings supply functions.

All researchers modeled the same policy change: a switch to a flat-rate consumption or income tax with an exemption for a fixed amount of wages. (The importance of controlling for policy can be seen in the study by Jorgenson-Wilcoxen, Chapter 3 in this volume, where output increases by 13 percent with a retail sales tax and 0.6 percent with a flat tax with an exemption.) All changes were revenue-neutral. The tax could be imposed as a VAT with a refundable wage credit, or its theoretical equivalent: a VAT with wages deducted by firms and taxed to individuals with an exemption – the flat tax. The effects of a retail sales tax should be similar to those of a VAT (which simply collects the tax in pieces at each stage of production).

As Table 2.1 shows, the projections varied widely. First-year projections ranged from a contraction in output of 2.3 percent to an increase of 7.8 percent. In the fourth year the range was even wider: from a 12.5 percent contraction to a 14 percent increase. Counting the last year of the Robbins estimates, output increases in the long run ranged from 1.7 to 16.9 percent.

The range in these estimates is far too large to be useful for policy making. However, understanding the reasons for these different results may help to exclude some results as unrealistic or inconsistent with empirical evidence and allow a narrowing of the range.

BASIC MODEL TYPES

The simplest models whose results are reported in Table 2.1 are the reduced-form growth models (Gravelle, 1997, and Robbins, 1997), which have supply functions for labor and for savings that are combined, via a production function and a growth framework (i.e., each increment of additional savings adds to the capital stock in the next period), to determine output. The effects in these models depend on the savings elasticity, the labor supply elasticity, and the factor substitution elasticity (the ease with which capital and labor are substituted in production).

The other reduced-form models are large-scale macroeconomic models, where any supply-side effects are of the reduced-form type. Effects in these models were also sensitive to demand-side effects, including possible contraction of output due to the costs of adjustment. These models include simulations by Roger Brinner (1997; DRI/McGraw-Hill) and Joel Prakken (1997; Macroeconomic Advisers), both well-known commercial forecasting models. The study also included simulations by John Wilkins (1997; Coopers & Lybrand).

The intertemporal models are more complex. These models are constructed from the basic building blocks of economic theory, including a mathematical function for expressing preferences for consumption (and, in most cases, leisure) over time. Factor supply functions are derived implicitly from these utility functions. Three of the models were the life-cycle models presented in the Brookings Institution study (Aaron and Gale, 1996), with simulations prepared, respectively, by Auerbach et al. (1997), Rogers (1997), and Engen and Gale (1997). The fourth intertemporal model, constructed by Jorgenson and Wilcoxen (1997), was an infinite-horizon model, which, rather than assuming many different age cohorts with finite lifetimes, assumed infinitely lived consumers.

At first glance, the simulation results seem chaotic: the smallest and largest results are from reduced-form models. The model rankings, by output effects, vary over time, and adjustment paths are quite different. Intertemporal models show positive effects, but one model reports short-run effects seven times those of another model. The macroeconomic models find small and even negative results initially, but eventually have positive results. This experiment shows that model results can differ dramatically, but not why.

Models with Unemployment and Short-Run Disequilibrium Effects

The reduced-form models with unemployment reflect short-term adjustment costs that vary across models and are one of the effects hardest to understand and to predict. Zodrow (Chapter 9 in this volume) discusses many of these issues in greater detail. The DRI/McGraw-Hill and Macroeconomic Advisers models are traditional aggregate demand models, similar to textbook ISLM models with many sectors. They also have supply-side aspects like the reduced-form growth models. It is less clear how the Coopers & Lybrand model incorporated these demand and supply factors.

Some short-run adjustment problems have received a great deal of attention. For example, the shift to a consumption tax will shift investment from currently favored owner-occupied housing to business, and employment would likely decline in the housing industry before it picks up in other industries. More important, when the locus of tax collection is changed dramatically, as in the VAT, it could cause considerable unemployment because wages and prices cannot easily adjust (or be adjusted) to accommodate the tax. With a VAT, firms would have much higher taxes to pay, and if they could not adjust their wages, they would need to pass the tax forward as higher prices. With sticky wages and prices, these adjustments may be difficult and costly. The contractionary effects in the DRI model are much higher in the case of the VAT form of the proposal.

Of course, understanding the source of this short-run contraction does not mean that we can easily predict it. But this issue has been largely ignored in the debate over fundamental tax reform (see, however, Bull and Lindsey, 1996, and Zodrow, 1997a). It is much more severe under the VAT and retail sales tax (RST) approaches: the latter would also shift the locus of tax collection – in this case, to firms engaged in retail trade. It is possible that the RST would be easier to accommodate than the VAT, because intermediate producers would not need to pass on the tax to those firms that they supply.

Changing the legal liability for most income taxes from individuals to firms is, by any standard, an enormous shift in tax liability. There is little to guide us on what to expect with a massive tax replacement of this nature. Although many countries have adopted VATs, they were largely substitutes for existing sales and excise taxes, as discussed in Tait (1988, pp. 191–213). Poterba, Rotemberg, and Summers (1986), however, found evidence that shifts to indirect taxes in the United Kingdom and the

United States were followed by both price increases and declines in output.

Can we reject the magnitude of the DRI/McGraw-Hill short-run results as unreasonable? These models are viewed with some suspicion, particularly when used for policy analysis. Several objections were enumerated by Reifschneider (1997) at the JCT conference: a weak correspondence between theory and model specification, limited treatment of expectations, and problems with identification. There is some flux in the theories regarding the causes of recessions (see Auerbach and Kotlikoff, 1995, for a summary). Nevertheless, the key predictions about short-run contractionary effects can be derived from simple logic and textbook analysis in a model with sticky wages and prices, a model that is still accepted by most economists. Moreover, an enormous price increase (on the order of 25 percent) would be needed to accommodate a VAT reform.

What is clear about the short-run disequilibrium attributable to the shift in the source of tax collection is that it has probably not been adequately studied – indeed, it has hardly been addressed – and yet it could be the most crucial transitional cost of reform. These contractionary effects may dominate supply-side considerations in the short run. This evaluation depends in part on the ability of the monetary authorities to steer the economy through the adjustment to the new tax regime, an ability limited by an imperfect understanding of the economy and the presence of other factors that are simultaneously affecting the important variables. Gravelle and Woodward (1998) suggest that the conduct of monetary policy is most precise when other disruptive influences are absent and that the appropriate policy will be extremely difficult to judge given direct pressures exerted on economic variables, such as interest rates, by the tax change. Clearly, if policy makers believe that output would fall by the amounts suggested in the DRI simulations, it is unlikely that they would consider the tax revision. Even the prediction of a slight recession may be enough to stall any tax reform effort. Either tax changes should be made more slowly, or the form of consumption tax would have to be the flat tax approach, where wages would continue to be taxed to individuals, rather than to firms, and changes in the legal liability for taxes would be minimal.

DRI/McGraw-Hill and Macroeconomic Advisers also found contractionary effects for the flat tax, albeit on a much smaller scale. These effects arise in part from sectoral disruption associated with the changes in relative prices. Eventually, output effects turned positive, reflecting supply-side considerations.

Short-run effects may be the most important focus for further research. Without some assurance that short-run disruptions can be controlled, a shift to a consumption tax may, in fact, be infeasible, particularly for a VAT or RST form of consumption tax. These considerations imply that a tax should be designed to approximate the legal liabilities imposed under the current income tax. However, further research may suggest ways to make a smoother transition, so it is worthwhile to consider the behavioral responses to a consumption tax reform in a full-employment model. If these responses are large and desirable, a case can be made for paying the price of short-run adjustment costs, whereas if these responses are very small, a shift to a consumption tax would seem less desirable.

FULL-EMPLOYMENT MODELS: FUNDAMENTAL FACTORS

The supply-side effects (and allocational effects) that are found in the full-employment models and, to some extent in the models with unemployment, also vary substantially, ranging from 0.1 to 7.8 percent.

One difficulty in assessing the models' effects is that they vary in many ways other than basic type. Of course, any model's outcome will be affected by the responsiveness of labor and savings supplies and how easily factors of production can be substituted in production. Models with low elasticities will have less pronounced effects, other things being equal. Some models, for example, keep labor supply fixed, as in the case of the early life-cycle model of Summers (1981a) and the infinite-horizon model of Chamley (1981). But the differences between models are not limited to the fundamental differences. Life-cycle models, for example, can vary in structural features that have important implications for their predictions (e.g., perfect foresight versus myopia; bequests; multiple or representative households and producers; open or closed economies; risk).

We begin this analysis with some fundamentals on how basic structural type affects outcomes, by holding elasticities across similar model types constant, based on work by three researchers participating in the JCT study (Engen, Gravelle, and Smetters, 1997). These researchers had access to versions of their own models and constructed an infinite-horizon model; they also fixed the labor supply in models with variable labor supply.

Their experiment was directed at understanding the basic structural causes of differing results: all models began with identical economies and simulated identical tax changes. The Engen et al. study compared life-cycle and intertemporal models, with certain variations, and a reduced-form growth model.

Reduced-form growth models directly incorporate savings elasticities with respect to the rate of return and labor supply elasticities with respect to the wage rate. In some models, there is simply an aggregate labor supply elasticity, which is technically only suitable for measuring a proportional tax change, because it cannot be decomposed into an income effect and a substitution effect. That is, an increase in the average wage increases income, which causes a decrease in labor supply because the income effect causes increased consumption of both leisure and goods. An increase in the marginal wage causes an increase in labor supply because the price of leisure has increased; this is the substitution effect measured by the substitution elasticity (a compensated elasticity). The labor supply response combines these offsetting effects in the uncompensated elasticity. Some models might have only this latter type of elasticity, which can be negative (a backward bending labor supply curve). The benefit of specifying both an income and a substitution elasticity is that flattening of tax rates, which alters both marginal and average wages, can be taken into account. (Properly speaking, labor supply response should also reflect changes in both hours and participation, and a savings response could reflect differential responses to changes in average and marginal rates of return, although none of the reduced-form models in these studies did so.)

The elasticities incorporated in the reduced-form model used in the Engen et al. study were intended to represent the typical estimates reported in the literature (summarized in Engen et al., 1997, and in the Gravelle contribution to the JCT, 1997, study). The model had a fixed labor supply and a compensated labor supply elasticity (substitution effect) of 0.2, identical to the assumptions in the Gravelle and Coopers & Lybrand models in the JCT project. A fixed labor supply is consistent with empirical evidence suggesting that labor supply is not very responsive to changes in the wage rate: the 0.2 substitution elasticity reflects the offsetting of small positive substitution and negative income effects.

The savings rate elasticity was 0.4, at the higher end of the range of directly estimated savings responses, which are generally close to zero (see Engen et al., 1997). (Note that Summers, 1981a, often cited in support of high savings elasticities, does not empirically estimate them but rather simulates them with a life-cycle model.) General-equilibrium effects are also determined by the substitutability of productive factors: the factor substitution elasticity of one falls within the range of estimated values (Engen et al., 1997, report a range 0.5 to 1.2).

In intertemporal models, the supply response is derived from intertemporal substitution elasticities (the elasticity of substitution between consumption bundles in different periods with respect to their price) and intratemporal substitution elasticities (the elasticity of substitution between the consumption of leisure and goods with respect to the wage rate within a given time period). Income effects appear in these implicit supply functions via budget constraints and the functional forms of preference functions. Labor supplies and savings are derived from these functions, and these derived elasticities are not necessarily the same from year to year. In the Engen et al. study, labor supply was backward-bending with respect to the wage rate, typical of most models. The intratemporal substitution elasticity was 0.8, the intertemporal substitution elasticity was 0.25, and the factor substitution elasticity was 1.0, values from the Auerbach and Kotlikoff (1987) model. The latter two values are similar to assumptions in the Engen-Gale model, which has a roughly fixed labor supply. Auerbach and Kotlikoff considered 0.25 to reflect empirical estimates of the intertemporal substitution elasticity (which ranged from 0.1 to 1).

Intertemporal models tend to dominate in the academic literature, and to most economists, a life-cycle model appears more realistic than an economy characterized by a single, infinitely lived consumer (or a group of infinitely lived consumers). The latter, with its simpler mathematics, has been used frequently, but has been criticized. Solow (1994), for example, stresses that this model was originally developed to represent the decision making of a social planner and not as a descriptive model of the economy. Moreover, a life-cycle model can reflect differences between the timing over a lifetime and distribution across age cohorts of consumption versus wage taxes that cannot be reflected in other models. Consumption taxes, for example, reduce taxes during periods of saving (when young) and increase them in old age, compared with an income or a wage tax. They also impose a lump-sum tax on the accumulated capital of older cohorts, while cutting lifetime tax burdens of the young. Yet, even though the more complex life-cycle models abstract from many important real-life characteristics, it is difficult to find empirical estimates that exactly match the relationships in the model, and model results are often at odds with historical observation.

The tax shift in the Engen et al. experiments was from a 20 percent flat income tax to a flat consumption tax, and a flat wage tax – changes that would eliminate taxes on the normal return to capital and would, in the first case, change wage rates very little (as taxes were collected on the slightly smaller consumption base) and, in the second case, reduce wage rates significantly in the short run as taxes were collected on the significantly smaller wage base. Sensitivity analysis was done to explore what causes the models to produce different results. Table 2.2 shows the Engen et al. consumption tax results, including not only the effects of different fundamental model types, but also the effects of fixing the labor supply response and of introducing myopia and uncertainty into the life-cycle models.

Table 2.2. Output Effects in the Engen-Gravelle-Smetters Simulation

Model Type	Year				Long Run
	1	4	10	25	
Reduced form	0.0	0.2	0.4	0.9	2.3
Infinite horizon	2.1	3.0	4.1	5.7	6.8
Infinite horizon, fixed labor	0.3	1.0	2.2	4.4	7.7
Life cycle, perfect foresight	3.4	4.3	5.4	6.5	6.9
Life cycle, perfect foresight, fixed labor	0.4	1.6	3.4	6.0	7.6
Life cycle, myopia, fixed labor	0.6	1.9	3.6	6.1	7.7
Life cycle, myopia, fixed labor, uncertainty	0.3	0.9	1.6	2.6	3.2

Source: Engen, Gravelle, and Smetters (1997, table 2A).

Short-Run Results

The factors driving the short-run results in the intertemporal models (although not in the reduced form models) may be surprising to most people.

In the reduced-form model, a shift from a proportional income tax to a proportional consumption tax has little effect on output in the short run, barring extreme savings elasticities, simply because it takes the capital stock a long time to accumulate. (No labor supply response occurs with a proportional tax shift because the uncompensated labor supply elasticity is zero.) The savings rate, given an assumed growth rate of 2 percent, could double and the capital stock would increase by only 2 percent, with net output increasing by only 0.5 percent. This modest effect is reflected in Table 2.1 for the Gravelle simulation results. Setting the uncompensated labor supply response to zero rather than at a higher elasticity does not dampen the response. Indeed, were the labor supply elasticity positive, there would be a contraction in the shift to a consumption tax because the wage rate falls initially as the tax rate rises (because the consumption base is smaller than the income base). In the Gravelle simulations for the JCT study this effect is offset because of the flattening of the rate structure, allowing a modest fall in marginal tax rates. Nevertheless, relying on small income and substitution effects that tend to offset each other, labor supply increases are modest.

Similarly, modest (although larger) output effects occurred in the intertemporal models when labor supply was fixed. Simply put, models that do not have a labor supply response, or have a small response, will not produce a large short-run result. Yet significant short-run output increases occurred in intertemporal models when labor was no longer fixed. What is surprising is why and how much labor supply expands in these models.

The labor supply expanded in the intertemporal models studied by Engen et al. that allowed for variable labor, but not because of higher marginal wages, which, in these models, tended to fall initially rather than rise because the labor supply expands faster than the capital stock. Rather, labor supply increases in response to higher rates of return. Individuals allocate consumption over time; in models with endogenous labor, consumption includes leisure. A higher rate of return causes individuals, other things equal, to allocate more consumption of goods and of leisure into the future. This effect is particularly pronounced in the infinite-horizon model which has an infinite planning period. To reallocate leisure to the future, it must be reduced today. An immediate increase in labor supply occurs, with the earnings, in turn, saved. This result follows from the basic model structure; however, there is no empirical evidence of a pronounced response of labor supply to a change in the rate of return.

In the infinite-horizon model with replacement of a flat income tax with a flat consumption tax, the labor supply initially expanded by 2.4 percent, leading to a 1.8 percent output increase. The remainder of the 2.1 percent increase in output (0.3 percent) came from an increased capital stock. With a fixed labor supply, output rises only 0.3 percent. This labor supply phenomenon explains much of the response in the Jorgenson-Wilcoxen type model and is illustrated with sensitivity analysis. When the intertemporal substitution elasticity falls to 0.05, output increase is only 0.1 percent in the first year; with elasticities of 0.5 and 1, it is 3.6 and 5.2 percent respectively. These results help explain the expansion in the Jorgenson-Wilcoxen model, shown in Table 2.1. Labor supply increased by the greatest amount in any model, 6.8 percent, but their model had an intertemporal substitution elasticity of one.

The labor supply effect is strong in part because of the nature of the function allowing a choice between leisure and consumption within a period. This function's mathematical form forces an income elasticity of one for both goods and leisure (creating a backward bending labor supply curve for changes in wages because the substitution elasticity is 0.8). But, in translating from leisure demand to labor supply, it is affected by another parameter that allows labor to be quite elastic: the availability of existing leisure hours relative to work hours, an independent number set by the researcher, usually without any particular empirical basis. This parameter is set relatively high in the base case model in the Engen et al. study, leading to larger responses (including responses to wage changes) than suggested by the empirical evidence on labor supply elasticities. If we adjust this parameter to reflect the consensus of a relatively inelastic labor supply with respect to wage changes (as set in the reduced-form model), by lowering the ratio of available hours to current work, the initial output effect is only 0.6 percent.

If the base case values are kept, however, and the tax shift is assumed to be from a currently progressive tax similar to the current income tax to a proportional tax, a simulation that maximizes the power of the labor supply response, the first-year effect is a 6.5 percent increase in output. Simulations with the Jorgenson-Wilcoxen-type model of a shift to a VAT, given the high intertemporal elasticity, could yield even larger initial responses – responses that are far in excess of observed shifts in the economy. Indeed, Jorgenson and Wilcoxen in this volume find a much larger effect: an increase in labor supply of close to 28–29 percent and an increase in output of 13 percent. (This simulation also reflects the replacement of state and local income taxes with a consumption tax.)

A second phenomenon affects labor supply in the life-cycle type of intertemporal models. In a life-cycle model, a shift to a consumption tax imposes a lump-sum tax on older individuals' wealth, out of which they consume; that is, there is a shift in tax burden from young to old that is not captured in an infinite-horizon model. In the Auerbach-Kotlikoff life-cycle model, endogenous retirement causes the hours of work to decline, with the last cohorts of individuals providing no hours of work. The endogenous retirement results from declining productivity with age; eventually the available wage becomes so low that individuals no longer wish to work. When some wealth is confiscated through the lump-sum tax, these individuals supply more labor and are responsible for much of the total labor increase. In the basic life-cycle simulation in Table 2.2, about half of the 3.8 percent increase in labor supply came from cohorts over sixty-five years of age.

This return to work happens quite naturally in the mathematical framework of the life-cycle model. But realistic retirement is more likely to reflect an increasing fraction of workers retired at each age. It is highly implausible that these workers would reenter the work force in large numbers, particularly after having been retired for a period of time. Yet, this effect is responsible for much of the large labor supply response in the life-cycle model. The increase in labor supply in the life-cycle model with variable labor is 3.8 percent, and the output effect is 3.4 percent: an increase of under 3 percent in output due to labor supply, with the 0.4 percent remainder due to the 2.3 percent increase in the capital stock. With a fixed labor supply, the increase in output is only 0.4 percent.

The life-cycle model is also affected by the interest rate effect on leisure, although less than the infinite-horizon model. With an intertemporal elasticity of 0.05, first-year output rises by a still significant 1.9 percent; with an elasticity of 0.5, the output effect rises to 4.7 percent.

The importance of labor supply can be seen by contrasting the consumption and wage tax shifts; the latter increases taxes on wages because the wage tax base is much smaller than the income tax base and there is no onetime windfall tax on existing capital. Labor supply and savings fall; output falls by 0.4 percent in the infinite-horizon model and by 1.7 percent in the life-cycle model.

Savings responses are large in the intertemporal models studied by Engen et al., compared to the small elasticities in empirical work that are often not statistically different from zero. The after-tax rate of return rises about 25 percent, which in the reduced-form model increases savings about 9.5 percent. In the infinite-horizon and life-cycle models with a consumption tax shift, savings increases by 81 percent and 105 percent, equivalent to elasticities of 3 or 4.

Savings responses are large in the models with fixed labor supply as well, although not as large: 50 percent and 87 percent for the infinite-horizon and life-cycle models, respectively. Even so, the savings responses are dampened by the assumption of perfect foresight, that is, that individuals know that future rates of return will fall as the capital stock increases. (The infinite-horizon model has perfect foresight by definition.) In the fixed-labor-supply, life-cycle model with myopic expectations (agents assume current rates of return will prevail), savings rate increases are larger, 127 percent, and the initial output effect is 0.6 percent.

These pronounced savings responses cause the output effects to grow over the first few years; by year ten, output in the infinite-horizon model increases by 4.1 percent (variable labor) and 2.2 percent (fixed labor). In the life-cycle model, output increases by 5.4 percent (variable labor) and 3.4 percent (fixed labor). With myopia and fixed labor supply, the output effect rises to 3.6 percent.

A final variation studied by Engen et al. is the introduction of uncertainty and a precautionary savings motive into a myopic, fixed-labor model. Because precautionary savings is much less responsive to the rate of return than life-cycle savings, the effects on savings and output are much smaller in this model, although even in this case the savings rate increased by 51 percent.

In sum, because the short-run effects in the intertemporal models tend to be outside the range of any empirically observed measures of behavioral response, a reduced-form model, employing these modest supply elasticities, would inevitably yield much smaller results. (The Robbins model, which is an outlier by any standard, has other factors driving it, which are discussed later.)

The Long Run

In the infinite-horizon model, an infinitely lived consumer allocates consumption (which can include leisure). A characteristic of this model is that the savings rate is infinitely elastic in the long run and the after-tax rate of return returns to its original value. The capital stock expands to achieve a fall in the original pretax return to the initial after-tax return when the tax on new investment is removed. This effect occurs because a small deviation in the rate of return will cause an infinitely large deviation in relative prices. The price of consumption in year t (with t running from zero to infinity) is $(1/(1 + r))^t$, where r is the after-tax rate of return; thus, a small change in the rate of return will cause a huge deviation in the ratio of consumption in periods that are far apart. The economy approaches a steady-state growth rate only as r approaches its original value. Thus, the model choice predetermines an important aspect of the long-run outcome. The effects on output are, however, affected by the substitution elasticity between capital and labor in production and by the supply response of labor (governed by the intertemporal substitution elasticity). When the factor substitution elasticity is low, the effects on output are low. The intertemporal substitution elasticity, however, affects the adjustment path.

There are also powerful forces in life-cycle models that push the rate of return back toward its original value, unless intertemporal substitution elasticities are quite small, because the lifetime horizon is very long. In fact, results from a standard life-cycle model were, in the long run, similar to those in infinite-horizon models in the Engen et al. experiments. Thus, the life-cycle model has built into it an implicitly high steady-state savings elasticity.

Contrast these effects with the long-run steady state in a reduced-form model that relies on empirical measures of savings elasticities. In such a model, the after-tax return can remain well above the initial return. Note also that the time path of adjustment tends to be slow in the reduced form model as compared to the intertemporal models; after twenty-five years, 40 percent of the adjustment in the reduced-form model has taken place, as compared to 80 percent or more in most of the intertemporal models. Part of that slow adjustment is due to the general path of change: in the intertemporal models, the savings elasticity is initially higher and declines over time, rather than being constant as in the reduced-form model. Adjustment also reflects the effects of fixing the labor supply response and of introducing myopia and uncertainty into the life-cycle models. (The steady state and time path of adjustment in Table 2.2 are in a closed-economy context; open or partially open economies can have important effects, as is discussed later.)

FULL-EMPLOYMENT MODELS: OTHER FEATURES
OF LIFE-CYCLE MODELS

The causes of differences among the full-employment reduced-form models are differences in elasticities, while there are many other features of life-cycle models that could affect outcomes. Most have been discussed and all are summarized in Table 2.3. Note that endogenous labor supply actually decreases output effects in the long run, because the shift in leisure over time causes a smaller long-run labor supply. Labor supply is also affected by changes in tax progressivity, and the pattern of a fall in long-run labor supply does not occur consistently.

Myopia

Life-cycle models can be myopic (individuals believe the prices they observe today will continue) or have perfect foresight. Myopia has no long-run effect, but myopic models have larger short-run effects because people do not realize that the rate of return will fall in the future as the capital stock grows. Thus, they perceive that future rates of return will be higher than they would be otherwise and overshoot their saving (and labor supply in endogenous labor models).

Bequests and Bequest Motives

Bequests and bequest motives affect outcomes. Altruistic bequests (taking into account the utility of children) lead to an infinite-horizon model where intergenerational redistribution does not occur. The "joy of giving" motive, where the bequest itself has utility and is treated as consumption, is not likely to have much of an effect on outcomes (Gravelle, 1991). Bequests due to uncertain life-spans tend to reduce retirement savings responses to interest rates. Bequests that are fixed and added to allow calibration (it is very difficult to calibrate a model without bequests to the actual economy) decrease the responsiveness of the model, as a smaller amount of the capital stock is due to interest-sensitive lifetime capital accumulation.

Existing Consumption Tax Treatment

The current tax system is a hybrid consumption-income tax system, as reflected in the Engen-Gale model. (Some limited consumption tax aspects are also in the Auerbach et al. model.) These consumption tax effects reflect the existence of accelerated depreciation and consumption tax treatment of certain types of retirement savings; taking these features into account reduces the effects of the tax shift.

**Table 2.3. Effect of Model Features as Compared with
Simplified Life-Cycle Model**

Feature	Effect on Output		Characteristic of These Models[a]
	Short Run	**Long Run**	
Infinite-horizon form	Lower	Higher	JW
Endogenous labor	Higher	Lower	FR, JW, AKSW
Myopia	Higher	None	FR, EG
Uncertainty	Lower	Lower	EG
Bequest objective			
Altruistic	Lower	Higher	JW
Joy of giving	Little effect	Little effect	AKSW
Uncertain life-span	Lower	Lower	EG
Calibration (fixed)	Lower	Lower	FR
Existing consumption			
tax treatment	Lower	Lower	EG
Lower substitution elasticities			
Intertemporal	Lower	Sometimes lower	FR .15, .5, AKSW .25, EG .3, JW 1.0
Intratemporal	Higher	Lower	FR .15, .5, all others 0.8
Factor	Lower	Lower	EG, AKSW 1.0, FR 0.8, JW 0.2
Stone-Geary	Lower	Lower	FR
Depreciation	Lower	Lower	FR, JW
Fewer leisure hours	Lower	Higher	FR
Multisector model	Higher	Higher	FR, JW
Transition relief			
Depreciation recovery	Lower	None	
Through wage tax	Lower	Lower	
Open economy	Uncertain	Uncertain	

Notes: The simplified life-cycle model is a certainty model with no bequests and fixed labor, similar to the Summers (1981a) model. Evaluation of features and characterization of models relies on a variety of sources including the findings of Engen et al. (1997), discussions of the models by authors and others in the JCT study (1997), and conversations with various modelers, as well as the author's own knowledge of these models. Note that there is a much more extensive discussion of the Fullerton-Rogers model in Fullerton and Rogers (1993).

[a] Abbreviations for the models: AKSW = Auerbach, Kotlikoff, Smetters, and Walliser; EG = Engen and Gale; FR = Fullerton and Rogers; JW = Jorgenson and Wilcoxen.

Elasticities

A lower intertemporal substitution elasticity tends to lead to smaller effects, at least in the short run, as can be easily seen in the Fullerton-Rogers results for high and low elasticities. Long-run effects depend on model structure. The intertemporal and factor substitution elasticities can also play an important role in determining output effects. In the Engen et al. simulation of the infinite-horizon model, a lower intertemporal substitution elasticity produced a larger labor supply response in the short run, probably because the after-tax wage fell (with a smaller tax base), and because the less substitutable consumption and leisure are, the smaller the offsetting contraction in labor supply due to a lower wage. (Labor supply still rises, however, because of the intertemporal effect, that is, the desire to move leisure from the present to the future.) The reverse effect occurs in the long run. Lower factor substitution elasticities dampen both short-run and long-run effects. The normal pattern for an endogenous labor model is a short-run rise and long-run fall in labor, while the capital stock rises continually. Relative supply shifts in factors can be accommodated more easily the more substitutable are factor inputs.

Other features that alter supply responses are Stone-Geary utility functions (requiring a minimum consumption each period), depreciation that reduces the price effects of changes in the rate of return on the marginal product of capital, and changing initial leisure (which was smaller in the Fullerton-Rogers model than in the Auerbach et al. model and the Jorgenson-Wilcoxen model).

Multiple Sectors

Multiple sectors can affect gross output levels when capital is reallocated to less durable business capital and out of housing. If the model accounts for depreciation, the gross marginal product of less durable capital is higher, other things equal, to account for depreciation; hence gross (although not necessarily net) output is increased. There can also be small efficiency gains from reallocating capital more efficiently that show up in increased output. The ability of the economy to substitute labor and capital increases in a multisector model, because resources can be shifted across sectors with different capital intensities.

Transition Relief

Transition relief can also affect the output levels under reform (see Zodrow, Chapter 9 in this volume). A consumption tax is a lump-sum tax on old capital along with a tax on wages. For a VAT or sales tax, the value of existing capital falls in terms of purchasing power if prices are allowed to rise. With any consumption tax without price accommodation, the value of equity capital falls (and hence the stock market falls).

One method of providing relief from this lump-sum tax is to continue to allow depreciation deductions and basis recovery on sale. This method provides only partial relief because depreciation deductions are recovered over a period of time, but it slows and reduces the imposition of the lump-sum tax. This relief reduces the initial labor supply response of the elderly in the life-cycle model and also requires higher marginal tax rates on labor income during transition. The output effects are delayed, but there is no long-run effect. An alternate method of providing transition relief is to use a wage tax, which eliminates the wealth effect on the old and reduces the short-run output effects, as well as permanently lowering the tax base, and thus reducing long-run effects.

Open Economy

It is possible to modify life-cycle models and allow a small open economy with perfect capital mobility; such a modification was made for the Engen-Gale model in the JCT study. These and other attempts to model open economies are discussed by Ballard (Chapter 5 in this volume). The open-economy assumption would actually have uncertain effects, however, because it tends to keep interest rates from falling as much as in the closed-economy simulations. Open-economy assumptions may not work well in models that do not distinguish between debt and equity, and it is ideal to model explicitly consumer behavior and portfolio choices in other countries. It is also difficult to allow perfect mobility of capital in an infinite-horizon model or its equivalent, a model with a utility-based bequest motive, because the after-tax rate of return must return to a particular value and inconsistencies between differential tax rates, mobile capital, and fixed after-tax returns in different countries can arise, as noted in Mendoza and Tesar (1998).

The Intertemporal Model Results Revisited

Clearly, it is virtually impossible to sort out the effects of these features in the different models used in the JCT study, although some insights are possible. First, the reasons for the small responses from the Engen-Gale model are clear: relatively fixed labor supply response, uncertainty regarding earnings and life-span, and the modeling of existing consumption features of the current system, especially with respect to retirement income (e.g., pensions).

The Auerbach et al. model, however, has significant effects typical of a one-sector life-cycle model, with a large long-run increase in the capital stock and output, and a small increase in labor supply in the short run that disappears over time.

The other two models are difficult to disentangle. The Fullerton-Rogers low-elasticity model (where both intertemporal and intratemporal substitution elasticities are 0.15) yields small results, and that model also has some other features, such as bequests, Stone-Geary utility functions, limited initial leisure, and depreciation that limit supply responses. These effects are much larger with higher elasticities of 0.5. It also seems likely that output is increased by the reallocation of capital from housing into business uses in this multisectoral model. In the short run, before the capital stock has increased, assets are probably shifted from housing into business; business assets have larger depreciation rates, and this shift increases GDP. (Short-run output effects cannot be fully explained by labor supply increases, which in the short run are 0.3 percent for the low-elasticity case and 3.7 percent for the high-elasticity case.) As capital expands and the rate of return falls, capital probably shifts back into the less durable assets, thereby lowering gross output from reallocation. (There are also some efficiency gains that affect output.) This shift into less durable assets with higher depreciation-inclusive marginal products does not increase welfare by the amount of the increase in output, because more output would be devoted to depreciation; such discrepancies are a problem with using output measures. The Fullerton-Rogers model also has disaggregated households and, in general, is such a complex model that it is difficult to isolate the forces driving its results.

The Jorgenson-Wilcoxen results are also not easy to explain. The capital stock increases very little, which is unexpected in an infinite-horizon model. The low-factor substitution elasticity, however, may play an important role in constraining the long-run increase in capital and output, given the large labor supply response (which could derive from both interest rate and wage rate effects). Because an infinite-horizon model has representative individuals, there are no income effects to moderate labor supply response to lower marginal tax rates. There is a reallocation of capital from housing to business use, which accounts for some output effects and makes some capital available to combine with labor in production, allowing output to expand despite a very low factor substitution elasticity. The Jorgenson-Wilcoxen study of the flat tax and the retail sales tax in this volume suggests that the personal exemptions in the flat tax play an important role in restricting the economic effects of the tax shift.

Other Limitations of Intertemporal Models

This brief tour of the features of intertemporal models serves to illustrate the complexity of these models and how difficult it is to explain their results. It also explains how easy it is in an intertemporal model to obtain either large or small results with plausible model features, making it difficult to rely on these models for predicting the effects of reform and for policy guidance.

Table 2.3 does not address some other troubling aspects of these intertemporal models. Intertemporal models are highly driven by their functional forms. For example, the elasticity of substitution between consumption bundles in different periods is always the same, even though in reality individuals would probably not see consumption thirty years apart as equally substitutable with consumption one year apart. Consider an individual planning a trip, when a temporary airline ticket tax is imposed. Equal substitution elasticities suggest that one might be just as willing, or even more willing, to delay the trip for thirty years as for one year. Most of us would find this preference function implausible.

The fundamental shortcoming of some of these intertemporal models, however, is that they tend to generate results that are at odds with empirical evidence about the responsiveness of savings and labor supply to changes in factor prices, a point also stressed by Charles Ballard (Chapter 5 in this volume).

The Contrast between Efficiency and Output

Economists would consider efficiency gains rather than increases in output the relevant measure of the desirability of tax changes. Other things equal, efficiency gains tend to be greater when elasticities are greater; however, efficiency gains cannot be determined by examining output effects, because output changes do not account for forgone leisure and consumption. Indeed, output gains may be positive in a life-cycle model with negative welfare effects, if output increases arise from income effects (e.g., increased labor of older individuals).

Most of the JCT studies did not report efficiency gains. Fullerton and Rogers reported a welfare gain of approximately 0.96 percent of lifetime income with high elasticities and a loss of 0.04 percent with low elasticities. Because older individuals lose and younger and future ones gain, this measure is the present discounted value of welfare gains of all generations. (Note, however, that lifetime income is larger than lifetime output or consumption, because it also includes leisure.)

In the earlier Brookings studies, Auerbach (1996) and Engen and Gale (1996) reported efficiency gains. For a flat tax proposal, Auerbach found that output rose by 2.7 percent in the short run and 6.1 percent in the long run, while welfare gains were 1.4 percent of lifetime income. These welfare gains were obtained with a simulation that used lump-sum transfers to keep the utility of transitional generations fixed, so it is larger than a weighted average of welfare gains over all individuals because individuals already alive had, by construction, no welfare gain.

Engen and Gale report welfare gains across cohorts; they find a long-run gain of 0.4 percent for a flat tax with transition rules and a personal allowance and a gain of 1.0 percent without these features. Most older generations have smaller and, in the latter case, negative welfare effects. Thus, efficiency gains across all cohorts are likely to be quite small.

Without a consistent method of summing welfare gains, it is difficult to compare models. Auerbach and Kotlikoff (1987) and Auerbach (1996) overstate the overall average gain, but simply reporting gains for each cohort leaves one without an overall measure. The most meaningful single efficiency gain would be one that devised a lump-sum redistribution method to provide for the same proportional welfare gain for all cohorts. No measures account for the cost of redistribution of income, which can occur across generations and across incomes. A social welfare function that incorporates a preference for equality would probably yield a lower value than the preceding measures of efficiency gain.

FULL-EMPLOYMENT REDUCED-FORM MODELS AND THE ROBBINS RESULTS

Most of the reduced-form models in the JCT study are limited to shorter-run projections and employ small supply-side elasticities. The Gravelle and Coopers & Lybrand models have zero uncompensated labor supply elasticities with respect to the wage rate (that are composed of offsetting income and substitution elasticities of 0.2). The other models have larger uncompensated labor supply elasticities (0.2 for DRI/McGraw-Hill, 0.3 for Macroeconomic Advisers, and a lagged elasticity of almost 0.4 for the Robbins model). Gravelle and Coopers & Lybrand have savings elasticities of 0.4, while DRI/McGraw-Hill and Macroeconomic Advisers have elasticities of 0.2; Robbins has an elasticity of 1.0. All of the models except Coopers & Lybrand have factor substitution elasticities of 1; the Coopers & Lybrand model has a factor substitution elasticity of less than 0.3.

Higher labor supply elasticities play some role in larger output effects in some of the reduced-form models (and these elasticities, ranging from 0.2 to 0.4, are on the higher side of the range observed in the empirical evidence). However, another important effect that interacts with this labor supply effect is the possibility of inflows of capital from abroad. By far the most powerful effects are in the Robbins model. Allowing capital to flow in from abroad can potentially increase output, and having an open economy is a reasonable assumption. The magnitude of the effects of an open economy are quite large, however, especially in the Robbins model, which essentially assumes an infinite savings elasticity with a very short adjustment period. That is, the after-tax rate of return returns quickly to its preexisting value, thereby driving down the pretax rate of return substantially (because the tax has been removed). This infinite elasticity assumption requires a dramatic increase in the capital stock, which is magnified because of an assumption that productivity will be further enhanced through an independent advance in productivity with a larger capital stock. This larger capital stock also increases the wage rate and, via the labor supply elasticity, the amount of labor. This model also does not address the effects on debt finance which would go in the opposite direction. Gravelle and Engen-Gale – both in JCT (1997) – found much smaller effects from an open-economy assumption.

Moreover, there is considerable reason to reject the assumption of perfect substitutability of capital around the world. That assumption is only appropriate for a small country; tax changes in the United States would have significant general-equilibrium effects on worldwide interest rates. Moreover, because of various risk and information characteristics, there are strong reasons to believe that investments in different countries are imperfect substitutes (see Gravelle and Smetters, 1998, for a survey; see also Ballard, Chapter 5 in this volume). For that matter, if debt is more mobile than equity across countries, a shift to consumption taxes could cause a capital outflow.

If the Robbins model results are deemed outside the reasonable range of responses, there is more agreement among the reduced-form models. Some models allowed capital inflows and the Macroeconomic Advisers model allowed for transition relief, which tends to dampen any supply response in the short run. The low Coopers & Lybrand factor substitution elasticity could also constrain their effects, but was relatively unimportant because both labor and capital expanded at similar rates. In addition, except for the Gravelle model, all of the reduced-form models had multiple sectors, so that gross output could grow because of reallocation of capital to less durable types; net national product would probably experience a much smaller increase.

OTHER ISSUES OF DISPUTE

This section discusses several other issues of dispute regarding the possible economic consequences of a shift to a consumption tax. Some have been the subject of intensive study, whereas others have barely been addressed at all.

Asset Values: The Stock Market

Although not explicitly modeled in the dynamic models, the stock market should fall substantially in those cases where price accommodation does not occur, as would presumably be the case for the flat tax (where no accommodation is needed). This fall in price would be permanent: the value of equity claims would be smaller than the market value of the firm's net assets.

A consumption tax is a tax on old capital plus a tax on wages. Whenever an asset is sold and converted into consumption, the tax applies. Moreover, in the case of the flat tax, all of the burden of the asset effect (for both debt and equity finance) falls on equity capital. As explained by Gravelle (1995), if a third of capital is financed by debt, a 20 percent tax would lead to a 30 percent fall in the stock market (.2/(1 − .33) times 100 percent).

The burden will fall on all business assets in cases where a price accommodation is allowed, as would be needed in order to avoid an economic contraction in the case of a VAT or retail sales tax. In these cases, nominal asset values (stock market equities and bond prices) would be unchanged, but their purchasing power in terms of consumption goods would fall.

Despite this rather straightforward theoretical finding, some economists have suggested that stock market values may not fall following the imposition of the flat tax and, indeed, may go up (see Gale and Hassett, 1998; Auerbach, 1997; Lyon and Merrill, 1999). The arguments made for this finding are both theoretical (adjustment costs, short-run demand considerations, and advantages to existing firms) and empirical (previous episodes of allowing incentives to new investment, such as the investment tax credit, have not resulted in asset price declines).

It is important to understand the implications of asset price effects for the response to a consumption tax. If asset prices never fall, there is, for corporate capital investment, no elimination of tax on new investment. (If asset price effects are delayed or reduced, these consumption tax effects are delayed or reduced.) Corporate taxes would remain and, despite their lower rates, may well be nearly as large as their preexisting values. For firms growing at moderate rates, the value of expensing is not much larger than the value of depreciation. Thus, much of the increased rate of return in the corporate sector (arising from a corporate consumption tax base) would not occur. This effect would be increased by the disallowance of the interest deduction, unless interest rates fell enough to offset loss of the tax deduction. There would be no wealth effect on older individuals and no complete elimination of the tax at the margin. To the small extent that corporate taxes fell, the effects would be the same as a reduction in capital income tax rates. The modeling in all of the studies discussed thus far would be incorrect. Models that allowed transitions would also be incorrect because in these models asset prices still fall (implicitly), but with a delay.

There are some legitimate reasons why the full stock market price reduction would not occur. One is suggested by Auerbach (1996), who points out that the current system is not characterized by a pure income tax. Because depreciation is not indexed but is accelerated, a capital investment is taxed first below and then above the statutory rate. As a result, because old capital is subject to higher rates than new capital investment, there should be an existing discount, which he estimates at about 8 percent, about 40 percent of the asset price reduction. (This amount is declining because of the longer lives adopted, especially for buildings, in 1986 and 1993; steady-state calculations by this author using data from Gravelle, 1994, suggest a 4 percent discount, or about 20 percent of the total.) Although this argument is legitimate, it also suggests that consumption tax effects may have been overstated in life-cycle models.

A second reason for the failure of the stock market to fall is adjustment costs, or lags. These effects would act to delay the short-run effects calculated in life-cycle models that arise from the wealth effect. Note, however, that adjustment costs do not refer to the adjustment to a new level of capital stock (which can take decades); the fall in the stock market could occur very quickly (even overnight) because it is a financial rather than a physical adjustment. Indeed, a fall in the stock market should *precede* the behavioral response that ultimately leads to an expansion of investment.

Empirical estimates that suggest the stock market did not adjust in the past would be inconsistent with Auerbach's discounting mechanism for existing asset values (because firms should issue stock when the value rises above the cost of replacing assets and individual investors should shift their portfolios to firms that are growing more rapidly and have higher rates of return). Empirical estimates of these types of stock market effects are extremely difficult to make, because it is difficult to control for other factors. These results may arise from adjustment costs. If, however, there is some fundamental failure of markets to adjust, the estimates of the effects of a shift to consumption tax are overstated. Consumption tax effects will still occur with unincorporated business capital, where taxes are imposed directly. Accepting a theory that stock market prices will not fall will not only suggest that the growth effects of a consumption tax are unlikely to occur, but also suggests that investments in unincorporated business capital and housing will continue to be favored relative to corporate investment, and thus that much of the efficiency gain from a reallocation of capital would not occur. If we believe this argument, a consumption tax is hardly worth considering, which makes doubts about the fall in the stock market important to resolve.

Risk and Excess Returns

Another thread of research that questions whether consumption taxes are really the equivalent of exempting the tax on capital income has been advanced by Glenn Hubbard in a number of presentations and discussed by Gentry and Hubbard (1997a) and by Hubbard in this volume. Much of their discussion is aimed at distributional analysis, but it is also relevant to growth. Basically, the notion they advance is that income and consumption taxes are similar in their treatment of much of the return to capital – namely, the portion that represents risk and the portion that represents excess returns. (The issue of the treatment of risk in a consumption tax has also been addressed by Zodrow, 1995.)

These insights suggest that behavioral responses to changes in tax treatment are less powerful than those in models without risk, because they suggest that the income and consumption taxes are not as different as depicted in those models.

Interest Rates

There has also been considerable debate about the effect of consumption taxes on interest rates (see Feldstein, 1995b; Gravelle, 1996a; Auerbach, 1996; R. Hall, 1996a, 1997; and Zodrow, Chapter 9 in this volume).

In the simplest world, with only debt finance, no risk, and all income measured correctly, a firm pays no tax on earnings. Income is taxed, but all income is paid out as deductible interest. If a consumption tax is imposed, the cost of capital for the firm is unchanged: interest is no longer deducted, but cost of a new investment is expensed, the equivalent in present value terms of deducting interest. If there is no savings response (because the after-tax return has increased), the interest rate is not affected.

This simple analysis does not account for three effects: the possibility of savings and growth; substitution between debt and equity; and the imperfect measurement of income. The first effect suggests a decline in the interest rate, because individuals will increase their savings as the after-tax rate of return rises, and that supply increase will drive down interest rates. If equity income is initially taxed more heavily than debt, simple portfolio effects would predict a shift from debt to equity finance; to return to a financial equilibrium, this shift would likely be accompanied by a rise in the interest rate. This effect cannot be precisely determined, because both firms and individuals shift their supplies and demands for different types of finance. That is, the demand for debt finance by firms and the supply by individuals both contract simultaneously.

(This analysis assumes, as discussed earlier, that the stock market falls, and equity capital becomes more attractive to investors.)

Gravelle (1996a) suggests that a more powerful effect is the combination of inflation and the deduction of nominal interest. Although taxable income is close to economic income before interest deductibility (because accelerated depreciation roughly offsets the failure to index depreciation allowances for inflation), nominal interest deductibility means that deductions are too large. In effect, debt-financed capital is subject to a subsidy, rather than a tax, at the firm level. If interest deductibility is removed, that subsidy is lost, leading to a much more powerful contraction of the demand for debt finance. A significant fall in interest rates would almost certainly occur simply to keep the cost of debt finance from rising dramatically. Gravelle finds, using a portfolio substitution model, that interest rates are likely to fall about a percentage point.

One caveat about interest rates has to do with international capital flows. If debt were perfectly mobile internationally and the United States were a small country, the interest rate could not change because the United States would be a price taker. Even with these assumptions relaxed, the fall in the interest rate may be limited by supply and demand forces in the international capital market.

Asset Prices: Owner-Occupied Housing

Because owner-occupied housing is not treated as a business, it should not suffer the permanent lump-sum tax that falls on owners of assets. In the case of a flat tax without price accommodation, the price of housing would be unaffected as in the case of capital goods in general, and there would be no additional tax upon sale. With a VAT and price accommodation (but not the RST) the price of capital goods would rise; housing prices would rise in nominal but not real value. Under a retail sales tax the price of new housing would rise to reflect the tax, because the sellers must recoup taxes; hence, owners of existing housing will experience a rise in price. It would also be possible to exempt housing from these taxes (by rebating the VAT and not imposing the sales tax; housing prices would fall in real, but not nominal, terms).

Most of the attention to owner-occupied housing has, however, reflected concerns about the implications for house prices of short-run reductions in demand for housing, which loses its tax-favored status. Such contractions could cause general economy-wide disruption. The attention to housing prices in the short run was addressed in studies by DRI/McGraw-Hill (1995, 1996), Capozza, Green, and Hendershott (1996), Foster (1996), and Gravelle (1996a). The first two of these studies predicted very significant declines in housing prices. Foster and Gravelle suggested that the effects would be much smaller.

In large part, the reasoning behind the first two of these studies is that demand will contract for a commodity that is relatively inelastic in supply, causing a large fall in housing prices. Gravelle (1996a) questions these results on a variety of grounds, among them, the possibility that supply is not inelastic in the short run and is clearly not so in the long run (when the housing stock shrinks and land can be put to other uses). Even if the stock of housing is in more or less fixed supply in the short run, housing offered for sale may be quite responsive to price, particularly if the reduced demand is seen as temporary. Even a modest degree of elasticity in the supply curve, particularly coupled with factors that limit the contraction in demand (such as an expected fall in the interest rate, adjustment costs that limit the attractiveness of business investment, and cash flow effects that might actually benefit liquidity-constrained investors), could result in much smaller price effects. The possibility that most first-time home purchasers are constrained not by lifetime income and alternative investment options but by current cash flow limitations is particularly important, because both the reductions in direct tax rates for these individuals (which offset the loss of mortgage interest and property tax deductions) and the possibility of lower interest rates could alleviate most contractionary effects. Gravelle presents historical data that suggest that significant changes in the cost of housing capital have had relatively modest effects on housing prices.

Pension Plans and Other Forms of Retirement Saving

Earnings on much retirement savings in the United States are already effectively exempt from income tax. Employer pension plan investments are treated in the same fashion as they would be under a consumption tax: contributions are deducted, and taxes are not imposed until funds are withdrawn (presumably for consumption purposes) in the future. Traditional individual retirement accounts (IRAs) are treated in the same way, although the new "back loaded" individual retirement accounts simply exempt earnings from tax. Certain types of plans offered by life insurance companies also allow for deferral of taxes.

Two important characteristics of these tax favored plans differentiate them from saving in general. First, most of these assets cannot be withdrawn prior to retirement (or leaving a job); IRA contributions can be withdrawn but there are penalties in some cases. Thus, these funds are not readily available for emergencies or to spend for some purchase prior to retirement. Second, most of the employer plans require participation of lower-compensated employees (antidiscrimination rules). It is possible that there is some saving on the part of less compensated workers as a result of being carried along with these plans, which might disappear if there are no special tax incentives to employer plans (see Samwick, 1998).

Could the shift of saving to forms with fewer strings attached and the reduction of pension coverage for lower-income individuals reduce retirement income, and even aggregate saving? Such an outcome might be possible. If retirement funds are readily available to individuals, their need to save for precautionary reasons might decline. This issue has barely been explored.

Other Allocational Effects

Many types of economic activities are encouraged by the current income tax structure and would presumably decline under a consumption tax system. These issues deserve greater attention. The Brookings study included papers on two activities: charitable contributions (Clotfelter and Schmalbeck, 1996) and employer-provided health insurance (Gruber and Poterba, 1996). Both of these authors predicted potentially significant effects, while acknowledging considerable uncertainty about the relevant elasticities. Many economists believe that such activities should be subsidized because of the spillover effects in charitable contributions and the way in which employer health care plans help to deal with adverse selection in the market for health insurance. Some other types of activities that are often viewed as desirable would lose relative attractiveness under a consumption tax plan, including investment in research and development and in human capital formation. In the former case, these expenditures are already treated on a consumption tax basis and are eligible for a tax credit. For human capital investment, investment in the form of forgone earnings and training is effectively expensed, and there are tax credits and subsidies for direct expenditures.

Of course, the removal of many subsidies may be viewed as desirable from an efficiency standpoint (including those to owner-occupied housing, already discussed). The loss of various subsidies to state and local governments (tax exemption of bond interest, deduction of certain state and local taxes) would increase the cost of state and local spending and investment. Shifting to a consumption tax could, however, complicate tax administration, because state and local authorities rely on federal resources for compliance. These issues, though discussed briefly by Zimmerman (1995) and Strauss (1996), have not been addressed in detail. Moreover, many other allocational effects arise from the existence of subsidies. (See the Senate Budget Committee's 1998 tax expenditure compendium for a brief discussion of the approximately 120 special provisions identified in the income tax.)

CONCLUSION

A consumption tax reform represents a major tax revision that would take us in directions we cannot predict without clear benefits. A reasonable alternative is to reject that tax revision in favor of more modest steps. I suspect that is what we face, given our current state of knowledge. Could a dramatic shift in relative prices arising from fundamental tax reform cause a recession? At least two macroeconomic modelers believe that is the case. Could a shift in the location of tax collections, as would occur with a shift to a VAT or RST, cause a short run economic disaster? At least one modeler believes that is the case. Until some better consensus can be reached on this issue – and very little attention has been paid to it thus far – serious contemplation of fundamental tax substitution, particularly of the more radical type, is probably unrealistic.

There is a further question of what we might gain in "supply-side" effects and efficiency gains if we risk this type of turmoil. Despite the predictions of large supply effects from models both simple and incredibly complex, the evidence that we can gain from direct observation of saving and labor supply does not support these results. The survey of these models indicates that they can be designed to produce any type of result, and that most of the mechanisms that lead to large effects in the foreseeable future would not be plausible. As Charles Ballard says in his discussion of intertemporal models, any model that relies on a labor supply response to interest rates is "shooting in the dark" (Joint Committee on Taxation, 1997, p. 155). Moreover, many of the gains estimated are not pure welfare gains. The value of consumption in the future is gained at the cost of less consumption in the present. Output from a larger labor supply is gained at the cost of a reduction in leisure. Output gained by shifting capital to less durable uses may be largely required to replace depreciating assets. Capital imported from abroad must eventually pay returns to foreign owners.

There are potentially significant gains from more neutral treatment of capital income. Distortions between investments in corporate business, noncorporate business, and owner-occupied housing, along with distortions between debt and equity finance, between dividends and retained earnings of corporations, and portfolio distortions arising from the lock-in effect of capital gains taxes are responsible for welfare costs that may be around 1 percent of output, depending on the model used (Gravelle,

1994, chap. 4). However, most of these gains could be achieved through an income tax reform rather than a consumption tax substitution.

The dangers of significant short-run disruptions and the lack of evidence on significant longer-run efficiency gains from shifting to a consumption tax make such a reform a questionable policy. Perhaps the most compelling need for information is on the short-run macroeconomic effects of such a tax shift. In the absence of compelling evidence that such short run disruptions would be minimal, it is probably prudent to pursue tax reform through more incremental revisions to the existing income tax.

Chapter 3

The Economic Impact of Fundamental Tax Reform

Dale W. Jorgenson and Peter J. Wilcoxen

In this chapter we present a new intertemporal general equilibrium model for analyzing the economic impact of tax policies in the United States. We preserve the key features of more highly aggregated models like that of Jorgenson and Yun (1990, 1991a). One important dimension for disaggregation is to introduce a distinction between industries and commodities in order to model business responses to tax-induced price changes. We also distinguish among households by level of wealth and demographic characteristics, so that we can model differences in household responses to tax changes and examine the distributional effects of taxes.

We model demands for different types of capital services in each of thirty-five industrial sectors of the U.S. economy and the household sector. These demands depend on tax policies through measures of the cost of capital presented by Jorgenson and Yun (1991b) that incorporate the characteristic features of U.S. tax law. The cost of capital makes it possible to represent the economically relevant features of highly complex tax statutes in a very succinct form. The cost of capital also summarizes information about the future consequences of investment decisions required for current decisions about capital allocation.

To illustrate the application of our new model, we simulate the economic impacts of fundamental tax reforms. We focus on the effects of substituting a tax on consumption for corporate and individual income taxes at the federal, state, and local levels. We consider two alternative methods for implementing a consumption tax: the flat tax proposed by House Majority Leader Dick Armey and Senator Richard Shelby (H.R.

We are grateful to Richard Goettle for performing the simulations reported in this chapter. This research was supported by the Alliance to Save Energy and is reported in more detail in Norland and Ninassi, *Price It Right* (1998). The authors retain sole responsibility for the views expressed in this chapter and any remaining deficiencies.

1040 and S. 1040) and the national retail sales tax proposed by Chairman Bill Archer of the House Committee on Ways and Means.

AN OVERVIEW OF THE MODEL

In Jorgenson and Wilcoxen (1993) we describe the econometric implementation of an intertemporal general equilibrium model of the U.S. economy. In this section we outline our model, emphasizing the new features that are critical in assessing tax policy impacts. We have constructed submodels for each of four sectors of the U.S. economy: business, household, government, and the rest of the world. Because tax policies affect industries in very different ways, we begin our presentation with the business sector.

Producer Behavior

Modeling the response of producers to changes in tax policies requires distinguishing among industries with different capital intensities. Accordingly, we have subdivided the business sector into the thirty-five industries shown in Table 3.1. Each of these corresponds, roughly, to a two-digit industry in the Standard Industrial Classification. This level of industrial disaggregation makes it possible to measure the impact of alternative policies on relatively narrow segments of the U.S. economy. We have also divided the output of the business sector into thirty-five commodities. Each one is the primary product of one of the industries. Many industries produce secondary products as well; for example, the textile industry produces both textiles and apparel, so that we have allowed for joint production. Each commodity is allocated between deliveries to satisfy intermediate demands by other industries and deliveries to satisfy final demands by households, governments, and the rest of the world.

We represent the technology of each industry by means of an econometric model of producer behavior. In order to estimate the unknown parameters of these production models we have constructed an annual time series of interindustry transactions tables for the U.S. economy for the period 1947 through 1985.[1] The data for each year are divided between a *use* table and a *make* table. The use table shows the quantities of each commodity – intermediate inputs, primary factors of production, and noncompeting imports – used by each industry and final demand category.[2] The make table gives the amount of each commodity

---

[1] Our data integrate the productivity accounts described by Jorgenson (1990) with an accounting system based on the United Nations (1993) System of National Accounts.

[2] Noncompeting imports are imported commodities that are not produced domestically.

Table 3.1. The Definitions of Industries

Number	Description
1	Agriculture, forestry, and fisheries
2	Metal mining
3	Coal mining
4	Crude petroleum and natural gas
5	Nonmetallic mineral mining
6	Construction
7	Food and kindred products
8	Tobacco manufactures
9	Textile mill products
10	Apparel and other textile products
11	Lumber and wood products
12	Furniture and fixtures
13	Paper and allied products
14	Printing and publishing
15	Chemicals and allied products
16	Petroleum refining
17	Rubber and plastic products
18	Leather and leather products
19	Stone, clay, and glass products
20	Primary metals
21	Fabricated metal products
22	Machinery, except electrical
23	Electrical machinery
24	Motor vehicles
25	Other transportation equipment
26	Instruments
27	Miscellaneous manufacturing
28	Transportation and warehousing
29	Communication
30	Electric utilities
31	Gas utilities
32	Trade
33	Finance, insurance, and real estate
34	Other services
35	Government enterprises

produced by each industry. In the absence of joint production this would be a diagonal array. The organization of the use and make tables is illustrated in Figures 3.1 and 3.2; Table 3.2 provides definitions of the variables appearing in these figures.

The econometric method for choosing the parameters of our model stands in sharp contrast to the calibration method used in previous

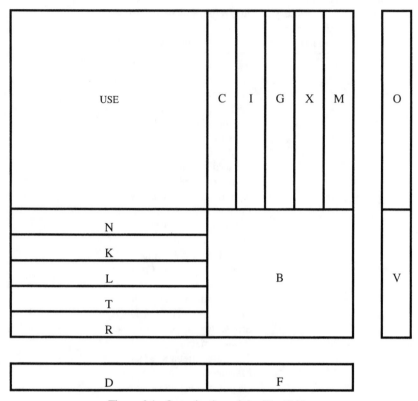

Figure 3.1. Organization of the Use Table

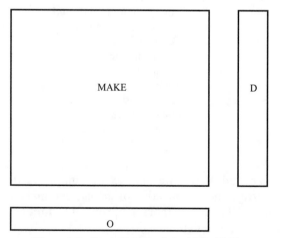

Figure 3.2. Organization of the Make Table

Table 3.2. Use and Make Tables

Category and Variable	Description
Industry-commodity flows	
USE	Commodities used by industries (use table)
MAKE	Commodities made by industries (make table)
Final demand columns	
C	Personal consumption
I	Gross private domestic investment
G	Government spending
X	Exports
M	Imports
Value-added rows	
N	Noncompeting imports
K	Capital
L	Labor
T	Net taxes
R	Rest of the world
Commodity and industry output	
O	Commodity output
D	Industry output
Other variables	
B	Value-added sold directly to final demand
V	Total value-added
F	Total final demand

general equilibrium models of tax policies. Calibration involves choosing parameters to replicate the data for a particular year.[3] Almost all general equilibrium models employ the assumption of fixed "input-output" coefficients for intermediate goods, following Johansen (1960). This allows the ratio of the input of each commodity to the output of an industry to be calculated from a single-use table like the one presented in Figure 3.1; however, it rules out substitution among intermediate goods, such as energy and materials, by assumption. It also ignores the distinction between industries and commodities and rules out joint production.

The econometric approach to parameterization has several advantages over the calibration approach. First, by using an extensive time series of data rather than a single data point, we can derive the response of production patterns to changes in prices from historical experience.

---

[3] Jorgenson (1986) describes the econometric approach, whereas Mansur and Whalley (1984) present the calibration approach.

This approach is particularly important for the analysis of tax policies, because these policies have changed substantially during our sample period and tax rates have varied widely. The extensive time series evidence on behavioral responses to changes in tax policy is ignored in the many parameters that are estimated solely from data taken from the benchmark year under the calibration approach.

A second advantage of the econometric approach is that parameters estimated from time series are much less likely to be affected by the peculiarities of a particular time period. By construction, parameters obtained by calibration are forced to absorb all the random errors present in the data for a single benchmark year. This poses a severe problem when the benchmark year is unusual in some respect. For example, parameters calibrated to the year 1973 would incorporate into the model all the distortions in energy markets that resulted from price controls and the rationing of energy during the first oil crisis. Econometric parameterization greatly mitigates this problem by reducing the influence of disturbances for a particular time period.

Empirical evidence on substitutability among inputs is essential in analyzing the impact of tax policies. The effects of these policies will be very different depending on whether it is easy for industries to substitute among inputs or substitution is limited. Calibration avoids the burden of data collection required by econometric estimation; moreover, calibration models that assume fixed coefficients rule out substitutability among inputs by assumption. This can easily lead to substantial distortions in estimating the impacts of alternative tax policies. By contrast the econometric approach determines the extent of substitutability on the basis of empirical evidence.

Consumer Behavior

The substitution of a consumption tax for an income tax would affect relative prices faced by consumers. This substitution, however, would have different impacts on different households. To capture these differences, we have subdivided the household sector into demographic groups that differ by family size, age of head, region of residence, race, and urban versus rural location. We treat each household as a consuming unit, so that the household behaves like an individual maximizing a utility function.

We represent the preferences of each household by means of an econometric model of consumer behavior. Our models of consumer behavior incorporate time series data on personal consumption expenditures from the annual interindustry transactions tables for the U.S. economy represented in Figure 3.1. The econometric approach to parameterization enables us to derive from historical experience the response of household expenditure patterns to changes in prices. Empirical evidence on substitutability among goods and services by households is essential in analyzing the impact of alternative tax policies. The effects of these policies will be very different depending on whether it is easy for households to substitute among commodities or substitution is limited.

The econometric approach to modeling consumer behavior has the same advantages over the calibration approach as those we have described for modeling producer behavior. Our models of consumer behavior incorporate detailed cross-section data on the impact of demographic differences among households and levels of total expenditure on household expenditure patterns. We do not require that consumer demands must be homothetic, so that patterns of individual expenditure change as total expenditure varies, even in the absence of price changes. Consumer demands also depend on the demographic composition of the population. These features of our model capture important characteristics of household expenditure patterns often ignored in general-equilibrium modeling.

Finally, we aggregate over individual demand functions to obtain a system of aggregate demand functions. This makes it possible to dispense with the notion of a representative consumer. The system of aggregate demand functions allocates total expenditure to broad groups of consumer goods and services. Given prices and total expenditure, this system allows us to calculate the elements of the personal consumption column in the make table of Figure 3.1. We employ the model to represent aggregate consumer behavior in simulations of the U.S. economy under alternative tax policies.

To determine the level of total expenditure, we embed our model of personal consumption expenditures in a higher-level system that represents consumer preferences between goods and leisure and between saving and consumption. At the highest level each household allocates *full wealth*, defined as the sum of human and nonhuman wealth, across time periods. We formalize this decision by introducing an infinitely lived representative agent who maximizes an additive intertemporal utility function, subject to an intertemporal budget constraint. The allocation of full wealth is determined by the rate of time preference and the intertemporal elasticity of substitution. The representative agent framework requires that intertemporal preferences must be identical for all households.

We model the household allocation decision by assuming that full consumption is an aggregate of goods and leisure. Our model of consumer behavior allocates the value of full consumption between personal consumption expenditures and leisure time. Given aggregate expenditure on goods and services and its distribution among households, this model then allocates personal consumption expenditures among commodity groups, including capital and labor services and noncompeting imports. Finally, the income of the household sector is the sum of incomes from the supply of capital and labor services, interest payments from governments and the rest of the world, all net of taxes, and transfers from the government. Savings are equal to the difference between income and consumption, less personal transfers to foreigners and nontax payments to governments.

Capital Formation

Our investment model, like our model of saving, is based on perfect foresight or rational expectations. Under this assumption the price of investment goods in every time period is based on expectations of future capital service prices and discount rates that are fulfilled by the solution of the model. In particular, we require that the price of new investment goods is always equal to the present value of future capital services.[4] The price of investment goods and the discounted value of future rental prices are brought into equilibrium by adjustments in future prices and rates of return. This incorporates the forward-looking dynamics of asset pricing into our model of intertemporal equilibrium.

In each of the thirty-five industrial sectors and the household sector the demand for capital services is first subdivided between the corporate and noncorporate subsectors. Within each of these subsectors, the demand for capital is further subdivided between short-lived assets or equipment and long-lived assets structures, inventories, and land. The prices for these different types of capital services reflect provisions of U.S. tax law for the taxation of capital income in the corporate, noncorporate, and household sectors. These prices also include tax provisions that affect short-lived and long-lived assets differently, such as depreciation allowances and investment tax credits. A detailed description of these tax provisions, based on Jorgenson and Yun (1991b), is given in the following section.

In our model the supply of capital in each time period is perfectly inelastic, because the available stock of capital is determined by past investments. An accumulation equation relates capital stock to investments in all past time periods and incorporates the backward-looking dynamics of capital formation into our model. For tractability we assume there is a single capital stock in the economy that is perfectly malleable and mobile among sectors, so that it can be reallocated among industries

---

[4] The relationship between the price of investment goods and the rental price of capital services is discussed in greater detail by Jorgenson (1996a,b).

and final demand categories at zero cost. Under this assumption changes in tax policy can affect the distribution of capital and labor supplies among sectors, even in the short run.

Government and Foreign Trade

The two remaining categories of final demand in our model are the government and rest-of-the-world sectors. We determine government consumption from the identity equating income and expenditure for the government sector.[5] The first step is to compute total tax revenue by applying exogenous tax rates to all taxable transactions in the economy. We then add the capital income of government enterprises, which is determined endogenously, and nontax receipts, also determined exogenously, to tax receipts to obtain total government revenue.

The key assumption of our submodel of the government sector is that the government budget deficit can be specified exogenously. We add the deficit to total revenue to obtain total government spending. To arrive at government purchases of goods and services, we subtract interest paid to domestic and foreign holders of government bonds together with government transfer payments to domestic and foreign recipients. We allocate the remainder among commodity groups according to fixed shares constructed from historical data. Finally, we determine the quantity of each commodity by dividing the value of government spending on that commodity by its price. Government consumption is not included in our representation of the preferences of the household sector.

Foreign trade has two quite different components – imports and exports. We assume that imports are imperfect substitutes for similar domestic commodities.[6] The goods actually purchased by households and firms reflect substitutions between domestic and imported products. The price responsiveness of these purchases is estimated from historical data taken from the import and export columns of the use table, Figure 3.1, in our annual interindustry transactions tables.

Exports, on the other hand, are modeled by a set of explicit foreign demand equations, one for each commodity, that depend on exogenously given foreign income and the foreign price of U.S. exports. Foreign prices are computed from domestic prices by adjusting for subsidies and the exchange rate. The demand elasticities in these equations are estimated

---

[5] Our treatment of government spending differs from the U.S. national accounts in that we have assigned government enterprises to the corresponding industry wherever possible. We include the remaining purchases by the government sector in final demands by governments.

[6] This approach was originated by Armington (1969). See Ho and Jorgenson (1994) for further details on our implementation of this approach.

from historical data. We assume that U.S. firms are price takers in foreign markets. The alternative approach of modeling imperfections in international markets would require firm-level data, not only for the United States, but also for all of its international competitors.

The key assumption of our submodel of the rest-of-the-world sector is that the current account is exogenous and the exchange rate is endogenous. The current account surplus is equal to the value of exports less the value of imports, plus interest received on domestic holdings of foreign bonds, less private and government transfers abroad, and less interest on government bonds paid to foreigners.

PROVISIONS OF U.S. TAX LAW

The purpose of this section is to introduce the characteristic features of U.S. tax law into the calculation of the cost of capital.[7] We distinguish among assets employed in three different legal forms of organization: households and nonprofit institutions, noncorporate businesses, and corporate businesses. Income from capital employed in corporate business is subject to the corporate income tax, while distributions of this income to households are subject to the individual income tax. Income from unincorporated businesses – partnerships and sole proprietorships – is taxed only at the individual level. Income from equity in household assets is not subject to the income tax. Capital utilized in all three forms of organization is subject to property taxation.

Although income from equity in the household sector is not subject to tax, property taxes and interest payments on household debt are deductible from income for tax purposes under the individual income tax. The value of these tax deductions is equivalent to a subsidy to capital employed in the household sector. Interest payments to holders of household debt are taxable to the recipients. Capital gains on household assets are effectively excluded from taxable income at the individual level by generous "roll over" provisions for owner-occupied residential housing. Capital gains on owner-occupied housing are not included in income so long as they are "rolled over" into the same form of investment. In addition, certain gains are excluded altogether.

Income from capital employed in noncorporate businesses is taxed at the level of the individual. Income from noncorporate equity is treated as fully distributed to equity holders, whether or not the income is actually paid out. Interest payments to holders of debts on noncorporate

---

[7] The incorporation of provisions of U.S. tax law into the cost of capital is based on Jorgenson and Yun (1991b, chap. 2). Jorgenson and Yun (1990, 1991a) have employed the results in analyzing the impact of the Tax Reform Act of 1986. The cost of capital in nine countries is compared in a volume edited by Jorgenson and Landau (1993).

businesses are subject to taxation. Property taxes and interest payments are treated as deductions from revenue in defining income from non-corporate businesses for tax purposes. Revenue is also reduced by deductions for capital consumption allowances. Until 1986 tax liabilities were reduced by an investment tax credit that was proportional to investment expenditures. Capital gains on noncorporate assets are subject to favorable treatment as outlined in this chapter.

Property taxes and interest payments are treated as deductions from revenue in defining corporate income for tax purposes. Revenue is also reduced by allowances for capital consumption, and an investment tax credit has been directly offset against tax liability. At the individual level distributions of corporate income in the form of interest and dividends are subject to taxation as ordinary income. Capital gains realized from the sale of corporate equities are subject to special treatment as outlined here. Interest payments to holders of corporate bonds are also taxable.

The special treatment of capital gains arises from three separate features of U.S. tax law. First, capital gains are taxed only when they are realized and not when they are accrued. This feature makes it possible to defer tax liability on capital gains until assets are sold. Second, capital gains have often been given favorable treatment by including only a fraction of these gains in income defined for tax purposes. Finally, capital gains taxes on assets received as part of a bequest are based on their value at the time of the bequest. Capital gains accrued prior to the bequest are not subject to tax.

In this chapter we have described the characteristic features of U.S. tax law in terms of the cost of capital and the rate of return. We have modeled provisions of U.S. tax law on corporate income taxes, individual income taxes, and property taxes. We have also incorporated the effects of the financial structure of the firm on the taxation of capital income. The financial structure determines the form of distributions of capital income to owners of financial claims. We have distinguished between equity, associated with distributions in the form of dividends and capital gains, and debt, associated with distributions in the form of interest payments.

In order to analyze the impact of changes in tax policies, we simulate the growth of the U.S. economy with and without changes in these policies.[8] Our first step is to generate a simulation with no changes in policy that we call the *base case*. The second step is to change the exogenous variables of the model to reflect a proposed policy change. We then produce a simulation that we refer to as the *alternative case*. Finally, we

---

[8] Methods for solving intertemporal general-equilibrium models are surveyed by Wilcoxen (1992).

compare the two simulations to assess the effects of the change in policy. Obviously, the assumptions underlying the base case are of considerable importance in interpreting the results of our simulations.

FUNDAMENTAL TAX REFORM

The debate over fundamental tax reform is both a challenge and an opportunity for economists because economic research has already generated much valuable information about the impacts of tax policy. Provided that the economic debate can be properly focused, economists and policy makers will learn a great deal about the U.S. economy and its potential for achieving a higher level of performance. Substitution of a consumption tax for existing individual and corporate income taxes would be the most drastic change in federal tax policy since the introduction of the income tax in 1913. It should not be surprising that the economic impact could be large.

Issues in Tax Reform

The first issue that will surface in the tax reform debate is progressivity or the use of the federal tax system to redistribute resources. Our recommendation is that this issue be set aside at the outset. Fiscal economists of varying persuasions can agree that progressivity or the lack of it should be used to characterize all of government activity, including both taxes and expenditures. Policies to achieve progressivity could and should be limited to the expenditure side of the government budget. This initial policy stance would immeasurably simplify the debate over the economic impact of fundamental tax reform. We view this radical simplification as essential to intellectual progress, because there is no agreed-upon economic methodology for trading off efficiency and equity in tax policy.

The second issue to be debated is fiscal federalism or the role of state and local governments. Because state and local income taxes usually employ the same tax bases as the corresponding federal taxes, it is reasonable to assume that substitution of consumption for income taxes at the federal level would be followed by similar substitutions at the state and local level. For simplicity we propose to consider the economic impact of substitution at all levels simultaneously. Because an important advantage of a fundamental tax reform is the possibility, at least at the outset, of radically simplifying tax rules, it does not make sense to assume that these rules would continue to govern state and local income taxes, if the federal income tax were abolished.

The third issue in the debate will be the economic impact of the federal deficit. Nearly two decades of economic dispute over this issue have failed to produce resolution. No doubt this dispute could continue well into the next century and preoccupy the next generation of fiscal economists, as it has the previous generation. An effective rhetorical device for insulating the discussion of fundamental tax reform from the budget debate is to limit consideration to deficit-neutral proposals. This device was critical to the eventual enactment of the Tax Reform Act of 1986 and is, we believe, essential to progress in the debate over fundamental tax reform.

Consumption Taxation

A useful starting point for the definition of consumption is personal consumption expenditures (PCE) in the U.S. national income and product accounts. However, the taxation of services poses important administrative problems reviewed in the U.S. Treasury (1984a) monograph on the value-added tax. First, PCE includes the rental equivalent value of the services of owner-occupied housing but does not include the services of consumers' durables. Both are substantial in magnitude and could be taxed by the "prepayment method" described by David Bradford (1986). In this approach taxes on the consumption of the services would be prepaid by including the original investment in housing and consumers' durables rather than the corresponding flows of consumption services in the definition of the tax base.

The prepayment of taxes on services of owner-occupied housing would remove an important political obstacle to substitution of a consumption tax for existing income taxes. At the time of the substitution all owner-occupiers would be deemed to have prepaid all future taxes on their dwellings. This is equivalent to excluding not only mortgage interest, but also capital gains, which might be taxed upon the sale of a residence with no corresponding purchase of property of equal or greater value. Of course, taxation of these capital gains is relatively modest under the current law.

Under the prepayment method purchases of consumers' durables would be subject to tax. This would include automobiles, appliances, home furnishings, and so on. In addition, new construction of owner-occupied housing would be subject to tax, as would sales of existing renter-occupied housing to owner-occupiers. Because these issues are politically sensitive, it is important to be clear about the implications of prepayment as the debate proceeds. Housing and consumers' durables must be included in the tax base in order to reap the substantial economic benefits of putting household and business capital onto the same footing.[9]

---

[9] See, for example, Jorgenson and Yun (1990).

Other purchases of services especially problematical under a consumption tax would include services provided by nonprofit institutions, such as schools and colleges, hospitals, and religious and eleemosynary institutions. The traditional, tax-favored status of these forms of consumption would be defended tenaciously by recipients of the services and even more tenaciously by the providers. Elegant and, in some cases, persuasive arguments could be made that schools and colleges provide services that represent investment in human capital rather than consumption. However, consumption of the resulting enhancements in human capital often takes the form of leisure time, which would remain as the principal untaxed form of consumption. Taxes could, however, be prepaid by including educational services in the tax base.

Finally, any definition of a consumption tax base will have to distinguish between consumption for personal and business purposes. Ongoing disputes over home offices, business-provided automobiles, equipment, and clothing, and business-related lodging, entertainment, and meals would continue to plague tax officials, the entertainment and hospitality industries, and holders of expense accounts. In short, substitution of a consumption tax for the federal income tax system would not eliminate all the practical issues that arise from distinguishing between business and personal activities in defining consumption. However, these issues are common to the two tax systems.

Implementation

In hearings on replacing the federal income tax, held by the Committee on Ways and Means (1996), testimony focused on alternative methods for implementing a consumption tax. The consumption tax base can be defined in three alternative and equivalent ways. First, subtracting investment from value added produces consumption as a tax base, where value added is the sum of capital and labor incomes. A second definition is the difference between business receipts and all purchases from other businesses, including purchases of investment goods. A third definition of the tax base is retail sales to consumers.

The three principal methods for implementation of a consumption tax correspond to the three definitions of the tax base that follow.

The Subtraction Method

Business purchases from other businesses, including investment goods, would be subtracted from business receipts, including proceeds from the sale of assets. This could be implemented within the framework of the existing tax system by integrating individual and corporate income taxes, as proposed by the U.S. Treasury (1992). If no business receipts were excluded and no deductions and tax credits were permitted, the tax return could be reduced to the now familiar postcard size, as in the flat tax proposal of Majority Leader Dick Armey and Senator Richard Shelby.[10] Enforcement problems could be reduced by drastically simplifying the tax rules, but the principal method of enforcement, auditing of taxpayer records by the Internal Revenue Service, would remain.

The Credit Method

Business purchases would produce a credit against tax liabilities for value-added taxes paid on goods and services received. This method is used in Canada and all European countries that impose a value-added tax. From the point of view of tax administration the credit method has the advantage that both purchases and sales generate records of all tax credits. The idea of substituting a value-added tax for existing income taxes is a novel one. European and Canadian value-added taxes were added to preexisting income taxes. In Canada and many other countries the value-added tax replaced an earlier and more complex system of retail and wholesale sales taxes. The credit method would require substantial modification of collection procedures, but decades of experience in Europe have ironed out many of the bugs.

National Retail Sales Tax

Like existing state sales taxes, a national retail sales tax would be collected by retail establishments, including service providers and real-estate developers. An important practical difficulty is that only sales to households would be covered by the tax, whereas sales to businesses would be excluded. A federal sales tax would require a new system for tax collection; one possibility is to subcontract that collection to existing state agencies. The Internal Revenue Service could be transformed into an agency that would manage the subcontracts. Alternatively, a new agency could be created for this purpose and the IRS abolished. Enforcement procedures would be similar to those used by the states.

The crucial point is that all three methods for implementing a consumption tax could be based on the same definition of the tax base, which would greatly simplify the tax economist's task, because the economic impact would be the same for all three approaches. However, the Armey-Shelby flat tax incorporates a system of individual exemptions for labor income that have the effect of setting the marginal tax rates equal to zero up to the exempt amount of income. After that point the marginal tax rate is constant at a flat rate that is also applied to business cash flow.

---

[10] Economists will recognize the flat tax proposal as a variant of the consumption-based value-added tax proposed by Robert Hall and Alvin Rabushka ([1985] 1995).

The purpose of these exemptions is to introduce progressivity in the rate structure; although the marginal tax rates are either zero or equal to the flat tax rate, the average tax rates decline gradually from zero to the flat rate.

Simulation Results

We have simulated the impact of implementing two different versions of a consumption tax at the beginning of 1996. The first is the Armey-Shelby flat tax. The Armey-Shelby proposal levies taxes on the difference between business receipts and the sum of business purchases and business payrolls. Labor income is taxed at the individual level. An important feature of the proposal is the system of personal exemptions at the individual level that we have described.

The second proposal we have considered is the national retail sales tax. The tax base is the same as in our simulations of the flat tax. However, the method of tax collection is different. The Armey-Shelby flat tax preserves the existing structures of the corporate and individual income taxes but alters the tax base. The national retail sales tax eliminates corporate and individual income taxes; retail establishments would collect the taxes. This would require a broad definition of these establishments to include real-estate developers and providers of services, such as medical, legal, and personal services. Most important, no personal exemptions are provided.

We have summarized our conclusions in a series of figures. We express all the impacts of alternative tax policies relative to the base case of U.S. economic growth under current tax law.

Figure 3.3 provides our base case projection for the period 1996–2020 of the U.S. gross domestic product (GDP) – valued in billions of 1987 dollars – under current tax law. Gross domestic product is the sum of consumption, investment, government, and net exports, equal to the difference between exports and imports.

Figure 3.4 compares the consumption tax rates for revenue-neutral substitution of the Armey-Shelby flat tax and the national retail sales tax for existing income taxes. The flat tax rate is 25.1 percent in the year 1996 and remains virtually constant through the year 2020. The national retail sales tax rate rises from only 15.7 percent in 1996 to 21.4 percent in the year 2020. Only the flat tax includes a system of personal exemptions, so that the tax rate is considerably higher, especially at the initiation of the tax reform. Second, the consumption tax base for the flat tax grows at nearly the same rate as government expenditures, whereas the tax base for the sales tax grows more slowly, reflecting the increased importance of investment.

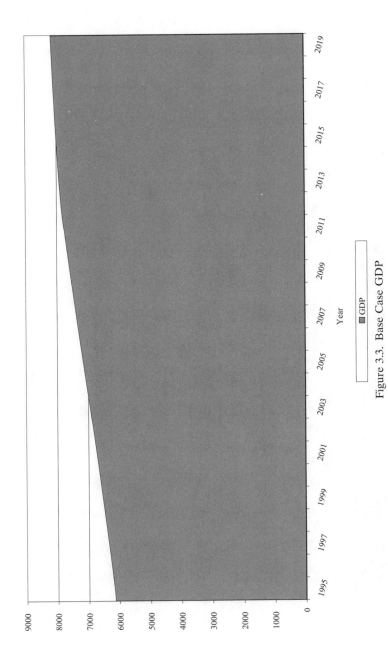

Figure 3.3. Base Case GDP

71

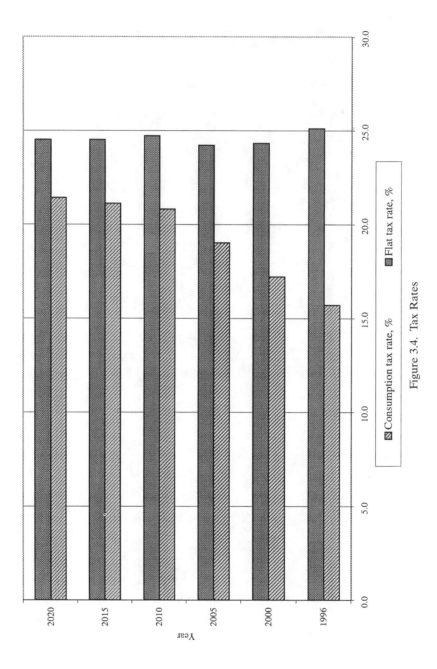

Figure 3.4. Tax Rates

Figure 3.5 compares the impacts of the flat tax and the sales tax on GDP. Under the flat tax the GDP is only 0.6 percent higher than the base case in 1996; the impact of this tax reform on GDP gradually rises, reaching 1.3 percent in 2020. Under the sales tax GDP jumps by 13.2 percent in 1996, but the impact gradually diminishes over time, falling to 9.0 percent in the year 2020. The short-run differences between these two tax reforms are due mainly to the impacts on labor supply, while the long-run differences also reflect the impacts on capital accumulation.

Figure 3.6 compares the impacts of the two tax reform proposals on consumption. The impact of the flat tax in 1996 is to increase consumption by 3.5 percent, relative to the base case. This impact gradually diminishes over time, falling to 1.3 percent by 2020. While it may seem paradoxical that consumption increases with a rise in the consumption tax, the marginal tax rate for low-income taxpayers is reduced to zero, stimulating consumption. By contrast the sales tax curtails consumption sharply in 1996, resulting in a decline of 5.6 percent, relative to the base case. However, the level of consumption overtakes the base case level in 1998 and rises to 5.5 percent above the base case in 2020.

Figure 3.7 compares the impact of the two tax reform proposals on investment. The impact of the flat tax in 1996 is to depress investment by 8.6 percent, relative to the base case. Investment recovers over time, eventually reaching a level that is only 1.7 percent below the base case in the year 2020. Substitution of the sales tax for existing income taxes generates a dramatic investment boom. The impact in 1996 is a whopping 78.5 percent increase in the level of investment that gradually gives way by the year 2000 to a substantial increase of 16.5 percent, relative to the base case.

Figure 3.8 compares the impacts of the tax reforms on exports, while Figure 3.9 compares the impacts on imports. It is important to keep in mind that net foreign investment, the difference between exports and imports in nominal terms, is exogenous in our simulations, while the exchange rate is endogenous. The flat tax results in a very modest decline in exports of 0.5 percent in 1996, relative to the base case, but exports recover rapidly and exceed base case levels in 1997, rising eventually to 4.6 percent above these levels in 2020. Imports initially rise by 2.0 percent, relative to the base case, in 1996, but this impact declines to only 0.3 percent by 2020. The sales tax generates a substantial export boom; the level jumps to 29.2 percent about the base case level in 1996 but declines by 2020, reaching 18.9 percent of this level. Imports in 1996 exceed the base case level by 2.5 percent but fall to 1.3 percent below this level in 2020.

Figures 3.10 and 3.11 give the impacts of the tax reforms on the prices of investment goods and consumption goods and services. The

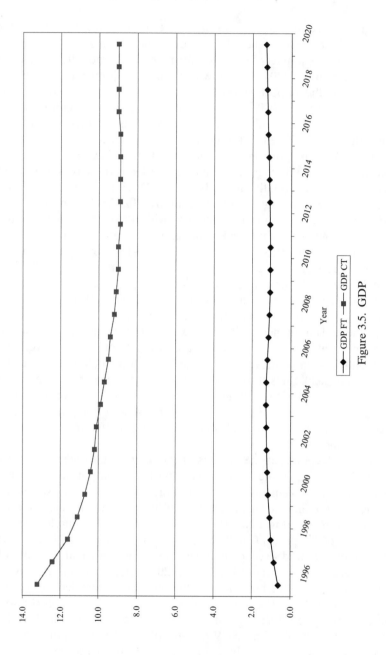

Figure 3.5. GDP

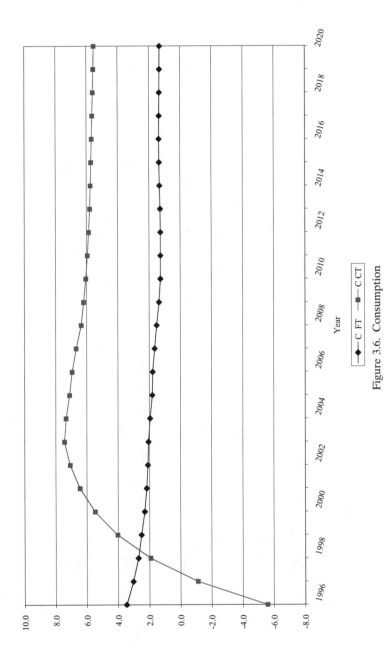

Figure 3.6. Consumption

75

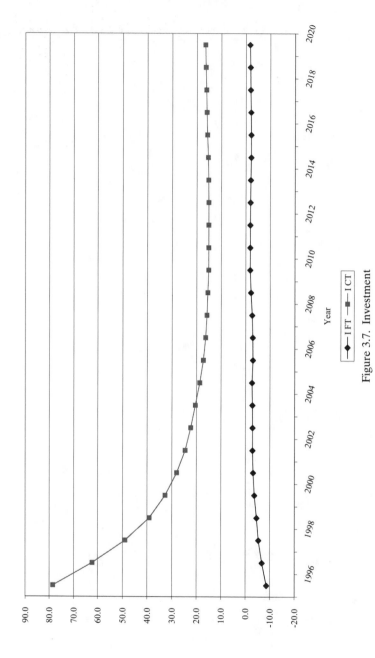

Figure 3.7. Investment

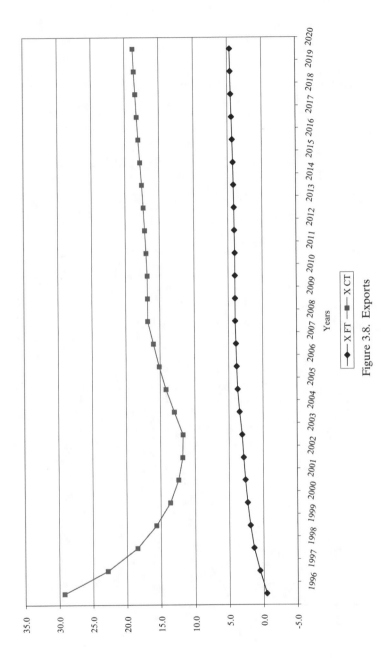

Figure 3.8. Exports

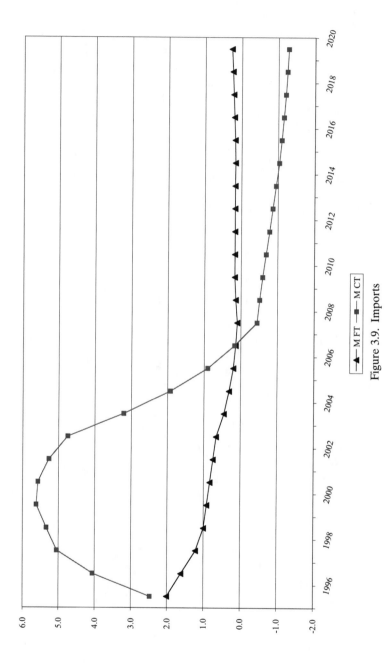

Figure 3.9. Imports

78

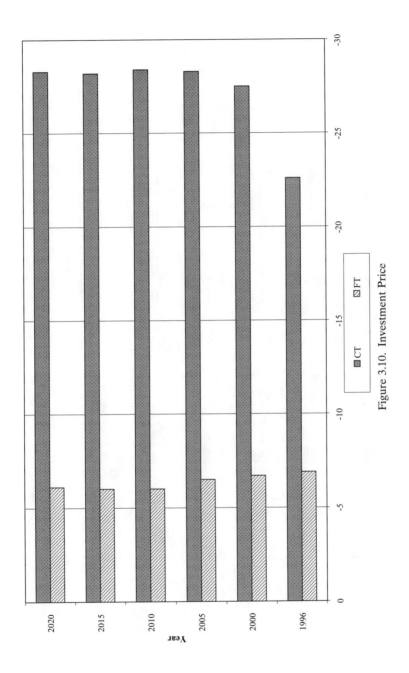

Figure 3.10. Investment Price

79

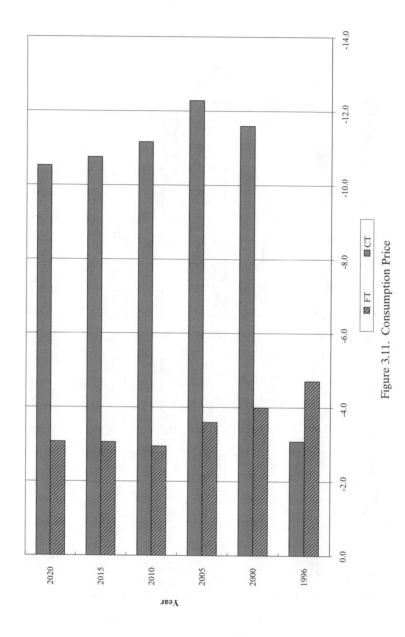

Figure 3.11. Consumption Price

80

intertemporal price system provides the mechanism for reallocations of resources in our simulations. Under the flat tax the price of investment goods drops by more than 6.8 percent in 1996 and the price decline continues, falling only modestly to a little over 6 percent by 2020. The sales tax produces a reduction in investment goods prices exceeding 20 percent in 1996, rising gradually to between 25 and 30 percent over the period 2000–2020. Under the flat tax prices of consumption goods and services decline by more than 4.5 percent in 1996, but this price reduction falls over time to around 3 percent in 2020. The sales tax reduces the price of consumption by a little over 3 percent in 1996, but this price decline increases to more than 10 percent by 2020. Despite the fact that both tax reform proposals reduce the marginal rate of taxation on capital income to zero, there are important differences in the impacts of these proposals on the prices of consumption and investment goods. It is useful to consider these price changes in analyzing the impacts of the proposals on consumption and investment, presented in Figures 3.6 and 3.7 above.

The implied subsidy to leisure time equals the marginal tax rate on labor income and would be significantly reduced when the individual income tax is abolished. Individuals sharply curtail consumption of both goods and leisure under the sales tax. Figure 3.12 shows that labor supply (and demand) jumps initially by 30 percent in 1996. This labor supply response recedes to a level of around 15 percent by 2020. By contrast the flat tax generates an increase in both consumption and labor supply. The labor supply response is only 2 percent in 1996 but gradually rises to more than 5 percent by 2020.

Figure 3.13 shows that, because producers would no longer pay taxes on profits or other forms of income from capital and workers would no longer pay taxes on wages, prices received by producers under the sales tax would fall by an average of 20 percent in 1996. Figure 3.14 shows that prices received by producers would fall by an average of 25 percent by 2020. The impact of the flat tax on prices received by producers is much less dramatic. Prices decline in the range of 6 to 8 percent for most industries in 1996 and 5 to 7 percent by 2020.

Figures 3.15 and 3.16 give the simulation results for quantities of output at the industry level for both tax reform proposals. The sales tax produces substantial increases in output levels for most industries shown in Figure 3.15 for 1996. This reflects the size of the impact for the sales tax on overall economic activity. By 2020 (Figure 3.16) the changes in outputs of the individual industries have increased by around 15 percent, again reflecting the impact on aggregate economic activity. The flat tax results given in Figure 3.15 for 1996 are much more modest; increases in the outputs of industries oriented toward consumption are partially offset by decreases in the outputs of industries contributing to

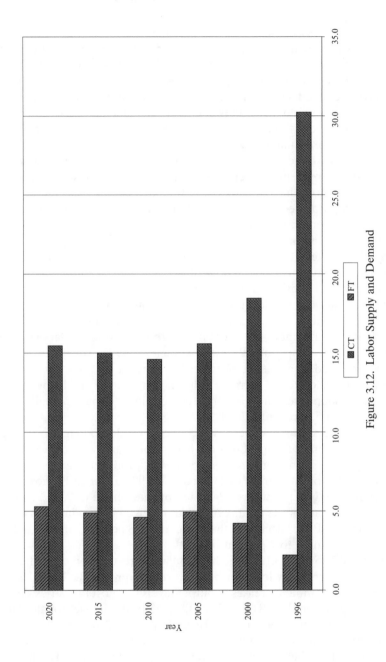

Figure 3.12. Labor Supply and Demand

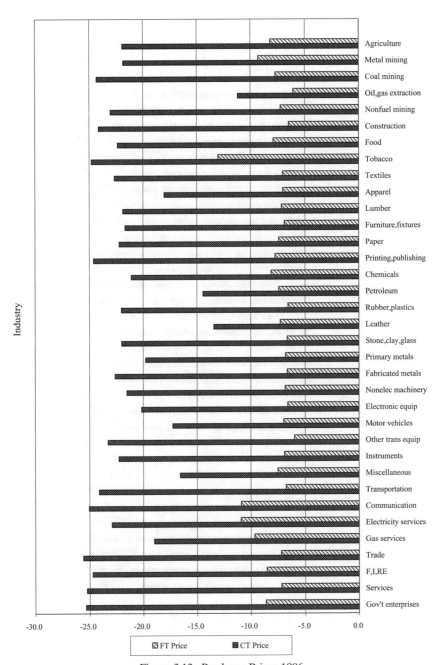

Figure 3.13. Producer Prices 1996

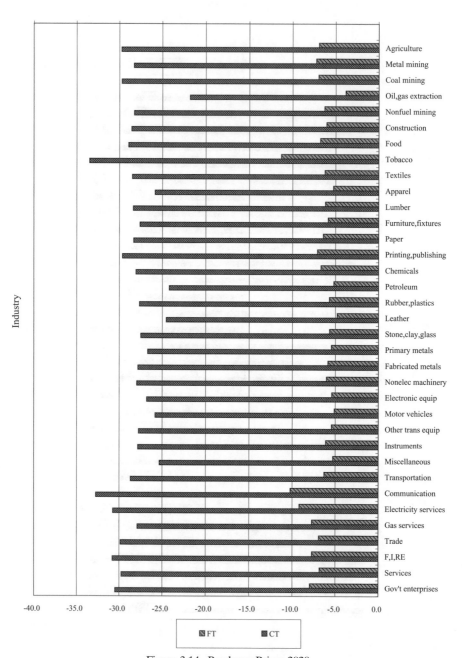

Figure 3.14. Producer Prices 2020

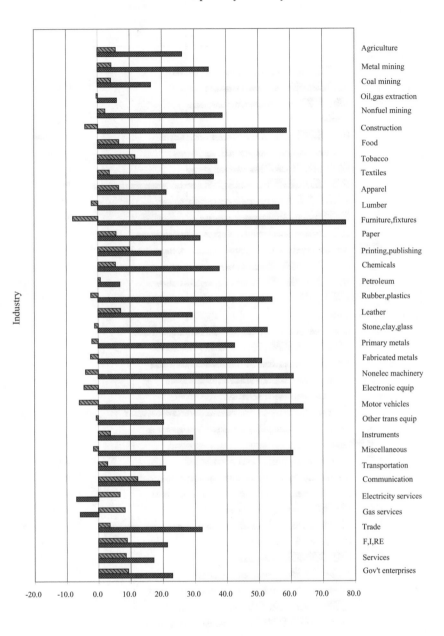

FT CT

Figure 3.15. Industry Production 1996

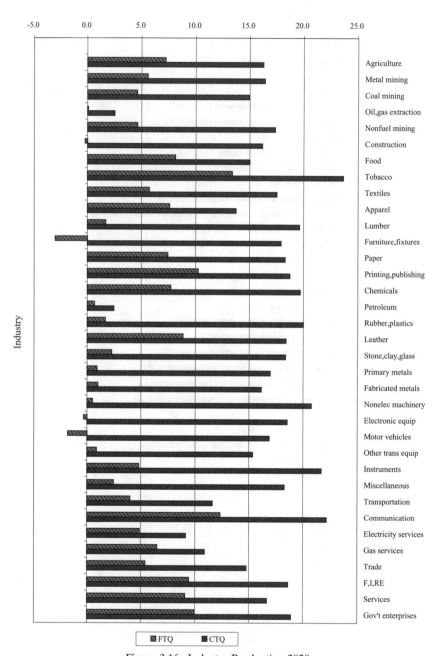

Figure 3.16. Industry Production 2020

investment. By 2020 (Figure 3.16) the flat tax produces modest increases in almost all industrial sectors.

In summary, the sales tax generates a substantial acceleration in the rate of economic growth, initially through a sharp rise in labor supply, because the capital stock is fixed in the short run. In the longer run a higher level of economic activity is generated by a higher rate of capital formation under the sales tax. The sales tax also produces drastic changes in relative prices with a sharp fall in the price of investment goods and a much smaller decline in the price of consumption goods and services. The flat tax generates a very modest rise in the level of economic activity through an increase in labor supply. Under the flat tax investment falls initially and remains below base case levels.

Both the flat tax and the consumption tax reduce the implicit subsidy to the consumption of leisure in the U.S. personal income tax. However, there is an important difference between the flat tax and the consumption tax. The flat tax includes a system of personal exemptions, so that a much higher initial tax rate is required to produce revenue-neutrality for the government sector. The flat tax produces only a modest reduction in the price of consumption, so that the response of leisure demand is negative, as expected, and the response of labor supply is positive but modest in size. These responses remain relatively small throughout the period of our simulation.

The response of consumption to the introduction of the flat tax is positive, but also modest in size. Saving and investment initially decline, but are ultimately almost left unchanged by the flat tax. As a consequence, the level of the GDP rises initially in response to the increase in labor supply and consumption, but remains only slightly above the base case level. The lack of response of saving and investment is a consequence of the relatively small changes in the prices of consumption and investment goods. The household sector works harder, consumes more, and saves less, but all these responses are small.

By contrast the low initial rate of the consumption tax results in a decline in the consumption price after tax reform. However, the price of investment declines dramatically, resulting in a sharp rise in real investment. As additional capital is accumulated, the price of consumption also begins to decline. Anticipating these developments, the household sector substitutes away from present consumption toward future consumption, as well as from present leisure to future leisure. Labor supply initially jumps and remains at a much higher level throughout the period of our simulations, while consumption declines initially, before rising to levels well above those in our base case.

After introduction of the consumption tax the substitutions among time periods by the household sector reflect the evolution of the price of consumption over time. Consumption of goods and leisure is very expensive immediately after introduction of the consumption tax, relative to later in our simulation period. At first households work harder, save more, and consume less. Later they continue to work harder and save more, but are able to consume more as well. This reflects the fact that the higher rate of capital accumulation under the consumption tax generates the productive capacity for more consumption as well as more investment.

CONCLUSION

We conclude that intertemporal general equilibrium modeling provides a very worthwhile addition to methodologies for analyzing the economic impact of tax reforms. The neoclassical theory of economic growth is essential for understanding the dynamic mechanisms that underlie long-term and intermediate-term impacts. The econometric implementation of this theory is critical for understanding the changes in economic behavior that would result from tax reforms. The wealth of historical experience, interpreted within an intertemporal framework, provides valuable guidance in the formulation of tax policy.

Intertemporal general equilibrium modeling provides a natural framework for economic analysis of the impact of taxes. The organizing mechanism of these models is an intertemporal price system balancing demand and supply for products and factors of production. The intertemporal price system links the prices of assets in every time period to the discounted value of future capital services. This forward-looking feature is combined with backward linkages among investment, capital stock, and capital services in modeling the dynamics of economic growth. Alternative time paths of economic growth depend on taxes through their impact on capital formation.

Although the intertemporal general equilibrium approach has proved to be useful in modeling the impact of alternative tax policies, much remains to be done to exploit the full potential of this approach. As an illustration, the model of consumer behavior employed by Jorgenson and Wilcoxen (1990b) successfully dispenses with the notion of a representative consumer. An important feature of this model is that systems of individual demand functions can be recovered from the system of aggregate demand functions. The consumer preferences underlying these individual demand systems can be used to generate measures of individual welfare for evaluating the distributional consequences of changes in tax policy, as described by Jorgenson, Slesnick, and Wilcoxen (1992).

Chapter 4

Capital Income Taxation in Tax Reform: Implications for Analysis of Distribution and Efficiency

R. Glenn Hubbard

Many recent proposals for fundamental tax reform have advocated replacing the current tax system with a broad-based consumption tax. Economists' support for such proposals centers on the gains in economic well-being made possible by tax reform. Three sources of efficiency gains would, in principle, accompany a switch to consumption taxation. First, the removal of the current tax on returns to new saving would eliminate distortions of savings decisions, augment capital accumulation, and, eventually, per capita consumption. Second, a pure consumption tax would remove distortions in the allocation of capital across sectors and types of capital. Third, a broad-based consumption tax would avoid potentially costly distortions of firms' financial structures. Recent estimates suggest that the efficiency gains from consumption tax reform could be quite substantial (see, e.g., Auerbach, 1996; Jorgenson, 1996c; Jorgenson and Wilcoxen, Chapter 3 in this volume; and Gravelle, Chapter 2 in this volume).

Another group of proposals has suggested reforming capital taxation under the income tax, in particular toward taxing broad measures of income once (see, e.g., American Law Institute, 1993; and U.S. Department of the Treasury, 1992). Although the debate between these "income tax reforms" and "consumption tax reforms" often characterizes the differences between the two options for reform as significant, I argue that for distributional analysis, and possibly for efficiency analysis, the distinction between reform toward a broad-based income tax and reform toward a broad-based consumption tax is not as large as that suggested by models conventionally used to analyze tax reform. This is not to say

Financial support from the American Enterprise Institute is acknowledged. I am grateful to William Gale, William Gentry, Jane Gravelle, Kevin Hassett, Dale Jorgenson, Peter Mieszkowski, Michael Palumbo, George Zodrow, and conference participants at the Baker Institute for Public Policy for helpful comments and suggestions.

that there are not important efficiency and distributional consequences of moving from the current tax system to a broad-based consumption tax. Instead, I argue that many of these consequences could be obtained with reform of the income tax.

In public policy circles, however, concern over consumption tax reform (and, to a lesser extent, over income tax reform) has centered substantially on fairness. Critics often claim that, as a tax base, consumption is less fair than income because the benefits of not taxing capital income accrue primarily to high-income households. This claim, of course, depends critically on the time frame for analyzing fairness; consumption taxes may be less regressive from a lifetime perspective than an annual perspective (see, e.g., Davies, St. Hilaire, and Whalley, 1984; Poterba, 1989; and Fullerton and Rogers, 1993).

My point here is a different one.[1] Despite the common perception that consumption taxation eliminates all taxes on capital income,[2] consumption and income taxes actually treat similarly much of what is commonly called "capital income." In fact, not all of what is commonly called capital income escapes the consumption tax. This observation affects economic analysis of tax reform in at least two ways. First, conventional distributional comparisons of income tax reform and consumption tax reform overstate the differences between the two. Second, assessing the distributional and efficiency consequences of tax reform would be helped by further research into certain non-life-cycle saving decisions.

In this chapter I suggest a working definition of fundamental tax reform and distinguish between broad-based income tax and broad-based consumption tax reforms; explore implications for distributional analysis of tax reforms; and I consider consequences for broader research on the effects of tax reform on saving.

DISTINGUISHING BETWEEN INCOME AND CONSUMPTION TAX REFORMS[3]

Defining Tax Reform

To fix ideas, I consider a "fundamental tax reform" proposal as one with the following characteristics:

---

[1] Here I build upon my research program with William Gentry (Gentry and Hubbard, 1997a, 1998a,b, 2000; and Hubbard, 1997).

[2] This perception is fostered in part by conventional economic analysis of tax reform in life-cycle models (see, e.g., Auerbach and Kotlikoff, 1987).

[3] The analysis in this section draws on Gentry and Hubbard (1997a, 1998a) and Hubbard (1997).

1. The tax system is a combination of a business-level tax (with either business cash flow or business income as the base) and a household wage tax.
2. For an income tax version of reform, we assume that inflation-adjusted depreciation allowances are as close to economic depreciation as possible; for a consumption tax version of reform, businesses will deduct capital expenditures.
3. The business-level tax does not distinguish between debt and equity financing.
4. In order to minimize the differences in marginal tax rates across business entities and investments, firms carry net operating losses forward with interest.[4]
5. Marginal tax rates are lower, with a single marginal tax rate across business entities and households; the household tax can have a personal or family exemption.

Because fundamental tax reform implies either income tax reform or moving to a consumption tax, I distinguish between consequences of tax reform that do not depend on the choice of tax reforms from effects that differ between two reform proposals. In what follows, I focus on a single uniform-rate income tax and a single uniform-rate consumption tax.

Income and Consumption Tax Prototypes

Within the context of broad-based income tax reform, the U.S. Treasury Department's (1992) Comprehensive Business Income Tax (CBIT) proposal generally followed this model. The goal of CBIT is to tax business income once. CBIT is a business-level tax on the return to capital of businesses. Broadly speaking, the business-level tax base under CBIT is revenue from the sale of goods or real assets less wages, material costs, and depreciation allowances for capital investments. To conform to standard income accounting principles, the CBIT base uses depreciation allowances that follow economic depreciation as closely as possible. Because CBIT includes a tax on capital income, it runs afoul of the standard income tax accounting problem of adjusting for inflation. To tax real, rather than nominal, capital income, the cost recovery system (depreciation allowances) must be indexed for inflation. CBIT does not distinguish whether investment is financed by debt or equity. That is, relative to the current tax system, CBIT would not allow businesses to

---

[4] The proposals I consider do not include interest for tax-loss carry-forwards. These proposals would probably maintain something like the current tax rules that allow limited carry-backs and carry-forwards of current tax losses without an adjustment for the time value of money. With such rules, effective tax rates can still vary across firms even when all firms face the same statutory marginal tax rate.

deduct interest payments from their tax base. Because CBIT taxes business income at the entity level, there is no need for investor-level taxes on capital gains, interest, or dividends received.[5]

CBIT can be thought of as the capital income tax component of a broad-based income tax that collects taxes from labor income through a household-level wage tax. We assume, for simplicity, that the marginal tax rate in CBIT is the same as the marginal wage tax rate. With this assumption, capital and labor income face the same tax rate. If the wage tax rate differs from the CBIT rate, then labor and capital income face different tax rates; however, capital income from different types of assets faces a common tax rate regardless of whether it is financed by debt or equity.

On the consumption tax side, consider a subtraction-method value-added tax (VAT), under which each business has a tax base equal to the difference between receipts from sales of goods and services and purchases of goods and services from other businesses. This measure of value added is then taxed at a fixed tax rate. Transactions among businesses generate offsetting increases in the tax base of sellers and decreases in the tax base of buyers, so that no net revenue accrues to the government. Net revenue arises when goods are sold by a business to a nonbusiness entity, generally households. Because the aggregate business tax base equals the aggregate sales by business to nonbusiness, the tax base is equivalent to aggregate consumption. As long as tax rates are uniform, this subtraction-method value-added tax is equivalent to the familiar European-style credit invoice value-added tax.

Converting CBIT into a consumption tax is straightforward. Instead of measuring business income through depreciation allowances, a consumption tax would allow businesses a deduction for capital investments when assets are purchased. This adjustment converts the combination of CBIT and a wage tax into the flat tax proposed by Hall and Rabushka (1983, [1985] 1995). I use the flat tax as the model of the consumption tax for the purposes of this chapter.[6] The key difference between the

---

[5] This treatment implies that two of the key problems of accurately measuring income in an inflationary period – indexing interest income and expense and capital gains – disappear; see also Cohen, Hassett, and Hubbard (1999). As a consequence, inflation indexing problems are much less severe under CBIT than under the current income tax, reducing the disadvantage of an income tax relative to a consumption tax in this regard.

[6] In principle, alternative forms of broad-based consumption taxes are economically equivalent; see, e.g., Auerbach (1996); Gentry and Hubbard (1997a); and Mieszkowski and Palumbo (Chapter 6 in this volume).

"Flat tax" proposals, generally modeled on Hall and Rabushka (1983, [1985] 1995), include those by then Treasury secretary Nicholas Brady (1992) and Representative Richard Armey. One could also consider a national retail sales tax, supported by, among others, Representative Bill Archer and Senator Richard Lugar. Recent value-added tax

CBIT and the flat tax is that the former depreciates capital expenditures, whereas the latter deducts capital outlays.

Single Risk-Free Return to Capital: What Is Taxed?

Traditional descriptions of the taxation of capital income under a cash flow tax or consumption tax assume that all income from capital is exempt. To explain this view, assume that investment projects offer a single riskless rate of return. One can then decompose the base of the flat tax into two parts: the first is a business cash flow tax whose base is $R - I$, where R is receipts from sales of goods and services less purchases for labor, raw materials, and services, and I is expenditure on capital goods.[7] The second is a wage tax, whose base is wages, W. (The subtraction-method VAT combines the two pieces, with a base equal to $R + W - I$.) While the wage tax burden is borne by labor, how should one think about the burden of the cash flow tax?

Under the cash flow tax, the user cost of capital is independent of tax parameters. In this case, the present value of one dollar's worth of depreciation deductions (expensing) is one dollar, whereas the present value of depreciation deductions is less than one dollar under the income tax. The present value of depreciation allowances depends on the depreciation schedule prescribed by the tax code for the firm's assets and the discount rate that the firm uses to discount the future tax savings from the depreciation allowances. Hypothetically, depreciation schedules reflect the useful life of different assets. For the case of a riskless investment project, the tax savings from depreciation allowances represent riskless cash flows that the firm would discount at the safe (nominal) rate of interest.

Inframarginal Returns: What Is Taxed?

The foregoing example assumed a single riskless return available on investment projects. Now suppose that, in addition to having access to riskless investments, certain entrepreneurs have access to investments

---

proposals include the plan by former representative Sam Gibbons to introduce a subtraction-method value-added tax in the United States.

The Unlimited Savings Allowance (USA) Tax (described in Alliance USA, 1995), introduced in April 1995, proposes a proportional tax on business value added. The individual-level tax in the USA system is a "consumed income tax" which excludes net saving from taxable income.

[7] The business cash flow tax has a long pedigree among economists seeking to apply consumption tax principles to business taxation. An early exposition appears in Brown (1948); implementation issues are discussed in King (1975), Institute for Fiscal Studies (1978), Aaron and Galper (1985), and Hubbard (1989).

with inframarginal returns. Such returns are associated with rents to ideas, managerial skill, or market power. By construction, the scale of these projects or opportunities is limited.

Extending the first example, what is taxed are rates of cash flow in excess of the firm's discount rate for depreciation allowances (the riskless rate of return under our hypothetical tax systems). Cash flows representing inframarginal returns are taxed equivalently under the broad-based income tax and the cash flow tax (or consumption tax). As long as the scale of inframarginal projects is limited and entrepreneurs' project selection is optimal,[8] the tax savings from expensing should be invested in another riskless asset. For the case of inframarginal projects, then, only the component of the return representing the riskless rate is untaxed under the cash flow tax (or consumption tax).

Risky Investments: What Is Taxed?

Thus far, the discussion has abstracted from risk in project returns. Introducing risk adds two complications. First, risky investments have a higher ex ante required rate of return than riskless investments, reflecting the risk premium required to compensate savers for bearing risk. Second, risky investments generate ex post high or low returns to investing. When we look at the distribution of capital income across households, some variation reflects this ex post good or bad fortune. The component of capital income that represents luck after a risky investment decision has been made can be treated like the inframarginal return in the hypothetical income tax and cash flow tax. Ex post returns in excess of the ex ante expected return are taxed under both the income tax and the cash flow tax; assuming similar loss-offset provisions, low ex post returns also generate the same tax consequences under the two systems.

Whether either tax system levies a tax on the ex ante risk premium depends upon how one defines a "tax." If a tax is defined as an increase in expected government revenues, then both the income tax and the cash flow tax include the ex ante risk premium; if, in contrast, a tax is an increase in the discounted present value of government revenues, then neither tax system includes the ex ante risk premium. This distinction is most easily seen for a cash flow tax with full loss offsets. By levying such a tax, the government shares equally in the costs and revenues of investment projects; this feature of the tax system leads to the analogy of the government as a "silent partner" in the investment. Suppose that the government taxes two projects with the same costs but with different

---

[8] That is, entrepreneurs exhaust all investments earning rents and invest at the margin in a riskless investment. If entrepreneurs face costly external financing ("financing constraints"), they may underinvest in the project that yields inframarginal returns. In this case, the firm's tax savings from expensing may be invested in the inframarginal project.

expected returns (because one project is riskier than the other). Neither project has expected inframarginal returns. As do private investors, the government would expect a higher return on its investment (cost sharing) in the riskier project. However, if expected returns compensate for risk, the "market value" of this extra-expected revenue would be zero because it compensates the government for the added riskiness of the revenue stream; that is, the government does not increase the discounted present value of its revenue by taxing pure risk.[9]

In contrast to the cash flow tax, an income tax provides depreciation allowances rather than expensing for capital purchases. This difference does not affect the treatment of the uncertainty about costs and revenues as long as the two tax systems have similar loss-offset provisions. By providing depreciation allowances rather than expensing, the government pays a smaller share of the cost of investment projects because the investor recoups the government's share of the cost in the future rather than at the time of the outlay. The present value of the loss to the investor (and, conversely, the gain to the government) depends on how the tax savings from depreciation allowances should be discounted. Under the assumption of full loss offsets and constant tax rates under both tax systems, the government's promise of depreciation allowances gives the investor a safe, predictable cash flow that warrants discounting at the default-risk-free rate of return.[10]

---

[9] One can argue that, absent frictions in portfolio transactions and capital-market imperfections, the government cannot bear systematic risk beyond that obtained in market outcomes (see, e.g., Bulow and Summers, 1984, and Gordon, 1985). For the purposes here, the point is simply that, for a given level of systematic risk, the government can bear the risk under both income and consumption taxes. Hence the experiment considered here still permits an analysis of differential tax incidence.

[10] This conclusion is not really at odds with Kaplow's (1994) arguments that an income tax is equivalent to a wage tax plus an ex ante wealth tax and that a consumption tax is equivalent to a wage tax; the apparent difference arises from Kaplow's assumption about the government's portfolio behavior. Both the example here and that used by Kaplow are obviously highly stylized. The treatment of the risk premium under an income tax or under a consumption tax will differ from what is suggested in these setups if borrowing or short-sale restrictions are present, if loss offsets are not perfect, and if tax rates change over time. It is not obvious, however, that these modifications would affect the equivalence of the tax on the risk premium under the two systems. Kaplow concludes that neither an income tax nor consumption tax taxes risk because the government offsets the effects of both taxes on the uncertainty of government revenue by decreasing its position in risky assets and increasing its position in safe assets. In Kaplow's model, the government can achieve the same effect as a tax on risk by, in effect, swapping safe assets for risky assets (which Kaplow argues is not a tax). Such a swap would increase the government's portfolio (i.e., the transaction generates a zero market value in an efficient financial market). In comparing a switch between the two tax systems – and holding the tax rate constant – the government portfolio rebalancing of Kaplow's framework is unnecessary because both tax bases include the return to risk taking. (Zodrow, 1995, also discusses the relative treatment of risk under alternative tax bases.)

R. Glenn Hubbard

In either case, the key point is that the stylized income and consumption tax bases treat both the ex ante and ex post components of the return to risk taking similarly. Because traditional ex post distributional analysis includes the returns to risk taking in household income and the consumption purchased from such returns (which is relevant, for example, for analyses that distribute consumption tax burdens in accordance with consumption), the distributional analysis I describe here assumes that the income and consumption tax bases include the returns to risk taking. That is, taxes are allocated based on the distribution of either expected or realized income.

This analysis suggests that income and consumption tax bases are similar with respect to the returns to risk taking, whereas conventional treatments (e.g., Auerbach and Kotlikoff, 1987) claim that a consumption tax is equivalent to a wage tax plus a tax on the value of "old" capital.[11] Relative to an analysis assuming that a consumption tax is borne in proportion to wage income and ownership of old capital, the inclusion of the returns to risk taking implies that households with relatively more risky assets or assets that earn inframarginal returns will bear more of the consumption tax. If attitudes toward risk or ownership of assets generating inframarginal returns vary across income or wealth groups, then including the return to risk taking and inframarginal returns in the consumption tax base can affect the distribution of taxes across income or net worth classes.

By putting these arguments together,[12] what is often called the return to capital can be thought of as the sum of the riskless return (opportunity cost or return to waiting), inframarginal returns (economic profits), the ex ante risk premium on risky investments (payment for bearing risk), and ex post realizations on risky investments (luck). Unlike the consumption tax base, the income tax base includes the opportunity cost of capital, which equals the rate of return on a marginal riskless project. If the consumption tax does not change the rate of return on investment, for investments with the same opportunity cost, the owner of the investment with a high rate of return will pay more in taxes than the owner of the investment with a lower rate of return. Because households that save benefit from eliminating the tax on the opportunity cost of capital, they

---

[11] The equivalence in the conventional view is true for analyzing the present value of government revenues provided the government discounts the uncertain revenues generated by a consumption tax at the risky market-determined rate of return (see Zodrow, 1995). However, distributional analysis is typically done on the basis of realized outcomes. From this perspective, two investors with identical wage income but different portfolios will have different tax liabilities under either an income tax or a consumption tax but not under a wage tax.

[12] See also Bradford (1996a).

benefit from this tax reform. However, because inframarginal returns to saving are still taxed, the distributional effects also depend on separating "opportunity cost" returns to saving from inframarginal returns and returns to risk taking.

IMPLICATIONS FOR DISTRIBUTIONAL ANALYSIS OF TAX REFORM

Distribution of "Non-Opportunity-Cost" Returns

Again, a key difference between fundamental income tax reform (as embodied in CBIT) and fundamental consumption tax reform (as embodied in the flat tax) is the taxation of the opportunity cost return to capital. For savers, relative to CBIT, the consumption tax favors households investing primarily through marginal projects. Accordingly, one way of capturing the long-run distributional differences between the two types of proposals is to examine the distribution of marginal projects.[13]

Although publicly traded companies may have inframarginal profits, the expected future value of those profits should be capitalized into share prices when investors buy equity. It is more likely for the purpose at hand that inframarginal projects are concentrated in holdings of active businesses. Gentry and I (1997a) showed that these active business assets are overwhelmingly concentrated among the top of the wealth distribution; in the 1989 cross section of the Federal Reserve Board's Survey of Consumer Finances, the top 5 percent of the net worth distribution owns fully 84 percent of active business assets. This is potentially an important point for analysis of the distributional consequences of tax reform. To the extent that households in the bottom and middle of the distribution of household net worth generate most of their returns through marginal projects (e.g., by holding financial assets) and by owning relatively few assets with potential inframarginal returns, they would benefit relatively more from removing opportunity cost returns to capital from the tax base. The rich would still pay taxes on their economic profit. This conclusion is consistent with the notion that households get rich by having good ideas (or good luck) rather than by saving through publicly traded financial assets.

In principle, one could focus directly on the empirical question of which households would benefit if the tax on the opportunity cost return to capital were repealed. By measuring differences in households' average Q (the market value of business assets relative to their replacement cost), one could describe the distribution across households of

---

[13] Here I am abstracting from short-run "transition" issues; see Gentry and Hubbard (1997a); and Zodrow (Chapter 9 in this volume).

inframarginal projects. Because a high Q value reflects inframarginal returns to ideas, patents, or market power, using Q values for household businesses, one could study whether inframarginal projects are concentrated among the well-to-do.

Using data from the 1989 Survey of Consumer Finances, Gentry and I (1997a) constructed average Q proxies for active business holdings.[14] For both net worth and current income groupings, median Q values are substantially higher in the top 5 percent of the respective distributions. This variation does not simply reflect age differences among business owners; median Q values do not vary much across age groupings.

Such a pattern is consistent with the idea that projects with economic profits are more concentrated among high-net-worth households than assets expected to return the opportunity cost of capital (e.g., bonds or liquid assets). To the extent that economists assume that all returns are untaxed in their analysis of the distributional consequences of a switch to consumption taxation, they understate the progressivity of the consumption tax.

Consequences for Distributional Analysis in Practice

In the context of distributional analysis in (Washington) practice, this understatement is significant.[15] The discussion of CBIT and the flat tax in the preceding section argues that the consumption tax should be thought of as a combination of a wage tax and a cash flow tax on returns from existing capital and returns from inframarginal and risky investments. Calculations by the Joint Committee on Taxation (1993) indicate that, if the burden is assigned to real wages and income from existing capital as earned, the burden of a 5 percent broad-based consumption tax is approximately proportional to (a broad concept of) income. If, instead, the burden is assigned as consumption occurs, the same tax appears more regressive. Moreover, even the Joint Committee's approach of distributing the burden of the consumption tax on returns to labor and existing capital understates the progressivity of the tax. In conventional distribution tables, distributing the burden of the tax to wage income and old capital income would increase the progressivity of taxes at low- and high-income levels relative to the case of distributions by consumption.

Gentry and I (1997a) pursued these distributional issues further by constructing measures of differences in tax burdens across tax regimes

---

[14] To calculate Q, we divided the sum of the household's market value of different active businesses by its share of the businesses' book value.

[15] For an overview of conventions used by Treasury Department and congressional staffs in distributing the burden of income and consumption taxes, see Hubbard (1995).

under different incidence assumptions for broad-based consumption taxes. The current tax base differs from a consumption tax both because the opportunity cost of capital is taxed and because of differential capital taxation, so we compared four different tax regimes: (1) a comprehensive income tax with uniform capital income taxation; (2) a (stylized) version of the current income tax base capturing the principle features of differential capital taxation; (3) a broad-based consumption tax under the assumption that the burden of the consumption tax falls on wages;[16] and (4) a broad-based consumption tax under which the tax base includes inframarginal returns and returns to risk taking but excludes the opportunity cost of capital from the tax base. We analyzed a flat-rate structure for the tax systems (with the same marginal tax rate for households and businesses) in order to concentrate on differences among the tax bases. We also estimated tax burdens under a flat-rate structure with a household exemption in order to mimic some of the progressivity introduced by graduated tax rates.

For each tax regime or incidence assumption, Gentry and I computed a measure of the tax base for each household in the Survey of Consumer Finances. Labor income includes wages, salaries, and pension benefits. We encountered more difficult issues in measuring both capital income and the share of capital income to include in each tax base. Because reported capital income excludes many items such as unrealized capital gains and imputed rent on owner-occupied housing, we constructed measures of expected income using each household's stock of various assets and expected rates of return on different assets. The different tax bases included varying portions of imputed capital income depending on the tax rules and our incidence assumptions.

For classifying household income, Gentry and I used imputed full household income, the tax base for the comprehensive income tax. By including the imputed income from owner-occupied housing, the inside buildup on defined contribution pension plans, and unrealized capital gains, this measure of household income is closer in spirit to the "family economic income" measure of the Treasury Department's Office of Tax Analysis than the income definitions used by the Joint Committee on Taxation or the Congressional Budget Office. We used this broad

---

[16] Recall that the conventional description of the imposition of a proportional consumption tax is the combination of a proportional wage tax and a proportional tax on cash flow from existing projects – a tax on "old" capital (see, e.g., Auerbach and Kotlikoff, 1987). Any tax on old capital would be included in the consumption tax base (as conventionally described as excluding all capital income) and in the modified tax base (which includes some capital income). Hence abstracting from the tax on old capital does not affect the difference in the distribution of taxes paid under the two depictions. Alternatively, one could assume full transition relief for old capital.

measure of income because the focus is on a broad spectrum of capital income.

Considering first uniform-rate taxes with no exemptions, we found that the significant decrease in the share of taxes paid by the top 5 percent (by income) of households under a conventional description of a consumption tax relative to an income tax is reduced by more than one-third after recognizing that only the opportunity cost of capital is exempt (see Gentry and Hubbard, 1997a, tables 7 and 8). We also calculated the distribution of the tax burden across income groups for a tax system with exemptions (again, to mimic progressivity). Incorporating these exemptions did not materially change the earlier conclusion. The decline in the fraction of taxes paid by the top 5 percent of the income distribution from moving to a broad-based consumption tax was again about one-third less under the assumption of a consumption tax excluding only the opportunity cost return on capital rather than the assumption of a consumption tax exempting all capital income. When we examined the distribution of tax burdens over the distribution of net worth, the same pattern emerged: the decrease in the fraction of taxes paid by the top 5 percent of the net worth distribution accompanying a switch to a broad-based consumption tax is about one-third smaller, under the assumption that the consumption tax base includes a portion of capital income.

The analysis in Gentry and Hubbard (1997a) using household data from the 1980s almost certainly understates the difference between the distributional effects of a conventionally described consumption tax and the definition I propose here. This is because at the present time, default-risk-free nominal interest rates are much lower than during the 1980s. As a consequence, an even smaller amount of capital income would be taxed by the income tax and not by the consumption tax.

IMPLICATIONS FOR ANALYSIS OF EFFECTS ON SAVING

Incentives to Save in a Life-Cycle Setting

As noted in the introduction, economists' analyses of the efficiency consequences of fundamental tax reform have centered largely on incentives for saving and investment and the responsiveness of saving and investment decisions to those incentives. Much of our intuition for describing distributional[17] and efficiency consequences of tax reforms is shaped by dynamic life-cycle models of the economy, with overlapping generations

---

[17] Shaviro (2000) provides a thoughtful review of economic and legal research on the distributional consequences of tax reform.

of representative agents (see Auerbach and Kotlikoff, 1987, and the more recent application in Auerbach, 1996). Regarding the shift from income to consumption taxation, such models imply that returns to new saving become tax-free, stimulating savings, capital formation, and steady-state output and consumption per capita. A consumption tax also raises revenue by imposing a transition tax on "old" capital (which, in representative agent life-cycle settings, falls on old people). Saving decisions in these models reflect consumption smoothing over the life cycle (e.g., saving for retirement). More complex life-cycle models also incorporate "precautionary saving" against uninsured idiosyncratic risk (see, e.g., Deaton, 1991; Hubbard, Skinner, and Zeldes, 1994, 1995; and Engen, 1994). In general, the assumption that a shift to consumption taxation eliminates the tax on saving leads to large estimated effects on saving in simple life-cycle models,[18] but much smaller effects in models incorporating precautionary saving.[19]

In addition, if only the opportunity cost return to capital (the default-risk-free interest rate) is exempt under a consumption tax relative to an income tax, the stimulus to domestic household saving from consumption tax reform per se may not be that large. Nevertheless, the reforms of the income tax embodied in the CBIT proposal (including reductions in marginal tax rates and elimination of double taxation of corporate equity investment) may have significant effects on the generation of economic profits and the saving of certain wealthy households.

Business Decisions and Non-Life-Cycle Household Saving

It is well known that simple life-cycle models fare poorly in explaining the aggregate capital stock or the distribution of wealth among households (see, e.g., the review of studies in Hubbard et al., 1994). While even more sophisticated dynamic models emphasizing insurance and capital-market imperfections can explain much of the heterogeneity in saving among U.S. households (see, e.g., Hubbard et al., 1994, 1995; Aiyagari, 1994; and Huggett, 1996), those models do less well in explaining the saving of high-income or high-net-worth households. That failure is a problem when one realizes that the top 1 percent of households in 1989 owned about 29 percent of total household wealth (based on data from the Panel Study of Income Dynamics, or PSID) or about 36 percent (based on the Survey of Consumer Finances).

---

[18] See, for example, Feldstein (1978), Summers (1981a), Evans (1983), Auerbach and Kotlikoff (1983, 1987), Auerbach, Kotlikoff, and Skinner (1983), and Hubbard and Judd (1986).

[19] See, for example, Hubbard et al. (1994, 1995) and Engen (1994).

Although the rich may be different from the rest of us for many reasons,[20] the foregoing discussion lends to a natural emphasis on active business ownership or entrepreneurial activity. Assessing how important entrepreneurs are in aggregate saving requires a definition of entrepreneurship. Focusing on entrepreneurship as combining an upfront investment with entrepreneurial skill to realize an uncertain return,[21] Gentry and I (1998b) find that the 8.6 percent of households we defined as active business owners in the 1989 Survey of Consumer Finances own about 39 percent of total household net worth. Moreover, active business assets are concentrated among wealthy households, and the propensity to own these assets rises dramatically with wealth. We find that wealth-income ratios and saving rates (using the 1983–89 panel data from the Survey of Consumer Finances) are significantly higher for entrepreneurial households even after controlling for age and other demographic variables. We also find portfolios of entrepreneurial households, even wealthy ones, are very undiversified, with the bulk of assets held within active businesses. Finally, upward mobility in the distributions of household income and wealth is much greater for entrepreneurs than for nonentrepreneurs.

These patterns are difficult to reconcile within a life-cycle framework, in which saving occurs for consumption smoothing and precautionary purposes. Based on the definition of "active business ownership" to which I referred earlier, there is good reason to believe that entrepreneurs' investment decisions differ markedly from the portfolio decisions of nonentrepreneurs. Starting and remaining in business likely require upfront investments (in, say, fixed or working capital) to realize potentially high returns from ideas, skill, or market power. While such expected returns may exceed those obtained from financial assets (returns typically used to study household saving decisions), entrepreneurs must often finance investments with personal assets or income. The potentially high returns available to entrepreneurs – coupled with constraints on external financing – could, in principle, lead to very high saving rates for entrepreneurs out of marginal income.

---

[20] A number of non-(simple)-life-cycle stories may help explain the saving of the very affluent, including: (1) differences in the importance of pensions and Social Security across income groups (see Hubbard et al., 1994, 1995); (2) bequest motives; (3) precautionary saving (see Hubbard et al., 1994, 1995); (4) differences in rates of time preference (see Lawrance, 1991; and Dynan, 1994); (5) differences in attitudes toward risk; (6) nonhomothetic preferences (see Attanasio and Browning, 1995; and Atkeson and Ogaki, 1996); and (7) differences in whether households derive direct utility from holding wealth (see Carroll, 1998). Dynan, Skinner, and Zeldes (1998) present evidence suggesting that saving rates rise with income and review some reasons why saving rates may vary with income.

[21] We thought of an entrepreneur as someone whose income is derived from earnings on upfront business investments; we applied a minimum business asset cutoff of $5,000.

A substantial body of research has analyzed the importance of costly external financing on the timing and level of capital investment (see, e.g., the review in Hubbard, 1998). These studies emphasize that, to the extent that information and incentive problems in capital markets raise the cost of external financing relative to internal financing, changes in internally generated funds can influence investment, even after controlling for measures of underlying investment opportunities. Moreover, the anticipation of binding future financing constraints can lead firms to accumulate retained earnings to finance future investment.

Interestingly, while most empirical studies have focused on the investment decisions of relatively large firms, the decisions of entrepreneurial ventures actually correspond more closely to underlying theories (see, e.g., Evans and Jovanovic, 1989; Holtz-Eakin, Joulfaian, and Rosen, 1994; and Gentry and Hubbard, 1998b). Entrepreneurial businesses offer at least three sets of decisions which could be affected by costly external financing: (1) entry into (or exit from) entrepreneurship, (2) the choice of technology (i.e., labor-intensive versus capital-intensive), and (3) the level of investment. Under costly external financing, the saving and investment decisions of business owners are likely to be closely related.

Household Saving and Business Entry

Past saving decisions are likely to affect entry into entrepreneurship. Models of entrepreneurial selection generally focus on the individual's decisions about whether to work for someone else for wage income or for himself or herself as an entrepreneur (see, e.g., Evans and Jovanovic, 1989). Under perfect capital markets, an individual's wealth is irrelevant for entrepreneurial decisions: the individual would enter entrepreneurship if expected entrepreneurial earnings exceed expected wage income. Costly external financing distorts the entry decisions for potential entrepreneurs with low net worth. If entrepreneurial ability is held constant, entrepreneurial earnings depend on capital invested. When external financing is costly relative to internal financing, both the probability of entry and the size of the capital stock increase with initial assets (see Gentry and Hubbard, 1998b).

An empirical question arises: given that a household is nonentrepreneurial in one period, do initial assets influence the probability of becoming an entrepreneur by the next period, after controlling for household characteristics and work experience? The answer appears to be yes. Using the Survey of Consumer Finances data described earlier, Gentry and I (1998b) show that higher initial assets raise the probability of entry into entrepreneurship, except for very high levels of initial assets. Such a pattern is consistent both with an "entrepreneurial ability" story (in which variation in entrepreneurial ability among households not seen by the researcher is correlated with initial assets) and with a "costly external financing" interpretation. Support for a role for costly external financing is provided by the heavy internal financing of businesses (as indicated by relatively less diversified portfolios) and the relatively high saving rates for entrepreneurial entrants prior to entering.

Household Saving and Entrepreneurial Investment

What about the decisions of continuing entrepreneurs? Under perfect capital markets, nonbusiness asset holdings should not affect business investment decisions. Using different data sets, Evans and Jovanovic (1989), Holtz-Eakin et al. (1994), and Gentry and Hubbard (1998b) find that a household's nonbusiness assets affect the growth of its business income, a finding inconsistent with perfect capital markets for entrepreneurs. In addition, Holtz-Eakin et al. (1994) and Gentry and Hubbard (1998b) find that the probability of continuing as an entrepreneur is positively related to nonbusiness asset holdings.

These results suggest strongly that entrepreneurial saving and investment decisions are not independent. To the extent that entrepreneurs expect higher returns on funds invested in active businesses than on financial assets, they have an incentive to invest their assets in their business and, if their achievable capital investment is less than the desired capital stock, increase their saving to finance business investment. These connections suggest that a reasonable analysis of the effects of tax policy or tax reform on entrepreneurs must go beyond the textbook perfect-capital-market stories.

Tax Reform and Entrepreneurial Decisions

Again, one can think of a tax reform shifting from the current tax system to a broad-based consumption tax as a two-step process: (1) income tax reform (rate reductions, base broadening, and elimination of differential capital taxation), and (2) the shift from a broad-based income tax to a broad-based consumption tax. Both steps affect the non-life-cycle household saving decisions of active business owners.

Income Tax Reform and Changes in Marginal Income Tax Rates

In addition to their effects in conventional life-cycle models, reductions in marginal income tax rates would likely provide a substantial stimulus to entrepreneurial activity and investment. First, reducing progressivity at the top of the earnings distribution makes it more likely that individuals with high entrepreneurial ability will become entrepreneurs, as opposed to working for someone else.[22] This outcome is likely both because entrepreneurial earnings are more variable than earnings from employment and because successful entrepreneurs are more likely to face the highest marginal tax rates. From the perspective of the would-be-entrepreneur, the extent of progressivity (measured by the slope of the tax schedule) is a determinant of the decision of whether to become an entrepreneur or to work for someone else (see, e.g., Gentry and Hubbard, 2000). Second, lower marginal tax rates increase after-tax entrepreneurial earnings. To the extent that entrepreneurs face costly external financing, the greater after-tax earnings increase the pool of internal funds for reinvestment in the business.

These effects of lower marginal tax rates on entrepreneurs' decisions are much larger than those measured by conventional analyses of effects of tax policy on labor supply and investment. Traditionally, specialists in labor economics and public finance focus on hours worked as a measure of labor supply. Under this definition, losses in economic well-being from progressive labor income taxation are generally estimated to be modest for men (whose hours worked tend to be relatively insensitive to changes in marginal tax rates) and greater for married women. Recently, Feldstein (1995a) has argued for shifting the focus to income, in order to measure effects of tax distortions on job selection, effort, amenities, and so on; he estimates much larger losses in economic well-being from high marginal income tax rates. For entrepreneurs, high marginal income tax rates can significantly reduce entrepreneurial entry and continuation, suggesting much larger losses in economic well-being from high marginal tax rates than those obtained by focusing solely on the decisions of employees.[23]

---

[22] Working in the other direction is the argument that greater progressivity may offer more insurance for risky entrepreneurial ventures; this argument would be more compelling, however, with more perfect loss offsets than those permissible in the current U.S. tax system.

[23] As with the case of a reduction in marginal income tax rates, a reduction in the tax rate on capital gains would likely affect entrepreneurs more than nonentrepreneurs. First, a lower capital gains tax rate can, in principle, stimulate both entrepreneurial participation and entrepreneurial investment. Second, a lower capital gains tax rate reduces the "lock-in" effect of capital gains taxation on entrepreneurial ventures. Third, a lower capital gains tax rate can increase the supply of funds for entrepreneurial ventures from taxable investors (e.g., angels or venture capitalists).

Focusing on entrepreneurial business assets as opposed to passive asset holdings represented by the employees' saving suggests greater potential gains from capital gains tax reductions than indicated by conventional empirical analysis. This difference partially reflects the first two channels discussed earlier. The effect of capital gains taxation on entry into and exit from entrepreneurial ventures is ignored in conventional measures of losses in economic well-being from capital income taxation. In addition, lock-in effects

In addition, the effects of tax policy on investment by entrepreneurs are likely to be large. Traditional analysis of tax policy on investment stresses the effects of income taxes on the marginal return to investment. That is, a reduction in marginal income tax rates, all else being equal, raises the marginal return to investing, and increases business investment (see, e.g., Carroll et al., 1998, and the review of evidence in Hassett and Hubbard, 1997). To the extent that entrepreneurs face costly external financing, an additional tax effect emerges; lower marginal tax rates increase internal funds and the ability to finance investment.

Changes in the Tax Base under Fundamental Tax Reform

It is often maintained that fundamental income or consumption tax reform offers the greatest potential for tax policy to stimulate saving and investment. As I have argued, the truth in this argument can principally be traced to reductions in income tax rates and capital gains tax rates made possible by income tax reform.

Beyond reducing marginal tax rates, a critical element of fundamental reform of the income tax is the integration of the corporate and personal income tax systems – the goal of the Treasury Department's CBIT proposal. Going further – to a broad-based consumption tax – would eliminate tax on the opportunity cost return to capital, delivering a smaller incremental effect on incentives for saving and investment than in the standard treatment in which such a reform eliminates taxation of all capital income.

Implications for Research on Tax Reform

The simple points I am raising here suggest the need for additional research on dynamic models of household saving decisions. By quantifying more precisely the roles played by risk taking and pursuit of economic profits in households' portfolio decisions, such additional research could shed more light on the relative magnitudes of the various components of "capital income" and on the broader question of households' motives for saving and on the sensitivity of those motives to tax changes.

Recent adaptations of the life-cycle model emphasize the importance of uninsured idiosyncratic risk (of earnings, life-span, or medical expenses) and lending-market imperfections (or borrowing constraints); see, for example, Hubbard et al. (1994, 1995). While such models can

---

are more costly for entrepreneurs for two reasons. First, selling entrepreneurial businesses is often an "all or nothing" decision – that is, the choice is often to sell the entire business as opposed to a small fraction, as, for example, with the sale of a portion of a passive stock portfolio. Second, lock-in makes it costly for entrepreneurs to exploit business development skills by selling one business and starting another.

explain many aggregate and distributional features of U.S. wealth accumulation, they are not well suited to explaining saving related to business ownership. That is, though such models incorporate decisions about labor supply and investment in financial assets, they do not incorporate decisions about entrepreneurial entry, saving, and investment. The inclusion of such margins is likely to be useful for explaining wealth accumulation, given the empirical significance for total wealth of business owners' household wealth accumulation decisions.[24]

Quadrini (2000) has embarked on one research program in this area. He nests a formalization of entrepreneurial choice within an intertemporal general equilibrium model of an economy of infinitely lived households. The production sector has both large firms and small firms, the latter being "financially constrained" (in the spirit of Fazzari, Hubbard, and Petersen, 1988; and Gertler and Gilchrist, 1994). Potential entrepreneurs face higher costs of external financing than for internal financing (their own saving). Calibrating the model using data from the PSID, Quadrini does relatively well in matching the variation on wealth-income ratios by income class for entrepreneurs and nonentrepreneurs and the distribution of wealth and income for the model economy and the PSID data. Moreover, he finds that eliminating the entrepreneurial selection and investment margins significantly reduces the model's ability to explain the observed concentration of wealth and income. Additional research along these lines will enhance the ability of dynamic equilibrium models to explain the level and distribution of saving and its responsiveness to tax policy.

CONCLUSION

The desirability of fundamental tax reform – proposals to shift the U.S. tax system to a broad-based consumption tax – will be judged on the basis of how reform changes the efficiency, simplicity, and fairness of the tax system. Of this trinity, fairness has generated most of the controversy over consumption tax proposals. Recent research suggests that this controversy may be misplaced. Most elements of consumption tax reform are consistent with moving to a pure income tax with uniform capital taxation. Moving from this pure income tax to a consumption tax only requires replacing depreciation allowances for physical investment with expensing of capital assets.

---

[24] Such research must also confront the sources of saving differences of business owners (e.g., distinguishing between the talent-cum-costly-external-financing story and stories emphasizing differences in risk-taking behavior for business owners and workers) and the effect of the current tax system (as opposed to the broad-based income tax) on risk taking.

Herein lies the qualification to distributional analysis. Despite the claim that consumption taxes fail to tax capital income, replacing depreciation allowances with expensing only eliminates the taxation of the opportunity cost of capital. Because more affluent households receive a larger portion of what is often termed capital income in forms treated equivalently by broad-based income and consumption taxes (ex post returns to risk taking and inframarginal returns), a consumption tax is less regressive than would be suggested by assuming that a consumption tax exempts all parts of capital income. This qualification substantially alters the distributional analysis of tax reform generally undertaken by congressional and Treasury Department staff members.

The point that, relative to income taxation, consumption taxation removes from taxation only the opportunity cost return to capital has potentially important consequences for economic analysis of the effects of tax reform on household saving decisions (and, by extension, steady-state per capita output and consumption). Such analysis is typically conducted in models that consider only life-cycle consumption-smoothing motives for saving and assume that a consumption tax eliminates taxation of all capital income. The focus on opportunity-cost versus non-opportunity-cost returns to capital suggests the significance of understanding the saving decisions of households with non-opportunity-cost returns – which are typically households of business owners – and how the saving decisions of those households are affected by tax policy. This is a useful and emerging area for research.

Chapter 5

International Aspects of Fundamental Tax Reform

Charles L. Ballard

Proposals for fundamental tax reform have attracted considerable attention in recent years. Most of the discussion has focused on domestic problems of administration and compliance,[1] or on the effects of tax reforms on labor supply and capital accumulation within the domestic economy.[2] International issues have been given relatively little attention. As the world economy becomes increasingly integrated, however, a focus on international issues becomes increasingly appropriate.[3]

This chapter has two closely related objectives: to survey the potential effects of fundamental tax reform in the United States on the international economy, and to assess the ways in which estimates of the economic effects of fundamental tax reform would be altered as a result of changes in the economic modeling of the foreign sector. International capital flows will be given particular attention.

A description of the current tax treatment of foreign-source income opens the chapter. I also describe how these tax rules would be changed

I thank Jim Hines, Taejoo Kim, Peter Mieszkowski, Leslie Papke, John Karl Scholz, and George Zodrow for helpful comments. Any errors are my responsibility.

[1] Andrews (1974) and U.S. Department of the Treasury (1977) were among the most important early contributions to the modern literature. These authors, and others such as Aaron and Galper (1985), have emphasized the adminstrative advantages of a cash flow consumption tax.

[2] A number of authors have simulated the effects of moving toward consumption taxation (while abstracting from issues of administration and compliance), including Fullerton, Shoven, and Whalley (1983), Auerbach and Kotlikoff (1983, 1987), Auerbach et al. (1997), Ballard (1990), Engen and Gale (1997), and Rogers (1997), as well as the chapter in this volume by Jorgenson and Wilcoxen. These authors have generally found that heavier reliance on consumption taxation will lead to welfare gains in the long run. For further discussion, see Chapter 2 by Gravelle in this volume.

[3] Recently, some researchers have begun to study the international implications of major tax reforms. These include Grubert and Newlon (1995), Hines (1996), Mendoza and Tesar (1998), and Thalmann, Goulder, and DeLorme (1996).

and how administrative and compliance issues would be affected if fundamental tax reform were enacted. Next I survey the evidence on the international mobility of capital as it relates to fundamental tax reform and show how our understanding of the incidence of the corporate tax can change when we consider international flows of goods and capital. Then I evaluate recent attempts to assess the efficiency gains from fundamental tax reform, both in models of closed economies and open economies.

THE TAX TREATMENT OF FOREIGN-SOURCE INCOME IN THE UNITED STATES

All countries assert the right to levy taxes on income generated within their borders, including the income of foreign multinational corporations.[4] However, different countries take different approaches to taxing the income of domestic citizens and corporations that is generated abroad. Some countries, such as Belgium, France, the Netherlands, and Norway, adopt a system that is largely a "territorial system," under which they do not tax income generated outside their borders. However, the United States (like Italy, Japan, and the United Kingdom) taxes on a "worldwide residence basis," under which the foreign-source income of U.S. citizens, permanent residents, and corporations is subject to tax by the U.S. government. Since foreign governments also tax this income, there is a possibility of substantial double taxation. The problem of double taxation could be reduced by either of two methods. Under the first method, U.S. firms could be allowed to deduct the taxes paid to foreign governments. The second method would allow a credit for foreign taxes paid. The choice made by the United States, as well as by other countries such as Greece, Italy, and the United Kingdom, is to use a credit system.

The Credit System

Although the credit system greatly reduces double taxation, it leads to another problem: if no limits were placed on the tax credits, the U.S. Treasury would effectively be offering an unlimited subsidy to foreign governments. If credits were unlimited, foreign governments would have an incentive to tax U.S. corporations at extremely high rates, knowing that the corporations would be completely reimbursed by the United

---

[4] Readers who are interested in more details on the tax treatment of foreign-source income can find helpful discussions in Froot and Hines (1995), Goodspeed and Witte (2000), Hines (1988, 1996, 1999a), and Slemrod (1990b). Hines (1997) contains a recent and very comprehensive review of the empirical literature that deals with these aspects of the tax law.

States government. Therefore, U.S. tax law only allows a credit for foreign taxes up to a limit, equal to the amount of tax that would be paid if the income in question were taxed according to U.S. tax rules.[5]

Figure 5.1 represents the combined effective tax rates that prevail under a system with foreign tax credits. First, let us consider a U.S. firm that operates a subsidiary in a country with a tax rate such as t_L in Figure 5.1, which is *below* the U.S. corporate tax rate. At first, the firm's income will be taxed by the foreign government at the rate t_L. Then, the firm's income will be taxed by the U.S. government at the rate t_{US}. (Currently, for all but the smallest corporations, the marginal tax rate under the U.S. corporate tax is 35 percent.) However, a credit will be given for foreign taxes paid. The combined effective tax rate will be the U.S. tax rate, t_{US}, but the U.S. government will only collect net revenue associated with the *difference* between the U.S. tax rate and the foreign tax rate, t_L. Thus, if the foreign government's tax rate is 20 percent, a U.S. multinational firm with $100 of foreign-source income will pay $20 to the foreign government and $15 ($35 − $20) to the U.S. Treasury, for a total of $35 in tax payments.

If a U.S. firm operates only one foreign subsidiary, and if that subsidiary is located in a country with a tax rate such as t_L, the firm will not have reached the limit for the foreign tax credit. A firm in this situation is said to be in a "deficit-credit" or "excess-limitation" position. However, in many cases, a firm's potentially creditable foreign taxes will be greater than the limit on credits to be taken in a given year. In this case, the firm will have exhausted its foreign tax credits, and the firm is said to be in an "excess-credit" position.[6]

Figure 5.1 also illustrates the situation facing a firm that is in an excess-credit position. Consider a U.S. firm that operates only one foreign subsidiary, which is located in a country with a tax rate such as t_H in Figure 5.1, which is *above* the U.S. corporate tax rate. The U.S. government does not collect any net revenue in a case like this. The combined effective tax rate is equal to the foreign tax rate, t_H. For example, if the foreign government's tax rate is 50 percent, a U.S. multinational firm with $100 of foreign-source income will pay $50 to the foreign government. Its $35

---

[5] Some other restrictions also apply. To qualify for the foreign tax credit, a U.S. firm must own at least 10 percent of a foreign affiliate. In addition, income taxes and withholding taxes are the only foreign taxes that are eligible for the foreign tax credit. Under the current interpretation of the U.S. tax laws, a cash flow consumption tax levied by a foreign country is not eligible for the foreign tax credit. See McLure and Zodrow (1998) for a discussion.

[6] Excess credits may be carried forward for five years, or backward for two years, to offset tax liabilities in other years. However, the tax code does not allow any interest accumulations on these carry-forwards and carry-backs, and they are not adjusted for inflation.

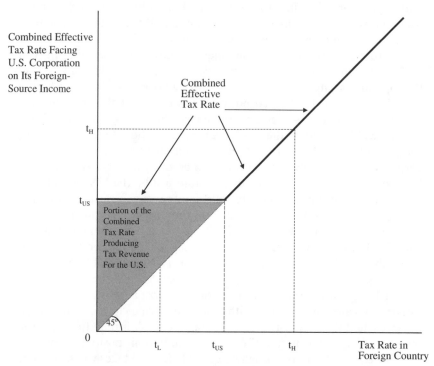

Figure 5.1. Effective Tax Rates Facing a Multinational Corporation

of U.S. taxes will be completely offset by a foreign tax credit of $35, so
that its net payments to the U.S. Treasury are zero, and its total tax payments are $50.

In spite of the limitations on foreign tax credits, they add up to a
substantial amount of money.[7] During most years of the 1980s and early
1990s, foreign tax credits were roughly $21–23 billion per year. As a result
of increases in worldwide income, the foreign tax credits taken by
U.S. firms rose to $30.1 billion in 1995. In a typical recent year, foreign
tax credits have amounted to about 70 percent of all of the tax credits
taken by U.S. corporations.[8]

---

[7] The tax code contains many attempts to limit foreign tax credits (several of which are
described in this section). However, despite the fact that these provisions make the tax
code very complicated, it is not clear that they have increased net U.S. tax revenues by
a substantial amount. In fact, since the early 1980s, foreign tax credits have regularly been
more than 90 percent of current-year foreign taxes. See Nutter (1997).

[8] See table 13 of "Selected Historical and Other Data" in Internal Revenue Service (1997),
and Nutter (1997).

In order to give some perspective on the magnitude of these figures, we can compare them with the total taxes paid by U.S. corporations. For example, in 1993, U.S. corporations received foreign tax credits of $22.9 billion, and paid a total of $119.9 billion in taxes (after credits). However, about half of these taxes was paid by firms with no foreign tax credits. If we focus exclusively on firms with positive foreign tax credits, the relative size of the foreign tax credits is even greater. In 1993, these firms paid $59 billion of U.S. tax, after credits, so that their foreign tax credits amounted to more than one-third of their ultimate tax liability in the United States (see Nutter, 1997).[9]

Other Features of the Tax Treatment of Foreign-Source Income

The Overall Limitation

Figure 5.1 was drawn under the implicit assumption that the U.S. firm operates subsidiaries in only one foreign country. In reality, many firms operate foreign subsidiaries in several different countries. A pure system of foreign tax credits would require firms to calculate their foreign tax credits separately for each foreign country in which they operate. However, since 1976, U.S. companies have been required to add together all of their worldwide income when calculating the limit on foreign tax credits. A firm will only have excess foreign tax credits if the *sum* of its taxes paid to all foreign governments is greater than this overall limit. Under such a worldwide averaging system, firms are said to be subject to an "overall limitation" on foreign tax credits, rather than a "per-country limitation."[10]

Deferral

We have already described a fairly complex system of taxation. In fact, however, the foregoing description only scratches the surface of the enormous complexity of the U.S. tax treatment of foreign-source income.

---

[9] The system of foreign tax credits is further complicated by the corporate alternative minimum tax (AMT). Lyon and Silverstein (1995) report that the AMT is quantitatively significant: for firms that filed for foreign tax credits in 1990, more than half of all assets and foreign-source income are accounted for by corporations paying AMT. As discussed in Lyon and Silverstein, the AMT has several effects on U.S. multinationals. Under one important provision, the total of AMT foreign tax credits and net-operating-loss deductions may not be used to reduce AMT liabilities by more than 90 percent. It should also be noted that, because the AMT rate is only 20 percent, firms subject to the AMT are more likely to be in an excess-credit position than otherwise comparable firms that do not face the AMT.

[10] See Frisch (1983) for simulations of the effects of replacing the overall limitation with a per-country limitation. U.S. Department of the Treasury (1984b) proposed a per-country limitation, but this proposal was not enacted.

One additional element of complexity is the provision for "deferral." The earnings of foreign *branches* of U.S. firms are immediately taxable in the United States. However, for foreign operations organized in the form of separately incorporated *subsidiaries*, U.S. taxes on foreign-source income may usually be deferred until the income is repatriated to the parent firm in the United States.[11] This leads to an incentive for subsidiaries in low-tax foreign countries to delay the repatriation of income. Frisch (1983) reports that foreign subsidiaries repatriated only about 41 percent of their income in 1972, and Hines and Hubbard (1990) report that 42.1 percent of income was repatriated in 1984.[12] For a recent discussion of deferral and repatriation, see Hines (1999b).

In an attempt to prevent the indefinite deferral of these profit remittances, the "Subpart F" provisions of the tax code require that certain types of income be treated as "deemed distributed" to the American parent firms (and therefore immediately taxable), regardless of whether the income is actually repatriated.[13] Passive income is the most important category of income covered by Subpart F: under this part of the tax law, nonfinancial foreign subsidiaries are prevented from avoiding taxes by making passive financial investments abroad. Subpart F also prevents foreign subsidiaries from avoiding taxes by investing their income in U.S. property, or by insuring risks in the United States. However, if a controlled foreign corporation reinvests its foreign earnings in active businesses abroad, it can continue to defer its U.S. tax liability.

One important question is whether the deferral of taxes in the home country has a marginal effect on the investment decisions of foreign subsidiaries. Hartman (1984, 1985) suggests that, for some foreign subsidiaries, it makes no difference whether home-country taxes are deferred. Hartman's argument draws a distinction between the "immature" foreign subsidiary, which must rely on transfers of funds from its parent, and the "mature" foreign subsidiary, which can finance investments with retained earnings.

Hartman argues that, if a subsidiary has already earned income in a foreign country, it has already incurred a tax liability in the foreign country. That tax liability is unaffected by the timing of home-country taxes. Thus, for a mature firm that makes its marginal investment out of retained earnings, foreign taxes have already been paid before the retained earnings are invested. However, if the parent firm is consider-

[11] These repatriations are typically referred to as "dividends," but they are more accurately described as "profit remittances." For discussions of deferral, see Hines and Hubbard (1990), Altshuler and Newlon (1993), and Altshuler, Newlon, and Randolph (1995).
[12] However, Hines and Hubbard also report that 84 percent of foreign subsidiaries did not repatriate *any* dividends in 1984.
[13] Subpart F applies only to *controlled* foreign corporations, in which U.S. parents own at least 50 percent of the foreign firm, with each U.S. parent owning at least 10 percent.

ing whether to transfer funds to a subsidiary in a foreign country, those funds have *not* already been subject to foreign tax. The parent firm should recognize that the returns on those transferred funds will be subject to foreign income taxes and withholding taxes. As Hartman puts it (1984, p. 478), "When the funds are already in the hands of a . . . subsidiary, a tax on transferring funds back to the parent firm becomes an unavoidable cost, and does not influence the firm's optimal investment decision. On the other hand, the same tax is avoidable if the funds are not already located in the [country where the subsidiary operates], and, therefore, [the tax] serves to some extent as an investment disincentive." In his empirical work, Hartman finds some support for this theory.[14]

Separate Baskets

Another source of complexity is the set of rules that are given the name "separate baskets." The U.S. tax code identifies nine "baskets" or types of income.[15] Foreign taxes imposed on taxable income in a particular basket can only be used to offset U.S. taxes that are due on income in that same basket.[16] One of the purposes of the separate-baskets rules is to prevent firms from reducing their taxes by averaging types of income that generate large amounts of foreign taxes with other types of income that generate smaller amounts of foreign taxes. The separate-baskets rules are somewhat analogous to the per-country limitation. Thus, in a sense, the U.S. tax law is inconsistent, in that it restricts averaging across different baskets of income but does not restrict averaging across different countries. From the perspective of the U.S. Treasury, it is reasonable to try to augment revenues by restricting the foreign tax credit, but the separate-basket rules create a very significant degree of complexity.[17]

Source Rules[18]

In principle, foreign tax credits are limited to the amount of tax that would have been paid if the income were taxed according to U.S. tax

---

[14] Hartman's ideas regarding the effects of deferred home-country taxes on investments by foreign subsidiaries are similar to the "new view" of dividend taxation. See Zodrow (1991) for a discussion of the "new view" and the "traditional view" of dividend taxation.

[15] The baskets are (1) investment interest income, (2) dividend income from domestic international sales corporations, (3) foreign-trade income of foreign sales corporations, (4) distributions from foreign sales corporations, (5) shipping income, (6) high-withholding-tax income, (7) financial-services income, (8) dividends received from foreign operations that are not controlled foreign corporations, and (9) all other foreign-source income.

[16] Thus, it is possible for a firm to find itself in an excess-credit position with respect to some baskets, but in an excess-limitation position with respect to other baskets.

[17] An interesting discussion can be found in Desai and Hines (1999).

[18] This subsection draws on Slemrod (1990b).

rules. However, as with so many other aspects of the tax code, this feature is subject to manipulation. If the limit on foreign tax credits is increased for any reason, certain firms can reduce their U.S. tax liability. This is true regardless of whether the increase in the limit has any clear connection with the principle on which the foreign-tax-credit limitation is based.

For example, if a firm is in an excess-credit situation, it can reduce its worldwide taxes if it can increase the limit on its foreign tax credits. Regardless of the *actual* source of a multinational firm's income, the firm may gain from any artificial rule that results in a higher portion of its income being classified as foreign source, *for U.S. tax purposes*.

One such rule involves the reclassification (for U.S. tax purposes) of a portion of the income from *domestic* production of export goods. Currently, up to 50 percent of the income from domestic U.S. production of export goods can be allocated to foreign-source income. This has the effect of increasing the limit on foreign tax credits. For a multinational firm that has excess foreign tax credits, this rule dramatically reduces the effective tax rate on domestic investments that lead to the production of export goods.

Transfer Prices

Regardless of the country in which income is *actually* generated, multinational corporations have an incentive to shift as much of their *taxable* income as possible from high-tax countries into low-tax countries. One way to do this is to engage in artificial "transfer pricing," by overstating the prices of intermediate goods that are sold from affiliates in low-tax countries to affiliates in high-tax countries, or by understating the prices of intermediate goods that are sold from affiliates in high-tax countries to affiliates in low-tax countries. In order to prevent this type of manipulation, U.S. law requires that these transactions occur at "arm's-length" prices – that is, at the market prices that would be charged between unrelated firms. Of course, the relevant market prices are sometimes difficult or impossible to determine, especially in the case of intangibles.[19] Considerable administrative and compliance costs are necessary to enforce the arm's-length rules.

In spite of these administrative and compliance costs, however, it appears that the tax authorities have not succeeded in stopping artificial transfer pricing. Grubert and Mutti (1991) present evidence that is consistent with artificial transfer pricing among affiliates in high- and low-tax countries. Harris et al. (1993) present evidence that is consistent

[19] For example, in some cases, the unique characteristics of patent rights may make it very difficult to trade them in markets, so that their fair-market value cannot be determined. See Hines (1997).

with artificial transfer pricing between the United States and other countries. Grubert, Goodspeed, and Swenson (1993) suggest that foreign firms operating in the United States may also be engaging in successful transfer-pricing schemes. On the other hand, the rules are probably not completely ineffective in reducing transfer-pricing schemes. See Hines and Rice (1994).

Interest-Allocation Rules[20]

Transfer-pricing schemes are not the only means of "income shifting" by which firms can reduce their tax liabilities. Another way is to arrange debt transactions to maximize the tax savings from interest-expense deductions.[21]

Foreign governments generally do *not* allow U.S. firms to deduct their interest expenses from U.S. loans against their taxable income in the foreign country. If a U.S. multinational is in an excess-limitation situation (i.e., the firm has not used up all of its foreign tax credits), small changes in the allocation of the firm's interest expenses on U.S. loans will not have any effect on the firm's total tax liabilities. This is because, if an extra dollar of interest expense is allocated against the income of a foreign subsidiary, the reduction in U.S. tax owed on the foreign-source income will be offset exactly by a decrease in the foreign tax credit.

If a firm has excess foreign tax credits, however, it will not owe any net U.S. tax on its foreign-source income. For a firm in an excess-credit position, if an extra dollar of interest expense is allocated against the income of a foreign subsidiary, the firm will still owe zero U.S. tax on its foreign-source income, but its deductions against U.S. income will have decreased. Therefore, the firm's taxes on its U.S. income will rise. Consequently, if a U.S. multinational is in an excess-credit position, the firm can benefit by allocating as much as possible of its interest expenses from U.S. loans against its U.S. income.

The tax authorities in the United States have long recognized the incentives for this type of income shifting. Generally speaking, American firms with foreign-source income are *not* permitted to take a deduction against U.S. taxes for all of the interest expenses they incur from loans originating in the United States. Instead, for the purposes of U.S.

[20] This subsection draws on the discussions in Altshuler and Mintz (1995) and Froot and Hines (1995).

[21] It should be noted that many of the issues associated with the allocation of interest expenses are also relevant for our understanding of research and development (R&D) expenditures, since R&D expenditures must also be allocated. This chapter does not discuss R&D explicitly, but see Hines (1993, 1994, 1995) for analysis of the R&D decisions of multinational corporations.

tax law, multinationals are required to allocate their interest expenses between U.S. income and foreign income.

The Tax Reform Act of 1986 altered the landscape of the interest-allocation rules in several important ways. First, the 1986 act reduced the marginal tax rate for most corporations from 46 to 34 percent. This raised the stakes associated with the interest-allocation rules, by pushing more firms into an excess-credit position. At the same time, the law restricted the ability of firms to manipulate the allocation of their interest deductions. Before 1986, multinationals had the choice of allocating interest expenses on the basis of *either* assets or income (within certain limits). This meant that, if the income of a foreign subsidiary was zero or negative, the multinational would choose to allocate its interest expenses on the basis of income, and all interest expenses would be charged against U.S. income. This practice was eliminated by the Tax Reform Act of 1986, which required that interest expenses could only be allocated on the basis of assets. Basically, the fraction of its interest payments that a U.S. multinational must deduct from its foreign-source income is equal to the fraction of the firm's worldwide assets that is expected to generate foreign-source income.[22]

Before 1986, interest expenses were determined separately for each company within a group of foreign subsidiaries that are controlled by the same parent firm in the United States. In practice, however, multinationals were able to circumvent the intent of the law by placing debt in a wholly owned domestic subsidiary that holds no foreign assets or income. In this way, U.S. firms were able to deduct 100 percent of their interest expenses against U.S. taxable income. The Tax Reform Act of 1986 attacked this practice by establishing a "one-taxpayer rule," under which the allocation of interest expenses between foreign and domestic income depends on the attributes of *all* members of a controlled group of firms, regardless of whether they are owned directly by the parent firm, or indirectly through one or more subsidiaries.

Froot and Hines (1995) present evidence suggesting that the Tax Reform Act was somewhat successful in reducing the tax deductibility of U.S. interest expenses for some U.S. multinationals. Once again, however, this result appears to have been very costly in terms of admin-

---

[22] By requiring that interest expenses must be allocated on the basis of assets, the Tax Reform Act of 1986 provided an incentive to U.S. parents to issue loans to their subsidiaries, in order to reduce the net value of foreign assets. This possibility was restricted by another provision of the Tax Reform Act, called the "netting rule." For a discussion of the netting rule, see Altshuler and Mintz (1995). However, the netting rule does not prohibit the foreign subsidiaries from reducing their assets through local borrowing. Altshuler and Mintz present evidence that foreign subsidiaries have indeed increased their local borrowing since the Tax Reform Act of 1986.

istrative complexity. Moreover, for better or worse, the current U.S. tax system allows deductions for some interest payments. Consequently, if one believes that interest deductions are appropriate at all, then serious questions can be raised about the interest-allocation rules, regardless of their effects on U.S. tax revenues. If the foreign government does not allow a deduction for these interest expenses, then an accurate calculation of U.S. taxable income would seem to require deductibility. However, many tax reform proposals would eliminate the interest deduction altogether, in which case the interest-allocation rules would be rendered irrelevant.

Proposals for Fundamental Tax Reform

The tax treatment of foreign-source income is extremely complicated, but this highly complex system does not appear to raise much revenue. Not surprisingly, many of the recent proposals for tax reform include dramatic changes in the tax treatment of income earned abroad.

In the current debate, three proposals have received the most attention. One of these is the flat tax proposal of Hall and Rabushka ([1985] 1995, 1996), a modified version of which has been advocated by Representative Dick Armey (R.-Texas) and Senator Richard Shelby (R.-Alabama). Another widely discussed proposal is the "Unlimited Saving Allowance" proposal, advocated by Senator Sam Nunn (D.-Georgia) and Senator Pete Domenici (R.-New Mexico), which is described in Weidenbaum (1996). A third proposal is for a national retail sales tax. This type of reform has been advocated by Representatives Bill Archer (R.-Texas), Dan Schaefer (R.-Colorado), and Billy Tauzin (R.-Louisiana), and Senator Richard Lugar (R.-Indiana). Although they differ in some important details, each of these proposals involves converting the current U.S. tax system to a territorial system. Each would eliminate the taxation of income earned overseas. Consequently, in this chapter, I focus on the implications of proposals that move to a territorial basis.[23]

In addition to the proposals for consumption taxation, there is also a long tradition of proposals for moving toward a purer income tax.[24] In several ways, proposals for fundamental income tax reform are similar

---

[23] By their very natures, a value-added tax or a national retail sales tax would not attempt to tax foreign-source income. The particular flat tax proposals that are currently being debated would also not attempt to tax foreign-source income. On the other hand, a flat tax proposal could be designed in such a way that it would continue to tax foreign-source income. Even if a flat tax proposal did continue to tax foreign-source income, the rate of capital tax would be reduced substantially. Therefore, much of what is said here would apply to the case of a flat tax that does tax foreign-source income, although it would apply less strongly.

[24] For example, see Break and Pechman (1975).

to proposals for a consumption tax. For example, the article in this volume by Hubbard discusses the similarities between a pure income tax and a pure consumption tax. Also, the article in this volume by Gale and Holtzblatt suggests that a simplified income tax would lead to many of the improvements in administration and compliance that could also be achieved under a flat tax or a national retail sales tax. In the sections that follow, I concentrate on consumption tax proposals, but some of the discussion also has implications for fundamental reform of the income tax.

ADMINISTRATIVE AND COMPLIANCE ISSUES

Simplifications That May Be Achieved by Fundamental Tax Reform

Clearly, much of the complexity of the current U.S. tax treatment of foreign-source income would disappear if the United States were to move to a territorial system. U.S. corporations would no longer be required to pay U.S. tax on the income earned by foreign subsidiaries. Presumably, firms would still desire to keep track of their foreign-source income and their taxes paid to foreign governments for internal accounting purposes. However, they would no longer need to determine the tax they would have paid if the income had been generated in the United States. In addition, firms would no longer be eligible for a foreign tax credit. Therefore, they would no longer need to average the income and taxes earned in different foreign countries, for the purpose of determining the amount of the foreign tax credit, and they would no longer need to keep track of the income flowing through different "baskets."

If the United States were to adopt a territorial system, foreign-source income would no longer be taxed in the United States, regardless of whether it is repatriated to the parent company in the United States. Therefore, the U.S. Treasury would no longer be concerned with the timing of repatriations, and the Subpart F rules would no longer be necessary. Moreover, firms would no longer have any incentive to alter the timing of their repatriations because of tax considerations. The choice of whether to repatriate to the parent company, or reinvest in the foreign subsidiary, or invest elsewhere, would be made solely on the basis of profitability.

Most of the current tax-reform proposals would eliminate the deductibility of interest expenses. Even in the absence of international considerations, this would eliminate much of the huge potential for tax arbitrage that exists under the current tax system.[25] Moreover, fun-

---

[25] Slemrod and Gordon (1988) provide a good discussion of the tax arbitrage opportunities brought about by the combination of interest deductibility and the fact that the marginal tax rate on interest income is different for different taxpayers.

damental tax reforms that convert the tax system to a territorial basis would eliminate the need for the complex interest-allocation rules that exist in the current tax system. This would greatly reduce the compliance cost of the tax system.

Administrative and Compliance Problems That Will Remain

Some of the problems associated with international income flows would remain, however, even if the tax system were shifted to a territorial basis. Under either a territorial system or a worldwide system, firms have an incentive to manipulate transfer prices to shift the *apparent* source of income out of high-tax countries. The tax authorities in the United States would still be concerned with transfer-pricing schemes, even if the Armey-Shelby flat tax or the Nunn-Domenici USA Tax were adopted.[26]

Of course, the extent to which manipulative transfer-pricing schemes are seen as a problem for the revenue authorities of any given country will depend on the level of tax rates in that country, relative to the tax rates in other countries. If U.S. tax rates are relatively low, then firms will have an incentive to shift income *into* the United States, and the U.S. Treasury would not be particularly concerned about transfer pricing, although foreign governments might be very concerned. This discussion serves to highlight a point of crucial importance: if we are to evaluate the effects of a change in the tax treatment of foreign-source income, the domestic tax rate can be just as important as the rules governing income earned abroad.

Today's proposals for fundamental tax reform point toward reduced taxation of capital income generally, and of corporate capital income in particular. The extreme case is the national retail sales tax, which would completely eliminate the taxation of normal returns to capital.[27] The flat tax would also reduce the taxation of corporate capital income: a portion of the burden currently borne by corporations would be moved to non-corporate firms, because the flat tax equalizes the tax treatment of corporate and noncorporate enterprises. In addition, the flat tax allows for expensing of capital investments, which will lead to a substantial reduction in tax burdens for many corporations.

---

[26] As mentioned earlier, there is evidence that firms are able to engage in some artificial transfer pricing, despite the government's attempts to enforce arm's-length rules. This has led some to suggest that the United States should abandon its current system of determining the international allocation of income, even if it were to continue to use the worldwide residence basis. Instead, it might be simpler and more effective to adopt some worldwide apportionment formula, or to impose a minimum level of presumptive corporate income tax on foreign-source income. See Mutti (1993).

[27] See Hubbard's article in this volume for a discussion of the distinction between taxation of normal returns to capital and taxation of "inframarginal" returns.

Therefore, in a sense, these proposals can be seen as converting the United States into an international tax haven. If fundamental reform were implemented, tax rates in the United States would presumably be lower than the tax rates of all of our major trading partners. Under some of the proposals for fundamental tax reform, U.S. tax rates might still be higher than those of a few tax havens, but these are likely to be of minor importance.[28] Consequently, if fundamental tax reform were to become a reality, both foreign and domestic firms would have incentives to use transfer prices to shift the apparent location of income into the United States.

Under a tax system like the flat tax, corporate capital income that is declared in the United States would be taxed, although at reduced rates. Therefore, if we hold the U.S. tax rate constant at its new, lower level, the amount of revenue collected by the U.S. Treasury would *increase* whenever transfer-pricing schemes are used to shift the apparent location of income from high-tax countries to the United States. Under a national retail sales tax, the incentive to shift the apparent source of income to the United States would be even greater, because such income would not be taxed at all in the United States. However, the U.S. government would not derive any revenue from this shifted income. It is difficult to predict the amount of resources the United States would devote to transfer-pricing enforcement in these situations. Perhaps the United States would decide to enforce transfer-pricing regulations because of the need to maintain good working relationships with foreign governments, or because of a recognition that transfer-pricing schemes are socially costly, regardless of whether any particular government gains revenue from them. However, experience suggests that the most powerful incentive for U.S. tax authorities to resist transfer-pricing schemes is the need to defend the tax base.

In summary, the essence of a transfer-pricing scheme is that different countries tax income at different rates, even though they may use the same rules for defining taxable income. If all countries recognize a particular deduction as being valid, then the firm has an incentive to take as

[28] Hines and Rice (1994) provide an interesting discussion of the activities of forty-one countries or regions that are categorized as tax havens. The seven most important tax havens are Hong Kong, Ireland, Liberia, Lebanon, Panama, Singapore, and Switzerland. Most of the countries in the list are very small, such as Andorra, Bahamas, Cayman Islands, Liechtenstein, and Vanuatu. Despite their small size, these countries do provide a home for a disproportionate share of the assets of the foreign operations of U.S. multinationals. However, that share would be expected to drop after fundamental tax reform in the United States, because the gap between the U.S. tax rate and the tax-haven tax rates would be reduced significantly. In some cases, the U.S. tax rate might actually be lower than the rates of some countries that are now characterized as tax havens.

much of the deduction as possible in the country with the highest tax rate. One of the most important effects of fundamental tax reform will be the reduction in tax rates in the United States, which will give businesses an incentive to shift the apparent source of income into the United States through transfer-pricing schemes.

However, there is a very different set of incentives when the definition of taxable income is different in different countries. Under a territorial system, domestic taxes would be reduced whenever domestic-source income is classified as being foreign-source income, *for the purposes of U.S. taxation only*. If income is actually generated in the United States, so that it is not subject to taxation abroad, it can avoid taxation altogether if it is declared by the United States to be foreign-source income. Therefore, if the U.S. tax system were switched to a territorial basis, there would doubtless be political pressure to reclassify domestic-source income as originating in foreign countries, as long as firms believe that foreign governments will not recognize the reclassification.

So far, this section has concentrated exclusively on the effects of fundamental tax reform on the classification of foreign-source *income*. In addition, fundamental tax reforms have implications for the border-tax adjustments that accompany foreign *trade*. If the United States were to institute a value-added tax, border-tax adjustments would be made in the same straightforward way in which they are already made in other countries. (In fact, the ease with which border-tax adjustments can be handled within a value-added tax is one of the strongest arguments in favor of value-added taxation. This has played a major role in the successful adoption of the value-added tax by the countries of the European Union.) As pointed out in the chapter by Cnossen in this volume, a national retail sales tax would not require border-tax adjustments, but it would generally *not* be neutral.

The value-added tax is a destination-based tax. This is the source of many of the advantages of the value-added tax. However, a flat tax is an origin-based tax. A flat tax would apply to exports, but not to imports. In the short run, at least, this might reduce the international competitiveness of a country that adopts a flat tax. In the long run, however, adjustments in exchange rates are likely to offset this disadvantage.

The Responses of Foreign Governments

Much of the discussion in this section has been based on the assumption that, because of fundamental tax reform in the United States, tax rates in the United States would be substantially lower than the tax rates of most other countries. However, this effect could be muted for any of several reasons. For example, U.S. tax rates might remain high temporarily, due to transition rules.[29] In addition, other countries could respond to the U.S. tax reform by reducing their own income tax rates. A worldwide reduction in income tax rates is likely to enhance worldwide welfare by more than a unilateral tax change in the Unites States. If the capital tax rates of all major countries were equalized at a modest level, we would most likely observe an increase in capital investment around the globe. In addition, if tax rates were equalized, multinational corporations would no longer have an incentive to devote resources to transfer-pricing schemes. Although transfer-pricing schemes are valuable for corporations that face different tax rates in different countries, they are socially unproductive, and their elimination would allow resources to be devoted to other more productive uses. More important, equalization of capital tax rates would lead to a more efficient allocation of the world's capital stock.

Predicting the responses of foreign governments is very difficult. In surveying responses to the Tax Reform Act of 1986, Whalley (1990) finds that some countries did adopt reforms that were similar to the ones undertaken in the United States. However, it appears that this may have resulted from common intellectual influences, rather than from the pressure of tax competition from the United States.

If the United States were to undertake a fundamental tax reform, my very tentative prediction is that some foreign governments would respond by making some similar changes. Overall, however, it seems reasonable to predict that the reduction in U.S. tax rates would not be fully matched by rate cuts elsewhere.

Summary of Effects on Administration and Compliance

Even in the absence of international considerations, simplification is one of the strongest arguments in favor of many of the proposals for fundamental tax reform, and the argument is only strengthened when we include the simplifications brought about in the international sphere. If the U.S. tax system were converted to a territorial basis, however, major simplification will only occur if fundamental tax reform is carried out fully. In fact, recent history does not provide any examples of dramatic simplification of the tax code, so it is probably inappropriate to be too optimistic on this score. In addition, major tax reforms almost always provide for transition rules, which can often be very complicated.[30] We should certainly expect that the move to a flat tax or a national retail

---

[29] Under many of the proposals for fundamental tax reform, the marginal effective tax rate on a capital investment will be zero. However, the statutory tax rate is positive in some cases.

[30] See Chapter 9 by Zodrow, in this volume, for a discussion of transition rules.

sales tax would be accompanied by transition rules. It is entirely possible that the tax laws could become more complicated, at least during the transition period.

Studies that have calculated the compliance cost of the U.S. income tax system sometimes find that the compliance costs can be 5 percent of revenues, or greater. Blumenthal and Slemrod (1995) present evidence that the ratio of compliance costs to revenue is substantially higher for the international portions of the tax system than for the tax system as a whole.[31]

INTERNATIONAL CAPITAL MOBILITY

If the world's capital stock were allocated by a perfect and frictionless international capital market, then the saving undertaken in any given country would be widely dispersed across the globe. Therefore, we would expect that the rate of saving and the rate of investment would be nearly uncorrelated in an international cross section. According to Feldstein and Horioka (1980), however, savings rates and investment rates are highly correlated across countries, which suggests that the world capital market is far from perfect. Subsequent studies have generated similar results. For example, Mishkin (1984) finds evidence of persistent international differences in real interest rates, and French and Poterba (1991) find that the portfolios of individual investors tend to be highly specialized in domestic assets. All of these pieces of evidence support the idea that the international capital market has significant imperfections.[32]

Of course, the massive capital inflows into the United States during the 1980s were likely to weaken the results regarding international capital immobility. In addition, in the decade following the publication of the Feldstein-Horioka study, some of the legal barriers to capital mobility were relaxed in a number of countries. Therefore, it is not surprising that Feldstein and Bacchetta (1991) find that the propensity to retain savings in the domestic economy was reduced substantially from the 1960s to the 1980s. Nevertheless, the results of Feldstein and Bacchetta are still consistent with a substantial degree of international capital immobility. They find that, even in the 1980s, each additional dollar of domestic saving is associated with more than 50 cents of additional investment in

---

[31] Chapter 7 by Gale and Holtzblatt in this volume contains a thorough discussion of administration and compliance issues, although it is focused primarily on domestic issues. See Seltzer (1997) for an in-depth look at the compliance costs borne by one multinational corporation.

[32] This literature is summarized and discussed by Gordon and Bovenberg (1996), who suggest that asymmetric information may be the reason for the relatively small degree of international mobility of capital.

the domestic economy. Frankel (1991) and Obstfeld (1995) provide reviews of the literature spawned by Feldstein and Horioka.

A number of studies have documented the responsiveness of foreign direct investment (FDI) and direct investment abroad (DIA) to differences in rates of return. Hartman (1984, building on the theory developed in Hartman, 1985) provides the starting point for the recent empirical literature on the effects of taxes on FDI in the United States.

Hartman performs an aggregate time series analysis. His dependent variable is constructed using data from the U.S. Commerce Department's Bureau of Economic Analysis, for the period from 1965 to 1979. Hartman finds that U.S. taxes do have an effect on inbound FDI. The elasticity with respect to the net rate of return on U.S. investments is around unity. Hartman is careful to emphasize that this does not mean that international capital flows are extremely elastic. A modest cut in the U.S. tax rate would not lead to a truly massive capital inflow. However, Hartman's results suggest that FDI is fairly sensitive to incentives.

Boskin and Gale (1987) extend and update the work of Hartman, using a longer time series and a variety of different econometric specifications. In most of their estimates of FDI in the United States, they get results that are similar to those of Hartman. Boskin and Gale also provide estimates of the determinants of DIA by U.S. firms. They find that outbound capital flows are also influenced by net rates of return. In one case, they find that the elasticity of DIA with respect to rates of return abroad is about 1.4.

Boskin and Gale simulate the effects on international capital flows of the capital-tax reductions that were legislated in the United States in the early 1980s. They suggest that these tax rate changes may have led to a reduction of about 2 to 4 percent in DIA, as U.S. firms found it more profitable to invest domestically. They also suggest that the tax rate changes may have led to a significant increase of between 11 and 20 percent in FDI in the United States.

Boskin and Gale suggest that U.S. welfare would be enhanced by these capital inflows. The United States receives a claim on the rate of return to foreign capital, through its taxation of the income from FDIs.[33] In the context of the current debate on tax reform, this argument applies to the flat tax, but not to the national retail sales tax. Regardless of whether the income from capital inflows is taxed, however, the productivity of domestic workers will be enhanced by increases in the capital stock, which would also tend to improve domestic welfare.

Slemrod (1990a) extends the analysis, again assessing aggregate data but with a number of improvements. A measure of the marginal effective tax rate replaces the average rates that had been used in previous work. Slemrod also uses a better set of nontax explanatory variables,

---

[33] See Goulder et al. (1983) and Hartman (1984) for similar discussions.

including unemployment rates and foreign-exchange rates. The estimated coefficient for the exchange rate variable is usually negative and significant. This indicates that a low dollar reduces the costs of production in the United States relative to the costs in other countries, providing a stimulus to FDI in the United States. In fact, FDI fell briefly during the early 1980s, at a time when the dollar was high, and then surged again in the late 1980s, when the dollar had fallen back.

Slemrod's results generally continue to support the idea that higher U.S. tax rates have a negative effect on FDI. His other important innovation is to provide separate analyses for the seven most important countries that invest in the United States (namely, Canada, France, Italy, Japan, the Netherlands, the United Kingdom, and West Germany). The disaggregated results generally support the results from the aggregate time series. The disaggregation allows Slemrod to test the effects of home-country taxes, as well as U.S. taxes, on FDI. Interestingly, he finds that the home-country tax rate and the home-country system of alleviating international double taxation do *not* have an important effect on FDI, a finding consistent with the previously mentioned ideas of Hartman (1984, 1985), who argues that deferred home-country taxes act more as taxes on transfers of funds out of the country in which the subsidiary is located rather than as taxes on the earnings of capital as such. A recent study by Kim (2000) provides estimates that are broadly supportive of the earlier results of Hartman, Boskin-Gale, and Slemrod.

Figure 5.2 displays the data series used by Hartman, carried forward to 1995, and it also shows the comparable series for DIA by U.S. firms. The most striking thing about Figure 5.2 is the sudden and dramatic increase in both FDI in the United States, and in U.S. DIA, after the mid-1980s.

Auerbach and Hassett (1993) try to explain this surge in international investment activity. One possible explanation is that the Tax Reform Act of 1986 played a dominant role, but Auerbach and Hassett are skeptical of this. They point out that the United States received a roughly constant share of the total FDI undertaken by foreign countries after 1986. Therefore, the boom was not just a boom in the United States; rather, it was a global boom.

It is probably true that tax factors played a very important role in the tremendous surge of FDI in the United States in the last few months of 1986, as foreign firms rushed to acquire U.S. assets before certain new rules took effect.[34] However, Auerbach and Hassett emphasize that this temporary phenomenon is only a part of the story.

---

[34] In particular, the Tax Reform Act of 1986 repealed the "general utilities doctrine," which had given favorable tax treatment to acquisitions. When foreign firms came to believe that this favorable treatment was about to be removed, they had a strong incentive to acquire U.S. assets quickly.

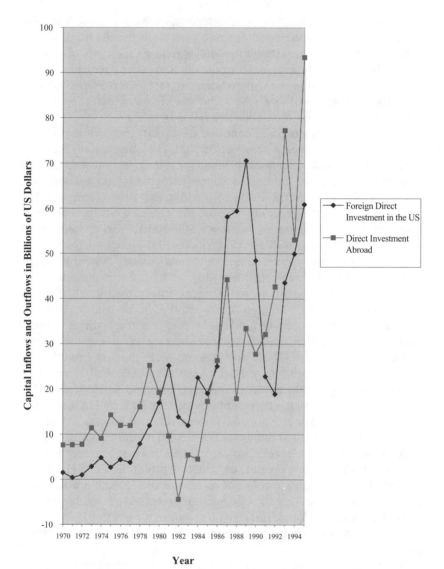

Year

Figure 5.2. Foreign Direct Investment in the United States and U.S. Direct Investment Abroad, 1970–95

The most important contribution of the analysis of Auerbach and Hassett is that they emphasize the differences between (1) establishments of new operations overseas, (2) new investment in plant and equipment by existing foreign subsidiaries, and (3) mergers and acquisitions. Even though theories of investment are best understood as dealing with the first two of these phenomena, much of the increase in FDI was concentrated in mergers and acquisitions. In their empirical work, Auerbach and Hassett distinguish between the different types of investment. Their results are something of a mix, and they find that no single theory is consistent with all of the facts. They conclude that, although taxes played a role, other influences such as exchange rate movements and the liberalization of world capital markets were also very important. As Poterba (1993) says in his comment on Auerbach and Hassett, "firms' actual incentives are difficult to describe with simple stylizations of the tax system. . . . once we recognize the details, it is difficult to draw broad conclusions."

Although it is risky to attempt to give a brief summary to this literature, I would offer these conclusions: first, international capital flows are affected significantly by tax incentives, although capital is less than perfectly mobile; second, and equally important, taxes are only part of the picture. As always, a great deal else is going on.[35] For example, exchange rate movements appear to play an important role.

THE INCIDENCE OF THE CORPORATE TAX

In a pathbreaking study, Harberger (1962) constructed a perfectly competitive, static, closed-economy general-equilibrium model to analyze the incidence of the corporate tax. The model has two sectors (corporate and noncorporate) and two factors of production (capital and labor). When a tax is levied on capital income in the corporate sector, competitive forces lead to a reallocation of the capital stock until the net-of-tax return to capital is the same in each sector. This leads to the result that the burden of the tax is borne by all capital, including capital that is not located in the corporate sector. The results in Harberger's model depend on the elasticities of substitution between capital and labor in the two sectors, the elasticities of demand for the two outputs, and the factor intensities in production. However, Harberger finds that his basic result is quite robust to changes in the parameters of the model.

Shoven (1976) extends the Harberger model to include twelve production sectors. Shoven, like Harberger, assumes perfect competition in a static context. Consequently, it is not surprising that Shoven's results are broadly supportive of Harberger's. However, the efficiency effects estimated by Shoven are larger than those estimated by Harberger. In effect, Harberger's assumption that there are only two sectors leads to

---

[35] Very similar results have been obtained in the literature examining the effects of state taxes on industrial location and expansion decisions in the United States. For recent surveys of that literature, see Wasylenko (1997), Mark, McGuire, and Papke (2000), and Zodrow (1999b).

an understatement of the intersectoral distortions caused by differential capital taxation. Fullerton et al. (1981) also assume perfect competition and the absence of international capital flows. However, they extend the model to nineteen production sectors, and they make the model dynamic. In the short to medium run, the results of Fullerton et al. are similar to those of Harberger (1962) and Shoven (1976): when the corporate and personal income taxes are integrated, the returns to capital increase throughout the economy. This implies that the corporate tax is borne by capital. However, the incidence picture changes dramatically when Fullerton et al. simulate the dynamic development of the economy. When the rate of return to capital is increased by the integration of the corporate tax, the rate of capital accumulation is increased. In the very long run, the capital stock is much larger when there is no corporate tax than it would have been in the presence of the corporate tax. This increased capital stock leads to higher real wage rates for workers, which means that labor bears a substantial portion of the burden of the corporate tax in the long run.

All of these studies assume a closed economy. When international flows of goods and capital are allowed, the results can change significantly. Harberger (1995) considers a static, perfectly competitive model in which there are international flows of goods and capital. Harberger assumes that the world capital market functions perfectly, in spite of the evidence of substantial international capital immobility. For a small, open economy, the net-of-tax rate of return to capital is fixed in the world capital market. Consequently, there is no way for domestic capital to bear the burden of the tax. Instead, capital will flow out of the domestic economy, raising the domestic gross-of-tax rate of return to capital, until the net rate of return to domestic capital is once again equal to the net rate of return to capital in the rest of the world. When the international flow of goods is also perfectly competitive, the brunt of the corporate tax must be borne by domestic labor.[36]

There are four main problems with Harberger's model of the corporate tax in an open-economy setting. First, the United States is not a small country. The analysis may be appropriate for Luxembourg, but it is not appropriate for the United States. Second, as discussed earlier, the international capital market is imperfect. Third, international goods markets may also be characterized by imperfect competition. Fourth, Harberger's analysis ignores the accumulation of capital over time.

Harberger addresses the first of these points. The United States is sufficiently large that it will have a significant effect on the world capital market as a whole. If the United States were to increase the corporate

---

[36] Feldstein (1994) gives a similar argument.

tax, rates of return to capital would be driven down around the globe. This means that capital owners throughout the world would bear a substantial portion of the burden of the corporate tax. However, domestic labor would still suffer, because of the decrease in the capital stock available for U.S. workers.

Gravelle and Smetters (1998) deal with the second and third of the objections to the model of Harberger (1995), by building a model with (1) imperfect substitutability between domestic and foreign products, and (2) imperfect portfolio substitution between domestic and foreign capital. We have already documented the imperfections of the world capital market, and there is also ample evidence of imperfections in world goods markets. Gravelle and Smetters find that these imperfections play an important role in limiting the amount of the corporate tax that is borne by domestic labor. In some cases, the burden on labor is eliminated entirely. The results of Gravelle and Smetters show a mild amount of sensitivity to changes in the parameters. For the parameter combinations that seem most reasonable, however, capital bears *at least* half of the burden of the tax and often significantly more.

One problem with the model of Gravelle and Smetters is its static character: the model is not used to study capital accumulation. Gravelle and Smetters make a strong case for the view that capital bears between 50 and 75 percent of the burden of the corporate tax in the short to medium run. If this is the case, then the corporate tax will cause some decreases in the rate of return to capital. Then, if saving responds at all to the decrease in the rate of return, there will be a decrease in the rate of capital accumulation. In the long run, the corporate tax will lead to a lower level of the capital stock. This, in turn, will lead to lower wage rates, so that labor will bear a portion of the burden of the tax.

If the world capital market operates perfectly (as suggested by Harberger), then labor will bear the burden right away. If Gravelle and Smetters are correct about the imperfections of the world capital market (and I believe they are), the amount of the burden borne by labor will increase over time. Sooner or later, however, labor does bear a significant share of the burden.

One of the objections to fundamental tax reform has been that the corporate tax is viewed as one of the most progressive elements of the tax system. Therefore, because most proposals for fundamental tax reform would reduce or eliminate the corporate tax, some worry that fundamental tax reform would lead to a major decrease in progressivity. If the analysis in this section is correct, however, labor really does bear a substantial part of the burden of the corporate tax. The tax may still be progressive but not as progressive as it would be if it were borne fully by capital. It is certainly legitimate to be concerned about the distributional effects of fundamental tax reform, but this analysis suggests that the regressive effects of fundamental reform may not be as serious as has been feared.

EFFICIENCY RESULTS FROM SIMULATION MODELS

Over the past twenty years, researchers have used increasingly sophisticated simulation models to study the economic effects of tax policy changes. Even though the focus of this chapter is on the international ramifications of tax reforms, the closed-economy models provide a good starting point for the discussion.

Closed-Economy Simulation Models

In the past two decades, a number of researchers have used simulation models to assess the effects of tax policy changes.[37] In these models, consumption is typically reduced in the first several years after the move to a consumption tax. However, the additional saving leads to a higher rate of capital accumulation, so that consumption is eventually higher under a consumption tax than under an income tax. The present value of the gain in consumption in the future is usually large enough to outweigh the loss of consumption in the near term. Thus, virtually all of the closed-economy simulation studies find that movements toward consumption taxation would yield welfare improvements.

Unfortunately, some of these simulation models imply very large savings elasticities, in spite of the fact that most econometric studies of consumption functions find that the savings elasticity is small. Thus, if a simulation model implies that the savings elasticity is enormous, the results of the simulation study must be viewed with caution.[38] In addition, some simulation models employ a utility structure that allows for unrealistically large labor supply responses. (The chapter by Gravelle in this volume contains a good discussion of the behavioral changes that might *actually* occur in response to fundamental tax reform.) This provides another reason for exercising caution in interpreting the results of some of the simulation models.[39]

Even though some of the simulation models imply that saving and labor supply are extremely, unrealistically responsive, it does not neces-

---

[37] For example, see Fullerton et al. (1981), Fullerton et al. (1983), Auerbach and Kotlikoff (1983, 1987), Ballard (1990), and Jorgenson and Wilcoxen (1997 and Chapter 3 in this volume).

[38] For example, the simulations of Auerbach and Kotlikoff (1983) suggest that the switch to a consumption tax would involve an increase in the savings rate from 10 to 42 percent.

[39] See Ballard (1990, 1997, 1999a,b) and Engen, Gravelle, and Smetters (1997) for additional discussion of the simulation modeling issues.

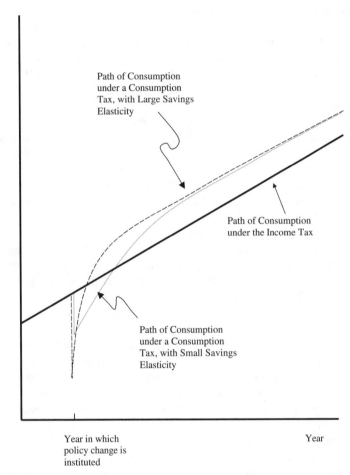

Figure 5.3. The Transition to a New Steady State after a Change from an Income Tax to a Consumption Tax

sarily follow that these models imply welfare improvements that are dramatically different from the welfare improvements that are simulated by models with more modest savings elasticities. As shown in Ballard (1990), very large increases in the savings elasticity are often only associated with small increases in the simulated welfare gains from moving toward a consumption tax. The reason for this is illustrated in Figure 5.3. In this figure, it is assumed that consumption grows at a constant rate under the income tax. (Therefore, the graph of the logarithm of consumption is a straight line for the income tax.) With a small savings elasticity, consumption drops when a consumption tax is instituted, and then recovers. Consumption eventually approaches a new steady state, in which the *level* of consumption is higher than in the base case, but the *rate of growth* is the same. With a larger savings elasticity, consumption drops farther when a consumption tax is instituted, and it recovers more quickly. However, consumption will approach the same steady state for either value of the savings elasticity. Thus, the consumption profiles for the large-elasticity case and the small-elasticity case are really quite similar. For the large-elasticity case, consumption is lower at first and then higher, and finally the levels of consumption in the two cases will converge to the same steady state. Consequently, the long-run welfare calculations may not be dramatically different.

Of course, comparing the results from different studies is often difficult, for at least four reasons. First, some analysts, such as Summers (1981a), report consumption gains in the long-run steady state, without considering the transition. Thus, the reported welfare gains are much larger (but also less useful) than those reported in other studies that consider the transition explicitly. Second, some analyses using overlapping-generations life-cycle models do not actually report a single number for the overall welfare gain from the switch to a consumption tax. Third, some studies (such as Fullerton, Shoven, and Whalley, 1983) begin with a very detailed description of the existing tax system, whereas others (such as Auerbach and Kotlikoff, 1983, 1987) start with a representation of the existing tax system that is highly stylized and highly unrealistic. If a study starts by overstating the degree of distortion in the present system, then it is likely that the study will generate unrealistically large welfare gains. Finally, papers differ in the nature of the proposed tax policy changes that they model.

With these caveats in mind, I offer the following conclusion: in closed-economy simulation models, the present value of the aggregate welfare gain from converting the income tax to a consumption tax is usually in the range of 1 to 3 percent of the present value of the stream of GDP in the base case (e.g., see Ballard et al., 1985, chap. 9).

Open-Economy Simulation Models

In addition to the closed-economy models just surveyed, some researchers have used open-economy models to simulate the effects of tax reforms. Before reviewing these models, it is important to note that they all employ *highly* simplified representations of the tax treatment of foreign-source income. These studies generally ignore Subpart F, separate baskets, the interest-allocation rules, and most of the other complications discussed earlier. These models also do not attempt to measure the reductions in administrative and compliance cost that will result from fundamental tax reform. Thus, their estimates of efficiency effects should be viewed as very rough approximations.

Goulder, Shoven, and Whalley (1983) begin with the General Equilibrium Model Taxation Analysis Package (for short, GEMTAP model), which they developed over a period of years, along with Ballard, Fullerton, and others.[40] The standard version of the GEMTAP model has a very cursory treatment of the foreign sector, but Goulder et al. modify the model to include international capital flows.

Their results depend critically on whether a particular reform leads to an increase or a decrease in the net rate of return (after corporate taxes) to capital in the United States, as perceived by foreign investors. For reforms that lead to an increase in this rate of return (such as corporate tax integration), the model suggests that the United States will receive capital inflows. As a result of these inflows of capital from abroad, the United States experiences significant welfare gains. The capital inflows lead to higher productivity and higher wages for U.S. workers. Also, even after the corporate and personal income taxes have been integrated, the U.S. government still collects capital tax revenues. When these revenues are collected from capital that is owned by foreigners, the U.S. government is able to export a portion of the tax burden.

Goulder et al. achieve rather different results for an increase in the percentage of domestic saving that is taxed on a consumption tax basis. This type of tax policy change increases the net-of-tax return for domestic savers, because they receive an increased tax subsidy when they save. However, foreign investors do not receive the tax subsidy, so that the immediate effect on their net rate of return is negligible. Over time, the increase in domestic saving leads to a decrease in the price of capital services. Thus, the rate of return received by foreigners who make investments in the United States will actually *decrease* when the subsidy to domestic savers is increased. Therefore, foreigners have less of an incentive to invest in the United States. In addition, some of the additional saving that is undertaken by U.S. residents will be invested abroad. When the results for this type of tax reform are compared with the results from the base case, the Goulder-Shoven-Whalley model usually finds that capital will flow out of the United States. These capital outflows lead to welfare losses, for the same reasons that capital inflows lead to welfare gains, as discussed earlier.

---

[40] For a detailed description of the standard version of the GEMTAP model, see Ballard et al. (1985). This model has the advantage that it can be calibrated to any desired savings elasticity, so that it avoids some of the problems of excessive intertemporal responsiveness, discussed in the previous section.

It should be understood that the results of Goulder et al. may be of only limited relevance for the current debate over fundamental tax reform. One reason for this is that the results are *highly* sensitive with respect to the values of the elasticity parameters that control the degree of international capital flows. Another reason is that the policies simulated by Goulder et al. bear only a modest resemblance to the fundamental tax reforms that are being debated today. They do not simulate the complete replacement of the existing individual and corporate income tax, and they restrict their attention to simulations in which the United States maintains its global, residence-based system of taxation, with full credits for foreign taxes paid. Thus, they never simulate a move to a territorial system. Nevertheless, the results of Goulder et al. demonstrate that our understanding of the effects of tax policy changes may be altered when we introduce international capital flows.

Thalmann, Goulder, and DeLorme (1996) assess the effects on the U.S. economy of tax policy changes in foreign countries. They use an infinite-horizon model that displays a larger degree of intertemporal sensitivity than does the model of Goulder et al. (1983).[41] Thus, in keeping with my earlier remarks, I would suggest some caution in interpreting the results of Thalmann et al. Nevertheless, their results are of some interest. For one thing, they explicitly incorporate imperfect substitutability between foreign and domestic assets, which is consistent with the evidence on international capital mobility.

Even for a fairly modest policy change (an increase in depreciation allowances in the rest of the world), the model of Thalmann et al. calculates a welfare improvement of 0.3 percent of GDP for the rest of the world.

Like the analysis of Goulder et al., the study of Thalmann et al. is limited in its applicability to the current debate over fundamental tax reform in the United States. Thalmann et al. focus on tax policy changes in the rest of the world, rather than on changes in the United States, and they do not consider a policy that is nearly as comprehensive as a truly fundamental tax reform. However, both of these studies find that, when a tax policy change leads to a higher rate of return, after corporate taxes, in the country undertaking the change, that country will experience capital inflows. These capital inflows, which may be substantial, tend to lead to welfare improvements. In all likelihood, the U.S. rate of return *will* be increased by fundamental tax reforms such as those currently

---

[41] Thalmann et al. report that the elasticity of first-period saving with respect to a permanent change in the rate of return is 0.71. This is high relative to the values found in the econometric literature, although it is much lower than the values generated by Ballard and Goulder (1985) with a simulation model that is rather similar in structure.

being considered in the United States. This is especially true of the national retail sales tax. Therefore, we can expect inflows of productive capital, which will lead to a higher level of output and a higher level of long-run welfare. (Of course, as discussed earlier, these effects would be muted if other countries were to respond by reducing their tax rates.)

Mendoza and Tesar (1998) use a simulation model to assess the difference between the effects of fundamental tax reform in a closed economy and in an open economy. Thus, in terms of the kind of policy experiment considered, their analysis is more relevant to the current tax reform debate than is either Goulder et al. or Thalmann et al.

On the other hand, Mendoza and Tesar employ some extreme assumptions. First, they use a model with an infinitely lived consumer. A model of this type is likely to produce simulated consumer behavior that is unrealistically responsive to changes in rates of return. Indeed, when Mendoza and Tesar simulate the effects of replacing the U.S. capital income tax with a consumption tax in a closed-economy setting, they find that the impact effect is for consumption to decline by 8.3 percent. Not since the period from 1929 to 1933 has consumption fallen by anything like this. If a percentage change like this is evaluated against today's level of personal consumption expenditure in the United States, it would mean a decrease of more than $400 billion, which seems extremely large and unrealistic.

The second extreme assumption employed by Mendoza and Tesar is that they consider a world in which international capital markets are "fully integrated"; that is, capital is assumed to be perfectly mobile. Thus, their simulations are likely to overstate the extent of the international capital flows that would be caused by fundamental tax reform in the United States.

Mendoza and Tesar emphasize that the simulated welfare gain from replacing the U.S. capital income tax with a consumption tax is greater when the simulations are carried out in an open-economy context than in a closed-economy model. In their closed-economy model, U.S. welfare increases by 2.16 percent. In the open-economy model, the United States gains by 2.89 percent. However, in the open-economy model, the rest of the world suffers a small welfare loss when the United States undertakes a unilateral tax reform of this kind. If these numbers are taken at face value, they suggest that the gains to the United States from fundamental tax reform are about one-third larger in an open-economy model than in a closed-economy model. Whether this difference is thought to be large or small will depend on the standard against which a comparison is made.

On the basis of the results reported here, I am prepared to say that a fundamental tax reform in the United States would lead to aggregate welfare gains, and that these gains would be larger in an open-economy context than they would be if the United States were the only country on earth.

CONCLUSION

I began this chapter by describing the current tax treatment of foreign-source income. The rules are extraordinarily complex, and they generate a great deal of administrative and compliance cost, in spite of the fact that they yield a surprisingly small amount of tax revenue for the U.S. government. Consequently, one of the most attractive features of fundamental tax reform is that it would greatly simplify the tax treatment of foreign-source income. If the United States were to adopt the territorial basis for taxation, the amount of resources that are devoted to administration and compliance would be reduced greatly.

Over the past quarter century, one of the strongest arguments for consumption taxation has been that it would simplify the tax structure, which would reduce the costs of administration and compliance. For the most part, this argument has been made in the context of a closed economy, but we have seen here that the argument is reinforced when international issues are included in the analysis. Thus, in the sphere of administration and compliance at least, the case for consumption taxation is somewhat strengthened when we consider international issues.

The other main thrust of the argument for consumption taxation has been that consumption taxation will lead to efficiency gains. Once again, this argument has been made primarily in a closed-economy context. And once again, the evidence suggests that international forces may strengthen the result. This statement must be interpreted with caution, however. I have emphasized that only a few simulation studies have attempted to consider fundamental tax reform in an international context, and the studies that exist have other flaws. At this point, it seems important to avoid making exaggerated claims about the efficiency improvements that will be brought about by fundamental tax reform, especially when international issues are involved. Yes, fundamental tax reform will probably improve the efficiency with which the economy operates, and the extent of the improvement may be modestly larger in an open economy. But fundamental tax reform will not, by itself, lead to a radical transformation of the U.S. economy. In the long run, the nation will probably be more prosperous with fundamental tax reform than without it, but it is not as if we will all be rich in either case.

At the end of the day, international considerations may change the minds of a few participants in the debate over fundamental tax reform. However, my guess is that most participants will probably not change sides as a result of the international issues discussed here. Presumably, proponents of fundamental tax reform have reached a favorable conclusion because of their concerns regarding administrative costs, compliance costs, and economic efficiency. These people will certainly continue to be in favor of fundamental tax reform when international issues are considered for the first time. However, I doubt whether many opponents of fundamental tax reform will change their minds due to international considerations. Presumably, opponents of fundamental tax reform have reached their conclusion because of distributional concerns, or because of the desire to preserve some particular tax preference. It is not clear to me that the good news on the international front will be sufficient to sway many of those who were not already swayed.

In short, for those who favor fundamental tax reform, international considerations may represent one card out of a potentially winning hand. However, the international card is not the most important one in the hand. In any event, the hand must be played astutely in the political arena if the pot is to be raked in.

Chapter 6

Distributive Analysis of Fundamental Tax Reform

Peter Mieszkowski and Michael G. Palumbo

How regressive will a general, single-rate consumption-based tax system be *relative* to the existing federal income tax system? The popular perception is that the introduction of a national retail sales tax (NRST) or a Hall-Rabushka type flat tax (FT) in place of existing federal income taxes will significantly increase the tax burden on low- and middle-income groups, while decreasing it at the high end of the income distribution. Three reasons are usually given: (1) the progressivity of the rate structure under the individual income tax will be reduced, (2) the elimination of the corporate income tax will lower the effective tax rate on capital income, and (3) the switch to a consumption base will lower taxes on affluent households who typically save a relatively large proportion of their incomes.

The research surveyed in this chapter, including our own recent work, supports the view that a move to consumption-based taxation would shift tax burdens as just described. For example, our results on the introduction of an NRST indicate that flattening the rate structure decreases the tax burden on high-income families. After estimating the proportion of income saved at different levels of income, we find that a consumption-based tax system is regressive relative to a proportional income tax, though significant gains are found only for the very rich.

These results on saving and consumption are obtained using a newly released panel of households from the Survey of Consumer Finances (SCF) for the years 1983–89. This panel includes extensive financial and income information for the same households at two points in time.

We are grateful to Joe Barnes, Ron Soligo, and George Zodrow for extensive comments and discussions, to Dae Il Kim for helping us access Current Population Survey two-earner wage data, and to Anna Witas and Alexei Zarovnyi for excellent programming assistance. Research support from the National Tax Research Committee is gratefully acknowledged.

The SCF oversamples families at high-income levels, including a significant number of those households with very high income that own the most wealth and contribute the most to aggregate private savings. Tax burdens for the current tax system are based on a file of individual income tax returns from 1993 prepared by the Internal Revenue Service (IRS).

Our conclusions depend on three key assumptions and procedures. First, households are ranked by *annual* income rather than by an estimate of lifetime income or current consumption. Second, we assume that the burden of the corporate profits tax is proportional to *all* real capital income, which implies that the elimination of the corporate tax will significantly increase the after tax return to capital. This assumption makes no allowance for the international mobility of capital, though it can be argued that if the United States eliminates the corporate tax, and other major industrial nations do not follow suit, a substantial portion of the resulting gains will accrue to labor, rather than capital, as capital will flow into the United States and increase the real wage. Third, estimated consumption by income level is used to allocate the tax burden of an NRST. Although this method is in accord with the procedure used by other studies of an NRST, it conflicts with the common characterization of a consumption tax as a tax on income from wages and old capital. For example, researchers investigating the distributive effects of the value-added tax (VAT), such as the Joint Committee on Taxation (JCT) (1993), allocate tax burdens on the basis of factor income. Furthermore, the factor-income procedure is commonly used in the analysis of the effects of an FT.

We establish that the allocation of tax burden according to factor income rather than by consumption will temper but not reverse our basic conclusions on the distributive impact of an FT or an NRST. Because of the importance of this issue for distributive analysis, it is discussed at some length before the presentation of the empirical results. Whether the burden of a consumption-based tax should be allocated by consumption or by factor income is closely related to whether single-rate, broad-based consumption taxes are equivalent in their behavioral and distributional effects. At least two writers (McLure, 1993, and Gravelle, 1996b) have argued that they are. If these taxes are essentially equivalent, their effects should be consistently analyzed. For example, the distributional impact of *both* an NRST and an FT should be allocated either by consumption or by factor income. Either both systems are taxes on consumption or they are taxes on factor incomes. This issue also has practical significance as data on factor incomes are much more plentiful and accurate than are data on savings and consumption, especially for high-income households.

Moreover, if different consumption taxes are equivalent, the choice between them should be based on administrative, compliance, and short-run transitional considerations, not on the basis of long-run allocative and distributional factors. There is greater administrative familiarity with the VAT and FT than with the NRST. Indeed, some skeptics (Slemrod, 1996, and Gale, 1998b) argue that a high-rate NRST could not be administered effectively.

Accordingly, the next section examines the equivalence of the NRST, VAT and FT, and a personal consumption tax (PCT) and argues that they are equivalent in their fundamental economic effects. We then address whether factor income is preferred to consumption as the basis of tax burden allocations, as well as the appropriateness of invoking a life-cycle budget constraint to justify the allocation of consumption tax burdens according to factor income. After reviewing several earlier studies of the distribution of tax burden, we discuss the estimation of saving rates from SCF data and present our results on the distributional effects of fundamental tax reform.

ON THE EQUIVALENCE OF ALTERNATIVE CONSUMPTION TAXES

It is generally agreed that the various forms of consumption-based taxation, direct and indirect, are equivalent in their distributive and allocative effects.[1] For a single-rate, fully comprehensive tax system without personal exemptions, the tax bases for a personal consumption tax, a national retail sales tax, a credit-method value-added tax, and a flat tax are all equal to the consumption of the individual household.

Most observers of these equivalencies find them self-evident. For example, an NRST and VAT are characterized as equivalent because a VAT collects tax at various stages of the production process and also produces offsetting tax credits at each preretail stage; no *net* tax is collected under this tax system until consumption goods and services are sold to non-business entities, households. Analyses of broader sets of consumption taxes typically establish equivalence of aggregate bases at the economy-wide level, but do not consider equivalence at the individual or household level. Before presenting such a microlevel assessment, we briefly elaborate on an aggregate example developed by McLure (1993, p. 347).

[1] McLure (1993) has analyzed the similarities and differences among the NRST, VAT, and FT and concluded they are equivalent under a number of simplifying assumptions. Bradford (1986), Gravelle (1996b), and Slemrod and Bakija (1996) all remark on the equivalence between the NRST and VAT. Bradford (1996a) and Gentry and Hubbard (1997a) note the equivalence between the VAT and FT. Also, Cnossen (Chapter 8 in this volume) discusses the equivalence between a VAT and an NRST.

Equivalence between Consumption-Based Taxes
at the Economy-Wide Level

McLure considers a four-industry economy consisting of two interme-diate inputs, one capital goods industry, and one consumption good. Suppose that in the absence of taxes, value-added is equal to $1,000 and that deliveries to final demand are $600 worth of consumption and $400 of investment goods.

We first consider a flat-rate personal consumption tax of 10 percent. Personal consumption taxes equal $60. If savings remain unchanged, private consumption decreases from $600 to $540, and government expenditures or consumption are equal to $60. The replacement of a PCT of 10 percent with a NRST imposed at a tax-inclusive rate of 11.11 percent would have no real effects. The nominal price of consumption goods increases from $1.0 to $1.111 and nominal consumption expenditures increase from $600 to $666.66. But real private consumption remains unchanged at $540.

The NRST could also be replaced with a credit method VAT, also imposed at a tax-inclusive rate of 11.11 percent. Initially, taxes of $111.11 are collected on the value-added of $1,000. The $400 of investment has a nominal value of $444.44 under a credit method VAT. Of this, $44.44 is a refundable credit paid to the investing industry, autos, resulting in a net nominal tax revenue of $66.66, the same as under NRST.

Finally, the VAT could be replaced by an FT of 10 percent. In the first instance, $100 of tax is collected, but investment is equal to $400 and the industries making the investment receive a net rebate of $40 leaving $60 of taxes collected, the same as under PCT.

The net taxes collected under the FT are equal to the tax rate t multi-plied by the amount of consumption. The tax burden for this production period should be allocated in proportion to a household's consumption. Part of the taxes that are "paid" by net savers on their current-period factor income is rebated to them through the intermediation of enterprises that receive a $40 rebate on their $400 gross investment. Just as taxes collected on enterprise profits are imputed to individual stockholders and bond-holders, the taxes returned to firms should be imputed to the households making the savings that finance the investment. The real effects of an FT are equivalent to those of a VAT as well as a PCT and an NRST.

Equivalence between Consumption-Based
Taxes at the Individual Level

The fact that aggregate tax bases are identical for various forms of con-sumption-based taxation does not necessarily imply that the tax burdens for particular individuals are the same under different tax systems.

In a world of no inheritances, zero bequests, and constant tax rates, the present value of a tax on wages is equivalent to a tax on consumption. But the burden of a tax on wages will not be equivalent to a tax on consumption for particular individuals during a particular tax period. Gravelle (1996b, p. 6) notes that, even if total consumption equals total wages, the burden of a wage tax could differ greatly from a consumption tax for particular individuals. Similarly, in an overlapping-generations model with zero population growth and a steady state with zero net investment, aggregate consumption will equal aggregate net income. A consumption tax will differ from a tax on net income with respect to the burden it imposes on particular individuals and the steady state it establishes.

The burdens for particular individuals, however, are equivalent for the four types of consumption-based taxation, provided we abstract from transitional complications associated with differences in the debt-equity ratios of various households and the different absolute price-level adjustments that will probably accompany different types of consumption taxation. The essential arguments required for establishing equivalence are developed by the Joint Committee on Taxation (1993, appendix B), and Gravelle (1996b).

Both writers portray a broad-based consumption tax as a tax on wages and a tax on old capital. The JCT establishes that a PCT and a business transfer tax (BTT), a form of cash-flow-based VAT, are equivalent in their annual *tax burdens* for various individuals even though two particular individuals have different annual *tax liabilities* under a BTT and a PCT. It notes that two individuals *with the same wage income* but with different net saving rates – with one individual's savings financing both current new investment and the dissavings of the second individual – will pay different tax liabilities under a PCT. Under a BTT they will pay the same wage tax if aggregate net savings are equal to net investment, equal to current profit income. However, the future tax liabilities on the income expected to be earned on the capital that the dissaver sells the saver will be shifted onto the dissaver so that capital with market value of $1.00 to the firm will be worth only $1(1 - t)$ to the dissaver in the form of consumption. In effect, part of the wage tax remitted by the saver is actually "paid" by the dissavers.

Gravelle (1996b, p. 20) also points out that for a PCT a person who saves more pays a lower tax. She considers a simple economy in which there are two groups, the old and the young. The young have only wage income and save by buying surviving capital from the old and newly produced capital goods. Under a PCT, "They pay a tax on their wages which are used for consumption, but not on their wages which are used for asset purchases" (p. 20). Two other insightful statements about the young are:

"They defer the tax on the part of those wages that is not immediately consumed, until it is consumed" (p. 21). "Another way of thinking about this is that young individuals pay a tax on their wages, but then they receive a tax benefit on their savings (just as in the case of an IRA)" (p. 21).

We now determine that the same points apply to an FT. First, consider a situation in which no individual dissaves. Individual savings are either positive or zero. The equivalence between a PCT and an FT is transparent once it is recognized that the savings deductions granted individuals under a PCT have the same effect on individuals as the deductions sole proprietors or corporations receive under the FT. Aggregate investment is equal to aggregate savings. The tax base for a PCT for individuals equals wages + income from old capital $- \Sigma_j S_{ij}$, where $\Sigma_j S_{ij}$ are the savings placed by individual i directly or indirectly in firm j. The savings placed in firms is equal to the current net savings for an individual. The base for a flat tax with a common rate on individuals and firms is exactly the same as the base for a PCT, even though a PCT does not include firm deductions for investment. Taxes, deductions, or tax credits imposed or granted to an individual are equivalent to taxes or deductions imposed on or granted to a firm that invests on behalf of an individual. If the tax savings generated by deductions granted to current investments are prorated to individuals according to the amount of their current savings in various firms, the sum of the imputed deductions will total the aggregate savings of the individual.

Next, consider the more realistic situation where there are net savers and dissavers in the economy. The dissavers sell old assets to savers and use the proceeds to consume. The savers must be indifferent between buying old assets and new assets. Under an FT, they receive a deduction, directly or indirectly, on the purchase of new investment. No tax rebate is received on the purchases of old capital and savers know that taxes will have to be paid on the old assets as well as the new assets. Old assets must sell at a discount relative to new assets, equal to $(1 - t)$ for every dollar of expected future income. All of the net tax burden under FT is incurred in the current period by persons in proportion to their current consumption just as it is under the PCT or an NRST. All consumption-based tax systems (PCT, NRST, VAT, and FT) are equivalent for each individual on a period by period basis.

Does the Burden of Certain Consumption Taxes Fall on Certain Returns to Capital?

The equivalence between different consumption taxes implies that they are distributionally equivalent and that their effect on income distribution should be measured in the same way. Before considering how distributional allocations should be made, we consider the argument recently made by Gentry and Hubbard (1997a) and Hubbard (Chapter 4 in this volume) that the returns to risk taking and economic rent earned on new inventions and new real capital continue to be taxed under a consumption tax.

In evaluating these points it is useful to remind ourselves why the riskless rate of return is not taxed under a consumption tax. Consider the simplest situation where capital lasts only one period and each unit of capital – say, $100 – earns a before-tax return of $i + p$, where i is the riskless return and p is the risk premium. The income flows under an income tax and a consumption tax can be depicted as follows:

	Investment Period t_0	Income Period t_1
Income Tax	−100	$(100(1 + i + p) − 100)(1 − t)$
Consumption Tax	−100	$(100(1 + i + p)(1 − t)$
FT	+t100	0

Assume the tax rate t is 50 percent. For the consumption tax the depreciation allowance comes earlier during t_0 and the government is effectively "sharing" half of the cost of the investment in exchange for 50 percent of the *gross* proceeds. Under the income tax, the government puts no money up front, but shares in only 50 percent of the *net* income earned.

The effect of the difference in depreciation treatment under the two tax systems is to increase the after-tax profitability of a *specific investment*. The $50 received during t_0 can be invested in a safe asset and the $50i$ earned just offsets the taxes paid on i earned by the project. Only the risk premium p is taxed under this response to the accelerated depreciation associated with expensing.

Under the NRST, PCT, or FT the returns to risk taking, economic rents, above-normal earnings to entrepreneurial activity, and other investment activity will be taxed at the time the income is consumed. Successful entrepreneurs who sell their businesses and live off of the proceeds will pay tax on these profits exactly as a highly paid salary worker pays wage tax on the portion of wages consumed. The idea that certain types of capital income are taxed identically under income and consumption tax systems is useful, as is the point that a disproportionate share of these forms of capital income that are taxed under the consumption tax accrues to high-income groups. These results extend the earlier characterization of a consumption tax as a tax on wages and old capital.

Clearly, if the tax burdens of consumption taxes are allocated on the basis of factor incomes, it is important to distinguish, as argued by Gentry and Hubbard, between different types of capital income. Debt and equity should also be distinguished in assessing the distribution of the burdens of the tax on old capital. But it is important to note that consumption taxes on economic rents and risk taking will be paid only if and when this income is consumed.

To see this essential point, distinguish between a tax paid by an individual on the income earned from a specific asset or investment and the overall tax liability of a particular individual at a point in time. For a PCT, rents earned on a particular investment are reported as the cash flow income of the individual. If the individual saves all of this income, no consumption tax is paid and any tax liability on these rents is deferred until this wealth is consumed. Similarly, under an FT the firm or individual reports the income on an old investment and then offsets the tax liability by saving in old or new assets. This point applies to all forms of consumption-based taxation, in marked contrast to an ideal income tax, where an individual pays tax on economic rents as they accrue, independently of whether these rents are consumed or saved.

DOES CONSUMPTION OR FACTOR INCOME PROVIDE A BETTER MEASURE OF THE BURDEN OF CONSUMPTION TAXES?

If consumption and income information were available for individuals for many time periods (ideally over their lifetimes), it could be used to estimate the differential burden of income and consumption taxes. Multiperiod information would (1) allow the averaging of income so as to eliminate transitory elements in the income of individuals; (2) measure variations in the savings, consumption, and incomes of households over their life cycle; and (3) account for the bequests made by households and determine the extent to which bequests vary as a proportion of lifetime income by income level.

Consumption information would be especially valuable in measuring the burden placed on older households during the transition period. During this period consumption is a better indicator of tax burden than is income from old capital. Lifetime consumption and income would also be very valuable as a means of estimating bequests. Unfortunately, multiperiod information on consumption is very limited, especially for high-income individuals. The information on bequests is similarly scanty. Although several multiperiod, lifetime studies of tax burdens exist, most detailed tax burden studies, which classify households according to either income or consumption, are static, single-period studies that do not allow for behavioral responses to changes in tax regime.

The JCT has adopted a five-year horizon for some of its work on tax burdens. No behavioral responses are considered in this analysis. The JCT was the first government agency to allocate the burden of consumption taxes to income as it is *earned*, not as it is *consumed*. Their approach has several elements. First, the burden of consumption taxes is compared with the burden of income taxes. By allocating the burden of consumption taxes according to factor income, the JCT is able to maintain consistency in measurement and assumptions among alternative tax proposals. Second, there is the problem of temporarily low incomes for some taxpayers. When individuals are temporarily unemployed their current consumption may exceed their current income by large amounts. Allocating tax burdens on the basis of consumption will result in estimates for some taxpayers that are large relative to their current incomes, which understates permanent or life-cycle income; retired households with negative savings will have low current incomes relative to consumption. One way of dealing with this problem is to measure tax burden relative to consumption, not as a function of income. As the JCT uses income as its classification of economic well-being, it chooses to deal with problems of life-cycle variation and transitory fluctuations in income by treating a general consumption tax as equivalent to a wage tax plus an income tax on capital accumulated prior to the imposition of the consumption tax. Thus low tax burdens are estimated for periods of low income.

The principle assumption underlying this approach is that individuals consume all of their income over their lifetime: "The method utilized by the JCT staff also implicitly uses a lifetime perspective, because while it does not calculate lifetime income, it does use the lifetime budget constraint to convert consumption taxes on certain types of income" (JTC, 1993, p. 57). Gentry and Hubbard take a similar approach.

The factor-income approach to estimating tax burdens of consumption taxes does *not* calculate the consumption taxes actually paid in the current period but instead estimates the tax that would be paid in the current period by the individuals under a factor tax that is deemed to be equivalent to a consumption tax over the taxpayer's life cycle. *This assumes that the strict life-cycle budget constraint applies* – with no bequests. We question this approach, as there is considerable direct and indirect evidence that the life-cycle model does not apply for households, especially those with high incomes who receive capital income disproportionately.

Whom Does the Life-Cycle Budget Constraint Bind?

As noted, discussions and formal analyses surrounding issues of tax incidence assume a binding lifetime budget constraint for each tax-paying unit – an identity equating the discounted value of lifetime expenditures to the discounted value of lifetime labor earnings (in models that abstract from labor supply decisions).[2] In this subsection, we draw on some recent research emphasizing the failure of such an identity to bind for many, let all alone all, contemporary families. In particular, we consider the case in which some families leave bequests to children or other family members, receive inheritances and gifts, make substantial contributions to charity, or even establish foundations to carry out philanthropic objectives with their accumulated resources, rather than allocate all lifetime wealth to consuming goods and services themselves.

That very few people die in a zero-net-worth position seems obvious; of greater interest is some recent research demonstrating a strong tendency for saving rates to rise with lifetime income levels (Dynan, Skinner, and Zeldes, 1998) and for wealth to accumulate among the richest Americans (Carroll, 1998). Regardless of the factors motivating some families to consume less than they earn during their lives (we describe several possibilities later), the implication is that under consumption-based tax systems, as opposed to income taxes, individuals can postpone indefinitely the payment of tax. Moreover, it is inappropriate for analysts to allocate consumption-based tax burdens on the basis of factor incomes, rather than expenditures, in the absence of a binding lifetime budget constraint.

There is no controversy surrounding the fact that some American families find themselves quite wealthy at any given point in time. It might be constructive to reconsider the consequences of large current wealth for the likelihood that a rich family's lifetime budget constraint binds.[3] Intuitively, once a family has accumulated a large amount of wealth, however the means or whatever the reason, *decumulation*, in the form of private consumption, requires deliberate and consistent effort. At a 5 percent rate of interest, for example, reducing net worth from $5 million to $1 million during a 10-year period requires spending $541,000 every

---

[2] When analysts study models with endogenous labor supply, the discounted value of a person's time endowment is equated to the discounted sum of leisure (nonlabor market activity) and consumption of purchased goods and services.

[3] Throughout this section, the term "life-cycle budget constraint" refers to an identity between the discounted value of (private) consumption expenditures and labor earnings over a family's lifetime. That is, the life-cycle budget constraint is said to "bind" in the absence of bequests to family members or substantial charitable gifts.

year – *in the absence of additional labor earnings.*[4] Furthermore, the spending must take the form of nondurable (or rapidly depreciating) goods and services. To be sure, many individuals possess the creativity required for expenditures on this scale. Nonetheless, the modest point remains – compound interest works in reverse, so it takes the same type of commitment to *decumulate* a large stock of wealth as it takes some families to accumulate it in the first place.

As an empirical matter, data from the 1983–89 Survey of Consumer Finances imply that about 250,000 American families reported private, nonpension net worth exceeding $5 million in 1989 (measured in 1986 constant dollars). This represents only about one-third of 1 percent of all families living in the United States that year.[5] On the other hand, these few wealthy families own approximately 20 percent of total net worth as measured by the 1983–89 SCF Panel data base (about $2.9 trillion of $14.4 trillion, according to our calculations). A reformed tax system that relies exclusively on the generation of revenue from consumed resources, therefore, might require waiting a long period of time before substantial amounts are collected. Put another way, as a matter of analysis, allocating the incidence of a consumption-based tax system according to factor incomes can be expected to affect tax distribution tables substantially, as these wealthy families will be earning nearly $200 billion a year from the returns to capital, and they spend only a small portion of this income.

Recent Empirical Evidence

Two studies provide the most recent evidence casting doubt on the existence of a binding life-cycle budget constraint between consumption and labor earnings for all American families, especially those at the top of the lifetime income distribution. Dynan et al. (1998) present empirical analyses based on microdata from the Survey of Consumer Finances (the 1983–89 SCF Panel), the Panel Study of Income Dynamics (PSID), and the Consumer Expenditure Surveys (CES). Their results based on the SCF Panel, which most accurately represents behavior among the wealthiest Americans, reveal average saving rates of around 2 percent among the bottom quintile in the lifetime income distribution, which

---

[4] More generally, consumption expenditures must exceed labor earnings by $541,000 during each of the ten years to decumulate wealth sufficiently in this numerical example.
[5] These figures are based on the 1983–89 SCF Panel data and, thus only approximate the truth. As the Federal Reserve Board warns, the panel data do not exactly replicate the 1989 cross-section distribution of wealth in the United States. Using the sample weights, as is required for accurate analysis, the 1983–89 SCF panel covers about 81.9 million American families.

grow steadily to above 40 percent among the top 5 percent of families.[6] Thus, Dynan et al. conclude: "Using a variety of instruments for lifetime income, we find a strong positive relationship between personal saving rates and lifetime income." We view this finding to be important because it implies a highly concentrated distribution of wealth and is consistent with U.S. cross-section data in which wealth is disproportionately accumulated by high-lifetime-income families. Dynan et al. (1998) do not report any evidence to suggest dissaving among these richest families or a reversal in saving or income patterns of the magnitude that would be needed for the lifetime budget constraint to bind during their lives.

Such a conclusion is consistent with Carroll's (1998) complementary study that examines SCF surveys from 1983 through 1992, along with many additional sources of documentary evidence, to focus on how net worth changes with age among the wealthiest contemporary American families. Carroll's study demonstrates an empirical pattern that seems plausible, given the numerical example presented here. The very wealthiest American families seem to become ever more wealthy as they age. They do not typically increase their consumption expenditures to the amounts necessary to stem further wealth accumulation. Carroll finds no evidence to indicate a strong motivation for wealthy families to spend all or even most of their accumulated resources exclusively on private consumption during their own lives.

Carroll and Dynan et al. reach convergent conclusions independently. Carroll's analysis questions the relevance of a binding life-cycle budget constraint for personal consumption expenditures as a description of the economic circumstances and experiences of the richest Americans: "I argue that a direct wealth accumulation motive is indispensable in explaining at least some of the observed behavior of the very wealthy" (Carroll, 1998, p. 2). Dynan et al. (1998, p. 28) conclude similarly: "It seems likely that characterizing saving rates in an empirically consistent manner requires either intended or accidental bequests."

As we describe later, these authors do not agree on how to specify the "best" alternative model, but that is not important for our current purposes. Any candidate model implying income-elastic estate values upon death suffices to make our point. Invoking the life-cycle budget

---

[6] Note that Dynan et al. report greater average saving rates and saving rates that rise more quickly with income than we report here, despite using the same 1983–89 SCF Panel data base. The apparent difference comes from using different definitions of household saving. Dynan et al. refer to "saving" as the change in household net worth during the 1983–89 period. We subtract an imputation of passive capital gains from the observed change in net worth to measure "active" saving, as the difference between income and outlays during the six-year period. Our basic objective in this study is to use this measure of active savings to calculate current consumption.

constraint definitely serves to clarify many issues surrounding the incidence of various tax systems. A potential concern, however, arises with
regard to the universal manner in which this tool of specific (and limited)
use seems to be applied in the literature. At the least, a study directed
at the consequences of nonbinding budget constraints for the distribution of lifetime tax burdens seems warranted.

Theoretical Discussion

As mentioned earlier, Dynan et al. and Carroll agree, in the interest of
explaining why the richest families seem to continue to accumulate
wealth, that models in which the only purpose of wealth is to finance
future consumption should be replaced with frameworks that allow
income-elastic intergenerational transfers or charitable gifts and wealth
for its own sake. Dynan et al. leave open the possibility that transfers by
the wealthiest Americans to their heirs might be motivated either by
accidental or by operative bequest motives. Carroll, on the other hand,
makes the case for models of "capitalist spirit," in which rich families
accumulate additional wealth for its own sake (to acquire the status or
power perceived to be associated directly with wealth) rather than to
provide for their own potential emergencies or the consumption of their
direct descendants.

In one of the alternative models outlined by Dynan et al., accidental
bequests result when assets saved for precautionary reasons are not completely spent before death. Furthermore, accidental bequests can be
income-elastic if, for example, mortality rates decline with wealth and the
hazard of expensive, high-quality health care (skilled nursing received at
home or in a residential facility) rises with age. The former empirical tendency is documented recently by Hurd, McFadden, and Merrill (1998);
the latter by Palumbo (1999). In practice, Carroll doubts the ability of
accidental bequests to explain completely the saving behavior among the
wealthiest American families, apparently because he considers a relatively modest estate (a few million dollars prudently invested, perhaps)
sufficient to finance both old-age consumption and high-quality health
expenditures.

Alternatively, in most of the large literature evaluating models with
operative, as opposed to purely accidental, bequest motives, specifications are such that the size of bequeathed estates is sensitive to lifetime
income. In their survey, Dynan et al., for example, cite works by Becker
and Tomes (1986) and Mulligan (1997) that recognize both the endogenous nature of labor earnings (as a function of a person's accumulated
human capital) and the multidimensional nature of intergenerational
transfers (financial gifts made by parents and support for their children's

human capital formation). The models emphasized by Becker and his colleagues differ in specific respects but carry similar implications for financial transfers in the form of bequests from parents to their children, which rise disproportionately with parental lifetime earnings.[7]

A third class of models capable of predicting income-elastic transfers from parents to their children poses operative bequests through dynastic family utility functions. According to dynastic models, households care about their own lifetime consumption levels plus the consumption of their descendants. Carroll builds a case that dynastic models fail to describe accurately the motivations for wealth accumulation among the wealthiest American families.[8] Perhaps his most persuasive evidence is the finding that wealthy elderly families with children, for whom the dynastic specification is potentially relevant, exhibit the same accumulation tendencies as those without children.

Thus, whereas Dynan et al. (1998) leave open the possibility that various different models that ultimately give rise to income-elastic bequests might be suitable for understanding the saving behavior of the very rich, Carroll (1998) argues in favor of focusing on a specific formulation, referring to wealth accumulation as a consequence of the "capitalist spirit." A model of "capitalist spirit" contains two key features: first, all individuals have the accumulation of wealth, in addition to consumption, as an objective (i.e., wealth is a second direct argument in the utility function); second, the marginal utility associated with wealth ownership declines more slowly than does the marginal utility of consumption expenditures. Carroll's specification of preferences for private consumption and accumulated wealth imply that low- and moderate-lifetime-income families will spend their earnings during their own lives, while high-lifetime-income families will accumulate large estates. The model he proposes certainly seems capable of matching the empirical patterns that Dynan et al. and his own work identify, but it remains to be seen just how much the model contributes, quantifiably, to our understanding about the saving behavior of the very rich or whether another yet-unspecified framework provides a better explanation.

Regardless of which theory of (lifetime) income-elastic estate values one prefers or which eventually receives the most empirical support, our basic point is justified: virtually nobody in the contemporary United States dies without some net worth and a small minority of families

---

[7] In his critique of "standard" bequest models, Carroll (1998) does not explicitly judge the ability of models like Becker and Tomes (1986) or Mulligan (1997) to explain data covering the wealthiest American families.

[8] Carroll also notes that studies such as Altonji, Hayashi, and Kotlikoff (1992) do not find supporting evidence for dynastic models of bequests using samples representative of the U.S. population (Carroll, recall, focuses exclusively on the most wealthy Americans).

leaves enormous amounts to descendants or to charities. More important, the average discrepancy between the discounted value of lifetime earnings and consumption expenditures is strongly associated with a variable of primary interest to policy makers interested in designing fair tax systems – the level of lifetime income. The latter point, of course, is critical for the issues at hand. In particular, the equivalence of an allocation of tax liabilities on the basis of factor incomes and on the basis of consumption obtains only in the counterfactual economy in which bequests simply represent a fixed proportion of the lifetime income of all families.

REVIEW OF RECENT TAX BURDEN STUDIES

General Issues

Three general conclusions emerge from the studies on the distribution of tax burdens of consumption taxes using data for a single period: (1) consumption taxes are found to be quite regressive when households are ranked on the basis of annual income but less regressive when a lifetime measure of income is used or when total consumer expenditures are used as a proxy for lifetime income; (2) the distributions of tax burdens for a BTT or for the FT are less regressive when burdens are allocated on the basis of some measure of current factor income rather than current consumption; and (3) the studies based on income tax data that report tax burden by income decile and by top percentile all conclude that the tax burdens on the rich will be reduced if the present personal taxes were replaced by either the FT or NRST.

Analyses in Which Consumption Is Used as a Proxy for Lifetime Income

Poterba (1989, 1991) was the first to use annual expenditures as a way of eliminating the transitory and life-cycle effects associated with the use of annual income as an estimate of lifetime income. Poterba obtains the standard result that excise taxes paid on motor fuels, alcohol, and tobacco are all highly regressive relative to annual income, as the expenditure fraction of these goods falls with income. In contrast, expenditures on gasoline and alcohol expressed as a percentage of total consumer expenditures are constant for the lowest four income quartiles, though lower for the highest fifth. Taxes on tobacco remain regressive in Poterba's calculations, though less so.[9]

---

[9] Chernick and Reschovsky (1997, p. 254) have questioned the use of total consumer expenditure as a proxy for lifetime income and have used eleven years of income data from the PSID finding that "When people are grouped into 11-years income decile

Metcalf (1994) adopts Poterba's use of total consumer expenditures as a proxy for lifetime income to study the absolute incidence of a 5 percent VAT. When current total consumption expenditures are used as a measure of lifetime income, the tax burden of a 5 percent VAT, assumed to be shifted to consumers, is proportional to the measure of well-being. In contrast, when households are ranked by observed annual income, the burden of a 5 percent VAT is regressive throughout the income range, varying from 7.07 percent for the bottom decile to 3.15 percent for the tenth. In another study of the regressivity of the VAT, Casperson and Metcalf (1994) use wages and age level from PSID data to estimate lifetime income. For one of the measures of income, with a fixed effects adjustment, the VAT is found to be only mildly regressive, with effective tax rates ranging from 4 percent at the bottom to 3 percent at the top.

Metcalf (1997, 1999) uses Consumer Expenditure Survey data to study the distributive effects of introducing a broad-based retail sales tax. He ranks households by annual income and by annual consumption. Using annual income to rank individuals, he estimates that there will be a dramatic increase in the tax burden of the bottom five deciles and a 7 percent decrease in the burden of the top decile (1997). However, the use of consumption as a proxy for lifetime income results in a much smaller increase at the bottom and only a 2 percent decrease for the top decile.

Studies in Which Consumption Tax Burdens Are Allocated on the Basis of Factor Income

The JCT (1993) also concludes that the burden of a general consumption tax, a business transfer tax of 5 percent, is roughly proportional to income. This study uses annual tax data to construct a measure of extended income and reports income levels by income bracket that range from $0–$10,000 to $200,000. The JCT used data from the Survey of Consumer Finances to estimate savings by income level. These saving rates are then used to impute consumption at various levels of income, the same approach as in our study.

The JCT allocates burdens of a 5 percent VAT on the basis of factor income and on the basis of consumption. The most regressive distributional pattern is obtained for a consumption allocation coupled with a tax induced price increase;[10] estimated effective tax rates range from 3.70

---

average gasoline burdens are only slightly less regressive than annual burden." While eleven years is not a lifetime, the authors note that Lyon and Schwab (1995) find little or no change for alcohol and cigarette burdens when these are calculated on a lifetime basis and when a five-year burden measure is used.

[10] The differential impact of a consumption tax with and without a tax-induced price increase is discussed by Zodrow (Chapter 9 in this volume).

percent of income for the bottom decile to 1.76 percent at the top decile. For a factor income allocation at constant money prices, tax burdens are proportional to income.

The United States Treasury (1996), and Cronin, Nunns, and Toder (1996) analyze the distributive effects of the Armey-Shelby flat tax proposal as a replacement for current individual and corporate income taxes allocating tax burdens by factor incomes. This study is notable for its very broad definition of income. The top 5 percent begins at $145,000 and the top 1 percent at $350,000. The U.S. Treasury's primary conclusion is that the Armey-Shelby plan will increase the tax burden of the lowest four quintiles and decrease it for the top quintile. As expected, the percentage decrease in tax liability increases with income – 14 percent for the top 10 percent, 21 percent for the top 5 percent, and 36 percent for the top 1 percent.

Responding to Gentry and Hubbard's (1997a) point that supermarginal returns are still subject to tax under a consumption-based system and that this income is more likely to accrue to high-income individuals, the study by Cronin et al. finds that assets likely to yield supermarginal returns (holdings of active businesses and publicly traded equities) are only slightly more concentrated in the top quintile (81 percent) than are marginal returns to capital (67 percent). Their revised estimate of the change in tax burdens of substituting an FT for the current income tax reflects a reduction in taxes for the top 1 percent of taxpayers of 34 percent, rather than 36 percent. Cronin et al. also estimate that if transition relief is added to the FT by allowing for depreciation allowances for existing capital, the FT reduces the tax burden for the top 1 percent of taxpayers by 40 percent.[11]

Gravelle (1996b) also analyzes the incidence of fundamental tax reform, using JCT (1993) estimates of saving by income class, which show that saving rates are relatively large in higher income brackets. When she allocates tax burden on the basis of consumption, Gravelle (1996b, p. 35) concludes that "the effective tax burden for the flat tax at the highest level would fall from fourteen percent to eleven percent." This implies that the tax burden of the top 1 percent of taxpayers will fall by 46 percent, rather than by the original estimate of 36 percent.

[11] The results of a study on the incidence of the FT by Dunbar and Pogue (1998) are consistent with the U.S. Treasury's. Dunbar and Pogue conclude that a "switch to the proposed flat tax would increase the tax burdens of a majority of taxpayers and would significantly redistribute tax burdens, mainly from the top decile to other taxpayers" (1998, p. 303). Although the treasury found the tax share of the top 1 percent would decrease by 32 to 36 percent, Dunbar and Pogue estimate that the share for this group would decrease by 29 to 34 percent.

Gale, Houser, and Scholz (1996) study the distributive effect of replacing personal income taxes with an FT and confirm the sensitivity of the allocation of tax burden on the basis of consumption rather than factor income. Like JCT (1993) and the present writers, Gale et al. estimate savings for each household using data from the 1983–89 panel of Survey of Consumer Finances. The burdens calculated on the basis of imputed consumption, reported in Gale et al. (1996, table 8B-1) indicated a dramatic change in the distribution of tax burdens when an FT is distributed according to consumption. The change in the tax burden for the top 1 percent is estimated to be a reduction of 43 percent, rather than 16 percent.[12]

Feenberg, Mitrusi, and Poterba (1997) also use CES data to calculate the effects of implementing an NRST. They link the consumption data from CES to a more detailed income tax data base. The latter data set has much more detailed information on high-income households than the CES. Feenberg et al. (1997, p. 65) report, "The Consumer Expenditure Survey top-codes income and consumption flows and it is therefore likely to be particularly weak in describing the consumption behavior of high-income high-consumption households." These difficulties notwithstanding, Feenberg et al. carry out an ambitious match between data sets, adjust the data set to include nonfilers, and impute medical expenditures and corporate tax liabilities to households in their sample.

Feenberg et al. present four sets of results, two for the replacement of personal taxes with an NRST and two for the replacement of an NRST for personal and payroll taxes, with households ranked by income and by consumption. They calculate that, when federal income taxes are replaced with an NRST, the distributional effects are highly regressive for both the consumption and income ranking of households. When a demogrant is added to the NRST, the burdens on the middle- and upper-income groups are increased but the tax paid by the top 1.4 percent of households, ranked by consumption, is estimated to be only half of what it is at present. Under the income ranking with a demogrant, the top percentile, Feenberg et al. estimate, will pay one-third of the taxes it pays under the current tax system.

If both personal income taxes and the payroll tax are replaced by an NRST and a demogrant is provided, the reduction in tax burden at the top of the income distribution is decreased to 10 percent for the top 1.4

---

[12] Gale et al. find smaller distributive changes for the factor income allocation approach than the comparable results reported by the U.S. Treasury. One explanation for this difference is that they use data drawn from the Survey of Income and Program Participation rather than income tax data, a better source for high-income taxpayers.

percent ranked by consumption and to 50 percent for the top percentile ranked by income. This is accomplished, however, only at the cost of significantly increasing tax burdens on the upper middle class. The decile just below the top 1.4 percent ranked by consumption is estimated to have its taxes increased by 30 percent by the introduction of an NRST.

Intertemporal Lifetime Approaches to Distributional Analysis

Studies of the distributive effects of taxes based on the distribution of income for one year take the overall level of income and the distribution of before-tax income as given. There are three major weaknesses to this approach. First, no allowance is made for variations in the annual income levels of individual taxpayers over their life cycles. Second, adjustments in savings and changes in labor supply induced by tax reforms are not considered. Finally, the efficiency and distributional effects of the elimination of the distortionary effects of the corporate profits tax and other tax preferences are excluded from the analysis.

The most extensive studies of differential tax incidence from a life-cycle intertemporal perspective have been developed by Fullerton and Rogers (1993, 1996), using eighteen years of panel data on individual households obtained from the PSID. They use the wage data from the PSID and regression analysis to estimate the lifetime incomes of different income groups. Consumers maximize intertemporal utility by allocating their endowment to consumption and leisure. They allocate their aggregate consumption between seventeen commodity groups; on the production side there are nineteen producer goods. Fullerton and Rogers also use estimates on bequests from Wisconsin probate records, collected by Menchik and David (1982), to approximate the bequests of the twelve different income groups in their model.

Fullerton and Rogers (1996) use their model to simulate the overall welfare and distributional effects of eight tax reforms, including the adoption of a proportional VAT or a proportional income tax, with and without personal exemptions. They conclude that, in the long-run, the welfare effects of all the tax reforms are positive, ranging from 4 percent of lifetime income in *steady state* for a VAT, without personal exemptions or demogrants, to just under 2 percent for proportional income and wage taxes. However, the present value of the welfare gains from the adoption of a VAT that accounts for transitional effects is only about 1 percent of lifetime incomes.

Interestingly, the pattern of gains estimated by Fullerton and Rogers for different income groups is consistent with the results of static, single-period distributional analysis. The adoption of a VAT *without* personal exemptions for low-income groups decreases the welfare of the very poor; and results in small gains for other low- and moderate-income groups. The gains for the groups at the high end of the income distribution are significantly larger. The single-period analysis estimates indicate that what high-income groups *gain absolutely*, low-income groups *lose absolutely*. The adoption of a VAT, with personal exemptions, produces long-run gains for all income groups, with a U-shaped pattern of gains. The lowest and highest income groups gain the most. Similarly, in the single period studies reviewed earlier, the poor and rich gain at the expense of the middle class.

More recently, Altig et al. (1997) adapt the Auerbach and Kotlikoff (1987) model to analyze the distributive implications of fundamental tax reform. This study uses a single good model and follows Fullerton and Rogers in estimating lifetime income profiles from PSID data. In addition to being more aggregative, the Altig et al. contribution differs from Fullerton and Rogers in a number of respects. Nevertheless, there is a rough consistency between the two sets of studies regarding the long-run distributional effects of tax reform. Altig et al. confirm that adoption of a consumption tax without exemptions decreases the steady-state utility of the lower-income groups and increases that of affluent groups. They find that an FT with a personal exemption increases the long-run welfare of all groups. The lowest- and highest-income groups gain the most and the middle class gains the least. The rich gain from the flattening of the rate structure and the poor gain from higher savings and wages induced by tax reform.

Dynamic incidence analysis is important as it recognizes supply-side adjustments and the efficiency gains of tax reform. If the intertemporal and leisure-consumption elasticities are in fact at the levels typically used in the dynamic studies, fundamental tax reform will increase the long-run welfare of all groups. Dynamic and static studies of the distributive effects of a consumption tax reform with a personal exemption agree that the wealthy and the poor have the most to gain from a tax reform. It is the middle class that is most at risk, during the transition and in the long run, as the welfare level of this income group depends critically on the size of supply-side adjustments, including the magnitude of adjustment costs (see Zodrow, Chapter 9 in this volume).

A NEW DISTRIBUTIONAL ANALYSIS

Our study on the distributive consequences of fundamental tax reform contributes to the existing literature in one important respect. We rely on a new source of household-level data to estimate spending propensities by income group in the U.S. economy. The particular attraction of this new data source – the Federal Reserve's Survey of Consumer

Finances – is the overrepresentation of very-high-income families – that is, families that undertake a disproportionate amount of personal saving in the United States. These data allow us to disaggregate high-income families much more precisely than previous researchers could. Also, our analysis of fundamental tax reform focuses particular attention on the impact on tax distribution of broad-based demogrants; such demogrants are fundamental to any proposed single-rate tax system seeking to avoid enormous redistributions away from the lowest-income families, relative to the current federal tax system.

Our objective is to estimate the short-run distributive impact of substituting a fully comprehensive, single-rate NRST for the major federal taxes on personal income, estates and gifts, corporate profits, and payrolls. The estimates are based on a file of individual income tax returns for 1993 prepared by the IRS and a recently released panel of households from the SCF, with data from both 1983 and 1989. The SCF data are a useful new source for tax distribution analysis because high-income families are overrepresented in the SCF survey design and because the data provide information about household saving and income. For this study we assume that saving rates estimated during the sample period 1983–89 apply at the same level of real household income for the tax-paying units observed in 1993.

To separate the distributional consequences of changing from the current progressive rate structure to a proportional one from the effects due to changing the current tax base from income (a combination of income, wages, and consumption) to consumption, we proceed in three steps. First, we compare the present federal system to an equal-yield proportional income tax. Second, we compare this hypothetical proportional income tax to a proportional consumption-based tax. Finally, we compare the current federal tax system to these two proportional taxes under the inclusion of a refundable tax credit, or demogrant, allotted to all taxpayers to relieve the tax burden at the lowest income levels. We make no provision for exemptions of specific items, such as food or medicine, or for preferential treatment of owner-occupied housing, which might actually be part of potential NRST legislation.

Also, unless stated to the contrary, we assume that consumption tax is paid on all Social Security income and that there are no provisions for indexing other forms of transfer income. Browning (1978, 1995) and Browning and Johnson (1979) in contrast, argue that once transfer income is indexed for price-level adjustment, Social Security and other transfer income would not be subject to NRST. By postulating that an NRST is paid on Social Security income we assume that, if the price level increases by the amount of NRST, Social Security and other transfer income are *not* indexed. This assumption may be questionable in the absence of a demogrant, but coupled with a demogrant, indexation seems an overly generous means of protecting recipients of transfer income from the payment of NRST.

Estimating the Distribution of Tax Burdens under the Current Federal Tax System

The basic source of data on the characteristics of taxpayers is information on the 114 million tax-paying units enumerated in the 1993 IRS tax file. This information has to be supplemented with information on households that are nonfilers under the personal income tax, but will bear a tax liability under an NRST. Fortunately, the Current Population Survey (CPS) now imputes nonfiling status to persons. Accordingly, we use the March 1993 CPS and first extract adult individuals above the age of eighteen and all married persons. These individuals are then identified as members of specific families, with young persons living with nonfiling adults treated as dependents. Income information on nonfiling families is then used to estimate the Social Security and corporate taxes paid by nonfilers and to estimate their consumption. There were 12.97 million nonfiling households in 1993, consisting of 26.95 million individuals. Nonfilers are approximately 10 percent of U.S. households; as only 12 percent of nonfilers have incomes greater than $20,000, their addition has little effect on the results of the distributive analysis.

The proportion of total taxes paid by this population is assumed to remain unchanged by any modification in tax regime, so we carry out the distributive analysis without reference to national aggregates of taxes collected or income earned. We assume that the aggregate amount of federal taxes paid by tax-paying units in the tax file remains the same for an NRST as for the current system.[13]

The calculation of personal income tax liabilities for each tax-paying unit follows directly from the IRS tax file. Payroll taxes paid directly by the taxpayer and indirectly by employers can be approximated by applying relevant tax rates and earning limits under the 1993 statutes. Data from the CPS on the earnings of two-worker families are used to estimate payroll taxes for returns in which wages and salaries exceed the earnings limits for particular payroll taxes.

To impute corporate income tax liabilities to individual stockholders, we draw extensively on the work of Feldstein (1988), who in turn applies the theoretical results of Harberger (1962). Corporate profits tax

---

[13] Thus, corporate taxes currently paid by nonprofit and foreign entities must be collected from resident households under an NRST, an admittedly problematic assumption.

burdens are taken to be proportional to all real capital income – returns to corporate equity, rental income, and real personal interest.[14] Feldstein first modifies the return to corporate equity, dividends, and retained earnings by noting that a large portion of corporate pension plans take the defined-benefits form, whereby retirement benefits are defined by the wages of pensioners, not by the earnings of pension reserves. Thus if the corporate tax is eliminated, the higher after-tax earnings of pension reserves will accrue to stockholders. Feldstein's major contribution is to calculate carefully real interest earnings by making appropriate inflation adjustments to both interest received and interest paid. An important advantage of his approach is that he can isolate the estimated portion of corporate income tax liability paid by American households; the remainder is borne by nonprofit organizations and by foreign entities.

A disadvantage of the Feldstein procedure is that for some years – 1993 being an example – real net interest received is significantly negative for the large middle-income tax-paying groups who borrow heavily to finance home ownership. To avoid some peculiar implications of this fact, we proceed as follows. First, we note that Feldstein attributes 64 percent of total corporate tax liabilities to households. This estimate is quite close to the fraction of total dividends reported on personal tax returns, 62 percent, after adjusting the latter for possible underreporting (Park, 1986). Instead of estimating the corporate taxes paid by households during 1993, we *assume* the appropriate figure is 64 percent of total corporate taxes paid, or $95 billion. We distribute the $95 billion among families in proportion to capital income, as reported in the IRS tax file, and allocate an additional $500 million to nonfilers, also in proportion to their capital income.[15]

---

[14] This result derives from analysis that assumes a fixed supply of capital in the domestic economy and no international mobility of capital. Harberger (1995) has updated his analysis to allow for international capital mobility and now concludes that a substantial portion of the corporate tax imposed in the United States will be borne by American workers and foreign owners of capital. These considerations should be addressed in future work, especially as our conclusions about the progressivity of the current federal tax system at high levels of income depend in large part on allocating corporate tax liability to domestic owners of capital. Malcolm Gillis brought this issue to our attention.

[15] After adjusting for the earnings of pension funds, we use national accounts data to estimate the total return to corporate equity as $397.4 billion, rental income inclusive of mortgage interest as $325.5 billion, and real net personal interest as $63.4 billion, for a total capital income of $786.3 billion. Thus, we allocate 50.5 percent of $95 billion according to dividends received; 41.5 percent according to rental income; and 8 percent according to net nominal interest reported by the IRS tax filers.

From the *Survey of Current Business* (Bureau of Economic Analysis, 1994, p. 115), we calculate royalties and rental income to account for 75 percent of net rental income ($102.5 billion); 25 percent represents the return to equity in owner-occupied homes.

Finally, in allocating gift and estate tax liabilities we follow the method developed by Feenberg et al. (1997). We define capital income (CAP) to be the sum of dividends, interest, capital gains, and income from trusts, partnerships, Subchapter S corporations, rents, and royalties using the IRS tax file. We then construct CAP 30k to equal capital income exceeding $30,000. Limiting ourselves to households containing someone older than sixty-five years, we allocate gift and estate taxes in proportion to each household's share of CAP 30k.

Estimates of Household Saving from the 1983–89 Survey of Consumer Finances Panel Data

Our empirical analysis depends on balance sheet information from the Federal Reserve Board's 1983–89 SCF Panel data base. This section introduces this relatively new data source and describes our use of it. Released for public use in March 1996, the SCF Panel is the latest available information for measuring saving decisions among families in the United States during the mid-1980s. In 1989 a subset of families from the 1983 cross-section interview wave was reinterviewed to make up the 1983–89 SCF Panel data base. Like the cross-section SCF surveys, the panel data overrepresent families reporting high income and high wealth relative to the U.S. population. Thus, based on direct information about changes in net worth between the 1983 and 1989 surveys, one can estimate annual saving at the family level. As described earlier, we allocate consumption tax liabilities in relation to household expenditures in this incidence study, so knowledge of the distribution of family saving and income provides required information about expenditures.

Computing Family Net Worth in 1983 and 1989

Computing net worth for each family in the SCF Panel in 1983 is simple because the Federal Reserve Board has recoded (preprocessed) the original data on the public-use file. We compute net worth as the sum of financial assets, value of owned home, value of other owned property, value of collectible items (antiques, art, rare coins, etc.), and net business

---

An additional $223 billion can be attributed to mortgage interest on owner-occupied housing, so total rents earned on home ownership amount to $248.6 billion; total rental income including mortgage interest thus comes to $325.5 billion in 1993. As noted previously, 41.5 percent of $95 billion in corporate tax liabilities are then attributed to rental income. Of this amount, a fraction equal to 76.9/325.5 is allocated in proportion to net rental income represented on IRS tax returns, and 165.8/325.5 is allocated according to mortgage interest itemized on tax returns. The remaining portion, 82.8/325.5, which represents the share of rental income on owner-occupied homes of nonitemizers, is allocated in proportion to their incomes on the assumption that homeownership of nonitemizers is proportional to income.

equity minus financial liabilities (credit card debt and other consumer loans), and mortgage debt on owned home and other owned properties.

Financial asset categories included in the SCF Panel are: balances in checking accounts, saving accounts, Individual Retirement Accounts, money market saving accounts, certificates of deposit, mutual funds, corporate stock equity, balances in margin or brokerage call accounts, trust fund balances, and the cash value of whole life insurance policies. We also add the value of loans to other people for previous property transactions, as well as loans to family members. Net business equity can be computed from information in the SCF Panel pertaining to both actively and nonactively managed businesses owned (or partially owned) during 1983. On the public-use file, net business equity for all nonactively managed businesses is computed by the Federal Reserve Board. Net equity in actively managed businesses results from adding two components, the total current values of each SCF family's share and total amounts owed to the family due to past loans, and subtracting a third component, any loan amounts owed by the family to its businesses.

Computing Family Saving during the 1983–89 Sample Period

The retail sales tax incidence analysis we perform here requires information about saving, not simply changes in net worth. For each family each year, there are several ways net worth can increase. First, existing (1983) assets can increase in market value, even though the family engages in no new transactions with respect to these appreciating assets. Corporate equity, housing, other property, or business equity might frequently increase due to such unrealized capital gains. Second, families can use a portion of their (flow) incomes (from any source) to finance new investments in financial assets, physical assets or property. Third, families can use a portion of their incomes to reduce existing (1983) debts. The relevant definition of household saving for our tax analysis includes only the latter two categories for net worth changes. In the related literature, this saving sometimes is identified as "active" by, e.g., (Dynan et al., 1998). When families save actively, they explicitly reduce consumption expenditures below the level afforded by their incomes earned from all sources: wages, salaries, pensions, Social Security, royalties, rents, transfer payments, interest, dividends, and the like. As we are interested in measuring savings out of current income so as to infer consumption, our problem is to estimate changes in net worth due to unrealized capital gains and losses, and then to remove these from directly observable changes in net worth for families in the 1983–89 SCF Panel. The SCF data do not include all of the information required for this task to be accomplished perfectly for each family but we have developed methods to estimate active saving levels for SCF Panel households based on the available data.[16]

Patterns of Family Saving Rates and Income Levels in the 1983–89 SCF Panel

Our empirical analysis examines "active" saving during the six-year sample period as a fraction of annual income earned from all sources. (We estimate annual income during the period 1983–89 as six times the average annual family income between 1982 and 1988, which is available in the SCF Panel.)[17] In this subsection, we present bivariate analysis of saving and family income patterns represented in the SCF Panel data base. Ultimately, we use the bivariate relationship between saving rates and income levels in the SCF data to impute values to families in the IRS tax files.

The SCF data reveal a pattern familiar to consumption and saving analysts: there is extreme variation in levels and rates of saving across contemporary American families. It follows that some sample statistics (primarily sample means of saving levels and rates as well as ordinary least squares regressions) are sensitive to the impact of outlying observations partially generating variation in the data across families. Thus, we examine means and ordinary least squares regressions on the full (weighted) sample, as well as statistics based on trimmed samples and analysis of medians that are less sensitive to outlying observations. Table 6.1 summarizes the SCF data on levels of saving and income, as well as saving rates, for the full sample and the two trimmed subsamples.[18]

Our incidence study for the replacement of personal and corporate income taxes with a retail sales tax concentrates on the bivariate relationship between saving rates and income levels in the SCF Panel data. Descriptions of the bivariate relationship for several model specifications appear in Table 6.2 and panels 1a and 1b of Figure 6.1. Due to the

---

[16] Details are available from the authors upon request. Our procedures are very similar to those described by Kennickell and Starr-McCluer (1996).

[17] Dynan et al. (1998) examine similar saving rates using the SCF Panel data. They include "passive" (accrued capital gains) saving in the numerator of their saving rates but use the same income definition as we do in this study. In the same study, they examine "active" saving among families in the Panel Study of Income Dynamics using essentially the same definitions we employ here. Kennickell and Starr-McCluer analyze changes in net worth as a fraction of total earned income using the SCF Panel data. Our processed data base appears to resemble theirs closely.

[18] The first trimmed subsample keeps observations in the middle 96 percent of the full-sample distribution; the second trimmed subsample keeps the middle 90 percent of observations. Using SCF Panel weights, the full sample represents 81.9 million households, the first subsample represents 78.5, and the second subsample represents 73.7 million households.

Table 6.1. Summary of the Distribution of Saving Levels, Saving Rates, and Income Levels in the 1983–89 SCF Panel Data Base

Sample Statistic	Entire Sample N = 4,434	Trim Sample 1 N = 4,107	Trim Sample 2 N = 3,579
Average annual level of family saving, 1982–88, $			
Mean	3,026	2,546	1,403
Standard deviation	105,581	55,420	23,489
1st quartile	−114,473	−54,423	−41,267
10th quartile	−10,508	−8,273	−6,278
25th quartile	−1,987	−1,873	−1,657
Median	115	138	115
75th quartile	3,700	3,533	2,960
90th quartile	15,558	14,249	11,268
99th quartile	145,483	84,300	41,433
Average family total (gross) income, 1982–88, $			
Mean	36,650	33,223	32,267
Standard deviation	69,159	68,470	59,858
1st quartile	3,600	3,600	3,600
10th quartile	7,100	7,135	7,100
25th quartile	13,700	13,710	13,700
Median	24,000	24,000	23,900
75th quartile	40,000	39,750	39,545
90th quartile	60,600	59,850	59,650
99th quartile	184,990	184,990	177,950
Average rate of saving, 1982–88, %			
Mean	−1.2	1.4	1.0
Standard deviation	139.1	43.1	26.0
1st quartile	−284.3	−161.9	−82.9
10th quartile	−46.5	−38.3	−30.6
25th quartile	−9.7	−8.6	−7.5
Median	0.9	1.0	0.9
75th quartile	15.0	14.3	12.5
90th quartile	43.3	39.6	32.6
99th quartile	276.9	148.8	63.0

absence of any direct tax information in the SCF data base, saving is measured as a fraction of total family income (as it is throughout this section). Thus, to apply this saving information to the IRS tax files, we use effective tax rates to adjust gross saving rates to saving as a fraction of disposable income, which is straightforward.

Across all types of specified models, the positive relation between saving rates and the level of family income is quite strong. Table 6.2 and

Table 6.2. Empirical Function of SCF Saving as a Fraction: Total Family Income, by Level of Income

Total Family Income in Thousands	Median Spline Regression	OLS Spline Regression	Average[a]	Modified Median Spline	Modified OLS Spline
5	−0.0070	−0.0641	−0.0356	−0.0470	−0.0641
10	0.0017	−0.0299	−0.0141	−0.0383	−0.0299
20	0.0105	0.0044	0.0075	0.0105	0.0044
30	0.0157	0.0245	0.0201	0.0157	0.0245
40	0.0273	0.0375	0.0324	0.0273	0.0375
50	0.0421	0.0468	0.0444	0.0421	0.0468
60	0.0542	0.0544	0.0543	0.0542	0.0544
70	0.0645	0.0607	0.0626	0.0645	0.0607
80	0.0733	0.0663	0.0698	0.0733	0.0663
90	0.0812	0.0712	0.0762	0.0812	0.0712
100	0.0882	0.0755	0.0819	0.0882	0.0755
120	0.1003	0.0831	0.0917	0.1003	0.0831
140	0.1105	0.0895	0.1000	0.1105	0.0895
145	0.1129	0.0910	0.1019	0.1129	0.0910
160	0.1194	0.0950	0.1072	0.1194	0.0950
180	0.1272	0.0999	0.1136	0.1272	0.0999
200	0.1342	0.1043	0.1193	0.1342	0.1043
250	0.1491	0.1136	0.1313	0.1491	0.1136
300	0.1612	0.1211	0.1412	0.1612	0.1211
400	0.1803	0.1331	0.1567	0.1803	0.1331
500	0.1951	0.1423	0.1687	0.1951	0.1423
600	0.2072	0.1499	0.1786	0.2000	0.1500
1,000	0.2412	0.1711	0.2061	0.2000	0.1500

[a] Average of median spline regression and OLS spline regression.

Figure 6.1 show results from our preferred models. Using an extremely general statistical algorithm supplied by He and Ng (1999), we searched for the best-fitting (in terms of Schwartz information criteria), smooth function relating median saving rates by income level (measured in natural logarithms) in the SCF data.[19] The model selected according to statistical criteria (maximizing the goodness of fit) is a piecewise linear

---

[19] We appreciate assistance from Pin Ng with the implementation of this statistical algorithm. The algorithm searches over a very wide class of piecewise linear splines for household saving rates as a function of income (candidate models can use a dozen knots or more, if the data require such flexibility) and chooses a parsimonious representation that fits the data well. Model selection criteria are purely statistical and described in He and Ng (1999).

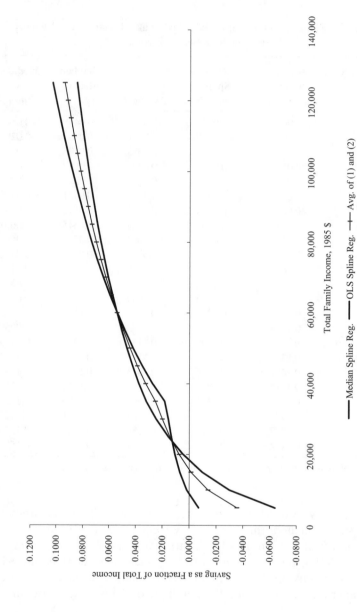

Figure 6.1a. SCF Saving as a Fraction of Total Family Income, by Income Levels

168

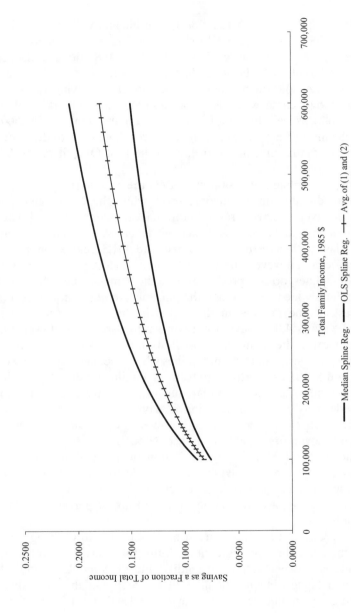

Figure 6.1b. SCF Saving as a Fraction of Total Family Income, by Income Levels

spline for saving rates as a function of log income with a single knot around $34,500. Thus, Figure 6.1a shows two log-spline functions connected at a "kink" income level of $34,500 (in 1985 dollars; also, see column 1 of Table 6.2). Using ordinary least squares (OLS), we estimated the same piecewise linear spline model for saving rates as a function of log income, which is reported in Figure 6.1a (and in column 2 of Table 6.2), as well. In the OLS specification, the "kink" at $34,500 is statistically insignificant. Thus, saving rates grow linearly with the natural logarithm of family income, according to the best OLS fit of the SCF Panel data.

The median spline regression model fits the middle (median) of the saving rate distribution, by income level, while the OLS spline goes through the average saving rate, conditional on income. If the distribution of saving rates at each income level were symmetric and homoskedastic, then estimated median and OLS regression models would coincide. However, the two estimated models, median and OLS regression splines, do not predict exactly the same saving rates, conditional on family income, although the patterns are quite similar. Among the lowest-income families in the SCF (the bottom 25 percent with income below $14,000), average saving rates are much lower than medians because the saving rate distribution is severely skewed to the left. Among the large majority of families whose incomes range between $20,000 and $110,000 (up to 98 percent of families), estimated median and OLS models are quite similar due to symmetry and conditional homoskedasticity in the distribution of saving rates by income level. As Figure 6.1b clearly documents, however, median saving rates are higher and grow more quickly with income among the upper 2 percent of families in the 1985 income distribution (incomes above $110,000). What lowers the average saving rates relative to the medians among this group of highest-income families is the observation of very large, negative saving rates among the bottom 10 percent of saving households.

OLS regression models are much more sensitive to outlying observations than are median regressions. Thus, there are relatively large discrepancies between estimated median and OLS models among the lowest- and highest-income families in the SCF. On the other hand, median regression models require larger samples than OLS for efficient estimation, which suggests the possibility of small-sample bias for the median regression models among the lowest- and highest-income families. Thus, in column 3 of Table 6.2 and in Figure 6.1, we compute intermediate fitted values for saving rates as a function of income levels that splits the difference between estimated median and OLS regression models.

At first glance, the saving rates shown in Table 6.2 seem to imply remarkably robust saving among households in the SCF between 1983 and 1989. However, it is important to recall how families are distributed across income levels in the data base. Measured in 1985 dollars, median total family income is only $23,900; family income averages only $32,267 (from column 3 in Table 6.1). Thus, the median-income family in the SCF Panel saved only 1.5 percent of total income during the period; the average-income family saved less than 2 percent (using the estimated median spline regression). Empirically strong saving rates in excess of 10 percent at the median and 8 percent on average are apparent among families whose incomes exceed $120,000. However, only 2 percent of American families meet this criterion during the 1983–89 sample period, according to the SCF Panel.

In the aggregate, saving rates from columns 1, 2, and 3 of Table 6.2 equal 5.2, 4.5, and 4.8 percent, respectively, for the SCF Panel. Calculations based on the National Income and Product Accounts during the same period are quite close: 4.8 percent during the entire period 1983 through 1989. In the aggregate, median-fitted saving rates (column 1) slightly overstate saving levels among the absolute highest-income families in the SCF Panel, whereas OLS-fitted saving rates are slightly too low for this group. These discrepancies appear among just the top 0.2 percent of the SCF income distribution – those families whose total incomes exceed $510,000 per year (in 1985 dollars). Thus, the "modified" median and OLS spline functions shown in columns 4 and 5 of Table 6.2 truncate maximum saving rates above $510,000 in family income. Additionally, because the median fitted values perhaps overstate saving among the very-lowest-income families, a downward adjustment to them appears in column 4 of Table 6.2. Thus, we have five similar, but slightly different, specifications for the relationship between household saving rates and income levels based on statistical evaluation of the SCF Panel data for use in our tax incidence study. Because of the similarity in the model specifications over the majority of the income distribution, however, our tax incidence calculations do not differ substantially across these specifications.

Calculation of Consumption and Savings for the Taxpayer Sample

The SCF Panel data base does not include information about tax payments. Thus, the saving rates we estimate from this source of data relate to before-tax income. Here, we describe how we use the estimated saving rates, by income level, from the SCF Panel to infer consumption and saving levels for the IRS taxpayer sample.

By definition, consumption equals gross income minus direct federal, state, and local taxes, and saving. We estimate consumption expenditures under the current tax system by applying this identity for each family in the IRS taxpayer sample for 1993. First, we directly observe federal taxes paid in the tax file. Second, direct state and local taxes are accounted for by subtracting state and local, personal income, corporate, and social security taxes and allocating them to households in proportion to their comprehensive income. Third, by multiplying the income-specific saving rate from Table 6.2 by adjusted gross income for each family in the tax-payer sample, we provide an estimate of the relevant saving level. Based on these three elements and observed adjusted gross income, we can estimate consumption for each family in 1993.

Estimating gross consumption expenditures under the retail sales tax regime requires two steps. First, for each family in the IRS taxpayer sample we augment adjusted gross income by current federal taxes paid indirectly by employers and corporations. There are two possibilities for the second step. Either we can apply the estimates of saving rates based on before-tax income to the broader definition of income and calculate savings or we can assume that the ratio of consumption to savings calculated for the present tax system will apply to the new retail sales tax regime. We adopt the first approach, which assumes that savings out of before-tax income remains unchanged. This assumption *minimizes* the difference between the income and consumption tax bases.[20] By imposing an equal-yield constraint on tax revenues, we are able to solve a simple two-equation system for the retail sales tax rate, on the assumption that each taxpayer faces the same tax on comprehensive consumption expenditures.

Tax Reform Incidence Results and Their Interpretation

Tables 6.3 and 6.4 report our estimates of the distribution of the tax burdens under the current federal tax system inclusive of payroll taxes. The overall burden is roughly proportional at low- and middle-income levels. Taxes as a percentage of income rise slowly to 23 percent for the $75,000 to $100,000 group. This income group borrows heavily to finance home ownership. Beyond this level of income, effective federal tax rates accelerate to a maximum average of nearly 38 percent.

Table 6.4 indicates that low- and moderate-income groups pay heavy social insurance taxes, moderate corporate taxes, and relatively small personal income taxes. Caps on wages subject to the social insurance tax rates make them regressive. The progressive elements in the federal tax system in the United States are the personal income, corporate income,

[20] Experimentation with both savings assumptions shows that, as the estimated saving rate for most income groups is quite low, the calculated tax burdens are very similar under both approaches. The exception is at the very top of the income distribution where the estimated tax burden is higher under the assumption we adopt.

Table 6.3. Distributions of Current Federal Tax Liability by Income Class

Income in Thousands[a]	Tax Units in Millions	Total Income in Billions	Total Federal Taxes[b] in Billions	Total Taxes as Percentage of Income
<0	0.81	−49.46	0.52	—
0–5	12.50	32.04	6.67	20.8
5–10	13.01	97.41	17.67	18.1
10–15	12.22	152.67	27.57	18.1
15–20	11.04	192.77	35.98	18.7
20–25	9.49	212.84	43.01	20.2
25–30	8.37	229.88	48.73	21.2
30–40	12.76	443.89	97.53	22.0
40–50	10.00	446.89	100.65	22.5
50–75	14.18	861.07	202.78	23.6
75–100	5.16	440.06	101.13	23.0
100–200	3.83	505.03	144.79	28.7
200–500	0.96	278.07	92.70	33.3
500–1,000	0.18	118.82	44.06	37.1
1,000+	0.08	217.69	82.37	37.8
TOTAL	114.60	4,180.17	1,055.19	25.24

[a] Income measure is adjusted gross income plus nontaxed social security benefits, plus various imputations, such as social insurance taxes paid, employers, corporate taxes, and corporate retained earnings.
[b] Personal income taxes, social insurance taxes, imputed corporate taxes, and inheritance taxes.

Table 6.4. Average Tax per Tax-Filing Unit

Income in Thousands	Average Income in Thousands	Personal Income Taxes	Social Insurance Taxes	Corporate Tax	Inheritance	Total Federal Taxes
<0	−60.8	380	1,196	−1,074	137	640
0–5	3.51	62	491	26	0	580
5–10	7.48	191	1,039	127	0	1,358
10–15	12.49	499	1,506	250	0	2,255
15–20	17.45	876	2,048	334	0	3,258
20–25	22.43	1,512	2,622	399	0	4,533
25–30	27.48	2,121	3,334	369	1	5,825
30–40	34.79	3,124	4,221	297	2	7,644
40–50	44.68	4,395	5,438	225	5	10,063
50–75	60.73	6,804	7,120	362	15	14,301
75–100	85.37	11,865	8,373	1,028	74	21,341
100–200	131.82	22,010	10,554	4,767	462	37,793
200–500	289.54	64,544	11,476	17,644	2,858	96,521
500–1,000	671.50	171,998	11,409	55,061	10,549	249,018
1,000+	2,602.06	685,405	11,448	223,188	64,577	984,618

Table 6.5. Distribution of Tax Liabilities for Various
Tax Systems by Income Class[a]

Income in Thousands	Current Tax System	Proportional Income Tax	Proportional Income Tax with Poverty-Level Demogrant	Proportional Consumption Tax	Proportional Consumption Tax with Poverty-Level Demogrant
0–5	6.67	7.99	–38.42	9.88	–37.11
5–10	17.67	24.29	–17.19	26.17	–14.53
10–15	27.57	38.07	5.67	40.79	8.99
15–20	35.98	48.06	24.67	51.32	28.68
20–25	43.01	53.07	38.05	56.46	42.28
25–30	48.73	57.31	48.62	60.82	53.00
30–40	97.53	110.69	107.43	117.06	115.50
40–50	100.65	111.44	119.50	117.42	127.18
50–75	202.78	214.72	250.58	222.79	261.27
75–100	101.13	109.86	136.56	111.11	138.70
100–200	144.79	125.93	164.87	122.76	161.75
200–500	92.70	69.33	95.37	62.21	86.95
500–1,000	44.06	29.63	41.68	23.88	34.70
1,000+	82.37	54.28	77.33	32.00	48.60
TOTAL	1,054.67	1,054.67	1,054.67	1,054.67	1,054.67

[a] For taxpayers with positive comprehensive income only.

and inheritance taxes, as shown in Table 6.4. The fact that average effective tax rates increase significantly on incomes in excess of $100,000 per year means that any reform that flattens the rate structure will inevitably reduce the tax burden on high-income families.

To separate the effects of changes in the rate structure from the distributive impacts of reforming the tax base, we present as a point of reference a comprehensive income tax levied proportionately at a 24.3 percent rate. Results from this experiment appear in the second column of Tables 6.5 and 6.6. According to our methodology, this tax is equivalent, in terms of implied distributional tax burden, to a comprehensive, flat-rate consumption tax *if the ratio of consumption to income is constant across families in different income groups.* Such a hypothetical tax proposal would lower burdens for every income group above $100,000, ranging from an implied effective tax cut of 15 percent for $100,000 to $200,000, 25 percent for $200,000 to $500,000, to about 33 percent for incomes above $500,000. Taxes at the bottom of the income distribution, on the other hand, rise by very large amounts in this income-proportional case.

Table 6.6. Taxes as a Percentage of Comprehensive Income[a]

Income in Thousands	Current System	Proportional Income Tax	Proportional Consumption Tax	Proportional Income Tax with Wage Demogrant	Proportional Consumption Tax with Wage Demogrant
0–5	20.8	24.9	30.8	—	—
5–10	18.1	24.9	26.9	—	—
10–15	18.1	24.9	26.7	3.7	5.9
15–20	18.7	24.9	26.6	12.8	14.9
20–25	20.2	24.9	26.5	17.9	19.9
25–30	21.2	24.9	26.5	21.1	23.1
30–40	21.2	24.9	26.4	24.2	26.0
40–50	22.5	24.9	26.3	26.7	28.5
50–75	23.6	24.9	25.9	29.1	30.3
75–100	23.0	24.9	25.3	31.0	31.5
100–200	28.7	24.9	24.3	32.6	32.0
200–500	33.3	24.9	22.4	34.3	31.3
500–1,000	37.1	24.9	20.1	35.1	29.2
1,000+	37.8	24.9	14.7	35.5	22.3

[a] For taxpayers with positive comprehensive income only.

When saving ratios vary by income class according to patterns estimated from the SCF Panel data, the adoption of a proportional consumption tax in place of a proportional income tax further increases the tax burdens on lower- and middle-income groups. Tabulations in Table 6.6 show about a 5 percent increase in tax burdens from this hypothetical proposal for families with incomes below $30,000 as a result of moving to a consumption-based tax system. In terms of percentage change, this represents about a quarter to a third of the increase in tax burdens resulting from transforming the present system into a proportional (broad-based) income tax. Among a large segment of families belonging to the upper middle class (incomes in the range $50,000 to $100,000), substitution of a proportional consumption-based tax for a proportional income tax increases their overall burdens by a modest amount.

For taxpayers reporting incomes above $200,000, moving to a proportional income tax without exemptions and deductions reduces tax liabilities from $219 billion under the current federal system to $149 billion – a decrease of 36 percent. Adopting a consumption-based system further reduces the burden of the affluent to $123 billion as saving rates rise steadily as income rises through the income distribution. It is of interest that 73 percent of the decrease of the tax burden on the rich is the result of broadening the tax base and flattening the rate structure and only 27 percent is the result of the change in the tax base.

One way of reducing the tax burden under a flat-rate system on low-income families is to exempt a fixed amount of income or consumption for all taxpayers. The government could provide a refundable tax credit, either as a fixed amount per person based on estimated taxes to be paid or one based on poverty levels of family income, which vary with the size of family.

A refundable demogrant serves as a useful vehicle for redistributing after-tax income to low-income groups, as Table 6.5 clearly shows. The two lowest-income groups, who report incomes below $10,000 per year (and who pay nearly $25 billion in taxes under the current federal system) would receive about $55 billion in net transfers under a poverty-level demogrant. Operating the demogrant is very expensive. In combination with the proportional consumption tax, the demogrant increases the tax rate from 28 to 41 percent.[21]

We have also experimented with a number of other demogrant systems, designed to lower the tax burden on low-income groups. One of these provides for a rebate on Social Security taxes. If the adoption of an NRST results in an increase in absolute prices, this is equivalent to the indexing of Social Security benefits for inflation. This approach has been combined with a wage demogrant that is gradually phased out. The wage demogrant provides for the return of all tax "paid" on the first $20,000 of wage income. The demogrant is then reduced at the rate, t, for every dollar of wage income above $20,000 so that the tax rebate becomes zero at $40,000 of wages.

A wage demogrant will require employers to report the wage and salary income of their employees. This consideration mitigates in favor of the partial, or full, retention of the existing wage taxes necessary to finance Social Security. In considering a wage demogrant we ignore administrative considerations and also abstract from the complications of two-earner households that were accounted in the allocations of existing Social Security taxes. The demogrant is calculated for family wage income.

In Table 6.6 we report the results for a Social Security and wage demogrant. We assume that the NRST is not paid on Social Security income and this provision is combined with the wage demogrant. This system is less expensive than the demogrant based on poverty levels. The

---

[21] As explained later, the net transfers to low-income groups under the poverty-level demogrant are probably overestimated.

tax rate is 38 percent relative to 41 percent for the poverty-based system. The large net transfers at the bottom of the income distribution disappear and positive net taxes are paid at incomes below $25,000, although they are smaller than for the existing tax system and significantly smaller than for an NRST without any tax relief.

The important point is that it is possible to design a demogrant system that will lower the tax burden on households with modest means and that is less expensive than the demogrant based on poverty level incomes. But due to the flat-rate tax system and the phasing out of the wage demogrant, its burden will fall largely on middle- and upper-middle-income groups. This is clear from a comparison of the tax burdens under the poverty-level and wage demogrants. The benefits of the lower tax rate of the wage demogrant accrue primarily to the upper end of the income distribution; some middle-income groups actually pay higher taxes under the less expensive wage demogrant. The burden could be partially shifted away from the middle to the top by phasing out the wage demogrant at a slower rate, or by beginning the phase-out at a higher level of wage income. The tax rate would have to be raised, and the tax burden in the middle and at the top end of the income distribution would be approximately the same as for the poverty-level demogrant.

CONCLUSION

Currently, the federal government collects taxes from a hybrid system in which the effective tax base is partly determined by wages, consumption, and capital income (not symmetrically). Like nearly all recent analysis on the topic, our calculations reveal a current federal tax system in which average effective tax rates are roughly proportional through most of the annual (comprehensive) income distribution, but rise strongly at very high levels of income. This pattern of progressivity at the top results from applying graduated marginal tax rates on personal income, explicitly taxing capital income, and taxing corporate income "twice." Proportionality at the bottom and through the middle of the income distribution largely arises from two offsetting factors: built-in regressivity from payroll taxes with earnings caps and generous exemptions and standard deductions in the personal income tax (as well as the earned income tax credit).

As a consequence of current federal tax progressivity, moving to a flat-rate, consumption-based tax system will reduce effective tax rates on families at the top of the (annual, comprehensive) income distribution. Effective tax rates are easily lowered to zero percent at the bottom of the distribution simply by implementing a lump-sum payment (demogrant) to all residents. An effective demogrant, however, is extremely expensive to operate. Put another way, financing both "ordinary" government activities and the demogrant requires very high marginal tax rates on consumption, which presumably mitigates the potential efficiency gains sought by many consumption tax reformers. With a demogrant included, our analysis and much other recent work on the topic reveal that financing government services will be accomplished by increasing the tax burden on a broad "middle class" of families reporting annual (comprehensive) income in the range of $20,000 to $200,000.

Chapter 7

The Role of Administrative Issues in Tax Reform: Simplicity, Compliance, and Administration

William G. Gale and Janet Holtzblatt

The basic administrative goals of tax policy are uncontroversial: taxes should be easy to understand and comply with, and they should be enforced and administered in a competent and fair manner. Despite nearly universal agreement on these goals, administrative concerns raise difficult issues for researchers and policy makers. Researchers have not reached consensus regarding many of the most basic questions about the existing tax system, such as the costs of compliance and the determinants of tax evasion. Even when research does produce reliable answers to these questions, policy makers face difficult trade-offs both among various administrative goals and between administrative goals and other widely held goals of tax policy, such as equity and efficiency.

Administrative issues have also been in the forefront of efforts to reform taxes in recent years. Perhaps the most common complaint about the existing tax system is the level of complexity. The nature of activities undertaken by the Internal Revenue Service has also proved highly controversial. The desire to address these issues generates much of the impetus for fundamental tax reform – replacing the current system with either the flat tax or a national retail sales tax.

This chapter examines the role of administrative factors in tax policy and tax reform. After summarizing conceptual and measurement issues relating to tax complexity and tax evasion, we explore why complexity and evasion continue to exist. In an examination of administrative issues in the income tax, we show that estimates of the costs of compliance,

We thank Edith Brashares, Jim Cilke, Lowell Dworin, Allen Lerman, Ed Nannenhorn, Jim Nunns, Emily Tang, and especially Peter Mieszkowski, Joel Slemrod, and George Zodrow for helpful comments. We thank Henry Aaron and Samara Potter for extraordinarily helpful comments on the penultimate draft of this paper. We also thank Jim Sly for research assistance. Views and opinions expressed in this chapter are those of the authors and do not necessarily represent the policies or positions of the U.S. Treasury Department or the staff, officers, or trustees of the Brookings Institution.

administration, and enforcement of the income tax vary widely, due in part to inadequate data. Our best estimate is that, in 1995, those costs ranged between \$75 billion and \$130 billion, or between 10 and 17 percent of revenues. The income tax evasion rate is about 17 percent, but varies significantly by type of income.

We also examine administrative issues in a national retail sales tax (NRST) and a flat tax. As proposed, the sales tax would greatly simplify taxes, but the NRST would actually require a much higher tax rate than is commonly proposed. Because the high tax rate would create strong incentives for (legal) tax avoidance and (illegal) tax evasion, the NRST may be neither administrable nor enforceable. The pure flat tax would greatly simplify taxes, and enforcement and administration would not prove difficult, but the flat tax could end up much more complicated than proposed, in response to tax avoidance behavior and political pressures.

However, an important caveat to any analysis of administrative issues in fundamental tax reform is that no country has successfully enacted or administered a high-rate national retail sales tax or a flat tax. Tax systems that exist in the real world have been forged through a combination of revenue requirements, political pressures, responses to taxpayer avoidance and evasion, lobbying, and other processes that any operating tax system would eventually have to face. Notably, all of these factors tend to raise complexity. In contrast, tax systems that exist only on paper – such as the NRST and the flat tax – appear to be simpler in significant part because they have not had to face real-world tests yet.

Tax simplification is a long-standing goal that garners widespread support, at least in principle, and is technically feasible. But the fact that most existing taxes turn out to be far more complex than originally proposed should serve as a caveat to the view that achieving tax simplification, in the existing system or in a new tax system, will prove easy or durable.

PRELIMINARY ISSUES[1]

Complexity

Tax complexity has many dimensions and could plausibly be defined in different ways. Following Slemrod (1984), we define the complexity of a tax system as the sum of compliance costs, which are incurred directly by individuals and businesses, and administrative costs, which are incurred by government. Compliance costs include the time taxpayers spend preparing and filing tax forms, learning about the law, and main-

---

[1] Slemrod and Yitzhaki (2000) provide an excellent summary and analysis of issues relating to tax avoidance, evasion, and administration.

taining record keeping for tax purposes.[2] These costs also include expenditures of time and money by taxpayers to avoid or evade taxes, to have their taxes prepared by others, and to respond to audits, as well as any costs imposed on any third parties, such as employers. Administrative costs, although incurred by government, are ultimately borne by individuals. These costs include the budget of the tax collection agency and the tax-related budgets of other agencies that help administer tax programs.[3]

Defining complexity as the total resource cost of complying with and administering a tax system provides a quantitative measure by which different tax systems can be compared, and by which the administrative aspects of a particular tax system can be evaluated relative to its impacts on equity, efficiency, and revenue. But the definition is not ideal. Slemrod (1989a) points out that a particular subsidy could be so complicated that few taxpayers use it. If it were simplified, and enough additional people used the subsidy, total resource costs would rise, even though the subsidy itself had become less complicated.

A number of issues arise in efforts to measure compliance and administrative costs. First, permanent and transitory costs may differ. A new tax provision may raise compliance costs temporarily, as people learn about the change, even if it reduces costs in the long term. Likewise, for administrative costs, the capital cost of upgrading IRS computers might appear as a current-year budget expenditure rather than being amortized over time. Second, only the *incremental* costs due to taxes should be included. Even with no taxes, firms would need to keep track of income and expenses to calculate profits, and individuals would engage in financial planning. The costs of these activities should be omitted from compliance cost measures. Third, an analysis of tax complexity alone may generate misleading conclusions. Governments can impose policies via taxes, spending, regulations, or mandates. Any tax provision can be made simpler by eliminating it, but if it then is recreated as a spending program, the overall complexity of government may rise.

The level of complexity can be influenced by structural elements – such as the tax base, the tax rate structure, and the allowable deductions, exemptions, and credits – as well as by administrative features of the tax code. The three most discussed tax bases are income, wages, and consumption. Holding the other features of the tax system constant, income is the most difficult of the three bases to tax. Income may be

---

[2] These items constitute the costs measured by the Paperwork Reduction Act of 1980 and printed in the instructions for federal tax forms.
[3] For example, the Department of Labor certifies employers as eligible for the Work Opportunity Tax Credit and the Welfare-to-Work Tax Credit.

decomposed into its sources (wages and capital income) or its uses (consumption and saving). For a wide variety of measurement and timing reasons, it is generally easier to tax wages than capital income, and easier to tax consumption than saving.

Tax rates are typically either graduated, like the current income tax, or flat, like the payroll tax. Flat-rate taxes can have lower compliance costs than graduated taxes. The presence of graduated rates gives taxpayers incentives to avoid taxes by shifting income over time or across people, while flat-rate taxes allow more efficient administrative structures. Taxes imposed at flat rates can be easily collected at source, because the rate does not vary across taxpayers.

Exemptions, deductions, or credits that are universal create little complexity. However, targeted provisions require clear definitions of eligible taxpayers and activities, and can create compliance headaches. Finally, different ways of administering taxes may affect complexity. For example, withholding taxes at source or eliminating the requirement to file a tax return could reduce compliance costs for individuals.[4]

This discussion suggests that, other things equal, the simplest system would tax consumption at a flat rate with universal deductions, credits, or exemptions and with withholding at source. Yet, the United States and many other countries tax income on a graduated basis, with numerous targeted credits and deductions, and with withholding at source only for certain types of income. Given the prevalence of these alternative systems, and the absence of any country that taxes only in the simplest way described earlier, it is instructive to ask why existing systems deviate so widely from the simplest structure.

We believe that three factors are paramount in explaining why tax systems are complex. The first is conflict among the consensus goals of tax policy. Although almost everyone agrees that taxes should be simple, most people also agree that taxes should be fair, conducive to economic prosperity, and enforceable. Even if all parties agree on these goals, they do not typically agree on the relative importance of each goal. As a result, policy outcomes usually represent efforts to balance one or more goals against the others. That is, sometimes a certain amount of complexity is created or permitted in order to help achieve other policy goals. For example, attempts to make taxes fairer often conflict with attempts to make taxes simpler. Most countries tailor tax burdens to the characteristics of individual taxpayers. This may improve tax equity, but it also creates complexity. It requires tracing income or consumption from the business sector to the individual. It requires reporting and documenting

---

[4] However, as we discuss later, some of those costs may be shifted to employers, other businesses, or government agencies.

individual characteristics such as marital status, number of dependents, and age, as well as the composition of expenditures or income. It allows tax rates that vary with individual characteristics, creating opportunities for tax avoidance.

The second factor that generates tax complexity is the political process. Politicians and interest groups have interests in targeted subsidies that reduce taxes for particular groups or activities. But targeted subsidies inevitably make taxes more complex by creating more distinctions among taxpayers and among sources and uses of income.

The third factor that creates complexity is the ability and willingness of taxpayers to avoid or evade taxes. Taxpayers have every right to reduce their taxes by any legal means possible. Such activity, however, inevitably creates issues about whether particular activities or expenditures qualify for tax-preferred status. Resolving these issues typically results in complex laws or regulations, developed in order to describe the limits of tax rules more fully, or complex transactions, undertaken to obtain favorable tax treatment, or both.

Recognition of these factors has at least three important implications for the study of tax complexity. First, the fundamental question is *not* the overall level of complexity, but whether particular tax provisions or tax systems provide good value for the complexity they create. This depends on the magnitude and incidence of the costs and *benefits* of tax complexity, where the benefits include the extent to which complexity aids in achieving other policy goals. Second, the factors that generate complex tax systems – policy trade-offs, politics, and taxpayers' desire to reduce their own tax burdens – are not features of tax policies per se. They will likely remain in force even if the tax system were reformed or replaced. As a result, an analysis of the extent to which policy changes can affect tax complexity should incorporate these factors. Third, there is an important distinction between private and social gains or costs. Suppose everyone had to fill out five extra lines of the tax form to receive a $1,000 tax cut. Each person might regard that as "good complexity," worth the cost of providing extra information. But, holding tax revenues constant, the revenue would still have to be raised from somewhere, so the net tax cut would be zero – that is, everyone's tax "cut" would be from a higher initial tax liability and net taxes would be the same. Thus, from a social perspective, the sum of all individuals' "good complexity" could be zero or negative.

Evasion

Tax evasion is simply the act of not paying taxes that ought to be paid. Evasion can be deliberate, when people choose not to report income or pay taxes due. It can also be unintentional, when people make mistakes in filing their taxes. In either case, evasion erodes tax revenues, and therefore requires higher tax rates to raise a fixed amount of revenue. Thus, evasion raises effective tax rates and burdens on taxpayers who comply with the system.

Like complexity, the extent of evasion is influenced by administrative and structural features of the tax code.[5] Withholding of taxes by third parties, such as employers currently do on behalf of employees, appears to reduce the evasion rate. In the absence of withholding, reporting of information by third parties to the government, such as firms currently do when they pay dividends, is associated with lower evasion rates. IRS enforcement actions may deter taxpayers from cheating on an ex ante basis and often root out evasion on an ex post basis. Structural features of the tax system also affect evasion. For example, higher tax rates increase the marginal payoff to the taxpayer from evasion. But they also reduce taxpayers' income and may make them more reluctant to cheat. The net effect is ambiguous, but the weight of available evidence suggests that lower tax rates reduce evasion rates (Alm, Jackson, and McKee, 1992; Andreoni, Erard, and Feinstein, 1998; Clotfelter, 1983; Feinstein, 1991; Slemrod and Bakija, 1996).

As noted, existing tax systems do not routinely achieve the minimum possible level of complexity. For similar reasons, they also typically do not achieve evasion rates of zero. For example, there are trade-offs involved in raising compliance rates. Some efforts to reduce evasion – such as increasing the number and intensity of audits – raise the level of intrusiveness of taxes in people's everyday lives. Other policies that reduce evasion – such as increasing reporting requirements – make taxes more complex. In addition, policy choices that generate more complexity may also raise evasion. Simpler tax systems are easier to comply with, and taxpayers may be more prone to make errors when they do not fully understand the rules.

ADMINISTRATIVE ISSUES IN THE INCOME TAX

The current tax system raises many administrative issues. Critics claim the system is bewilderingly complex, noting that the Internal Revenue Code and the regulations that interpret the code span thousands of pages and millions of words. Critics also argue that evasion rates are too high, and that the IRS has been reckless, if not abusive, in its enforcement of the law. All of these charges, however, are controversial. Most households face relatively simple tax situations, so that the implications of a

---

[5] Excellent discussions of the determinants of evasion may be found in Andreoni, Erard, and Feinstein (1998) and Slemrod and Bakija (1996).

lengthy legal code are not clear. The level of evasion and the behavior of the IRS raise several difficult issues. In this section, we examine complexity, evasion, and tax administration in the current tax system, focusing mainly on the income tax.

Complexity

The complexity, or total resource costs, of the current tax system can be divided into several components: the amount of time it takes individuals and businesses to comply with the tax system, the valuation of that time, the out-of-pocket costs incurred by taxpayers, and the administrative costs borne by government.

Three surveys, conducted during the 1980s and described in Table 7.1, provide data on the time taxpayers needed to comply with federal taxes. Slemrod and Sorum (1984) surveyed 2,000 taxpayers in Minnesota in 1983. Weighting the responses to reflect national averages, they estimated that taxpayers spent 2.1 billion hours filling out their 1982 federal and state income tax returns. Blumenthal and Slemrod (1992) repeated the survey in 1990 and found that time requirements for 1989 returns had increased to 3.0 billion hours. Unlike the earlier survey, the latter survey's estimates include time spent arranging financial affairs to minimize taxes.

The largest survey, commissioned by the IRS and conducted by Arthur D. Little Inc. (ADL, 1988), asked 6,200 taxpayers by mail about time spent preparing 1983 federal income tax returns. ADL also surveyed 4,000 partnerships and corporations and their paid preparers. ADL used the results to develop models that could be used with readily available data to estimate compliance costs in future years. To develop the models, the time for each activity (e.g., learning about tax law) associated with each form was assumed to be a linear function of the number of items on the form, the number of words of instructions and references to the IRC and regulations, or the number of pages in the form. Based on these models, ADL estimated that taxpayers spent 1.6 billion hours on 1983 individual income tax returns and 1.8 billion hours on 1985 returns. For partnerships and corporations, the estimates were 2.7 billion hours for 1983, and 3.6 billion hours for 1985.

The IRS currently uses the ADL models to estimate the time required to complete forms and schedules. These estimates are published with the tax forms as part of the "Paperwork Reduction Act Notice." For fiscal year 1997, the Office of Management and Budget (OMB, 1998) estimates that taxpayers needed 5.3 billion hours to comply with the requirements of all tax forms and IRS regulations. This estimate applies to businesses and individuals, and includes all federal taxes, not just income taxes.

Table 7.1. Surveys of Individual Taxpayer Time

Survey	Arthur D. Little	Slemrod and Sorum	Blumenthal and Slemrod
Data source	National random survey of 6,200 individuals[a]	Random survey of 2,000 Minnesota residents	Random survey of 2,000 Minnesota households
Response rate	65.3%	32.7%	43.4%
Sample size[b]	3,750	600	708
Types of returns	1983 federal income	1982 federal and state income	1989 federal and state income
Recordkeeping[c]	0.7	1.3	1.7
Learning[c]	0.3	0.2	0.4
Time with preparer[c]	—	0.4	0.2
Preparing return[c]	0.5	0.1	0.5
Sending[c]	0.1	—	—
Rearranging financial affairs[c]	—	—	0.3
Total hours[c]	1.6	2.1	3.0
Value of time	—	$10.65/hour in 1982$ $13.69/hour in 1989$	$10.09/hour in 1989$
Out-of-pocket costs	—	$44/return in 1982$ $57/return in 1989$[d]	$66/return in 1989$
Total costs for individuals	—	$26.7 billion in 1982$ $34.1 billion in 1989$	$37.6 billion in 1989$ $34.8 billion with same activities as 1982
Adjustments to survey (if any)	Survey results used to obtain models for estimating taxpayer burden; estimates above from models	Weighted nationally; accounting for biases in estimates, authors suggest estimates could be as low as $17 billion	Weighted nationally

[a] Arthur D. Little also surveyed 4,000 corporations and partnerships, with a response rate of 36.8 percent. Businesses were found to spend 1.6 billion hours on recordkeeping, 0.1 billion hours on learning, 0.1 billion hours on obtaining materials, 0.1 billion hours on finding and using a preparer, 0.7 billion hours on preparing the return, and 0.1 billion hours on sending. Total business time: 2.7 billion hours.

[b] The sample size was reduced by incomplete or inconsistent responses, as well as nonrespondents.

[c] Measured in billions of hours.

[d] Blumenthal and Slemrod report that the average out-of-pocket expenditure for 1982 taxpayers (in 1989 dollars) was $45. This appears inconsistent with the estimate shown in the Slemrod and Sorum study, which shows that the average out-of-pocket expenditure for 1982 taxpayers was $44 in 1982 dollars – which would be consistent with $56.5 in 1989 dollars.

Several features of the ADL/IRS model are problematic, however. Most obviously, complexity can be related to many factors other than the number of lines or words on a form. When complexity is related to the length of instructions on the form, the ADL model may get the sign wrong. For example, if instructions were moved off of a form and into a separate publication, the ADL model would show compliance costs falling when the change may well have actually increased compliance costs. Another set of concerns focuses on the business model (Slemrod, 1996). The model does not adjust its cost estimate for the scale of the business. Inexplicably, it overstates survey estimates of hours by partnerships, corporations, and their preparers by a factor of four or more. And the ADL study may not be very representative; it only includes one corporation with assets in excess of $250 million, and only nine with assets over $10 million.

Given an estimate of the number of hours individuals and businesses spend complying with the tax system, the next component of compliance cost requires placing a value on taxpayers' time. The surveys above did not inquire about this issue. Instead, analysts have generally imputed some measure of opportunity cost to individuals. Different methodologies result in widely varying estimates of the value of taxpayers' time (Table 7.2). Vaillancourt (1989) uses the taxpayer's pretax wage, on the grounds that this is the cost to society. Slemrod (1996) argues that taxpayers are more likely to forgo leisure than work to complete a tax return, and so uses after-tax wages. Payne (1993) and A. Hall (1995, 1996) value individual and business taxpayers' time by averaging the hourly labor costs of one of the major accounting firms and the IRS. This approach undoubtedly overstates the appropriate costs for individual taxpayers. The implicit assumption that a taxpayer and tax professional operate at the same level of efficiency when completing a tax return is doubtful and ignores the expertise the tax professional has developed. And most taxpayers do not face tax situations anywhere near as complicated as those seen by an accountant at a major firm or an IRS examiner.

Estimates of the total resource costs of operating the income tax vary widely (Table 7.2). Payne (1993) estimates costs of $277 billion (1995 dollars) for 1985.[6] A. Hall (1995, 1996) estimates costs of about $141 billion in 1995. Slemrod (1996) estimates costs of $75 billion in 1995. The differences between these estimates are driven largely by two factors: whether to use the results from the ADL business model or the business survey, and how to value the time spent by businesses and individuals.

---

[6] Payne calculates a total cost of $514 billion, but about $237 billion is primarily attributable to "disincentives to production," or the excess burden caused by distortions in relative prices. These costs are generally not included in compliance estimates.

Table 7.2. Estimates of Costs of Operating Income Tax System: 1995

Components	Slemrod 1995	Hall[a] 1995	Payne (1985 in 1995$)
Individuals			
Hours data	Blumenthal and Slemrod	OMB estimates of average hours (ADL models for 1995)	ADL models for 1985
Total hours	2.8 billion	1.2 billion	1.8 billion
Valuation	$15/hour (after-tax hourly wage)	$39.6/hour (average labor cost of IRS and Price-Waterhouse)	$40/hour (average labor cost of IRS and Arthur Andersen)
Value of time	$42 billion	$46 billion	$73 billion
Out-of-pocket	$8 billion	—	$8 billion
Total costs	$50 billion	$46 billion	$81 billion
Businesses			
Hours data	ADL survey in 1983	OMB estimates of average hours (ADL models for 1995)	ADL models for 1985
Total hours	800 million	2.4 billion	3.6 billion
Valuation	$25/hour	$39.6/hour (average labor cost of IRS and Price-Waterhouse)	$40/hour (average labor cost of IRS and Arthur Andersen)
Total costs	$20 billion	$95 billion	$145 billion
Other taxpayer costs	NA	NA	$27 billion[b] (avoidance, evasion) $18 billion (enforcement burden)
Total compliance costs	$70 billion	$141 billion	$271 billion
Total administrative costs	$5 billion	—	$6 billion
Total operating costs	$75 billion	—	$277 billion

Notes: ADL = Arthur D. Little Inc.; IRS = Internal Revenue Service; OMB = Office of Management and Budget.

[a] Hall includes individual income tax returns with Schedules C and F in the business category. The other estimates include these returns in the individual category.

[b] Payne would include $236 billion that he estimates represents the distortionary effects of the income tax. Such costs are not typically included in the operating costs of the tax system and are not included in the table.

Both Payne and Hall use the results from the ADL model, which appears to overstate the relevant costs. Slemrod uses the results from the survey. Both Hall and Payne value taxpayer time at the cost of tax professionals' time, which is problematic for the reasons stated. Slemrod values taxpayers' time at the after-tax wage.

Given the existing data, it is possible to suggest a range of plausible estimates of the annual costs of operating the income tax. Slemrod's $75 billion estimate provides a realistic lower bound. An upper-bound estimate of $130 billion is obtained by adjusting Hall's estimate for the value of time (using Slemrod's estimate of $15 an hour rather than Hall's estimate of $39.60), and adding individuals' out-of-pocket expenditures ($8 billion that Slemrod and Payne include) and tax administrative costs ($5 to $7 billion).

All of these estimates are based on taxpayer surveys. However, although they may provide the best available information to date, the survey results should be interpreted with caution. All of the surveys have low response rates. They do not distinguish between permanent and transitory costs. The surveys omit compliance costs imposed on taxpayers after returns are filed (except for Payne, who provides only a rough estimate of audit costs). It is unclear whether survey respondents have netted out the cost of nontax activities, or distinguished the costs of one tax from other taxes. In addition, the surveys were undertaken in the 1980s and are now dated. Several major and minor tax bills have become law over the past fifteen to twenty years. It is not evident that the IRS methodology captures these changes. Over the same period, technological change has generally worked to reduce compliance costs. For example, when the IRS initiated the first pilot of electronic filing in 1986, a handful of professional tax preparers electronically transmitted 25,000 returns. By 2000, over 35 million taxpayers filed electronically. In many cases, they filed from home by telephone or personal computer. The cost savings from electronic filing are not reflected in the compliance cost estimates.[7] All of these considerations suggest the need for a new, comprehensive survey of taxpayer compliance costs.

The Incidence of Complexity

Measures of resource costs indicate the total administrative burden of taxes, but provide no information about which taxpayers bear the biggest burdens. Just as the distribution of tax payments is central to policy discussions, the distribution of the burden of tax complexity is also worth considering.

---

[7] The IRS web site, launched in 1996, enables taxpayers to download forms and publications and registered 968 million "hits" during the 2000 filing season.

For most taxpayers, direct contact with the income tax is relatively simple. In 1998, 17 percent of taxpayers filed the 1040EZ, a very simplified version of the standard 1040 form.[8] An additional 21 percent of taxpayers filed the 1040A. Relative to the 1040EZ, the 1040A requires more information and contains several more complicated provisions, but it is still fairly simple.[9] The remaining taxpayers filed the standard 1040 form. About 8 percent of taxpayers filed the 1040 but were eligible to file a 1040A or 1040EZ. An additional 6 percent did not itemize their deductions, did not claim capital gains or losses, and did not have business income (defined to include business net income or loss, rents, royalties, farm net income, farm rental income, partnerships, S-corporations, estates and trusts). These figures show that in 1998, over half of taxpayers either filed a simplified form or filed the 1040 but did not itemize deductions, have business income, or report net capital gains. Thus, for most taxpayers, filling out an income tax form is relatively straightforward.

Survey estimates support these findings. Blumenthal and Slemrod (1992) found that, while the average taxpayer reported spending 27.4 hours on filing income tax returns and related activities, 30 percent spent less than 5 hours, and 15 percent spent between 5 and 10 hours. At the high end, 11 percent spent 50–100 hours and 5 percent spent more than 100 hours. Out-of-pocket costs averaged $66 (in 1989 dollars), but 49 percent of filers had no such costs and another 17 percent had costs below $50. Slightly over 7 percent spent more than $200. Expenditures of time and money were highest among high-income and self-employed taxpayers.

Information on the use of paid preparers may provide additional evidence on how complex individuals find the system to be. In 1998, 53 percent of tax filers used paid preparers. Among those who filed the 1040, 64 percent used preparers. Even among 1040A and 1040EZ filers, 35 percent used preparers. At first glance, these figures suggest that most taxpayers do not believe they have simple tax situations. However, it is

---

[8] To be eligible for the 1040EZ, taxpayers must be single or married filing jointly, have taxable income below $50,000, have income only from wages, salaries, tips, taxable scholarships, unemployment compensation, and interest, with taxable interest income below $400. Filers of the 1040EZ can claim personal exemptions, the standard deduction and the earned income tax credit (EITC) for workers who do not reside with children.

[9] To qualify for the 1040A, taxpayers' income must come only from wages, taxable scholarships, pensions, IRAs, unemployment compensation, social security, and interest and dividends. Taxpayers may report IRA contributions, student loan interest deductions, personal exemptions, the standard deduction, the EITC, the child tax credit, the child and dependent care tax credit, education tax credits, and the credit for the elderly and disabled, and exemptions for the elderly and blind. Taxable income must be below $50,000. Some of the issues arising for 1040A filers include head-of-household filing status, dependency rules, child-related credits, and, in rare cases, the alternative minimum tax (AMT).

not entirely clear how to interpret the figures. Some individuals use preparers to obtain quicker refunds through electronic filing. Also, with relatively high income and often little leisure, many families pay others to clean their homes, plan their retirement nest egg, and handle other tasks; that they have turned to professional tax preparers as well may not provide any evidence about complexity.

Complexity and Corporate Taxes

The factors most likely to create high compliance costs for large corporations include depreciation rules, the measurement and taxation of international income, the corporate alternative minimum tax, and coordinating federal and state income taxes (Slemrod and Blumenthal, 1996). In addition, the largest firms are almost continually audited, and final resolution of corporation tax returns can stretch over several years. Nevertheless, the magnitude of compliance costs and the impact of tax complexity on firm operations are controversial.

At one end of the spectrum, company representatives have testified in Congress that it cost Mobil $10 million in 1993 to prepare its U.S. tax return, which comprised a year's worth of work for 57 people. These costs sound astonishingly high at first glance, but closer examination suggests otherwise. In 1993, Mobil operated in over 100 countries and had worldwide revenues of $65 billion and profits of about $4 billion. Mobil's revenues exceeded the GDP of 137 countries and 22 of the states in the United States. Mobil's self-reported costs of compliance were about 0.015 percent of revenues and 0.25 percent of profits. Viewed in this context, the burden imposed by compliance with the U.S. income tax appears relatively small.[10]

In contrast, a recent study of the Hewlett-Packard corporation concluded that "a large U.S. multinational company can complete an accurate corporate tax return with the functional equivalent of three full-time tax professionals" (Seltzer 1997, p. 493). It would be interesting to know why Mobil's return required so many more resources than Hewlett-Packard's. To the extent that the problem lies in the tax system, it would be useful to know which features caused the problems.

Evasion

One measure of evasion is the "tax gap," the difference between taxes that should have been paid on income earned in legal activities and taxes that were paid on that income in a voluntary and timely manner. The tax gap does not include revenues lost to the underground economy. IRS

---

[10] In the same year, Mobil paid $19 million in U.S. income taxes and its total worldwide tax burden was $1.931 billion.

Table 7.3. Misreported Income on Individual Tax Returns, 1992

	Percentage of Total Misreported Income	Percentage of Tax Return Line Item Misreported
Subject to withholding and reporting requirements		
Wages and salaries	8.4	0.9
Subject to reporting requirements only		
Dividends	2.1	7.6
Pension and annuities	3.0	3.9
Interest	1.3	2.2
Unemployment compensation	0.8	6.7
Social Security	0.4	4.1
Capital gains	3.3	6.9
Not subject to withholding or reporting requirements		
Nonfarm proprietor income	26.1	31.3
Informal supplier income	21.5	81.4
Farm income	6.3	31.3
Form 4747	1.4	27.1
Other	25.5	—

Source: U.S. Department of the Treasury (1996). Estimates based on tax deficiencies ultimately assessed after all appeals and litigation have been completed.

estimates of the tax gap stem from audits in the Taxpayer Compliance Measurement Program (TCMP). The TCMP randomly selects taxpayers for audit. The most recent TCMP was conducted in 1988.

Based on the 1988 TCMP, the IRS (1996) estimates the tax gap in the individual income tax in 1992 was between $93 billion and $95 billion. This represents 17 percent of potential individual income tax liability, and 20 percent of actual revenue collected. About 61 percent of the gap is due to underreported income, 15 percent is due to overstated deductions and credits, and 14 percent comes from taxpayers who do not file returns but who should have. The rest comes from underpayment of tax liabilities that were correctly reported. The overall tax gap, including the corporate tax, was $128 billion, or 18 percent of potential revenues from the corporate and individual income taxes (Willis, 1997; General Accounting Office, 1998).

Evasion rates vary considerably by type of income. Compliance is highest for income subject to withholding by a third party. For example, employers subtract taxes from employees' paychecks and send the funds directly to government. As shown in Table 7.3, 99 percent of wage income earned by filers was reported to the IRS in 1992. Compliance rates are lower for income that does not have taxes withheld but that is reported separately to the IRS by a third party when payments are made. The underreporting rate is about 2 percent for interest income and between 4 and 8 percent for social security benefits, dividends, pensions, capital gains, and unemployment insurance. Compliance rates are lowest for income that does not have taxes withheld and is not reported separately to the IRS. About 30 percent of income from farms and nonfarm proprietors (i.e., small business) goes unreported. In the informal supplier sector (e.g., baby sitters and flea markets), underreporting exceeds 80 percent.

These results suggest that there are currently two enforcement tiers. For taxpayers who receive most of their income from wages, the IRS is able to match virtually all returns to wages reported by the employer and verify the existence of their dependents by checking social security numbers. In contrast, individuals with significant income from sole proprietorships or farms have much greater opportunities to evade taxes.

Administering the Tax System: The Internal Revenue Service

Popularity may not be possible for an organization such as the Internal Revenue Service that is charged with making sure that people regularly surrender a sizable fraction of their incomes. But at least grudging acceptance of the IRS's legitimacy is essential because effective tax collection is possible only if the vast majority of citizens voluntarily complies with the laws. To achieve and sustain such compliance, filers must feel they are paying taxes for a government they fundamentally support under a tax system that is perceived as fair and efficient. That sense of justice and efficiency requires that the IRS has the capacity to detect abuse and enforce the tax laws without needlessly harassing honest filers.

In recent years, an external commission and congressional investigations have revealed several shortcomings in IRS administration that call justice and efficiency into question. In congressional hearings, taxpayers accused the IRS of abusive behavior, while IRS employees charged the agency with treating taxpayers unfairly. Complaints were also heard regarding the lack of long-term planning (due in part to the short tenure of IRS commissioners) and poor customer service (arising from inadequate training and supervision and insufficient use of computer technology).

The IRS Reform and Restructuring Act of 1998 instituted various corrective measures to address these problems. The law gave the commissioner of the IRS, its chief executive, a fixed five-year term, and broadened the commissioner's powers to replace top management. It established an external supervisory board, consisting of public and private members, to oversee the work of the IRS. It extended a Taxpayer Bill of Rights that proscribes revenue quotas for auditors, limits the authority of the IRS to seize property, and protects people from being held responsible for the tax liabilities of former spouses.

Given all of the complaints, some important facts regarding the IRS tend to be downplayed. First, enforcement activities bring in a substantial amount of revenue. The IRS estimates that it raised $14.9 billion through enforcement actions on 1992 individual income tax returns. By way of comparison, the entire IRS budget in fiscal year 1993 was $7.1 billion, of which only $3.8 billion was spent on tax law enforcement. Second, although audits are discussed frequently and are clearly a concern of many taxpayers, fewer than 2 percent of individual tax returns and fewer than 3 percent of corporate returns are audited. The proportion of returns that are audited has fallen over time, in part because the IRS has become more efficient at choosing returns for audit. In the 1960s, the IRS did not make any tax changes on more than 40 percent of audited returns; since then, the "no change" rate has fallen to between 10 and 15 percent. Finally, the Government Accounting Office (GAO) (1999) found no evidence to support some of the most egregious charges of unfair treatment of taxpayers made during the congressional hearings.

The continuing reform of the IRS raises fundamental and difficult questions about the proper managerial stance for the nation's revenue agency. Abusive practices create public anger and can erode voluntary compliance. But so too can administrative laxity that permits people to cheat with impunity. If the IRS is unduly draconian, it courts the first risk. Procedural hurdles that prevent it from aggressively pursuing evaders raise the second risk. Although there can be no doubt that the IRS needed administrative modernization and that taxpayer rights must be protected, recent legislation will need careful monitoring to ensure that the agency retains the power to do an inherently unpopular job.

Modifying the Existing Tax System

Besides the IRS reforms discussed thus far, modifications to the structure and administration of the existing tax system could have significant effects on complexity and evasion rates. For example, broadening the base by eliminating targeted preferences and taxing capital gains as ordinary income directly removes major sources of complexity. Using the revenue raised to increase standard deductions removes people from the tax system, and using the revenue to reduce tax rates reduces the value of sheltering and cheating. Increasing the number of people who face the same "basic" rate facilitates withholding of taxes at the source, which further simplifies taxes and raises compliance. In short, broadening the base and reducing the rates, which in general may be considered efficiency-enhancing, would also simplify taxes (see Pechman, 1990; Slemrod, 1996; Slemrod and Bakija, 1996; Gale, 1997, 1998c).

Slemrod (1996) refers to such plans as "populist simplification." That is, they make taxes simpler for a large number of taxpayers, but the overall saving in compliance costs may not be very large. He estimates that simplification could reduce individual and business compliance costs by 15 and 5 percent, respectively. If so, the cost saving would be about $8.5 billion, compared to his $75 billion estimate of overall resource costs.

Not all structural reforms, of course, have the same impact on compliance costs. Slemrod (1989b) found no significant saving from changing to a single-rate tax structure. In contrast, eliminating the system of itemized deductions would result in a substantial reduction in expenditures on professional assistance; the impact on total compliance costs, though, varied depending on the model used.

Notably, proposals that simplify the tax system would likely raise compliance rates as well. The combination of lower rates, less variation in rates across sources and uses of income, and increased withholding, which would be facilitated by a flatter rate structure, could reduce both intentional and unintentional tax evasion.

Another strategy for reform is to focus on reducing filing burdens. Thirty-six countries use some form of a return-free system for at least some of their taxpayers (GAO, 1996). In these countries, an end-of-year filing requirement was replaced with greater reliance on withholding throughout the year and end-of-year reconciliation by the tax agency. Gale and Holtzblatt (1997) found that 52 million U.S. taxpayers could be placed on a return-free system with relatively minor changes in the structure of the income tax. These include taxpayers who have income only from wages, pensions, social security, interest, dividends, and unemployment compensation; do not take itemized deductions or credits other than the child tax credit and the earned income tax credit; and are in the zero or 15 percent tax bracket.

Nevertheless, the net cost savings may not be great. Over 80 percent of the affected taxpayers currently file the relatively simple 1040A and 1040EZ returns and the others file 1040s but have relatively simple returns. Taxpayers subject to a return-free system would still have to provide information to tax authorities on a regular basis. Some administrative costs would merely be shifted from taxpayers to employers, other payers, and the IRS. And if state income taxes were not similarly

196   *William G. Gale and Janet Holtzblatt*

altered, many taxpayers would still need to calculate almost all of the information currently needed on the federal return.[11]

Lastly, procedural changes in the tax policy process might indirectly help to simplify taxes by raising the visibility and explicit consideration of simplicity and enforcement issues. For example, the recent IRS restructuring legislation requires the IRS to report to Congress each year regarding sources of complexity in the administration of federal taxes. The Joint Committee on Taxation (JCT) is required to prepare complexity analysis of new legislation that impacts individuals or small businesses. Another way to increase the visibility of simplification issues is for the U.S. Treasury or a congressional agency to release an annual list of simplification proposals. A U.S. Treasury "blue book" released in 1997 contained over fifty proposals for simplification, two of which were enacted later that year. The IRS restructuring act requires the JCT to include simplification proposals in biennial reports on the state of the federal tax system.

ADMINISTRATIVE ISSUES IN THE NATIONAL RETAIL SALES TAX

A national retail sales tax has been proposed recently by Congressmen Dan Schaefer (R.-Colorado) and Billy Tauzin (R.-Louisiana) and by a group called Americans for Fair Taxation (AFT).[12] The sales tax base would include almost all goods or services purchased in the United States by households for consumption purposes. The imputed value of financial intermediation services would also be taxed.[13] To tax households' consumption of goods and services provided by government, all federal, state, and local government outlays would be subject to federal sales tax. The tax would exempt expenditures abroad, half of foreign travel expenditures by U.S. citizens, state sales tax, college tuition (on the grounds that it is an investment), and food produced and consumed on farms (for administrative reasons).[14]

[11] Another option is to subsidize electronic filing (Steuerle, 1997). Electronic filing may help reduce error rates because returns are often prepared using computer software programs with built-in accuracy checks, and it prevents key punch errors that could otherwise occur at the IRS. The IRS restructuring act establishes a goal that 80 percent of tax returns should be filed electronically by 2007. In February 2000 the Clinton administration proposed a temporary refundable credit for electronic filing of individual income tax returns to help achieve this goal. The proposal was not enacted in 2000.

[12] See H.R. 2001 (1997).

[13] For example, households purchase banking services through reduced interest rates on their checking account, and the value of these implicit payments would be included in the tax base.

[14] Retail sales occur when a business sells to a household. Thus, purchases of newly constructed housing by owner-occupants would be taxable, but resales of existing homes would not be.

The sales tax would provide a demogrant to each household equal to the sales tax rate times the poverty guideline, the annual income level below which a family of a given size is considered in poverty. States would collect the sales tax, and businesses and states would be reimbursed for tax collection efforts. The IRS would monitor tax collection for businesses with retail sales in numerous states.

The required tax rate in a national retail sales tax merits attention. Tax rates can be described in two ways. For example, suppose a good costs $100, not including taxes, and there is a $30 sales tax placed on the item. The "tax-exclusive" rate is 30 percent, because the tax is 30 percent of the selling price, excluding the tax. This rate is calculated as T/P, where T is the total tax payment and P is the pre-sales-tax price. The "tax-inclusive" rate would be about 23 percent, because the tax is 23 percent of the total payment, including the tax. This rate is calculated as $T/(P + T)$. Sales taxes are typically quoted in tax-exclusive rates; this corresponds to the percentage "markup" at the cash register. Income taxes, however, are typically quoted at tax-inclusive rates. The reported tax-inclusive rate will always be lower than the tax-exclusive rate and the difference rises as tax rates rise.

The AFT proposal assumes a 23 percent tax-inclusive rate (30 percent tax-exclusive). The Schaefer-Tauzin proposal assumes a 15 percent tax-inclusive rate (17.6 percent tax-exclusive). The difference in rates in the two proposals is due to the different taxes slated for abolition. Both proposals would abolish taxes on individual income, corporate income, and estates. The AFT would also eliminate payroll taxes, which raise considerable sums currently, while the Schaefer-Tauzin proposal would eliminate excise taxes, which raise little revenue.

The actual required rates would be much higher, however, for several reasons (Gale, 1999). First, the plans stipulate that the government must pay sales tax to itself on its own purchases but fail to allow for an increase in the real cost of maintaining government services. Fixing this problem alone raises the required rate in the AFT proposal to 35 percent on a tax-inclusive basis and 54 percent on a tax-exclusive basis (Table 7.4). Second, the plans do not allow for any avoidance or evasion, though it is universally acknowledged that both will occur. Third, the plans propose to tax an extremely broad measure of consumption, but political and administrative factors would very likely require a narrower base. Conservative adjustments for these factors raise the required tax-inclusive rate to 48 percent and the tax-exclusive rate to 94 percent in the AFT proposal, and 35 percent and 54 percent, respectively, in the Schaefer-Tauzin proposal (Table 7.4).

The remainder of this section examines tax complexity, evasion, and tax administration in the context of a high-rate national retail sales tax. We find that complexity would not be an overwhelming problem in the

Table 7.4. Required National Sales Tax Rates, %

	Tax-Inclusive	Tax-Exclusive
To replace income, payroll, and estate taxes		
(1) AFT Proposal	23	30
(2) = (1) Adjusted to hold government constant	35	54
(3) = (2) Adjusted for 10% statutory base erosion	39	65
(4) = (3) Allowing for 17% avoidance and evasion rate	48	94
To replace income, estate, and excise taxes		
(1) Schaefer-Tauzin	15	18
(2) = (1) Adjusted to hold government constant	23	30
(3) = (2) Adjusted for 10% statutory base erosion	27	37
(4) = (3) Allowing for 17% avoidance and evasion rate	35	54

Source: Authors' calculations, using 1995 data and methods in Gale (1999).

NRST, but the ability to administer and enforce the tax may prove quite difficult.

Complexity

As a flat-rate consumption tax with a universal demogrant, the sales tax contains many of the features that generate simpler taxes. In principle at least, the simplicity gains could be impressive. Most individuals would no longer need to keep tax records, know the tax law, or file returns. The number of taxpayers who would have to file would decline significantly and would include only those sole proprietorships, partnerships, and S- and C-corporations that made retail sales. The complexity of filing a return would decline dramatically as well.

Nevertheless, a NRST could create new areas of complexity. The demogrant is based on the Health and Human Services (HHS) poverty guidelines, which rise less than proportionally with the number of family members. For example, in 1998, the poverty level was $8,050 for a single individual, plus $2,800 for each additional family member. Thus, the poverty level for a family of four was $16,450, just over twice the level for an individual. This structure will create incentives in many households for citizens to try to claim the demogrant as individuals rather than families. It is also not obvious from AFT descriptions how the demogrants would be administered, or even which agencies would be responsible for determining eligibility and monitoring taxpayers. Thus, the compliance and administrative costs of ensuring that the appropriate demogrant is paid could be significant.

Another area of potential complexity stems from tax avoidance and evasion behavior. The primary way to avoid sales taxes would be to combine business activity with personal consumption. For example, individuals may seek to register as firms or may seek to purchase their own consumption goods using a business certificate, and employers might buy goods for their workers in lieu of wage compensation (GAO, 1998). Ensuring that all business purchases are not taxed and all consumer purchases are taxed would require record keeping by all businesses, even though only retailers would have to remit taxes in a pure retail sales tax. The AFT proposal deviates from a pure retail sales tax by requiring that taxes be paid on many input purchases and that vendors file explicit claims to receive rebates on their business purchases. This would raise compliance costs further.

A second source of tax avoidance and evasion concerns the importation of goods and services from abroad. Imported purchases of up to $2,000 per year per taxpayer would be exempt from the sales tax. This feature is likely to be exploited fully by many taxpayers, not because they travel abroad but because it would be very simple for firms to set up off-shore affiliates, warehouses, or mail order houses and ship goods to domestic customers. Moreover, it would be very difficult to monitor such arrangements and it seems quite likely that taxpayers could end up importing more than $2,000 per person on a tax-exempt basis. Some related evidence on the potential extent of these problems comes from the experience with state-level "use" taxes under which taxpayers voluntarily make tax payments on goods purchased in other states. Enforcement of such taxes has been "dismal at best" (Murray, 1997a). The development of electronic commerce could raise many additional avoidance and evasion problems for the sales tax.

There are no rigorous estimates of the compliance and administrative costs associated with a high-rate NRST. Some evidence is available with respect to state sales taxes. Slemrod and Bakija (1996) report that administrative costs were between 0.4 and 1.0 percent of sales tax revenues in a sample of eight states, and compliance costs were between 2.0 and 3.8 percent of revenues in seven states. A. Hall (1995) cites a Price-Waterhouse study that found that retailers spent $4.4 billion complying with state retail sales taxes in 1990. Adjusting for increased retail sales between 1990 and 1995, he asserts a NRST with no demogrant would have administrative costs of $4.9 billion.[15]

---

[15] Adopting IRS time estimates of the costs of completing the schedules for interest and dividends, the child and dependent care tax credit, and the EITC, Hall estimates that adding a demogrant would cost $6.3 billion and thus raise the total cost to $11.2 billion. A. Hall (1996) estimates that taxpayers would spend $8.2 billion to comply with the

Unfortunately, as Slemrod and Bakija (1996) note, compliance cost estimates from state sales taxes are likely to understate vastly the analogous costs in an NRST for several reasons. First, at 4 and 6 percent, state sales tax rates are an order of magnitude lower than the required rate in an NRST (Table 7.4). The higher rates in an NRST would encourage more taxpayers to engage in time-consuming taxpayer avoidance and evasion activities than under the existing state sales taxes, and this, in turn, would increase the required tax rate and compliance and administrative costs. Second, state sales tax bases are very different from the proposed federal base. States sales taxes typically include a significant amount of business purchases (Ring, 1999). This reduces compliance costs, because distinguishing business and retail sales is costly. To avoid taxing business in an NRST may require all businesses to file returns and receive rebates, which would raise costs. State sales taxes often exclude hard-to-tax sectors. All states exempt financial services from their retail sales taxes, but the NRST would not. Third, states do not provide demogrants.

On the other hand, states often exempt from taxation goods such as food, housing, rent, and health care, for political or social reasons. This increases compliance costs relative to taxing a broader base because defining the boundaries of the exemption (e.g., distinguishing "food" and "candy") can be difficult, and record-keeping requirements can be extensive. However, if an NRST required high rates, there would be massive political pressure to exempt goods like food, health care, and rent.

Evasion

Because the sales tax offers such drastic changes in the structure and administration of taxes, it could influence evasion in a number of different ways.

Rates of Evasion on Legally Generated Income

Several aspects of the sales tax would affect evasion rates relative to the current system. Simpler tax forms would reduce unintentional evasion. But any realistic formulation of the federal sales tax rate that holds the real size of government constant would be high compared with the 35 percent corporate income tax rate faced by larger corporations and the 39.6 percent tax rate faced by high-income sole proprietors (Table 7.4). Many corporations and sole proprietors, of course, face even lower rates in the current system. Higher marginal tax rates increase the return to

Schaefer-Tauzin NRST. The estimate was also based on experience with state sales taxes. It does not include the compliance costs of payroll tax credits, used in the Schaefer-Tauzin plan, to rebate sales taxes.

cheating and so plausibly would increase intentional evasion under the sales tax relative to the existing system.

As noted earlier, another important determinant of evasion is whether anyone other than the taxpayer withholds taxes or reports the tax liability to the government. Under the current system, most income and payroll taxes are collected via third-party withholding and reporting to the government, and feature extremely high compliance rates. Evasion rates on sole proprietorship income are much higher. The retail sales tax would be collected only from businesses that make retail sales, and there would be no withholding or reporting by anyone other than the business itself. That is, the entity reporting the tax payment would also be the entity legally responsible for the tax liability. This suggests that the possibility of high rates of evasion needs to be taken quite seriously. In addition, the parties that would be responsible for remitting taxes under an NRST have average or higher than average evasion rates under the existing system (Table 7.3).

Moreover, rates of 35 percent or more would make it very attractive to evade the NRST. Those with business certificates would have considerable incentive and opportunity to use them for nonexempt purchases. As a consequence, the tax system would need high audit rates and more information collected on the identity of the buyer of exempt goods. The lack of third-party withholding will also make it difficult to collect high-rate sales taxes from a number of small-scale service industries – taxi cab drivers, plumbers, handymen, painters, and maids are classic examples. Another potential concern is the possibility of many small tax-evading retailers, who are able to set up businesses (possibly offshore but also on the Internet) with low overheads and are effectively created by the prospect of being able to undercut legitimate retailers by 35 percent or more.

The precipitous decline in the number of filers under an NRST compared with that under the current system could also affect evasion. With fewer filers, and the same number of audits, each taxpayer faces a higher probability of audit and therefore is more likely to comply with the tax code. However, several factors would tend to offset this effect. First, in the sales tax (as in the current system), *all* businesses would potentially be subject to audit, not just retailers, to ensure proper use of business certificates. Second, under the sales tax, businesses would likely file monthly, which would vastly increase the number of returns filed and would offset much of the gains from having fewer taxpayers. Third, audits at the firm level are probably more labor-intensive than audits for most individuals, so the number of business audits that could be performed would be smaller than the number of individual audits. Lastly, audits in the income tax appear to be well targeted; 85 percent or more of audits result in changes in tax payments. Audits of sales tax returns are likely to be less well targeted.[16] We conjecture that these four factors would offset much or all of the compliance gains that derive from having fewer tax filers under the NRST than under the existing system.

The Underground Economy

Sales tax advocates often claim the NRST would be more effective than the current system at raising revenue from the underground economy. The classic example is that of a drug dealer who currently does not pay income tax on the money he earns, but would be forced to pay sales taxes under an NRST if he took the funds and bought, for example, a Mercedes. The problem with this argument is laid out by Representative Richard Armey (1995). "If there is an income tax in place, he [the drug dealer] won't report his income. If there is a sales tax in place, he won't collect taxes from his customers" and send the taxes to government. In the end, to a first-order approximation, neither system taxes the drug trade.[17]

Estimates of the Overall Evasion Rate

Unfortunately, no reliable estimates of evasion rates exist for high-rate national sales taxes. Evasion does not appear to be a huge problem in existing state sales taxes. A study by the state of Florida estimated that about 5 percent of tax-free business purchases involved abuse or misuse of business exemption certificates, based on a sample limited to selected business sectors. GAO (1998) found that audit assessments accounted for between 1 and 3 percent of sales tax revenues in about twenty-two states in 1992. Mikesell (1997, p. 150) writes that "few believe [state-level] sales tax compliance rates to be a severe problem, although that belief stems more from faith rather than from research."

There is little reason, however, to believe that evasion rates in state sales taxes are a useful guide to evasion in a national sales tax. The most

---

[16] Income tax audits are well targeted in part because the IRS has become very efficient, with the use of administrative data and TCMP findings, in identifying questionable returns for further investigation. Under existing state sales taxes, the states with the best audit programs seem to rely heavily on cross-checking with income tax returns or using past compliance record data for the firm or industry (Due and Mikesell, 1995). If the U.S. replaced the income tax with a sales tax, the former source of information would disappear, and at least initially, there would not be much experience at the national level with the much higher-rate and broader-based NRST to identify firms or industries with potentially bad compliance records. On the other hand, publicly available financial information may be of some use to authorities as a cross-check.

[17] Some additional effects, though, may complicate the analysis. For example, the effective tax rate on drug dealers and their customers may differ, and the drugs may be purchased with income generated illegally.

obvious difference between the state taxes and a hypothetical national sales tax is that the latter would require substantially higher tax rates. In addition, states currently piggyback on federal enforcement efforts, which are in turn aided by the existence of an income tax with its various reporting requirements. These would vanish if the income tax were abolished.

Administration

Under the AFT plan, states would administer the federal sales tax, and the IRS, or some national tax agency, would only be involved in collecting taxes from firms that operate in many states. Although many states already have sales taxes, however, it seems extremely unlikely that states would be in a good position to administer and enforce a federal sales tax. Five states currently do not have state sales taxes and so would need to develop an entirely new tax apparatus. In addition, existing state sales taxes do not conform with each other and fall far short of the ideals laid out in the AFT plan. Although the AFT would allow states to keep 1 percent of the revenue they remit to the federal government, states would still have very weak incentives to collect federal taxes other than those that flowed in due to voluntary compliance. This problem would be reduced to the extent that states conformed their sales taxes to the federal base, so that they would collect state sales taxes on any additional sales found during audits for federal taxes. Even in this case, however, it would be an interesting issue to determine whether state or federal authorities would be responsible if federal revenues went uncollected. Finally, states differ considerably in their audit coverage and technical support of audit staff. This would seem to raise problems of tax equity in a federal system.

Summary and Discussion

It is difficult to predict the resource costs and evasion rates in a high-rate, national retail sales tax because no such tax has ever existed. Our reading of the available evidence, however, is pessimistic. We believe the combination of a required high sales tax rate, coupled with the ability to avoid and evade the tax, and the political pressure to exempt particular goods, will create a vicious cycle of sorts. For example, even if there is no avoidance or evasion, and no shrinkage of the tax base for political or administrative reasons, an NRST would require a tax-inclusive rate of about 35 percent (Table 7.4) to hold the size of government constant. This would correspond to a markup at the cash register in excess of 50 percent. These rates would create huge incentives to avoid and evade taxes, and there would be significant opportunities to do so, due to the possibility of importing tax-free from abroad and the lack of third-party withholding. There would also be huge political pressure to exempt certain goods – food, housing, health – which collectively account for a large portion of consumption. The resulting erosion of the tax base – due to avoidance, evasion, and political pressures – would in turn require higher tax rates to meet a given revenue target. This in turn would create more incentives to evade and avoid, and more political pressure to exempt other commodities, which would require higher rates, and so on.

Thus, in our view, it is quite possible that the NRST would prove to be unworkable. This conclusion is by no means extreme relative to previous analysis. Bartlett (1995), Casanegra (1987), McLure (1987), OECD (1998), Slemrod (1996), Tait (1988), and Tanzi (1995) also conclude that retail sales taxes in the 30–40 percent range would be unworkable. Retail sales taxes at higher rates, which Table 7.4 suggests would be required, would be even more difficult to enforce.[18]

To address administrative problems and other concerns with the retail sales tax, many countries have employed value-added taxes (VATs). VATs are paid by businesses and impose taxes on all sales, including business-to-business transactions. Each business owes taxes on its sales and receives deductions or credits to account for the taxes it paid on its purchases. Controlling for administrative factors, the net economic effect of a VAT should be the same as an NRST. The key administrative advantage of a VAT over an NRST is that the existence of a paper trail can improve compliance rates. The chief disadvantage is the added compliance costs created. See Cnossen (Chapter 8 in this volume) for further discussion.

Mieszkowski and Palumbo (1998) describe a "hybrid NRST" that would add the following features to a retail sales tax: taxes would be due on all sales of multipurpose goods and services used as final consumption goods or business inputs; businesses would file for rebates for the taxes collected on business inputs; and sales taxes would be withheld at preretail stages of production and distribution, such that taxes collected at one stage of production and distribution are credited at the next stage.[19] This system would improve compliance relative to the NRST by developing a more extensive paper trail to identify suspicious returns and facilitate tax audits. However, the tax would also be more complex. A system of cross-checks and cross-reporting would be needed to limit fraud. The number of firms required to file would rise much closer to VAT levels than NRST levels. And businesses would file more fre-

---

[18] OECD (1998), Tait (1988), and Tanzi (1995) present evidence that the experience of other countries is consistent with this view as well. See also Cnossen (Chapter 8 in this volume) for additional discussion of the experience in other countries.

[19] See also Gillis, Mieszkowski, and Zodrow (1996), and Zodrow (1999a).

quently, perhaps on a biweekly or even weekly basis, in order to claim refunds. Mieszkowski and Palumbo concur with those who claim, as we do here, that the compliance experience of state sales taxes is not very relevant for formulating cost estimates for a high-rate national sales tax. They note that the compliance costs of a hybrid NRST would likely be "several multiples" of the $20 billion compliance cost estimates they cite for an NRST. Note that if several equals "four," the costs of complying with and administering this system would be as high as Slemrod's estimated costs for the income tax.

ADMINISTRATIVE ISSUES IN THE FLAT TAX

Originally developed by Robert Hall and Alvin Rabushka (1983, 1995), the flat tax has been proposed in legislative form by Representative Richard Armey (R.-Texas) and Senator Richard Shelby (R.-Alabama).[20] Under the flat tax, businesses would pay taxes on the difference between gross sales (including business-to-business transactions) and the sum of wages, pension contributions, and purchases from other businesses, including the cost of materials, services, and capital goods. Individuals would pay taxes on their wages and pension disbursements, less exemptions of $21,400 for a married couple ($10,700 for single filers) and $5,000 for each dependent.

Both individuals and businesses would pay the same flat tax rate, estimated by the U.S. Treasury (1996) to be 20.8 percent (on a tax-inclusive basis). As with the sales tax, realistic versions of the flat tax will require higher rates. Unlike the sales tax, however, the required rate estimate for the flat tax already incorporates evasion and avoidance, does not assume that government tries to raise revenue by taxing itself, and is not intended to replace the payroll tax. The only significant adjustments are for transition relief and the possible retention of some major deductions and credits due to political pressures. Adjusting for those factors, the required rates range between 21 and 32 percent (Table 7.5).

In this section, we examine complexity and evasion in the proposed flat tax. With the sales tax, the main concern was the rate of evasion and the eventual administrability of the tax. The flat tax would not change the administration of taxes very much. Instead, the main issue is the potential for the flat tax to become significantly more complex than originally proposed.

Complexity

As with the sales tax, the flat tax would change the tax aggregate base to consumption, flatten tax rates, eliminate all deductions and credits in

---

[20] See H.R. 1040 and S. 1040 (1997).

Table 7.5. Required Tax Rates under the Flat Tax

Alternative	Flat Rate If Only One Adjustment Is Made	If All Flat-Rate Adjustments up to This Point Are Made
Armey-Shelby flat tax (no adjustments)	20.8	20.8
Allow transition relief	23.1	23.1
Retain mortgage interest deduction	21.8	24.4
Retain health insurance deduction (businesses only)	22.3	26.5
Retain charitable contribution deduction (households only)	21.1	27.0
Retain state and local income and property tax deductions (households only)	21.6	28.4
Retain earned income tax credit	21.1	29.0
Retain payroll tax deduction (businesses)	22.3	31.9

Source: Aaron and Gale (1997).

the tax code, and vastly simplify tax compliance. For taxpayers who were not self-employed, the individual filing requirement could probably be eliminated. For those that did have to file, the tax form could be a relatively short postcard with simple calculations. The tax would eliminate individual-level taxation of capital gains, interest and dividends, and the individual alternative minimum tax (AMT).

Any well-functioning business already retains records of wages, material costs, and investments, so tax filing would impose little additional cost. The flat tax would eliminate the differential treatment of debt versus equity, the uniform capitalization rules, the corporate alternative minimum tax, depreciation schedules, rules regarding the definition of a capital good versus a current input, depletion allowances, corporate subsidies and credits, the potential to arbitrage across different accounting systems, and a host of other issues. The tax distortions currently caused by inflation would vanish.

Nevertheless, the flat tax would retain some existing sources of complexity and exacerbate others. It would also create entirely new areas of complexity, and the types of complexity it would abolish could easily creep back into the code.

The Pure Flat Tax

Some areas of the existing tax code are also common to the flat tax and would prove just as difficult as ever. These include rules regarding independent contractors versus employees, qualified dependents, tax with-holding for domestic help, home office deductions, taxation of the self-employed, and nonconformity between state and federal taxes. The treatment of travel and food expenses might also cause problems. To the extent they are a cost of doing business, the expenses should be deducted in the flat tax. To the extent they are a fringe benefit, they should not. Making this determination may prove difficult. Graetz (1997) empha-sizes the numerous problems in the existing system that would be retained in the flat tax.

A potentially more troubling issue is that, because the flat tax makes different distinctions than the existing system does, the flat tax will create new "pressure points," and so could create a host of *new* compliance and sheltering issues. For example, under the existing income tax, a firm must pay taxes on interest income as well as income from sales of goods. In the business portion of the flat tax, receipts from sales of goods and ser-vices are taxable, but interest income is not. This creates an important incentive in transactions between businesses subject to the flat tax and entities not subject to the business tax (households, governments, non-profits, and foreigners): the business would like to label as much cash inflow as possible as "interest income." The other party (not subject to the business tax component of the flat tax) is indifferent to such label-ing. The same possibility occurs for cash outflows from businesses. Outflows that are labeled purchases of goods and services or capital investments are deductible, whereas outflows that are labeled interest payments are not deductible. This creates obvious incentives for busi-nesses to label as "purchases" as much of their cash outflow as possible, and possibly seriously erode the tax base and tax revenues. Thus, although it equates the tax treatment of debt and equity flows, the flat tax creates a new wedge between inflows labeled "sales" and those labeled "interest," and a new wedge between outflows labeled "pur-chases" and those labeled "interest expense." Concerns that these wedges would be easily manipulated led McLure and Zodrow (1996a) to conclude that the business tax "contains unacceptable opportunities for abuse."

Another new area of complexity concerns wages, fringe benefits, and current operating expenses. Under the current system, all are deductible to firms. Under the flat tax, however, fringe benefits are not deductible. Gruber and Poterba (1996) speculate that this wedge could bring back the "company doctor." In the flat tax, a firm's contribution for health insurance would not be deductible, but its payment for in-house doctors, nurses, and medical equipment would be deductible.

Some flat tax rules will exacerbate existing tax complexities. The sheltering of personal consumption, especially durable goods, through business would become more important due to the more generous deduction for expensing. Conversion of business property to individual use ought to generate taxable income for the business but would be hard to monitor.

The tax treatment of mixed business and personal use raises a number of issues. A family that rents rooms in its home or has a vacation home must currently follow fairly complex rules for allocating expenses and depreciation between personal and rental use. The flat tax is based on cash flow, however, so it is not clear how such items would be handled. Suppose a taxpayer bought a home in year 1 and in year 5 decided to begin renting a room in the house. What deduction for the cost of the capital good would the homeowner be able to take? The answer should not be none because depreciation is a legitimate business expense. Nor should the answer be "expensing" because the flat tax is based on cash flow and the house did not become a business property until year 5, during which there was no house purchase. But any other answer will lead to a potentially complicated new set of rules (or the same rules that currently exist). Also, if a deduction were allowed, then the decision to stop renting the room or the vacation home after a period of time would implicitly convert a business asset to personal use and so should be taxed at the business level under the flat tax (Feld, 1995).

Current law imposes limits on how taxes or losses may be allocated among different taxpayers. These provisions regarding consolidated returns, S-corporations, and partnerships stop firms from merging solely for tax purposes. They appear to have no counterpart in the proposed flat tax. However, as Feld (1995, p. 610) notes: "the logical conclusion of unregulated allocation of deductions would allow free transferability of losses. Historically, however, the outcry against the opportunity by wealthy businesses to purchases exemption from income tax has produced the existing restrictions on the transfer of loss corporations and repeal in 1982 of the finance lease provisions of the 1981 tax act." It thus seems likely that a complex set of laws would have to be imposed to stop such behavior.

Taxpayers may also create pressure to find ways to transfer income between wages and business income. Under the flat tax, business and wage incomes are recorded on separate forms. Thus, a business loss may be carried forward, but – unlike in the current system – it cannot be used to offset current wage income.

The flat tax would create several incentives regarding cross-border flows. Firms would have incentives to engage in transactions that shifted interest expense offshore and interest income into the United States. Transfer pricing would probably work to encourage firms to locate more profits in the United States, because the tax rate would be lower here

than in most other industrialized countries. Both of these issues would
be easy to exploit and would drain revenues from foreign countries.
Some sort of retaliation, adjustment, or treaty negotiation might be
expected, which would then require changes in the tax treatment of international flows under the flat tax (Hines, 1996).

Feld (1995) highlights a variety of additional concerns with the business tax, including the role of in-kind transfers to a corporation, the
definition of a business input (and the possible need to exempt passive
assets from the definition), and possibly complex rules for hedging transactions to distinguish those that are part of the business from those that
are investments by the individual.

Despite its apparent simplicity, the individual tax also creates some
potential areas of complexity (Feld, 1995). First, the flat tax would effectively renegotiate every alimony agreement in the country. Under the
flat tax and other reform proposals, alimony payments would no longer
be deductible and alimony receipts would no longer be taxable. Second,
suppose that a victim earns money and then a robber takes it away.
Under the flat tax, the victim is still liable for taxes, and the robber is
not. Under the income tax, it is the other way around. Third, prize money
won by contestants would be deductible by the sponsoring organization
as an expense but does not appear to be taxable as wages. Addressing
any of these problems would make the flat tax more complex.

Lastly, a new system will inevitably create unintended loopholes that
will need to be addressed via corrective tax measures. It would be a
mistake to underestimate the creative ingenuity of America's accountants, attorneys, and tax planners.

To be clear, all of the concerns noted here could be resolved by writing
carefully detailed rules covering each contingency. But, of course, that is
what the current system already does. There is little reason to believe
that the ultimate resolution of most of these issues will be simpler under
the flat tax than in the current system. Feld (1995) concludes that to
avoid losing revenues, the flat tax will either generate complicated business transactions (to skirt the simple rules) or complicated tax laws (to
reduce the gaming possibilities), or both. This conclusion seems quite
reasonable to us.

Modifications to the Pure Flat Tax

All of the foregoing discussion focuses on the pure flat tax. However, if
the flat tax were implemented, "we should expect near unanimity that it
will be necessary to provide transition relief" (Pearlman, 1996). Zodrow
(Chapter 9 in this volume) concurs that some transitional relief is
"virtually inevitable." Pearlman and Zodrow discuss the various types of
transition relief that could be provided, including compensating firms for

lost depreciation deductions and carry forwards of AMT credits, net operating losses, and foreign tax credits. The treatment of interest deductions will also require attention. More generally, because taxes are embedded in the fabric of existing legal contracts, transitioning to a new tax system could potentially affect numerous aspects of agreements in other areas. The effect on alimony, noted already, is one such example. Pearlman (1996, p. 419) concludes that "inevitably, any approach [to transition relief] will make the new law more complex for a long time."

Another potential source of complexity is the reintroduction of social policy into the tax code. The pure flat tax would be devoid of all social policy initiatives. Thus, the flat tax would not only change tax policy but also reduce the generosity of subsidies toward housing, the charitable sector, families and children, education, health insurance, and state and local governments.

For each existing deduction and credit, however, a political case would be made that the subsidy should be retained. To the extent that social policy creeps back into the flat tax, there will be added complexity. Notably, because the flat tax has an individual component – whereas the sales tax, for example, does not – social policy in the flat tax can be tailored to individual circumstances. However, credits for children, child care, and education all raise issues of eligibility, compliance, and phase-outs. Retention of popular deductions would require additional record keeping, reporting, and monitoring. Retention of the mortgage interest deduction, in a system that does not tax interest income, could create arbitrage opportunities and added record-keeping costs. Corporate subsidies for research, environmental clean-up, and other goals could easily wind their way back into the business tax. And, to the extent that the demand for any of these programs remained and the tax system was able to remain clean, there is a possibility that the programs would return as spending or regulatory initiatives, thus adding complexity.

A third source of complexity in a modified flat tax concerns the real and perceived distributional effects. Families in the highest income or consumption strata would see tax burdens fall dramatically (Gale, Houser, and Scholz, 1996). The flat tax would make poor families worse off, because it would eliminate the earned income tax credit, but the increased burdens on the poor would not be as large as the reduced burdens on high-income families. The difference would be made up by increased taxes on middle-class families (Dunbar and Pogue, 1998; Gale et al., 1996; Gentry and Hubbard, 1997a; Mieszkowski and Palumbo, Chapter 6 in this volume).[21]

---

[21] Fullerton and Rogers (1996) and Metcalf (1997) show that the distributional impacts over taxpayers' lifetime are not as extreme as those on an annual basis. The relevance of this finding for political support of the flat tax, however, is debatable.

It seems unlikely that these distributional effects will pass political muster. Retaining the earned income tax credit would reduce much of the distributional loss of the pure flat tax (Gale et al., 1996), but would raise compliance costs. Moving to a Bradford-style X-tax (which would use the flat tax base, but has graduated tax rates on wages and sets the business tax rate at the highest wage tax rate) would provide more progressivity but would also create administrative and compliance problems. It would significantly increase the revenue loss from transition relief. This would require higher tax rates on the remaining tax base. It would reintroduce taxpayer incentives and attempts to redistribute income across people or over time to exploit tax rate differentials. By raising tax rates at the high end of the income distribution, it would increase political pressure to restore popular itemized deductions.

A number of issues regarding what economists might describe as perceptions of fairness also arise. For example, there will be an inexorable tendency to compare the flat tax to an income tax because both are collected from individuals and businesses. Despite the fact that some taxes on capital income will be collected at the business level, the nontaxation of capital income at the individual level may upset citizens who are used to seeing people remit taxes directly to the government on the capital income they receive.[22]

Several perception issues arise in the business tax. Unlike the current corporate or individual business taxes, the business tax in the flat tax does not attempt to tax profits. Changing the entire logic and structure of business taxation will create several situations that will be perceived as problems by taxpayers and firms, even if they make perfect sense within the overall logic of the flat tax.

First, some businesses would face massive increases in their tax liabilities. For example, Hall and Rabushka ([1985] 1995) note that General Motors's tax liability would have risen from $110 million in 1993 under the current system to $2.7 *billion* under a 19 percent flat tax. Despite economists' view that individuals – not businesses – bear the burden of taxes, there will likely be massive resistance at the business level to such changes. Businesses who oppose such change will demand reductions in the tax base or other types of relief.

Second, some businesses with large profits will pay no taxes. Profit (before federal taxes) is equal to revenue from sales and other sources less deductions for depreciation, interest payments, materials, wages, fringe benefits, payroll taxes, and state and local income and property

---

[22] The flat tax would not tax the normal return to capital, only the excess return. That reduction in the effective tax rate on capital income may be a source of added controversy in the flat tax, but it is distinct from the issue addressed in the text, which concerns whether taxes on capital income are remitted by individuals or businesses.

taxes. The tax base in the business tax, however, is equal to revenue from sales minus materials, wages, pension contributions, and new investment. Thus, if a firm had large amounts of revenue from financial assets (i.e., not from sales of goods and services), it could owe no taxes or even negative taxes under the flat tax even though it reported huge profits to shareholders. This situation is consistent within the context of the flat tax. But, in the past, precisely this situation led to the strengthening of the corporate and individual alternative minimum taxes, which are universally regarded as one of the most complex areas of the tax code. It is hard to see why those same pressures would not arise in the flat tax.

The third issue is the flip side of the second: some firms with low or negative profits may be forced to make very large tax payments. For example, a firm with substantial amounts of interest expense, fringe benefits, payroll taxes, and state and local income and property taxes could report negative profits, but because these items are not deductible in the flat tax, the firm could still face stiff tax liabilities. Again, this makes sense within the context of the flat tax but will not be viewed as fair by firm owners who wonder why they have to pay taxes in years when they lose money and who will push for reforms. Misunderstanding of this point could be very important. For example, the *Wall Street Journal* editorial board (February 5, 1997), a strong supporter of the flat tax, nevertheless complains about a German tax that can force companies to pay taxes "even when they are losing money." The flat tax, however, would do exactly the same thing for some firms. This will lead to efforts by businesses to retain currently existing deductions for health insurance, payroll taxes, and state and local income and property taxes. Taken together, these deductions would cut the business tax base by more than half.

Estimates of Compliance Costs

Slemrod (1996) and A. Hall (1995) have attempted to quantify the compliance costs of the pure flat tax. Both authors' estimates ignore transition issues and the potential reemergence of social policy. Using the ADL model for taxpayer hours described earlier and valuing taxpayer time at $39.60 per hour, Hall estimates that the costs of record keeping, learning about the tax law, form preparation, and packaging and sending the return would equal $8.4 billion. The projected 93 million individual returns are estimated to take an average of 1 hour and 8 minutes. The projected 24.4 million business returns are estimated to take an average of 3 hours and 24 minutes to complete.

Hall's estimates seem both significantly too large in some respects and significantly too small in others. For example, valuing individuals' time at $15 per hour and business time at $25 per hour, as Slemrod does, would reduce the estimate by about half. On the other hand, some of the time estimates seem implausibly low, and possibly off by orders of magnitude. Individual taxpayers are estimated to spend an average of 2.4 *minutes* per year doing record keeping for tax purposes. Businesses are estimated to spend only 2.3 hours per year on record keeping for tax purposes. Remarkably, especially in light of the foregoing discussion on possible areas of complexity, businesses are estimated to spend an average of only 18 minutes learning about the tax law, and 24 minutes gathering all the relevant documents and preparing the return. In addition, Hall's estimate leaves out many components of compliance costs, such as tax planning and auditing.

Slemrod (1996, p. 375) concludes that "it is impossible to confidently forecast the collection cost of the business part of the flat tax on the basis of observable systems, because none exists." Instead, he offers an educated guess that the flat tax would cut business compliance costs (which were $17 billion in the individual income tax and $20 billion in the corporate tax) by one-third and cut individual filing costs by 70 percent (from $33 billion to $10 billion), for total compliance costs of about $35 billion. This is $35 billion less than his compliance cost estimate for the income tax, or about 0.5 percent of GDP in 1995.[23]

Evasion and Administration

Although there are several areas where the flat tax may become more complex than advertised, whether the flat tax could be enforced and administered, given the probable tax rates, does not appear to be an issue. The flat tax would inherit the administrative structure and withholding practices from the existing system and, on net, would likely simplify the system. As noted, reductions in compliance costs and clarification of rules can help reduce evasion. If the flat tax actually reduces marginal tax rates for most people relative to the current system, this should reduce evasion as well. Whether this occurs, of course, depends on the erosion of the tax base.

CONCLUSION

As a purely technical matter, tax complexity and tax evasion can be reduced, and tax administration can be made more just and efficient. As a political and policy matter, however, making these improvements has proved quite difficult. Efforts to simplify the tax system typically run up against conflict with other tax policy goals, political factors, taxpayers'

---

[23] Calegari (1998) and Weisbach (1999) make a variety of points similar to those presented here and extend the analysis in a number of directions in their insightful analyses of administrative issues in the flat tax.

efforts to avoid and evade taxes, and revenue requirements. Each of these factors tends to shape the base, credits, deductions, rate structure, and administrative aspects of the tax system in ways that raise complexity. Efforts to reduce evasion sometimes run into similar problems.

To the extent that simplicity is a goal of tax reform, many improvements could be made within the existing system. Pure versions of both the national retail sales tax and the flat tax could be vastly simpler than even an improved income tax. But realistic versions of the flat tax and especially the sales tax would require tax rates much higher than advertised by their proponents. These higher rates complicate tax compliance and enforcement. The sales tax would face potentially serious problems with enforceability and political pressure for exemptions. The flat tax would face the same political pressures, and although enforceability is not a major issue, the tax would likely become significantly more complex than currently proposed.

Thus, simplification is an important goal of tax reform, but lasting and significant simplification may prove difficult to establish. Policy makers and voters should, therefore, weigh the costs and benefits of simplification against the other goals of tax policy.

Chapter 8

Evaluating the National Retail Sales Tax from a VAT Perspective

Sijbren Cnossen

There is considerable interest in the United States both in academia and in politics, in "fundamental tax reform," defined as the replacement of the income tax (corporate and individual), the gift and estate tax, and, in some cases, the payroll tax by some form of consumption tax. Proponents believe that fundamental tax reform would result in a much simpler and fairer tax system. A consumption tax, it is argued, would also be more conducive to capital formation and economic growth than the current income tax.

A national retail sales tax (NRST) that would be applied to sales of goods and services by businesses to households is one of the alternatives being discussed.[1] Examples include H.R. 2001 (1997, 1999), introduced by Representatives Schaefer and Tauzin in 1997 (ST) and a similar proposal made by the lobbying group Americans for Fair Taxation (AFT). The tax base under both plans would, in principle, consist of all personal and government consumption expenditures on final goods and services. The main difference between the two plans is that AFT would replace the payroll tax in addition to the income tax and the gift and estate tax. The proposed NRST would be collected by the states, most of which have considerable experience with this form of consumption tax.

The author is grateful for stimulating comments made by Peter Mieszkowski, George Zodrow, and the students (especially Bernard Metz) and faculty participants in the 1999 New York University's School of Law Colloquium on Tax Policy and Public Finance.

[1] Other indirect consumption taxes that have received political support include the value-added tax (VAT) and the business transfer tax (BTT) pushed by the lobbying group American Council for Capital Formation; for a meticulous review, see Gillis, Mieszkowski, and Zodrow (1996). Direct consumption taxes that have been proposed include the personal expenditure tax, called Unlimited Savings Allowance tax or USA tax (for a review, see Seidman, 1997) and the flat tax, originally proposed by Hall and Rabushka ([1985] 1995). For a broad review of all of these approaches to taxing consumption, see Cnossen (1999c).

Outside the United States, extensive experience with retail sales taxes (RSTs) is confined to the Canadian provinces. At the federal level, Canada imposes a tax-credit invoice method value-added tax (VAT, but referred to as Goods and Services Tax or GST) that taxes all sales by businesses but permits businesses to take a credit for the tax on purchases from other businesses. Elsewhere, the Nordic countries and Switzerland used to have NRSTs, but all of these countries switched to VAT. VAT is also the preferred form of consumption tax in more than one hundred other industrial and developing countries.[2] Although the specific reasons for adopting the VAT differ from one country to another, the main argument has been that a properly designed VAT raises more revenue with lower administrative and economic costs than other broad-based consumption taxes.

Given equal coverage and tax rates, NRST and VAT are identical in their economic effects and in the distribution of their respective tax burdens (Mieszkowski and Palumbo, Chapter 6 in this volume). In essence, NRST and VAT are both comprehensive, destination-based forms of consumption tax that take domestic consumer expenditures, not producer goods, as their base, and that cover the retail stage, either by definition (NRST) or by design (VAT). NRST excludes producer goods through the suspension technique, while VAT achieves this objective through the tax-credit invoice method. In accordance with the destination principle, both taxes include imports in the tax base but free exports of tax. In principle, the only difference between the two taxes is the way in which the tax is collected by the tax authorities – in full from retailers under NRST and fractionally throughout the production-distribution process under VAT.

The choice between NRST and VAT, therefore, largely involves administrative and technical considerations, especially – in the present context – the ability to reach the retail sector with a tax levied at an unprecedented high rate. The proposed NRST would be levied at tax-exclusive rates of 17.6 percent (ST) or 29.9 percent (AFT).[3] But, as Gale and Holtzblatt (Chapter 7 in this volume) demonstrate convincingly, these rates would have to be raised to 30 percent and 53 percent, respectively, if real federal, state, and local government programs were to be held constant (i.e., if there were to be no cuts in the level of government

---

[2] See Cnossen (1998). Nearly all countries without VAT are small island economies in Oceania and the Caribbean, and oil-rich Middle Eastern countries. The only major country other than the United States without VAT at the federal level is India. Australia, a federal country like the United States, is the latest convert to VAT.

[3] The ST and AFT plans mention tax-inclusive rates of 15 percent and 23 percent, respectively, but the international convention is to express consumption tax rates on a tax-exclusive basis.

operations due to the increase in the consumer price level). Further increases in the NRST rates would be required if some statutory base erosion were allowed for and if, as might be expected, state and local income and sales taxes would conform to the federal model.

In light of these considerations, it is of crucial importance to choose the most robust form of consumption tax, NRST or VAT, which would have to be levied at the same rate. To put the choice in a real-world perspective, this chapter begins by reviewing the experience with RST's and VAT's in the G-7 countries, discussing the considerations that led various countries to prefer VAT over NRST, and examining the theoretical and actual tax bases of NRST and VAT, as derived from U.S. National Income and Product Accounts (NIPA). In light of the requirement that all consumer goods and services should be included in the tax base, special attention is paid to exemptions that are made on social or administrative grounds. Because NRST and VAT intend to tax consumer goods only, the chapter subsequently considers the comparative ability of NRST and VAT to exclude producer goods from the tax base. The administrative litmus test of a "good" consumption tax is the extent to which its operational costs can be kept low. Hence, the chapter includes a comparative analysis of administrative and compliance aspects and costs. Transition issues of fundamental tax reform are not considered, nor are issues, such as internet sales, shared by both taxes.[4]

EXPERIENCE WITH RSTs AND VATs

There is ample experience with RSTs and VATs. Of particular interest for the U.S. debate are the reasons that countries have advanced in choosing VAT over RST.

G-7 Countries

Table 8.1 lists the consumption taxes that are levied in the G-7 countries: by the United States and Canada, members of the North Atlantic Free Trade Agreement (NAFTA) along with Mexico; by France, Germany, Italy, and the United Kingdom, four of the fifteen member states of the European Union (EU) together accounting for 75 percent of the EU's total gross product; and by Japan, the single most important trading partner of the United States. As indicated, RSTs are found at the subnational level in the United States and Canada, but the EU member states, Japan, and – at the federal level – Canada, have a VAT (in addition, in Canada, the province of Quebec has a VAT).

---

[4] For transition issues, see Bradford (1996a) and Zodrow (Chapter 9 in this volume); for the taxation of electronic commerce, see McLure (1997).

Table 8.1. G-7 Countries: Consumption Taxes in 2000

Country	Type(s) of Consumption Tax[a]	Date(s) of Introduction	Rates[b] Standard	Rates[b] Lower[c]	Revenue as Percentage of[d] Total Tax Revenue	Revenue as Percentage of[d] GDP
NAFTA[e]						
United States						
Federal	—	—	—	—	—	—
State[f]	RSTs	1932–69	4.0–9.5[g]	X	7.6	2.2
Canada						
Federal	VAT (GST)	1991	7	0	6.9	2.6
Provincial[h]	RSTs/VAT	1937–67	5–12/7.5	X	7.1	2.7
European Union						
France	VAT	1968	20.6	5.5	17.5	7.9
Germany	VAT	1968	16	7	17.9	6.6
Italy	VAT	1973	20	10	14.2	6.1
United Kingdom	VAT	1973	17.5	0	18.1	6.7
Japan	VAT	1989	5[i]	—	8.9	2.5

[a] RST = retail sales tax; VAT = value-added tax, called goods and services tax (GST) in Canada.

[b] As percentage of the tax-exclusive value of taxable goods and services.

[c] The letter "X" means that essential products (mainly food items) are exempted. In addition to the lower rates shown in the table, France, Italy, and the United Kingdom levy special lower rates of 2.1 percent, 4 percent, and 5 percent, respectively. These rates, however, are only applicable to one or two products.

[d] Revenue figures, drawn from OECD (2000), relate to 1998 and are for all levels of government.

[e] Mexico is also a member of NAFTA (North American Free Trade Agreement). It has a VAT as its main consumption tax.

[f] Forty-five out of fifty states and the District of Columbia levy an RST. Alaska, Delaware, Montana, New Hampshire, and Oregon do not levy an RST at state level (but Alaska has local RSTs).

[g] Inclusive of (highest) local RST rates.

[h] Five out of ten provinces levy an RST. Quebec has its own VAT, while the small maritime provinces (New Brunswick, Newfoundland, Nova Scotia) have piggy-backed the national VAT. Alberta does not impose a consumption tax at provincial level.

[i] Inclusive of the special 1 percent local consumption tax that is levied on the same base and collected along with the VAT.

In the United States, RST is levied by forty-five out of fifty states,[5] accounting for on average 34 percent of total state tax revenue, or 7.6 percent of total national tax revenue (2.2 percent of GDP). The coverage of the various RSTs differs widely across states and is far from comprehensive. Half of all states, for instance, do not tax services, apart from the rental of tangible personal property, transient accommodation, and (selected) utility services. Other states with RST tax services on an ad hoc basis.[6] Furthermore, although all states tax food consumed outside the home, only eighteen states tax food purchased for home consumption. A number of states also exempt clothing and footwear in addition to food. Beyond that, all states include various producer goods in the tax base, which distorts the choice of production technique. Thus, twenty-two states explicitly tax industrial and agricultural machinery. Furthermore, nearly all states tax various dual-use goods and services, such as building materials, utility services, computers, small transport vehicles, office equipment, stationery, and various other items that can be used for business as well as private purposes.

In the EU, all fifteen member states – not just the four states listed in Table 8.1 – levy VAT, because its adoption is a condition for membership.[7] The VATs in the EU are much more comprehensive than the RSTs in the United States. Whereas the RST-bases cover on average 35 percent of total consumption expenditures, the harmonized EU-VAT base covers on average 67 percent.[8] In principle, all services are taxed.[9] Exemptions are limited to services provided in the public interest (health care, education, social services) or to services that are too difficult to tax for administrative reasons (tenant-paid rents and imputed rents of

---

[5] In addition, the District of Columbia levies RST, as well as some 7,000 local governments, including counties, cities, school boards, and police departments. Alaska, Delaware, Montana, New Hampshire, and Oregon do not levy RST at the state level (but Alaska levies RST at the local level). For a comprehensive treatment, see Due and Mikesell (1995).

[6] Only Hawaii, New Mexico, and South Dakota tax all services, except those specifically exempted. Of course, all states with RST tax the value of distribution activities, such as wholesaling and retailing, carried on in the normal course of selling goods. Also, the value of many services, although not taxed explicitly, is taxed indirectly if rendered to businesses that use the services to produce taxable goods.

[7] The VATs of the EU member states have been harmonized under the Sixth Directive on Value Added Tax agreed to by the Council of the European Economic Community in 1977. For an up-to-date version, see European Commission (1996).

[8] For the U.S. states, see Due and Mikesell (1995). For the EU, see Table 8.2. In calculating the tax base for the EU, residential investment has been taken as a proxy for tenant-paid rents and imputed rents of owner-occupied housing.

[9] As Kay and Davis (1990) point out, VAT is the first consumption tax that has successfully integrated the taxation of services with the taxation of goods.

owner-occupied housing, insurance, and banking). Food products are also taxed, albeit at lower-than-standard rates (exceptions are the United Kingdom and Ireland, which tax food purchased for home consumption at a zero rate). The tax-credit invoice system comprehensively eliminates the tax on producer goods. As indicated in Table 8.1, VAT rates in the EU are higher than RST rates in the United States. In conjunction with the much broader base, this means that VAT collections in the EU, as a percentage of GDP, are on average more than three times higher than RST collections in the United States.

In Canada, RST is levied by five out of ten provinces. The provincial RSTs resemble those levied by the U.S. states, although the tax base generally is somewhat broader. An exception is the province of Quebec which imposes its own VAT on the same base as the federal VAT (GST).[10] The Canadian VAT closely resembles the EU VAT, although the rate of 7 percent is lower than the average standard rate of 17.6 percent in the EU.[11] Noteworthy features of the Canadian VAT are the zero rating of basic groceries and prescription drugs; the partial rebates of VAT on purchases of inexpensive new homes and on purchases by the MUSH sector (municipalities, universities, schools, hospitals), which is exempt in the EU; and VAT refunds for lower-income groups (presumptively established amounts based on the previous year's income).

The base of the Japanese VAT is also similar to that of the EU VAT, but the rate of 5 percent is much lower. A noteworthy feature is the treatment of small businesses. An unusually generous exemption excludes two-thirds of all potentially VAT-liable businesses from tax coverage. To prevent cumulative effects from occurring when these exempt firms (not being able to claim a credit for the VAT on their taxable inputs) sell their output to registered firms, the latter are permitted to compute their input tax credits on the basis of presumptively tax-inclusive prices.[12] As a result of this arrangement, more tax than actually has been paid is refunded at the point of export and more tax than is actually being paid with respect to similar domestically produced goods is imposed on imports.

---

[10] For an interesting account of coordinating the Quebec VAT with the federal VAT, see Bird and Gendron (1998). Of the four other provinces, the three maritime provinces (New Brunswick, Newfoundland, Nova Scotia) have a joint federal-provincial VAT, while oil-rich Alberta levies neither RST nor VAT.

[11] Of course, the provincial VAT or RST rates have to be added for the comparison. In Quebec, for instance, this results in a combined rate of 15.025 percent, because the federal VAT of 7 percent is levied on prices inclusive of the provincial VAT of 7.5 percent. The combined VAT rate in the maritime provinces is 15 percent.

[12] This approach, which effectively exempts the value added by nonregistered firms, contrasts sharply with that of the usual VAT that increases the tax burden on nonregistered firms selling their output to registered firms, inducing them to register and pay VAT.

Considerations Affecting the Choice between VAT and RST

Experience indicates that most countries, when faced with the choice, have favored VAT over RST, taking the view that in practice VAT would be more broadly based than RST, better equipped to free producer goods of tax and facilitate trade, and easier to enforce. This can be illustrated by the experience in the EU, Norway, Canada, New Zealand, and Australia.[13]

In the 1960s, the then member states of the EU opted for VAT because, unlike the cascade type of turnover tax levied previously, VAT permits the precise and unambiguous computation of export rebates and compensating import taxes – called border-tax adjustments (BTAs; Cnossen and Shoup, 1987). Correct BTAs are considered to be an indispensable feature of any tax on goods and services that enter intra-EU trade. Subsequently, therefore, the adoption of VAT became a condition for EU membership. Although RST was considered by the Neumark Committee (1963) that was appointed to study the most appropriate consumption tax, it was rejected "on practical technical grounds . . . (given particularly the large number of small retailers of whom the majority are unable to maintain precise bookkeeping)."

Even before they became members of the EU, Denmark and Sweden – as well as the non-EU European countries of Iceland, Norway, and Switzerland – switched from RST to VAT. These countries cited foreign trade considerations as the main reason for the switch. RST was getting into exports indirectly through the taxation of certain producer goods, which implied that the equal-rate compensating import tax was under-taxing finished-goods imports relative to import-competing goods, whose price incorporated elements of the tax on producer goods. More generally, VAT's ability to tax goods and services more broadly and neutrally than RST's and an expectation that a shift to VAT would result in increased revenues – ostensibly, in many cases, as part of a general shift in emphasis from direct to indirect taxes – were cited in support of the switch.

Norway is the only country in which the debate on the relative merits of VAT versus RST continued long after VAT was introduced in 1970 (Due and Brems, 1986). Opponents of the VAT claimed that it was more costly for businesses and the tax administration than RST had been. The majority of a government-appointed committee that reported in 1975 supported their views. The committee also believed that the opportunity for fraud was somewhat greater under VAT. Accordingly, it recommended that the government revert to RST. Subsequently, the

---

[13] This section draws heavily on Cnossen (1987).

Norwegian Treasury was instructed to review the issues. Reporting in 1985, it concluded in favor of VAT, pointing out that the exclusion of producer goods was more comprehensive under VAT; that a large part of the tax was collected upstream from large firms with well-organized accounting systems, whereas under RST much of the tax would have to be collected from small retailers; that VAT had had a beneficial effect on accounting standards, with spillover benefits for the income tax and the property tax; that the number of businesses that had to be registered under VAT was not significantly larger than the number that had been registered under RST; that the transitional costs of a return to RST would be high; and, finally, that the claim that VAT was more costly to administer and to comply with than RST was ill-founded. At the end of the 1980s, the controversy was settled in favor of VAT.

Initially, the government of Canada did not take an explicit position on the relative merits of a national RST versus a national VAT. In June 1987 it put up for discussion the alternative of an integrated RST combining the existing provincial RSTs with a new federal RST or a separate national VAT without any link with the provincial RSTs.[14] Despite extensive negotiations with the provinces, the integrated RST proved to be beyond reach. It was simply not possible to reform nine different RST regimes and consolidate them into one unified system. Perhaps this was not surprising, because as the minister of finance opined: "this had never been accomplished before anywhere in the world." In April 1989, therefore, the government went ahead with the introduction of a federal VAT.

The choice between RST and VAT has also been debated in New Zealand and Australia. The government of New Zealand, which introduced VAT in 1987, took the view that VAT would be more effective than RST in ensuring compliance, owing to its multistage collection feature, its inclusion of imports in the tax base, and the more complete audit trail that the tax provided. Retailers, the least reliable participants in the collection process, would not be accountable for the full amount of the tax. Moreover, as in the EU, small taxpayers could be excluded by reference to their turnover, yet they would still pay tax on their inputs (being exempt, they would not be entitled to take credit for tax on purchases). This arrangement would minimize administrative and compli-

---

[14] This left open the question whether the direct subtraction method (taxation of the difference between sales and purchases) or the indirect subtraction method (credit for tax on purchases against the tax on sales) should be used. The study group appointed by the minister of finance initially favored the direct method (BTT) which, because of its resemblance to a business income tax, would minimize overlap and conflict with the provinces (with their RSTs).

ance costs. The government also concluded that, given a comprehensive tax base and a single rate, VAT would be a more flexible revenue instrument than RST (New Zealand, 1985).

In Australia, the RST-VAT debate waxed and waned for more than twenty years. The Asprey Committee, which reported in 1975 (and which was, perhaps, influenced by the recent introduction of VAT in the United Kingdom), favored VAT over RST, arguing that RST was more susceptible to evasion. In contrast, the Australian government's Draft White Paper, published in 1985, argued that RST had significant administrative and compliance advantages relative to VAT. The government believed that the self-policing properties of VAT (i.e., the ability to cross-check invoices) had been overstated. While it accepted the argument that producer goods and exports could be more readily freed from tax under VAT than under RST, the longer lead-in time of VAT persuaded the government that RST was the right choice. Subsequent governments, however, leaned toward VAT, which, finally, emerged as the consumption tax of choice in 1998, largely on the basis of the same arguments as used earlier in New Zealand (Howard Government's Plan, 1998).

TAXING ALL CONSUMER GOODS AND SERVICES

As Harberger (1990) has argued persuasively, there are good pragmatic reasons for including all goods and services in the tax base of a general consumption tax and to apply a uniform rate. Unlike the Ramsey-rule solution for optimal commodity taxation, uniform taxation does not require knowledge of demand and supply relations, which is generally not available. Moreover, uniform taxation is more robust to changes in tastes and technology. To what extent do NRST and VAT meet the standard of uniform taxation?

NRST and VAT Bases Compared

Table 8.2 shows the NRST tax base as derived from GDP, as well as the comparable tax bases of a very broad New Zealand type of VAT and a more narrow EU type of VAT – using U.S. National Income and Product Accounts (NIPA) data. The proposed U.S. NRSTs would reach 90 percent of personal consumption expenditures. This would be more than a New Zealand type of VAT, which taxes 86 percent, and considerably more than an EU type of VAT, which covers 71 percent. Each of these tax bases includes some investment expenditures and purchases of intermediate goods of exempt sectors – that is, housing (NRST: owner-occupied property only), medical care (EU VAT only), education and research (NRST and EU VAT), religious and welfare activities (NRST and both VATs), and financial services (VATs). Governments are taxed

Table 8.2. NRST and VAT Tax Bases (in billions of 1994 dollars)

	Components of GDP	NRST	VAT New Zealand	EU
Total tax base	6,936	5,616	5,146	3,948
Personal consumption expenditures	4,702	4,302	4,040	3,342
Food purchased for off-premise consumption	405	405	405	405[a]
Meals and beverages at restaurants	258	258	258	258
Clothing, accessories, and jewelry	311	311	311	311
Furniture and other household equipment	147	147	147	147
Utilities and other household operation	381	381	381	381
Local transit, tolls, and bridges	8	8	8	8
Other transportation expenditures	529	529	529	529
Clubs and fraternal organizations	12	12	12	0
Other recreation expenditures	363	363	363	363
Imputed rent of owner-occupied housing	508	207[b]	207[b]	207[b]
Tenant-paid rent	198	198	81[b]	81[b]
Employer-provided medical care	315	315	315	0
Government-provided medical care	327	327	327	0
Out-of-pocket medical care purchases[c]	192	192	192	192
Private education and research	105	61[d]	105	61[d]
Religious and welfare activities	131	76[d]	76[d]	76[d]
Imputed value of financial services	146	146	49[d]	49[d]
Brokerage and banking services	138	138	46[d]	46[d]
Other consumption expenditures	228	228	228	228
State and local government purchases	798	798	798	298[d]
Federal government purchases	516	516	308[d]	308[d]
Net export of goods and services	−94	0	0	0
Gross private domestic investment	1,014	0	0	0

[a] Zero-rated in Ireland and the United Kingdom.
[b] Residential investment.
[c] Assumed to be a proxy for medicines, medical aids, and health investment purchases.
[d] Excluding compensation of employees (author's estimate for financial services).

Source: Congressional Budget Office (1997a).

in varying degrees under NRST and the two VATs. In any case, taxing governments should not yield any net revenue if the real level of government expenditures is held constant.

The coverage of both NRST and VAT is limited, inherently, to products sold in the market. "Value added" outside business or government is not and cannot be taxed. Neither tax reaches the value of the labor involved in preparing meals at home, maintaining one's house, repairing one's car, or other activities that can be substituted for services provided by restaurants, plumbers, painters, carpenters, garages, and so forth – services that a comprehensive consumption tax should cover. Similarly, casual barter services performed by one individual for another individual cannot be taxed. As a result, both NRST and VAT encourage do-it-yourself substitution (as does the income tax).

Certain exclusions and exemptions from the NRST and VAT base, however, reflect either deliberate policy choices or the administrative inability to reach particular goods and services. Under the proposed NRSTs, an exemption is proposed for college education – presumably, purchases made by colleges would bear tax, but services provided would not be taxed. In the EU, all general education is exempted, because it is believed – in the words of the Sixth Directive on Value Added Tax (Article 9) – that services provided "in the public interest" should not be taxed.[15] Health care is exempted on the same grounds. By contrast, New Zealand includes both health care and education in its VAT base. NRST also exempts imputed rents of owner-occupied housing (but not tenant-paid rents), which would be difficult (and unpopular) to tax. Under the EU and New Zealand VATs, imputed rents and tenant-paid rents are both exempt. Administratively, furthermore, it has thus far not been considered feasible to tax financial services. Nonetheless, the NRST plans propose to include the imputed value of financial services in the tax base. Finally, some countries exempt or zero-rate food purchases for off-premise consumption.

Food and Other Essential Items

A broad-based, uniform-rate NRST or VAT would, by definition, have a proportional impact when measured with respect to an (annual) consumption base and a regressive impact when measured with respect to an (annual) income base, because savings as a proportion of income rises when income rises.[16] The proportional or regressive impact can be mitigated by a system of presumptive tax rebates (demogrants) targeted at

---

[15] This begs the question, of course, of why the tax on inputs is not refunded. If goods and services are not to be taxed, then zero rate rather than an exemption is the proper instrument to effect this policy choice. The choice between exemption and zero-rating is hardly relevant, however, if health and education are heavily subsidized and provided at administered prices.

[16] Many economists argue that savings are spent also when viewed over the individual's lifetime. The "true" notion of income, therefore, corresponds to their definition of "permanent income." One proxy for this is consumption, which is less likely than income to contain erratic and random movements or to be affected by life-cycle variations.

lower-income groups or provided to all households, or by zero-rating or applying lower-than-standard rates to essential goods that are disproportionately consumed by the poor.

Both NRST plans suggest that demogrants be provided to all households – calculated at the tax rate times the poverty line (or the minimum wage, if lower, under the ST plan).[17] The demogrants system resembles the refundable tax credit mechanism of the Canadian VAT. Simply by filing an income tax return, even if no income has been earned, lower-income households in Canada can obtain a refund (differentiated between adults and children) of the VAT that is assumed to have been paid on purchases of essential items of consumption. Various special-situation credits are also available. In addition, a zero rate is applied to basic groceries, a benefit available to all income groups.[18] Ireland and the United Kingdom also apply zero rates to food purchases for off-premise consumption, as well as some other essential goods. Most other EU member states, however, levy lower-than-standard rates on these items. Denmark is the only member state that taxes all goods and services at the same rate. It uses the social benefit system to compensate the poor for having to pay VAT.

Rate differentiation under VAT or NRST is not an effective way of alleviating the impact of the tax on the poor. Because the consumption patterns of low- and high-income groups have converged, tax burden studies show that rate differentiation changes the impact of a broad-based consumption tax less than might be expected when food is zero-rated (as in the United Kingdom) or taxed at a lower rate (as in the Netherlands).[19] Moreover, studies in Canada (Cnossen, 1999b) and Ireland (Commission on Taxation, 1984) have found that, although the poor spend relatively more of their income on food, the rich spend twice as much in absolute amounts as the poor, because they buy more expensive varieties of food, eat out more often, and tend to throw food away more often. This implies that zero-rating of groceries gives twice as much tax relief to high-income groups as to low-income groups – an odd and expensive way of alleviating the plight of the poor. In the same vein, and perhaps more telling, a study in Sweden showed that abolition of that country's standard rate on food would mainly benefit single people (yuppies) with higher incomes (Swedish Ministry of Finance, 1983).

---

[17] For an early discussion of individual rebates in the context of VAT, see Brashares, Speyrer, and Carlson (1988).

[18] Obviously, this makes little sense in conjunction with the demogrants system.

[19] See OECD (1988). This finding is corroborated by a CBO study (1993) that shows that the regressivity of a hypothetical U.S. VAT would be reduced by merely 18 percent if food were zero-rated.

Moreover, differentiated VAT rate structures increase administrative and compliance costs, particularly for small businesses.

For much the same reasons, Feenberg, Mitrusi, and Poterba (1997) find that exempting food and housing under an NRST alleviates little of the burden of this tax on the poor. A system of demogrants would be more cost-effective than is rate differentiation under VAT, because the benefit does not rise with income. But, as Mieszkowski and Palumbo (Chapter 6 in this volume) find, providing a poverty-level demogrant to all households is extremely expensive as it increases the tax rate of an NRST from 28 to 41 percent. If incomes are known, it would be advisable to put a means-conditioned program in place; such an approach, however, would add to the costs of administering NRST. Alternatively, the demogrants could be based on wage income as reported for payroll tax purposes. Arguably, the economic and administrative costs of the targeted approaches would be lower than those of a universal demogrant. A uniform NRST or VAT rate with a targeted demogrant system seems the best solution, therefore, to mitigate the tax impact on the poor.

Housing

The proposed NRST takes a second-best approach to the taxation of housing services by exempting imputed rents but taxing tenant-paid rents and new owner-occupied residential premises. Because the purchase price of a house may be taken to represent the present value of its future services, the tax on the purchase price may be considered a close proxy for the present value of the tax that should be levied on the future flow of housing services. The inevitable drawback of this approach is that substantial windfall gains are created for owners of residential real estate existing at the time of the introduction of NRST.[20] But there is no other feasible way to bring housing into the NRST tax base. As Table 8.2 indicates, imputed rents of owner-occupied housing constitute 11 percent of total personal consumption expenditures in the United States. This is too large a portion to ignore for tax purposes, particularly if tenant-paid rents are taxed.

Basically, VATs follow the same approach, but, ostensibly to provide equal treatment, tenant-paid rents are also exempt. There is an interesting difference, however, between the tax method followed in New Zealand (as well as Canada) and the exemption method adopted in the EU (Cnossen, 1996). Under the tax method, the construction, sale, rental,

---

[20] Existing residential real estate could be taxed at the time of sale subsequent to the introduction of NRST or VAT, but this would create severe lock-in effects. No country has ever taken this route.

and repairs of real estate are, in principle, taxable, but residential rents (and imputed rents of owner-occupied housing) are exempt, as is the sale of previously occupied residential property. Under the exemption method, by contrast, the sale and rental of all existing real estate is, in principle, exempt, but all newly constructed buildings, as well as alterations and maintenance of the existing building stock, are taxable. The exemption method needs a definition of specified nonresidential use (hotel accommodation, boarding houses, camping facilities, parking space) that is taxable. It must also offer the opportunity for optional registration and payment of tax on the commercial use and sale of real estate to avoid potential discrimination and cumulation of tax. The tax method requires a definition of residential use, but optional registration and payment of VAT is not an issue.

Clearly, the tax method, under which all leases and sales of commercial real estate are subject to VAT, is to be preferred to the exemption approach. Under the tax method, increases in the value of commercial real estate (and hence in the value of the services that the property renders) are always included in the tax base; thus, distortions are fewer and change-of-use rules are easier to apply. Under NRST, it will prove to be difficult to tax tenants but *appear* to exempt owner-occupiers. If tenant-paid rents as well as imputed rents of owner-occupied property are to be exempted, then the tax method is to be preferred over the exemption approach. Whatever is done, the proper treatment of housing is one of the thorniest (transition) issues under a high-rate consumption tax.

Health, Education, and Social Services

As indicated in Table 8.2, the NRST plans propose to tax employer- and government-provided medical care, as well as out-of-pocket medical care purchases. Furthermore, college education and religious and welfare activities will not be taxed on the labor element of services rendered, but presumably goods and services supplied by third parties will be taxed. In the EU, this treatment is applied to all health care, education, and social services (see Table 8.2), except that private clinics and educational (training) activities carried on for profit are taxed. This contrasts with the New Zealand VAT, which taxes all health and education services, whether or not provided by government. Only religious and welfare activities are exempted.

In the EU, nearly all health and education services are provided by government or by heavily subsidized institutions with administered prices. Hence, the taxation and subsidization of these services can be exactly replicated by the exemption. (This is also true for New Zealand, although it has chosen to tax health care and education.) In this situation, exemption seems to have the edge from a political perspective. The exemptions violate the neutrality criterion, however, to the extent that the exempt entities are induced to perform laundry, food, and administrative services themselves in order to save the payment of VAT on the labor element of the value of such services if purchased from registered businesses. Although most EU VAT's have an anti-avoidance provision under which such in-house services can be taxed, it is not invoked.

An issue of greater concern is that exemption precludes health and educational institutions from passing the tax on their inputs on to private sector companies, say, interested in undertaking pharmaceutical or marketing research with the exempt entities. These companies would be interested in the application of VAT to the services that are billed to them, because they would then be able to take a credit for that tax (and implicitly for the tax on the inputs of the exempt institutions) against their own VAT on sales. It is increasingly being recognized, moreover, that exempting education discriminates against other taxable forms of learning, such as reading and museum visits. Clearly, from a neutrality point of view, NRST is on the right track by taxing health care and most education. The drawback of the NRST approach is, however, that demogrants cannot be used to rebate the tax to the poor, because health care and, to a lesser extent, education are less evenly consumed by the poor than are food and other essential goods. In this event, zero rating of the services might be the better alternative.

Financial Services

Banking and insurance are other hard-to-tax sectors. The NRST plans propose to tax the imputed value of financial services. By contrast, the EU and New Zealand do not tax financial services under their VATs, because the intermediation charge that should be taxed cannot be separated from the pure interest rate, premium, or rate of return that should not be taxed.[21] Exemption means that financial institutions incur input tax on their purchases but cannot charge tax on their sales of financial services. Consequently, consumers of such services face effective tax rates that are lower than statutory rates, thus distorting their choice in favor of financial services. What is probably worse, the tax on inputs of financial institutions cannot be passed on to business users of their services in a way that does not distort producer choice.

---

[21] EU member states and New Zealand, however, tax secondary financial services, such as debt collection, keeping securities, and the rental of safety deposit boxes. New Zealand also taxes fire, general, and accident insurance premiums under its VAT. To confine the tax to the gross margin, insurers are allowed a credit for the tax fraction of any indemnity payments. For a survey of the actual treatment of financial services in EU member states (and other OECD countries), see KPMG (1996).

In practice, it has been difficult to define the scope of the exemption in VAT countries. To limit distortions and unequal treatment, various complementary services, such as legal counseling and accounting and tax advice, are taxable. If the complementary services were exempt, financial institutions would be induced to provide them "in house" rather than purchase them from specialized firms. But taxation means that complementary services must be segregated from financial services per se and that input taxes must be apportioned between taxable supplies and exempt supplies. The rules for doing so are inherently arbitrary.[22]

Various alternative approaches to the current VAT treatment of financial services that have been proposed in the tax literature would also be relevant to the NRST debate.[23] These alternatives include the zero-rating of financial services (rebates of all prior-stage tax), the optional approach (taxing financial institutions on a transaction-by-transaction basis, as is done in Germany), the addition method (taxing financial institutions on the sum of wages and business cash flow, as is done in France), the subtraction method (taxing the difference between lending revenues and borrowing costs, at one time proposed in Canada) and, most recently, the cash flow method (taxing the difference between cash inflows and cash outflows). So far, none of the alternatives seems to offer a viable way of taxing financial services in a simple and neutral fashion, because they either do not permit the tax on inputs to be passed on to taxable users, continue to exempt consumer use, or are too complicated.[24] In light of this, it will be interesting to see how the NRST plans intend to compute the imputed value of financial services and segregate taxable consumer use from exempt business use.

[22] The turnover basis is the most widely used apportionment basis. It divides the tax on inputs into deductible and nondeductible amounts in the same proportion as taxable (including zero-rated exports) and exempt supplies bear to total turnover.

[23] For a review and evaluation of these approaches and references to the relevant literature, see Cnossen (1999a). Interestingly, in the EU, the exemption of financial services causes few complaints by the financial community. One reason may be that some member states permit financial institutions to use the gross margin – that is, the difference between lending revenues and borrowing costs – instead of total lending revenues, as the denominator in the apportionment formula. This "bankers' method" significantly increases the amount of deductible input tax. Another way in which banks might be able to maximize their input tax recovery using the turnover method is to increase artificially the level of taxable supplies by transacting a small number of high-value zero-rated transactions (e.g., in gold).

[24] The cash flow method, proposed by Poddar and English (1997), seems the most promising alternative. Its major drawback is that it would require the valuation of assets and liabilities when introduced and when rates are changed.

Governments

Under the NRST plans, federal, state, and local government operations would be taxed under the addition method – that is, governments would pay tax on wages and nonpension fringe benefits of government employees, as well as on purchases of intermediate and investment goods. To prevent double taxation, purchases of property and services for resale would be exempt, as would cash and in-kind transfers. But household purchases of government-provided goods and services would be taxed – clearly, a form of double taxation. NRST proponents believe that the proposed treatment would increase the accountability and transparency of government operations.

In the EU, by contrast, governments are treated as exempt entities – that is, purchases of intermediate and investment goods are taxed, but there is no tax on governments' own value added in the form of wages and salaries. The philosophy is that it does not make much sense to require government departments to charge VAT on the "sale" of their services (in effect, their budgetary allocations) and, at the same time, to increase their funding. Beyond that, public-sector bodies generally are exempt if treatment as a nontaxable entity does not lead to significant distortions of competition with the private sector. However, economic activities such as the supply of water, electricity, gas, telecommunications, transport of goods and passengers, port and airport services are always taxable.

It does not appear to make much sense under NRST to tax activities that only the government can perform, and for which no price is charged or that are supplied at administered prices. This is almost always the case with federal (central) and state government operations. Local governments, however, more often produce goods and services that can also be supplied by the private sector. A case can be made, therefore, for taxing their operations, as is done in New Zealand. Alternatively, local governments can be permitted to claim refunds of tax paid on purchases of goods and services used for nonbusiness activities, as is done in France, Luxembourg, and the United Kingdom. It obviates the need to increase budgetary allocations from the central government to local governments upon introduction of the tax. A third approach, adopted in Canada, is to provide a rebate of 50 percent of the VAT on taxable purchases of municipalities (as well as universities, schools, and hospitals – the rest of the MUSH sector) and to zero-rate sales by businesses to provincial governments. Some arrangement for compensating the effect of a federal NRST on state and local governments' budgetary outlays would also have to be considered in the United States.

EXCLUDING ALL PRODUCER GOODS AND SERVICES

Which tax, NRST or VAT, does a better job in excluding producer goods from the tax base?

Dual-Use Goods and Services

NRST would have difficulty distinguishing between producer goods (that should not be taxed) and consumer goods (that should be taxed). How does a registered business know that a computer it supplies will be used for entertainment purposes at home (taxable), for resale (exempt), or as an (exempt) capital good for (taxable) hotel services? Exempting dual-use goods, such as building materials, utility services, computers, small transport vehicles, office equipment, furniture, and stationery, causes consumers to buy more of the exempt items than they would have done if the items were taxed. Taxing dual-use goods discourages capital-intensive production and hampers specialization. The problem may be ignored under a low-rate state type of RST, but represents a major shortcoming under a high-rate NRST.

This observation seems to be confirmed by what occurs under state RSTs in the United States. Raymond Ring (1999) has estimated that producer goods make up on average 40 percent of the RST base (with a range of 18 to 65 percent). Admittedly, it is somewhat difficult to know how much of this is attributable to deliberate policy choices rather than to RST's inherent inability to exempt producer goods. The practice of taxing producer goods may be so widespread in part because many RSTs grew out of gross receipts taxes. Revenue considerations too may have played a role, as well as concern that the harmful effects of taxing these goods would be limited if the rate were kept low. The current trend is to expand the exclusion of producer goods. It is doubtful, however, whether this exclusion can ever be as comprehensive as it is under VAT. Texas, for example, has made a serious effort to exclude many types of producer goods from the RST base. Nevertheless, recent estimates suggest that nearly one-half of the tax base is still business purchases (Zodrow, 1999b).

What applies to dual-use goods is even more relevant to the supply of services.[25] Many services have extensive dual use: they are sold for intermediate use as well as final use. This is especially true of professional services and of services provided by important sectors such as utilities, transportation, communications, and advertising. Outside of construction, hotels, catering, and services sold for intermediate use may account

---

[25] The difficulties of taxing services under state RSTs have been documented by Fox (1992) and Hellerstein (1988).

for 40–50 percent of the total output of service establishments (Kay and Davis, 1990). In many countries, moreover, sectors such as transportation, banking, and insurance are heavily involved in export activities, which may account for up to 30 percent of total output. It is of crucial importance, therefore, to segregate taxable consumer use of services from exempt business use. But this is extremely difficult to accomplish at the retail stage.

Dual-use goods and services pose far fewer problems under VAT than under NRST. Identification of the purchaser or an investigation into the objective of the purchase, imperative under NRST if cascading or under-taxation is to be avoided, is unnecessary under VAT. Whether the purchaser is subsequently entitled to take credit for tax is of no concern to the seller, but a matter between the purchaser and the tax authorities (who collect the corresponding tax from an upstream firm). Consider a simple service transaction – the purchase of a train ticket for a business trip. VAT does not require the ticket office to take the purpose of the trip into consideration. The proper application of NRST, on the other hand, would require not only the presentation of an exemption certificate but also an inquiry into the purpose of the trip. Clearly, the ticket office is not in a position to check such information. This example could be multiplied many times by others drawn from the fields of transportation, communications, advertising, and the professions.

To solve the problems posed by dual-use goods and services under NRST, the ST plan proposes to tax dual-use items, but to reimburse the tax to registered firms that use them for business purposes, similar to the tax credit and refund technique of VAT. Of course, there is nothing against incorporating some VAT features into NRST (or vice versa), but it is unlikely that this will improve the situation. At heart, the issue is that no proper consumption tax is feasible, unless it shifts the emphasis from defining and taxing (individual) products to taxing (summarized) transactions expressed in monetary amounts, and from exempt producer end-use to taxable consumer end-use. The proposed rebate feature would unduly complicate NRST, unless it would be expanded to include all producer goods, as under VAT.[26] Registered sellers, including retailers, could then simply be told to always charge tax, leaving it to buyers to obtain a tax credit if they are also registered (and placing the tax unequivocally on consumers who are not registered).

NRST and VAT both have problems with dual-use items of consumption. To prevent consumption "through the business," VAT denies the tax credit for purchases of food products, beverages, employee fringe benefits, and personnel transportation – even if made for business

---

[26] For a more favorable view on the tax rebate scheme, see Zodrow (1999b).

purposes, say, to entertain clients. Likewise, NRST would have to ensure
that consumption items bought exempt from tax are not diverted to personal use without payment of tax. VAT seems to be better placed to tax
dual-use consumption items, because it taxes purchases and, hence,
requires taxpayers to fraudulently claim a tax credit. NRST, on the other
hand, induces them simply to "forget" that tax should be charged. Finally,
both taxes stimulate the purchase of dual-use production goods, such as
furniture, upholstery, and similar products that also satisfy consumer
wants even if used for business purposes.

Border Tax Adjustments

The (in)ability to free producer goods and services of tax also has implications for foreign trade.[27] The entry of arbitrary elements of tax into
business costs and export prices under NRST should cause excise-type
effects that will not be uniformly eliminated by compensating exchange
rate movements. If these tax elements cannot be passed on to foreign
traders, they will have to be paid out of factor income (i.e., profits or
wages) – an outcome that contradicts the purpose of a consumption tax.
Even if producer goods are not widely taxed, the fact that the coverage
of businesses under NRST is less than comprehensive makes it likely that
some inputs will not be bought tax-free and hence that the tax on these
inputs will find its way into export prices. These distortions have their
mirror image on the import side of the ledger. Imports will be undertaxed relative to domestically produced goods if the tax on producer
goods that were used to manufacture imports is fully rebated in other
countries.

VAT too cannot completely free exports of tax. What are probably
the most significant distortions (albeit still minor) arise when registered
exporters have inputs of exempt banking and insurance services. To the
extent that the noncreditable tax on the inputs of these service sectors
enters the price banks and insurance companies charge for their services
to businesses, exports are not completely freed of tax. The same effect
occurs if exporting firms buy from small exempt firms (although rela-

---

[27] In reviewing these implications, it should be noted that it is generally agreed that goods
and services entering international trade should be treated on the basis of the destination principle (imports taxed, exports freed of tax) rather than the origin principle
(exports taxed, imports free of tax). In theory, neither principle affects real trade and
investment. Imports are exchanged for exports – hence, a tax on exports is a tax on
imports – and compensating exchange rate or price movements would restore the original position if one principle were substituted for the other principle. But the consumption distortions under the destination principle are thought to be less harmful than the
production distortions under the origin principle (Diamond and Mirrlees, 1971). The
origin principle, moreover, involves transfer pricing problems.

tively few are likely to do so). A small amount of VAT may also enter export prices as a result of the noncreditable status of the tax on some business inputs, such as personnel transportation, meals and lodging, and travel. A major difference between VAT and NRST is that at the import stage VAT is generally – though not invariably – payable immediately, as if it were an import duty, rather than, say, in the following month, along with the tax on domestically traded goods. In other words, at the import stage, the VAT becomes a tax on purchases rather than on sales. This implies that the importer may incur an interest charge on the "prepaid" tax. This feature discriminates against imports.[28]

Furthermore, under VAT, the existing arrangements for BTAs through border controls cannot deal effectively with nontangible services whose location of supply or purchase is difficult to determine. Obviously, international differences in tax rates will generate distortions if the liability to tax is determined by the country in which the service is supplied. But if the receiving firm's country is the taxing locus, it will be difficult to tax purchases by final consumers. The EU's Sixth Directive on Value Added Tax (Article 9) provides a workable solution by taxing services rendered mainly to final consumers in the country of supply, which in virtually all cases is also the country of destination. On the other hand, services exported by banks, insurance companies, professional firms, advertising agencies, and similar enterprises, which are rendered mainly to businesses, are considered supplied in the receiving firm's country (they are treated as if they were inputs supplied by the importing firm itself).[29] This means that these services are zero-rated when exported. NRST would have to face up to the same problems. Due to its less than comprehensive coverage of businesses, it would probably not do as good a job in taxing cross-border services as does VAT.

ADMINISTRATIVE AND COMPLIANCE ASPECTS

In view of the high rate at which the tax would have to be levied, administrative considerations should carry considerable weight in choosing between NRST and VAT. These considerations include collection enforcement, the number of taxpayers, susceptibility to tax evasion, and administrative and compliance costs.

---

[28] This discriminatory element is not present under current EU VATs, which have shifted border tax adjustments to the first inland trader under what is called the deferred payment system or transitional regime. Under this regime, the tax credit mechanism is relied on to tax imported goods at the first stage of use in the country of importation.

[29] This is called the reverse charge mechanism. Since 1993, this mechanism is also applied to goods in the EU (see note 28).

Collection Enforcement

VAT, just like NRST, is collected in full by the retailer from the consumer. The retailer, in turn, remits part of the full VAT – the part that is calculated as his own value added (simply defined as the difference between sales and purchases) times the tax rate – to the tax authorities. He pays the remainder of the full VAT, representing the tax on his purchases, to his suppliers who have billed him for this part of the tax. The suppliers, in turn, go through the same motions as the retailer. The only difference with NRST is, therefore, that the total tax paid by the consumer under VAT is remitted to the tax authorities by all businesses in the production-distribution process (instead of the retailer only) in proportion to their respective shares in the total value added (= retail price) embodied in the final product.[30]

But the multistage collection feature of VAT has important implications for the feasibility of the tax, particularly one levied at a high rate. In legal terms, this feature gives the tax authorities a lien, as it were, on suppliers for the tax payable by the retailer. Manufacturers and wholesalers have, in effect, been made tax collectors on behalf of the government – they remit part of the tax paid to them by retailers. Presumably, the rationale for this arrangement is that taxable retailers are less likely to default on tax invoiced by their suppliers than on tax payable directly to the tax authorities as is the case under NRST.

Furthermore, the multistage collection feature under VAT transfers part of the onus of proof regarding the tax liability to the taxpayer, whereas under NRST the onus rests fully with the tax authorities. A basic tax law rule is that for positive items – sales – the burden of proof lies with the tax office; it must prove that a business liable to tax has understated its sales. In this respect, NRST and VAT are similar. But for negative items, such as tax credits claimed under VAT on the strength of purchase invoices, the *onus probandi* lies with the taxpayer, who must

[30] Even the timing of net tax collections (and refunds) under a multistage VAT is identical to the timing of tax collections under a single-stage NRST. The only plausible assumption that needs to be made for this to be so is that the length of time required for remitting tax (and for processing any refunds) under VAT is the same as the average length of time required for settling accounts receivable and payable. Thus, under VAT, as under NRST, taxable businesses will not even bear the cost of financing carrying charges for tax paid on, say, inventory accumulation or capital equipment purchases. Under NRST, such items are exempt from tax; under VAT, the purchaser's right to a tax credit (and refund) arises at the same time that the supplier has to account for the tax. The result is that the tax authorities do not collect any net tax revenue under VAT with respect to transactions between registered businesses – just as under NRST. Net tax is collected only when taxable products leave the "ring" of registered firms and are sold to final users or consumers.

prove, to the satisfaction of the tax authorities, that he is entitled to the tax credits shown in his return because the goods and services purchased have been used in the course of the business. Under NRST, by contrast, registered vendors have to verify the status of buyers purchasing for resale and the end use of products sold. Because cheating a vendor, without doing him economic harm, presumably is less difficult than cheating the government, NRST places a lower price on dishonesty than VAT.

Number of Taxpayers

The number of taxpayers that has to be registered under NRST is not that much smaller (if at all) than the number that has to be put on the tax roll under VAT. The difference is not as large as expected, because NRST requires the registration of all businesses that sell at retail, not just retailers as such.[31] There are some 25 million business units in the United States. Of this number, some 10 million businesses would have to be registered under NRST, but the number under VAT would not have to be any larger if small businesses with sales of, say, $100,000 or less would be exempted.[32] Generally, this finding accords with an earlier U.S. Treasury (1984c) study that concluded that a broad-based NRST would require registration by three-fourths of the firms that would be subject to VAT. The estimate is also in line with that of an official report in the United Kingdom which estimated that the introduction of RST would involve the registration of 72 percent of the taxable businesses registered for VAT purposes.

Although the total number of registered firms would be about the same under NRST and VAT, the types of businesses would differ greatly. If a sizable small-business exemption is introduced, VAT would be largely confined to large business units which, generally, have good accounts. By definition, NRST would have to put most small-business units on the tax roll. Not taxing small firms would, in contrast to VAT, mean that all value added would go untaxed. Generally, the accounts of these units would not be as reliable as the accounts of large-business units and filing delinquency would be much higher. As a way out of this dilemma, Murray (1997b) and, in greater detail, Mieszkowksi and Palumbo (1998) have suggested that an NRST withholding system be introduced for small retailers at pre-retail stages of production and distribution. Retailers would then be allowed to credit the tax withheld

---

[31] In addition, businesses with exemption certificates would not have to register but would nevertheless have to be audited.

[32] Because inputs of small businesses would still be subject to tax, the revenue loss should not exceed 2.6 percent of total VAT proceeds. See GAO (1993).

against their own tax on sales.[33] Moreover, the paper trail would facilitate cross audit. But it would then become necessary to define who would have to withhold for whom. Just like the tax credit rebate scheme for dual-use goods, it would then be much more cost-effective to apply the withholding scheme to all stages of production and distribution, as does VAT.

The NRST plans do not envisage an exemption for small businesses. The argument is that fairness requires that everyone should contribute to the cost of government, just as under the income tax that is being replaced. Moreover, in the case of small businesses value-added consists largely of the proprietor's reward for working in his own business. This line of reasoning, however, bypasses the empirical finding that VAT (and NRST) compliance costs fall with exceptional severity on small businesses. Sandford, Godwin, and Hardwick (1989) found that the compliance costs of small businesses in the United Kingdom, as a percentage of turnover, were twenty times higher than the costs of large businesses. The comparable figure for New Zealand was fifty (Sandford and Hasseldine, 1992). If it is assumed that owners of small businesses have lower incomes, the burden distribution of compliance costs should be highly regressive. This regressivity can be mitigated by incorporating a small-business exemption under VAT, confining the tax to the inputs of the business. This is not possible under NRST.

Susceptibility to Tax Evasion

Because retailers have "prepaid" the tax on their purchases under VAT, it is often thought that they are less likely to succeed in evading the full amount of the tax. However, this would only be the case if a retailer operates entirely outside the tax system. Retailers with a permanent place of business would more likely underdeclare some portion of their sales but, under VAT, still claim a full credit for tax on all purchases. In this event, the same amount of tax would be at risk under VAT as under NRST.

Nevertheless, VAT has some features that make it a more robust tax than NRST. These features include the following:

- Under VAT, the invoice represents a "public declaration" of the tax liability with respect to a particular transaction, so that falsifying the invoice is fraud.

---

[33] Louisiana has some experience with such a scheme. Wholesalers are required to collect the tax in advance on their sales to retailers, which, in turn, can credit the payments against their RST liability.

- Buyers (who want the tax credit to be as high as possible) and sellers (who want the tax to be as low as possible) have opposing interests in the amount of tax to be shown on the invoice and hence are less likely to agree on a false invoice.[34]
- Invoices offer tax auditors the opportunity to cross-check purchases and sales more easily than is feasible under NRST.
- The onus of proof with respect to the tax liability is partly on the taxpayer who must prove that he is entitled to the tax credits claimed in his return.
- Claims for refunds of tax (that has already been paid by suppliers) provide a warning signal to the tax office that scrutiny is required.
- The wider coverage of VAT and the more extensive record keeping that is required offer greater opportunities for joint audit with other taxes and across business sectors.
- Wholesalers and manufacturers act as withholding agents for the government, so that retailers are less likely to default on tax invoiced by suppliers than they would be on tax payable directly to the tax office.
- VAT is partly collected on imports where the risk of evasion probably is smallest.

Generally, these points indicate that a high-rate VAT is more evasion proof than a high-rate NRST, although the strength of the arguments should not be exaggerated. Compliance under NRST can also be checked on the basis of information on purchases that is cross-checked with entries in the books of suppliers. Under both taxes, full-scale audits must be made to verify the reliability of the accounts of a business. Moreover, there are several hard-core areas in which both taxes seem to be equally evasion-prone (as under the income tax). These areas include most repair work (plumbing, painting, carpentry, garages), hotels and restaurants, and various professional services rendered to households. Perhaps the most important difference between the two taxes is that VAT is predominantly collected from large firms (in other words, by these firms from other smaller firms) that are typically not in the business of evading the tax.

Both taxes also have to police fraudulent appropriations of business purchases for consumer use. Such appropriations are nearly impossible to detect, particularly if turnover is large. Generally, VATs actually in use

---

[34] Of course, the dark side of this administrative method is that it is possible for the seller to issue counterfeit invoices, which may be difficult to detect if the seller understates the tax on the copy of the invoice that he uses for his own records and correctly states or overstates the tax on the copy of the invoice that he gives to the buyer.

disallow credit for prior-stage tax on consumer items, such as employee
fringe benefits, the provision of food and drink below cost, entertainment and luxury items, business gifts, motor fuel, car, and traveling
expenses, even if used in the course of business; however, the audit of
these items is probably not watertight. Barter arrangements that allow
both parties to evade tax are also hard to detect, as is the issue of false
invoices at the retail stage. The application of exemptions under NRST
makes the tax vulnerable to evasion through the misclassification of
sales. VAT has to cope with the problem of fraudulent refund claims,
which are especially hard to single out for scrutiny when they are filed
by exporters.[35] Under NRST, on the other hand, the practice of pro-
ducing counterfeit registration numbers to obtain tax-free goods would
be prevalent.

There are no studies on the estimated revenue loss through evasion
under a high-rate NRST.[36] In the EU, revenue losses under VAT vary
from country to country. Some older studies indicate that in the United
Kingdom the VAT revenue lost through evasion is estimated to be only
about 1.5 percent of potential revenue.[37] The smallness of the loss probably reflects two factors: the large number of commodities that are
zero-rated under the United Kingdom's VAT and the relatively small
number of small businesses in the country. In the Netherlands, by contrast, the total VAT lost through fraudulent practices is estimated to be
6 percent of total proceeds. Interestingly, the findings for this country
show that, although evasion is practiced slightly more often at the retail
stage than at other stages, the amounts of tax evaded at the retail stage
are substantially smaller. A 1989 French tax council report estimated that
VAT evasion in France amounts to 3 percent of the yield (Duverne,
1990).

No doubt, these figures should be adjusted upward if the rate would
be (much) higher than the rates of the European VATs. Agha and
Haughton (1996) report that a higher average VAT rate is associated
with lower compliance. A one-point increase in the rate at the level of
an average rate of 15.8 percent would imply a fall in the compliance rate
by 2.7 percentage points. This finding leads the authors to conclude that

---

[35] For a review of evasion practices under VAT, see Oldman and Woods (1983). Although
VAT is by no means evasion proof, these authors conclude that "an effectively administered VAT does seem to have some advantages over other taxes with respect to both
the amount of tax that can be evaded and the ease of detecting evasion."

[36] Some figures indicate that evasion of state RSTs with respect to interstate sales is on
the order of 1 to 2.5 percent of total collections; in-state evasion probably accounts for
another 2 to 3 percent of total proceeds. See Ulbrich (1985). For an analysis of potential evasion and avoidance problems under NRST, see Murray (1997a).

[37] See Hemming and Kay (1981). Tait (1988) puts this figure at 2–4 percent of revenue.

revenue would be maximized with a VAT rate of 25 percent, which, incidentally is the rate found in Denmark. The authors also found that administrative expenditure has a clear positive effect on compliance. For every extra dollar spent on administration, compliance would rise by twelve dollars. It is doubtful whether NRST could be levied at a 25 percent rate.[38] State RSTs avoid the enforcement problems associated with higher rates by widely taxing investment goods, just as they avoid the problems of hard-to-tax groups, such as the service sectors, by simply excluding them from the base.

Administrative and Compliance Costs

Although no studies on the administrative costs of a high-rate NRST have been done, several studies involving VATs have shown that their administrative costs in selected OECD countries are on average 0.027 percent of GDP.[39] Norway and Sweden – two countries with a simple rate structure – administer their VATs at a relatively low cost per registered business. Costs in Belgium and Ireland, on the other hand, are relatively high. A 1988 OECD report cites some fragmentary evidence that indicates that VAT revenues "can be collected at a lower average cost than income taxes for a similar amount of revenue."[40] This finding is based on experience in Sweden and the United Kingdom. In Sweden, the cost of collecting income tax is twice as high as the cost of collecting the same amount of VAT; in the United Kingdom, the cost of collecting income tax is 60 percent higher than the cost of collecting VAT. Furthermore, it was found that relative administrative costs increase with the complexity of the rate structure and decrease with the size of the small-business exemption.

In the United States, the Department of the Treasury (1984c), KPMG (1989), the Government Accounting Office (1993), and the Internal Revenue Service (1993) have estimated the administrative costs of a hypothetical VAT. Major design aspects that affect the costs of VAT administration were found to be the number of rates, the breadth of the

---

[38] Although there is little empirical evidence for the view that "10 percent may well be the maximum rate feasible under an RST" (Tanzi, 1995), retailing is undoubtedly the weakest enforcement link in the production-distribution process. The effectiveness of the fractional collection process under VAT can be compared with wage and capital income withholding schemes under a high-rate income tax.

[39] Due and Mikesell (1995) report that the costs of administering current state RSTs are "usually less than 1 percent of revenues." For a summary and analysis of reports on the administrative costs of VATs, see Cnossen (1994). See Gale and Holzblatt (Chapter 7 in this volume) for possible adminstrative costs of NRST.

[40] For references to the compliance costs of an income tax, see also the wealth of material found in Gale and Holzblatt (Chapter 7 in this volume).

tax base, and the number of registered businesses that are required to pay the tax or that are entitled to a refund. On the basis of these studies, Cnossen (1994) estimates that the ongoing incremental administrative costs of a single-rate VAT, otherwise similar in design to, say, the German VAT, would be on the order of 0.015 percent of GDP, or $1 billion in 1995. This assumes a basic exemption of $75,000 and an additional vanishing exemption of $50,000 (which would require registration). Administrative costs would be on average $100 per registered business, but this assumes joint audit with the business income tax (which, of course, would not be around under NRST).

Most studies indicate that the compliance costs of VAT should not be underestimated. Sandford et al. (1989) estimated that the compliance costs of the U.K. VAT were 3.7 percent of collections in 1986–87.[41] On the basis of the data generated by the U.K. study, Congressional Budget Office (1993) simulated the compliance costs of a hypothetical U.S. VAT levied at a rate of 10 percent. It estimated compliance costs at about $4 billion to $7 billion in 1988. Apart from assuming that the hypothetical VAT would be similar in design and operation as that in the United Kingdom, the CBO assumed that small businesses with annual sales under $25,000 would be exempted. By comparison, Slemrod and Sorum (1984) calculated the compliance costs of filing federal and state individual income tax returns at between $17 billion and $27 billion in 1982, or 0.6 to 0.8 percent of GDP. Whatever the level of the compliance costs per se, the data seem to indicate that it is lower than the compliance costs of the income tax.

WHAT IS THE PREFERRED CHOICE?

If an indirect consumption tax is to be adopted, what is the preferred choice? I conclude that VAT is inherently more robust than NRST. Inherent robustness is an important attribute in view of the high rate that would be required to serve the purposes of fundamental tax reform. VAT's technical superiority over NRST implies that it can be levied with fewer distortions than its rival and that it has a greater revenue potential. By far the most important difference between the two taxes is that VAT does not have to make a distinction between consumer goods and producer goods. Dual-use goods are not an issue. The exclusion of producer goods is fully integrated with the taxation of consumer goods. This feature results in a more even tax burden distribution under VAT than is possi-

---

[41] A 1982 study of seven U.S. states with RSTs found gross costs (inclusive of credits for collection costs) ranging from 2.03 percent of taxes collected in Missouri to 3.75 percent in Arizona. These figures are equivalent to 0.083 and 0.19 percent of gross receipts. See Peat Marwick Mitchell (1982).

ble under NRST. VAT has other useful attributes: it disperses the collection process (whose timing is generally the same under VAT as it is under NRST) over the whole of industry and commerce, it transfers part of the *onus probandi* for the tax liability to taxpayers, and it places a higher price on dishonesty than does NRST. This conclusion is supported by the experience of various countries that have switched from NRST to VAT.

The problems of NRST – that is, confining the tax to consumer goods and services and fully reaching the retail sector with a high-rate tax – are not adequately solved by the introduction of a tax rebate scheme for dual-use goods used for business purposes and withholding schemes for small retailers. As halfway stations on the road to VAT, these schemes would greatly complicate the operation of NRST, because they would involve numerous delineation issues and require additional audit oversight. To be feasible, the schemes would have to be extended to all goods and services and all businesses. This implies, of course, that NRST would be converted into VAT.

The NRST plans do not provide for a small-business exemption on the philosophy that the new tax replaces the income tax. But any high-rate, broad-based consumption tax would be difficult to administer properly without a small-business exemption. Under VAT, an appropriate exemption would eliminate some 60 percent of all potentially liable firms from the VAT register. But subject to optional registration, small firms would still pay VAT on inputs. In other words, the loss of revenue on account of the exemption would be very small. This would not be possible under NRST. Moreover, the compliance costs, measured against sales, which small businesses would have to incur if registered are much higher than for large enterprises and generally regressive if measured against proprietors' income. The (generous) small-business exemption that is possible under VAT mitigates this effect. An incidental, if welcome, side effect would be that VAT's small-business exemption would eliminate most of the operational overlap with state RSTs. It should be noted that it would not be possible to levy a national RST or VAT as a supplement to the state RSTs. A high-rate indirect consumption tax requires a centralized tax agency with nationwide powers of audit and enforcement (Mikesell, 1997; Mieszkowski and Palumbo, Chapter 6 in this volume).

These considerations support the view that VAT is to be preferred over NRST if the income tax and the gift and estate tax are to be replaced by a broad-based indirect consumption tax.[42] If the United

---

[42] This raises the question why there are so few serious proposals in the United States for VAT. An important reason, particularly for those interested in fundamental tax reform, may be that VAT is viewed as a money machine associated with "spendthrift" govern-

States were to give thought to adopting a VAT, it should be advised, however, to avoid the mistakes of the European VATs with their multiple rates, open-ended exemptions for health, education, and governments, and ill-considered treatment of agriculture, commercial real estate, and nonprofit organizations. Rather, the United States should look toward the New Zealand VAT, whose tax base more closely resembles the base proposed under the NRST plans. All goods and services, with the fewest possible exceptions, should be taxed at a single rate (only exports should be zero-rated). Tax burden distribution concerns could be addressed through targeted demogrants.

There is no real-world experience with the high rate at which the new tax would have to be levied. Among VAT countries, the highest rate is found in Denmark, which successfully imposes VAT at a single rate of 25 percent. In principle, there seems to be no reason why VATs cannot be levied at the same rates as business income taxes in countries, such as the United States, where there are few limits on administrative capacity. This implies that the rate could be raised to, say, 40 or 50 percent. As under the business income tax, however, the tax authorities would then have considerable difficulty in enforcing the tax on small business establishments, particularly firms that provide services to consumers. A high rate would also put downward pressure on the small-business exemption (with a concurrent increase in operational costs), because the inducement to split up business operations would become substantial. On balance, a 30 percent rate for a federal VAT might well be the maximum.[43]

Even this rate should probably not be introduced overnight. The abolition of the income and payroll taxes, the onetime rise of the general price level (if one assumes that the introduction of the VAT would be accommodated by the monetary authorities), and the switch from taxing exports to taxing imports would bring many uncertainties in their train. The risk-averse nature of the tax collection process is an argument to introduce the VAT at a moderate rate of, say, 10 percent. Over time, the rate could then be raised in tandem with a (further) reduction of the income, gift, and estate taxes. VAT would then become the primary revenue source for the federal government. To disassociate it from VATs levied elsewhere, it might be labeled NGST – national goods and services tax.

ments in Europe. Another reason is that the individualized flat tax (which would fit more easily in the U.S. federal tax system and involve fewer transition problems) with a basic exemption for wage earners has recently received most of the attention. The flat tax has not been considered in this chapter, because it is not an indirect consumption tax.

[43] Obviously, state RSTs would have to be added. In some states, this would bring the combined rate close to 40 percent.

Chapter 9

Transitional Issues in the Implementation of a Flat Tax or a National Retail Sales Tax

George R. Zodrow

Proposals for replacing the existing income tax with some form of consumption-based taxation, especially various versions of the Hall and Rabushka ([1985] 1995) flat tax or a national retail sales tax (NRST), have been the focus of much recent discussion in both the political and academic arenas. The debate regarding the desirability of such "fundamental tax reform" in the United States has proceeded in many dimensions.[1] In particular, there is a large literature on the relative merits of income-based and consumption-based taxes, as well as on the relative advantages and disadvantages of direct or individual and firm-based taxes like the flat tax and indirect or transaction-based taxes like the NRST. These issues are not revisited in this study. Instead, the analysis focuses on an issue that arises often in the discussion of fundamental tax reform – the transitional problems associated with moving from the

The opinions expressed in this chapter are those of the author, and should not be interpreted as reflecting the views of the Baker Institute for Public Policy. I would like to thank Peter Mieszkowski and Jane Gravelle for helpful comments and Craig Johnson and John Diamond for excellent research assistance.

[1] It is interesting to note that the same "fundamental tax reform" terminology was used to describe the Tax Reform Act of 1986 (TRA86), as well as its precursors, the two Treasury Department reports commonly known as Treasury I and Treasury II, even though these proposals generally attempted to move the tax system closer to one based on comprehensive income rather than consumption. (See McLure and Zodrow, 1987, for a comparison of these three proposals.) It is clear that the 1986 act did not provide reform that was "fundamental" enough for many observers and may have even provided some impetus for the current interest in consumption-based tax reforms. Indeed, Charles McLure, who was the chief economist on the team that developed the two U.S. Treasury reports, has argued that the complexity of TRA86 may demonstrate that taxation on the basis of income is impracticable and that a consumption tax is a preferable alternative; see McLure (1988), who argues for further consideration of a direct consumption-based tax such as that detailed in McLure et al. (1990) and Zodrow and McLure (1991), which is a variant of the Hall-Rabushka flat tax proposal. See also McLure and Zodrow (1996a,b).

current income-based tax system to a consumption-based tax, especially the tendency of such a reform to impose a onetime windfall loss on the owners of existing capital.

Concerns about transitional problems have long been an impediment to fundamental tax reform. In particular, the U.S. Treasury (1984a) cited transitional issues as one of the primary reasons that consumption-based taxes were not seriously considered in the process that led to the Tax Reform Act of 1986. More generally, Pearlman (1996, p. 395) observes that in legislative discussions of tax reform it is often the case that "attention is refocused entirely to the design of politically acceptable transition relief, depriving substantive changes of adequate analysis." Several recent essays have focused on the transitional problems associated with consumption tax reforms. In particular, this chapter draws heavily on Zodrow (1997a) as well as Sarkar and Zodrow (1993), and builds on the excellent analyses by the Joint Committee on Taxation (1993), Gravelle (1995), Bradford (1996a), Pearlman (1996), R. Hall (1996a), and Shaviro (2000).

Although these studies have identified a number of transitional problems raised by the implementation of a consumption tax, one issue has by far received the most attention. Specifically, the enactment of a consumption tax is sometimes described as the enactment of a tax on future wages plus a tax on existing capital. It is the latter component of the tax that gives rise to transitional concerns, because such a capital levy – if not mitigated or reversed by other reform-induced changes – would impose a potentially large onetime transitional windfall loss on the owners of existing capital. Moreover, because a disproportionate share of the existing capital stock is owned by the elderly, such a capital levy would result in significant intergenerational redistributions from the current elderly to current young and future generations.

This and other transitional issues associated with a movement toward a consumption-based reform are analyzed in this chapter, in the context of a movement to the flat tax or an NRST. I consider the likely effects of these reform proposals on the price level; discuss the potential "capital levy" or windfall tax on existing capital that is commonly associated with the implementation of a consumption tax; present alternative economic, legal, and political perspectives on the transitional problems caused by the implementation of tax reforms; and consider potential transition rules that might be used to reduce the reform-induced windfall losses and gains associated with a consumption tax reform.[2]

---

[2] This discussion focuses on domestic issues. For discussions of the international effects of consumption tax reforms, see R. Hall (1995), Hines (1996), and Ballard (Chapter 5 in this volume).

THE TWO PROPOSALS

The National Retail Sales Tax

Proponents of an NRST envision a tax levied at a single rate on an extremely comprehensive base that would include personal consumption of all goods and services, with very few exemptions on either distributional or administrative grounds.[3] Distributional concerns at the low end of the income distribution are addressed by providing individuals with a rebate sufficiently large to cover the NRST paid on expenditures equal to the poverty level of consumption.[4] The rebate is universal rather than means-tested, an approach that achieves simplicity and nonintrusiveness at a relatively high revenue cost.[5]

Proponents of the NRST do not envision extensive transition rules. However, the Shaefer-Tauzin bill provides a tax credit to retailers for inventories accumulated prior to the enactment of reform at the time such inventories are sold.

The Flat Tax

The flat tax is a direct tax that is similar in its basic structure to the existing income tax. It includes a business level tax, the base of which consists of all nonfinancial receipts with deductions for all nonfinancial business expenses, including purchases of capital and additions to inventories as well as wages. The primary difference between this cash flow approach to business taxation and the current income tax system is that the flat tax allows "expensing" or immediate deduction of all purchases of depreciable capital, whereas the income tax provides deductions for depreciation.

Wages are taxed at the individual level, after personal exemptions and a standard deduction, at a single rate. Hence, wages in excess of the exempt amount are taxed at a "flat" rate. Capital income is not taxed at the individual level.

---

[3] The following description generally applies to the NRST proposal put forward by the lobbying group Americans for Fair Taxation, which is broadly similar to the bill introduced in 1997 by Representatives Schaefer and Tauzin (H.R. 2001).

[4] For a comprehensive discussion of the distributional effects of consumption tax reforms, including the NRST proposal, see Mieszkowski and Palumbo (Chapter 6 in this volume) and the references cited therein, especially Feenberg, Mitrusi, and Poterba (1997).

[5] The subsequent discussion assumes that the goal of comprehensive coverage of personal consumption is attained under the NRST. However, experience with the sales tax suggests that such coverage would be difficult to achieve. For discussions of this point, as well as some proposals to deal with various administrative problems that arise under the sales tax, see Cnossen (Chapter 8 in this volume), Gillis, Mieszkowski, and Zodrow (1996), Mieszkowski and Palumbo (1998), and Zodrow (1999a).

The Armey-Shelby flat tax has no special transitional provisions, following the original Hall-Rabushka proposal. However, Hall and Rabushka (1995) discuss a number of possible transition provisions in the more recent version of their proposal. More generally, in commenting on Pearlman's (1996) discussion of transition rules, R. Hall (1996b, p. 431) concludes that, "Although the flat tax looks less attractive once it is combined with a reasonable transition plan, I concede that the factors considered by Pearlman mandate a serious consideration of the transition."

Price Level Effects

Because the flat tax is similar in structure to the existing income tax system, its implementation would have relatively little effect on the absolute price level. Both before- and after-tax wages would be roughly similar before and after reform, so that nominal prices remain roughly constant.

In contrast, the effect of implementing an NRST on the absolute price level is less certain. One possibility is that the tax would be fully shifted forward in the form of higher prices for consumption goods, with no change in the prices of investment goods, which are untaxed under the NRST. At the other end of the spectrum of possible responses, nominal prices could remain constant. Under this scenario, before-tax real wages would have to fall roughly to the level of prereform after-tax real wages in response to the elimination of the income tax. Intermediate responses between the "full price adjustment" and "no price adjustment" scenarios are of course also possible.

Choosing between these various scenarios requires making necessarily speculative assumptions about the response of the monetary authorities to the imposition of the NRST. However, most analysts assume that the monetary response would be sufficiently accommodating that the full price adjustment scenario would obtain.[6]

The primary rationale underlying this assumption is the view that the downward flexibility of nominal wages is quite limited, in part because most wage contracts and agreements are specified in nominal terms. Thus, a tax reform that required wage reductions to reach a new equilibrium would be quite costly as these wage reductions would initially be

---

[6] The mechanics of such a monetary accommodation would not be trivial, as stressed by Bull and Lindsey (1996). However, some lessons might be drawn from the European experience with the implementation of value-added taxes, especially in those cases that involved reduced income taxation; see Tait (1988). In addition, cost-of-living indices used to adjust wages should be defined to exclude the onetime reform-induced price increase; see R. Hall (1996a).

distributed unevenly across industries. This in turn might result in considerable unemployment in sectors characterized by rigid wages, as well as misallocations of labor, at least in the short run. Proponents of the full price adjustment view assume that monetary policy would be expansionary in order to avoid these costs.[7]

Most observers fall into the full price adjustment camp. For example, McLure (1996, p. 23) concludes that it would be "hard to imagine the monetary authorities not accommodating such an increase in prices." Gravelle (1995, p. 9) argues that full price adjustment is likely because a "national sales tax . . . would tend to produce an economic contraction if no price accommodation is made." In its analysis of the distributional implications of implementing consumption taxes, the Joint Committee on Taxation (1993, p. 59) concludes that, "Unless there are convincing reasons to assume otherwise, the JCT staff assumes the Federal Reserve will accommodate the policy change and allow prices to rise." Finally, Bradford (1996a, p. 135), in discussing the same issue in the context of a value-added tax, observes that, "It is commonly believed that introducing a value-added tax of the consumption type will bring with it a monetary policy adjustment that would result in a one-time increase in the price level . . . and no change in payments to workers in nominal terms."[8]

Nevertheless, opinion on this issue is certainly not unanimous. For example, the alternative assumption is implicitly made by Jorgenson and Wilcoxen (Chapter 3 in this volume), who argue that implementing a national sales tax would reduce producer prices on average by 25 percent.[9] Auerbach (1996) takes a compromise position by assuming partial price adjustment. In addition, European experience with the introduction of VATs is mixed, generally suggesting partial price adjustment.[10] On the other hand, Besley and Rosen (1999) find full (or even more than 100 percent) forward shifting of state sales taxes in the United States.

The analysis here follows the conventional wisdom on this issue, assuming that the implementation of the flat tax would have no effect

---

[7] Two other factors suggest that the full price adjustment scenario is relatively more desirable from a political perspective and is thus the more likely outcome. First, by engineering a full price adjustment, the government would effectively experience a windfall gain through a reduction in the real value of its debt. Second, as stressed by Gravelle (Chapter 2 in this volume), stock market prices would be much more likely to fall under the no price adjustment scenario, especially for highly leveraged firms.

[8] Full price adjustment is assumed in the recent studies by Feenberg et al. (1997) and Kotlikoff (1997).

[9] See also Jorgenson (1996c).

[10] See Tait (1988).

on the price level, whereas the implementation of an NRST would result in a onetime increase in the price level equal to the amount of the tax. Assumptions about the nature of the price response to the implementation of reform play an important role in analyzing the transitional effects of reform.

EFFECTS OF A FLAT TAX OR AN NRST ON THE OWNERS OF EXISTING CAPITAL

Much of the concern about the transition from an income tax to a consumption tax has focused on the potential capital levy or onetime windfall loss that such a reform might impose on the holders of existing capital assets.[11] In this section I examine the source of this potential windfall tax on old capital and how the specific nature of the loss would vary across the two alternative tax reform options; discuss other factors that would affect the holders of existing capital, many of which would act to offset such a windfall tax; and evaluate some simulation studies of the net effects of a consumption tax reform on asset values and on the distribution of welfare across generations.

Source of the Potential Windfall Loss to Existing Capital Owners

The implementation of any consumption-based tax, including the flat tax and the NRST, is often described as the enactment of a tax on wage income plus a onetime levy on the owners of existing capital.[12] This equivalence can be explained as follows. An essential feature of any consumption-based tax system is that the return to new saving is untaxed.[13] After the enactment of either reform, aggregate consumption in any time period must equal the sum of current wage and capital

---

[11] See, for example, Auerbach and Kotlikoff (1987), Kotlikoff (1995), Bradford (1996a), Joint Committee on Taxation (1993), Gravelle (1995), Pearlman (1996), Zodrow (1997a), and Zodrow and Williams (1998).

[12] For formal derivations of this result, see Joint Committee on Taxation (1993) and Gravelle (1995). Note, however, that this characterization – and the discussion that follows – is incomplete in that it ignores the taxation of above-normal returns to new (and existing) capital, and (arguably) the returns to risk taking, that would occur under a consumption tax and thus provide additional revenues beyond those obtained from the taxation of future wage income. (The equivalence result can, however, under certain circumstances be extended to returns to risky investments; see Zodrow, 1995.) As stressed by Hubbard (Chapter 4 in this volume), such taxation of above-normal returns is common to both income and consumption taxes. In addition, the following discussion does not apply to existing capital in the form of owner-occupied housing, which, due to its generous treatment under current law, is not subject to this onetime reform-induced capital levy.

[13] For a demonstration of this well-known proposition, see Zodrow and McLure (1991).

income (net of depreciation) less new net saving. However, given the exemption of the returns to new net saving under a consumption tax, the base of a consumption tax in all periods after the enactment of reform is just the sum of wage income plus the income earned on the capital stock existing at the time of reform. This in turn implies that the consumption tax base is effectively future wage income plus the value of the existing capital stock at the time of enactment of reform. The precise nature of the windfall loss experienced by the owners of existing capital, however, depends on the reform enacted and the nature of the price adjustment to that reform.

The NRST

Under an NRST with full price adjustment, asset prices would simply reflect the cost of investment goods, which would be roughly unchanged under the NRST, relative to the income tax, because the tax does not apply to such goods.[14] However, with full price adjustment, nominal prices of consumption goods would increase by the amount of the tax. Thus, under the NRST, the loss to capital owners would be reflected as the reduced purchasing power of existing assets, with no changes in the nominal prices of assets or after-tax producer prices.

This loss would be distributed uniformly across the holders of existing equity and debt. Because the reform-induced increase in the price level would lower the real value of outstanding bonds, the portion of the windfall loss on existing capital that is debt-financed would be borne by lenders (the bondholders) rather than by borrowers (the equity owners of the firm), for whom the decline in real value of their assets would be offset by the decline in the real value of their loan obligations. Note that under the full price adjustment scenario the windfall loss would extend to holders of government debt, unless some type of governmental accommodation were made to insulate them from the loss; and to transfer recipients, including Social Security beneficiaries, unless such transfers were indexed or adjusted for this onetime reform-induced increase in the price level.

This windfall loss for existing capital owners would not be avoided under the less likely "no price adjustment" scenario for the NRST. In this case, producer prices would decline and the correct relative prices between tax-free investment goods and taxable consumption commodities would be maintained only if the prices of new investment goods

---

[14] As shown by Auerbach (1983), asset prices under an income tax also reflect the cost of investment goods, as long as the tax code allows deductions for real economic depreciation; the implications of accelerated depreciation allowances under the current income tax are discussed later.

fell as well.[15] Arbitrage across new and old assets thus implies that existing assets would have to decline in value.[16] Thus, if monetary policy were tight in the sense of maintaining constant nominal commodity prices inclusive of the NRST, a windfall loss would still be imposed on the owners of existing capital, in the form of a decline in nominal asset prices.

Under the no price adjustment scenario, however, the distribution of the windfall loss across equity and debt owners would be quite different than that described with full price adjustment. In this case, lenders would be insulated from loss by the fact that their loans are fixed in nominal terms. Accordingly, the entire reform-induced windfall loss on existing capital would be borne by equity holders, who would experience losses equal to the product of the value of the capital stock and the tax rate, divided by the fraction of capital that is equity financed.[17] Such a concentration of losses would increase the likelihood of reform-induced bankruptcies for highly leveraged firms. These reform-induced effects would be viewed as highly inequitable and would greatly increase the probability that transitional relief would be granted.

The Flat Tax

Similar results would occur with implementation of the flat tax under the no price adjustment scenario. Implementation of the flat tax would imply expensing of all new business capital assets, which in turn implies an increase in the rate of return to such assets, relative to the income tax. Old assets would experience similar increases in their rate of return only if they were also allowed expensing – in the case of existing assets, expensing of all remaining (undepreciated) tax basis. However, the flat tax has no such provisions; indeed, it would not allow the remaining depreciation deductions scheduled under current law. Thus, the generous treatment of new investment under the flat tax implies that existing assets would be less valuable than new ones. For an equilibrium to exist, with equal after-tax rates of return on new and existing assets, the prices of existing assets would have to fall by the product of the value of the capital stock and the tax rate under the flat tax.[18] Moreover, this loss would be borne entirely by equity owners in the case of the flat tax;

---

[15] This decline would reflect the reduction in net cash flows attributable to the assets, given the reform-induced reduction in producer prices under the "no price adjustment" scenario.

[16] That is, if the gross return to an old investment (and the gross and thus net return to a new investment) is R, then the after-tax return to old capital initially valued at one dollar will fall to $R(1 - t)$; equilibrium requires an after-tax return of R, so the value of the old asset must decline to $(1 - t)$ dollars. See Gravelle (1995).

[17] See Bradford (1996a, p. 136).

[18] For example, see Gravelle (1995) or Bradford (1996a).

that is, the loss would equal the product of the value of the capital stock and the tax rate, divided by the fraction of capital that is equity financed.

Thus, unless this reform-induced windfall tax on capital were offset by other factors, implementation of the NRST or the flat tax would have a very negative effect on existing capital owners. Moreover, under the no price adjustment scenario (the likely outcome under the flat tax), the capital levy would be borne entirely by equity owners. By comparison, with full price adjustment (the likely outcome under the NRST), the capital levy would be distributed equally among holders of both debt and equity. The analysis thus far, however, has ignored a number of items that might offset the tendency of a consumption tax reform to impose the capital levy described earlier.

Factors Offsetting the Potential Windfall Loss to Existing Capital

If implementation of the flat tax or an NRST involved huge transitional costs in the form of a windfall loss to existing capital owners, reasonable opposition to the imposition of such arbitrary and capricious losses could easily doom any such reform. Other factors, however, would also affect the welfare levels of the owners of existing capital assets, many of which would offset this potential capital levy.[19] As a result, the net effects of the implementation of the flat tax or an NRST on asset values as well as on the welfare levels of the owners of existing capital are unclear.

Costs of Adjusting the Capital Stock

The foregoing analysis implicitly assumes away any costs of adjusting the capital stock in response to the relatively favorable tax treatment of capital income under the new consumption-based tax structure. In the presence of adjustment costs, however, the movement to the new equilibrium will take time. During the adjustment period, the owners of existing capital, as well as those making new investments (which will largely be the same firms and individuals, especially if they have better information regarding favorable investment opportunities under the new tax regime), will earn inframarginal rents. This will have a positive impact on the market values of existing assets – although, as stressed by Gravelle (Chapter 2 in this volume), it will also reduce the efficiency gains associated with a consumption tax reform.[20]

---

[19] Note, however, that in most cases these factors also imply that the efficiency gain from the enactment of a consumption tax reform would be smaller than implied by an analysis that ignored such factors.

[20] A variety of other factors would also affect the impact of reform on asset prices. In particular, asset values would tend to increase as reform-induced increases in saving drove up equity prices, but would tend to decline as the favorable treatment of investment generally and equity-financed investment in particular increased the supply of equities.

Empirical evidence regarding the effects on firm values of previous reforms might provide one way of resolving this theoretical ambiguity. Although no country has ever replaced an income tax with a consumption tax system, some relevant empirical evidence on this issue is provided by Lyon (1989a), who examines the effect on firm value of changes in the investment tax credit (ITC) for equipment. Lyon finds that increases in the ITC benefit equipment-intensive firms, which suggests that adjustment costs are important enough that the inframarginal rents earned by existing firms during the transition to a new equilibrium outweigh the negative effect on firm values associated with granting the ITC only to new equipment. Furthermore, empirical evidence presented by Lyon (1989b) and by Downs and Demirgures (1992) indicates that the introduction of the generous treatment of depreciable assets under the Economic Recovery Tax Act of 1981 had no appreciable impact on firm returns or values.

Although this evidence suggests that the offsetting changes in asset values that would arise with the implementation of a consumption tax reform might result in a net effect that would be quantitatively small, two important caveats must be noted. First, in the absence of adjustment costs, the reductions in firm value that would be predicted under a consumption tax reform would be considerably larger than those examined in these studies. It is thus unclear whether small net effects would also obtain with such a reform. Second, although early estimates of capital stock adjustment costs were quite large (e.g., Summers 1981b), more recent empirical work by Cummins, Hassett, and Hubbard (1994) provides significantly smaller estimates. This suggests that the move to a new equilibrium after the enactment of a consumption tax reform could be fairly rapid, which in turn implies that adjustment costs would have a relatively small effect in terms of moderating reform-induced windfall losses.

Firm Value Effects Due to Factors Other Than Tangible Assets

As stressed by Lyon and Merrill (1999), firm values reflect not only the value of tangible capital, but also the present value of future growth opportunities, the value of intangible assets, and the present value of economic rents that reflect market power. These factors are not affected by changes in the tax treatment of depreciation allowances. Their value would, however, increase to the extent that a consumption tax reform reduced or eliminated the taxation of the future cash flows of the firm, thus offsetting the negative effect on firm values described earlier.

Lyon and Merrill report that in October 1998, 70 (25) percent of firms in the Standard and Poor's 500 Index had a stock market value to book value ratio of 2 (5) or more, generally reflecting very valuable trademarks, reputations, and managerial and other skilled labor. Thus, this effect, which is ignored in current simulation studies of the transitional effects of a consumption tax reform, could be significant.

Effects of Reform on Interest Rates

An important factor in determining the effects on existing capital owners of the implementation of a consumption tax is the effect of such a reform on interest rates. In particular, the generous tax treatment of capital income under a consumption tax reform implies that the owners of existing assets will gain from higher postreform after-tax rates of return (to both existing and new saving) unless nominal interest rates fall immediately to their preenactment after-tax levels. As noted by Bradford (1996a),[21] such higher rates of return could also offset any reform-induced capital levy, with the importance of this effect increasing with the length of time the individual is able to defer consumption (or the making of gifts to future heirs).

The effect of the implementation of a consumption tax on nominal interest rates has been debated at some length in the literature. A common view is that a decline in interest rates would be expected with the elimination of the taxation of interest income and expense. For example, Hall and Rabushka ([1985] 1995) suggest that a decline of 2 percentage points would be a reasonable response to the elimination of the taxation of interest income and expense.[22] Hall (1997) suggests that the process of adjustment to an equilibrium interest rate close to the preenactment after-tax rate of return would take approximately ten years (which implies that existing capital owners would benefit from higher rates of return over that period).

As noted by Bradford (1996a), such an analysis is consistent with a highly elastic supply of capital such that after-tax returns received by savers are roughly constant and savings (and thus wealth holdings) expand to meet increased demands for capital investment by firms as interest rates decline. Note that this could be described as a "closed-economy" scenario, in that interest rates are determined domestically rather than fixed in an international capital market.

Alternatively, as also described by Bradford (1996a), a fixed before-tax rate of return is the more likely outcome to the extent that there is a highly elastic demand for capital at the going before-tax rate of return, and there are ample opportunities for increased investment, either domestically or abroad, to accommodate reform-induced increases in savings. Under this "open-economy" scenario, reform has little impact on before-tax rates of return.

---

[21] This point is also stressed in U.S. Treasury (1977). [22] See also Golob (1995).

In addition, Feldstein (1995b) stresses that the current income tax system favors debt finance, so that a consumption tax reform would reduce effective tax rates on equity-financed investment much more than on debt-financed investment, thus increasing relative returns to equity.[23] The fact that debt would become relatively less attractive would in turn put upward pressure on interest rates in order to maintain a financial equilibrium; that is, interest rates might rise even though the overall before-tax rate of return declines as a result of the consumption tax reform. Although this effect would be mitigated by increased savings in response to higher rates of return, Feldstein (1995b, p. 1) concludes that, "With plausible parameter values, the analysis suggests that the shift from an income tax to a consumption tax is more likely to raise rates than to lower them."[24]

Under the latter scenario, savers are rewarded to at least some degree with a higher after-tax rate of return even in the long run under the consumption tax regime. By comparison, this effect occurs only in the short run under the former (fixed after-tax return) scenario while the economy adjusts to the new lower-interest-rate equilibrium. In both cases, higher after-tax returns act to provide an offset to any windfall loss imposed on the owners of existing capital at the time of enactment of a consumption tax.

Most of the simulation studies of this issue, including those discussed later, have assumed a closed economy. In these studies, interest rates follow the general path described by Hall, gradually approaching an equilibrium interest rate close to the after-tax interest rate in the

---

[23] As discussed in Hall (1997) and Gentry and Hubbard (1997b), the marked differences in the views of Hall and Feldstein can to some extent be attributed to different views of equilibrium in financial markets. Hall's position is consistent with either (1) an equilibrium in which the tax advantage to debt finance under the current income tax implies that all investment is financed with debt at the margin, or (2) an equilibrium in which marginal investments are financed with retained earnings and the "new view" of the effects of dividend taxation holds so that individual-level dividend taxes have no effects on marginal investment decisions and the tax advantage to debt under the income tax is minimal. By comparison, Feldstein's view is consistent with the traditional view of dividend taxation, under which dividends affect decisions regarding marginal investments (which are financed with a combination of debt and equity) and in equilibrium after-tax rates of return on debt- and equity-financed investments are identical. Although the issue is still controversial, the current consensus in the profession seems to favor the traditional view of the effects of dividend taxation; see Zodrow (1991).

[24] In addition, Gravelle (1996a) notes that, in the presence of inflation, full deductibility of nominal interest expense implies that debt finance is subsidized at the firm level under the current income tax. She constructs a portfolio model of interest rate determination in which the reduction in demand for debt finance that would result from the elimination of this subsidy with a consumption tax reform puts sufficient downward pressure on interest rates to result in a decline of roughly 1 percentage point.

preenactment equilibrium. Thus, to the extent that these studies over-state the decline in interest rates that would follow reform, they under-state the gains to the owners of existing capital that would arise from postenactment higher after-tax rates of return.

The Role of Accelerated Depreciation under Current Law

The analysis underlying this discussion of the windfall tax on old capital implicitly assumed that the tax basis of assets equals their market value. Under current U.S. law, however, depreciation allowances are acceler-ated, relative to economic depreciation, although recent reforms have reduced the extent of acceleration. Such acceleration is provided pri-marily to offset the reduction in real value over time of depreciation deductions in the presence of inflation (which has of course also declined in recent years, reducing the need for such accelerated deductions). Accelerated deductions for depreciation imply that the income gener-ated by a depreciable asset is undertaxed during its early years and then overtaxed in its later years. This in turn implies that under the current income tax regime older assets should sell at a discount, reflecting the capitalized value of the higher effective tax rates on the cash flows gen-erated by the asset. Eliminating the corporate income tax as would occur under the NRST would eliminate this expected tax, and thus confer a windfall gain to the holders of existing assets. A similar but smaller effect would occur under the flat tax; that is, because the returns generated by existing assets would still be taxed, owners of such assets would benefit only to the extent that rates under the new business tax were lower than current income tax rates. Auerbach (1996) estimates that the existing cor-porate fixed capital stock should sell at a discount of roughly 8 percent due to this factor. This discount should disappear under the NRST, and be reduced significantly under the flat tax if its rates were as low as envi-sioned by its proponents.

Capitalization of Future Dividend Taxes in Stock Prices

The implementation of either the flat tax or NRST might also have a positive effect on asset values through the elimination of a second cap-italized tax (beyond that associated with deductions for accelerated depreciation), although this potential gain is considerably more tenuous. Specifically, under the controversial "new view" of the effects of dividend taxation, dividend taxes at the individual level have no effect on mar-ginal investment decisions financed with retained earnings.[25] Under this view, the present value of future taxes paid on the income earned by such

---

[25] For a discussion of the "new" and "traditional" views of the effects of dividend taxation, see Zodrow (1991).

investments exactly offsets the tax benefit obtained by retaining earnings and deferring individual-level dividend taxes and thus does not result in additional tax burden on such income. Moreover, this view implies that the market value of capital assets sells at a discount to reflect the capitalized value of future dividend taxes (net of the effective accrual capital gains tax rate that must be paid on such assets). Thus, elimination of the taxation of dividends at the individual level under either the flat tax or NRST reform should eliminate the associated undervaluation of corporate shares and thus act to offset any reform-induced windfall capital levy. Auerbach (1996) estimates that, assuming the validity of the new view, the associated discount on corporate shares under current law is 10 percent.[26]

This capitalization effect, however, is quite tenuous, as the consensus of the profession seems to favor the traditional view of dividend taxation, under which the effective tax rate on the income from all equity-financed investment is a weighted average of the dividend tax rate and the effective annual accrual rate on capital gains.[27] Under this view, there is no capitalization of dividend taxes in share values, and thus no windfall gain for shareholders would arise with the implementation of either the flat tax or NRST. Most tax reform simulation models, including those discussed later, ignore this "new view" capitalization effect. To the extent that the new view of the effects of dividend taxation is valid, these results thus overstate the capital levy associated with consumption tax reforms.

The Extent of Taxation of Capital Income under a Consumption Tax

Many discussions of consumption-based taxes argue that they "exempt" capital income from tax, and this result obtains in many simulations of fundamental tax reform. As stressed by Bradford (1996a), Gentry and Hubbard (1997a,b), and Hubbard (Chapter 4 in this volume), however, this characterization is accurate only for the "normal" return to saving and investment (the "return to waiting") that is untaxed as a result of expensing under the flat tax or because investment goods are not subject to tax under the NRST. By comparison, the three other components of capital income – inframarginal returns attributable to market power, good ideas, or managerial skill; the expected returns to risk taking; and

[26] Note, however, that the validity of the new view also implies that the existing level of taxation of capital is relatively low, which in turn implies that the efficiency gains from introducing a consumption tax are relatively low.

[27] This consensus is based primarily on the fact that empirical evidence generally supports the traditional view; see, for example, Gerardi, Graetz, and Rosen (1990). In addition, critics of the new view note that new-view models typically make the counterfactual assumption that share repurchases are precluded.

returns to risk taking in excess of the risk premium (or "good luck") – are all taxed similarly under both income and consumption taxes.

The extent to which returns to risk taking are "taxed" under either tax system is open to interpretation. It is clear that the expected value of government revenues is greater for risky investments. However, if the government discounts the uncertain revenue stream associated with risky investments at the same rate as the private sector, then such returns do not increase the present value of discounted government revenues.[28] Instead, they simply represent the return on the government's share of the risky investment as a "silent partner" in the venture, purchased through the "up front" deductions allowed with expensing. In any case, the tax treatment of such returns is the same under both income and consumption taxes. Thus, as stressed by Hubbard (Chapter 4 in this volume), the differences between the two taxes in terms of their tax treatment of capital income is much less than commonly assumed, especially in simulation analyses that ignore uncertainty and assume competitive markets. Recall that the source of the consumption tax reform-induced capital levy is the difference in the taxation of capital income before and after reform. Because this analysis indicates that this difference is smaller than under approaches that ignore imperfect competition and uncertainty, it suggests that the declines in the values of existing capital assets would be smaller than those implied by analyses – including most simulation studies of tax reform – that assume that all capital income taxation is eliminated with the implementation of a consumption tax.

Tax-Deferred Accounts and Unrealized Capital Gains

Another crucial factor in determining the transitional effects of a consumption tax reform is that the current system is not a pure income tax but a hybrid tax system that already has many features characteristic of a consumption tax.[29] In general, these features imply that the transition to a consumption tax would result in smaller reform-induced windfall gains and losses than if the current system were truly based on income. Indeed, because roughly 25 percent of total household assets are held in tax-deferred retirement plans and effectively all of net personal saving in the past twenty years has been in the form of tax-preferred retirement saving, models that ignore this factor significantly overstate the windfall losses imposed on the owners of existing capital attributable to the implementation of a consumption tax.[30]

---

[28] For example, see Bulow and Summers (1984) and Gordon (1985). In the consumption tax context, see Kaplow (1994) and Zodrow (1995).

[29] See Aaron, Galper, and Pechman (1988).   [30] See Engen and Gale (1996).

Most important, significant amounts of assets accumulated under the income tax are currently held in tax-deferred accounts, such as pensions, IRAs, Keogh and SEP plans, 401 (k) and 403 (b) plans. Assets in such tax-deferred accounts would be fully taxed upon withdrawal under continuation of the income tax; this implies that the owners of such assets do not suffer a windfall loss when such assets are taxed under a consumption tax. Under an NRST, the benefit of eliminating the direct tax on withdrawals of assets from tax-deferred accounts would, to a rough approximation, fully offset the reduction in real asset value attributable to the reform-induced price increase that occurs under the NRST. Under the flat tax, withdrawals from tax-deferred accounts would be included in the tax base as under the current income tax.[31] Indeed, under either consumption tax regime, the owners of existing assets would receive a windfall gain to the extent that reform resulted in a reduction in the tax rate applied to such withdrawals.

The existence of tax-deferred accounts, especially when coupled with the fact that owner-occupied housing is not subject to any onetime reform-induced capital levy, also has important implications for the intragenerational redistributional effects of reform. Specifically, a disproportionately large fraction of capital holdings for all households except those at the very top of the income distribution takes the form of either assets held in retirement accounts or owner-occupied housing. As noted by Diamond and Zodrow (1999), this implies that these households would, to a large extent, be sheltered from the capital levy aspect of a consumption tax reform, which would be concentrated at the top of the income distribution. As stressed by Mieszkowski and Palumbo (Chapter 6 in this volume) among others, however, a disproportionately large share of the economic benefits from moving from the current income tax to a flat tax or an NRST would also accrue to these very wealthy households. Thus, to the extent that the primary effect of any reform-induced capital levy is simply to reduce the gains from reform that accrue to the very wealthy, it is much less problematical than it would be if it were uniformly distributed among all capital owners. This is especially true since the wealthy have the greatest discretion in changing their bequest behavior to shift any reform-induced capital levy to their heirs (who will benefit from the long-run gains obtained from the enactment of a consumption tax regime).

---

[31] Note that transitional provisions designed to reduce or eliminate the taxation of withdrawals of assets accumulated in tax-deferred accounts prior to the enactment of reform would be a fairly straightforward way to reduce any reform-induced windfall losses on elderly capital owners associated with implementation of the flat tax.

Finally, owners of existing assets would benefit from the tax exemption of unrealized capital gains under the flat tax, which would also tend to offset any reform-induced windfall losses. The size of this benefit would be limited, however, by the fact that capital gains receive rather generous tax treatment under current law. By comparison, unrealized capital gains would be taxed when consumed under an NRST. Relative to current law, such treatment would result in longer deferral in some cases but eventual taxation of some gains transferred at death that would have been entirely exempt under current law.

The Role of Bequests

The relationship between reform-induced asset price changes and intergenerational redistributions depends on the nature of bequests and bequest motives. This is most obvious in the case of altruistic bequests, where the utility of one's children enters one's utility function. In this case, parents will realize that a consumption tax reform is redistributing wealth to their children and offset this with reductions in bequests. Under these circumstances, the elderly bear little if any of the burden of a reform-induced capital levy. In practice, this would be especially true for the very wealthy, who have the greatest discretion in affecting the intergenerational distribution of wealth (within their families) by effecting changes in bequests.

More generally, given any pattern of reform-induced asset price changes, the intergenerational redistributive effects of a consumption tax reform will depend on bequest behavior, and there is still a great deal of uncertainty in the literature about the nature of bequest motives.[32] Thus, it is difficult to predict how bequests would change in response to a consumption tax reform, and similarly difficult to predict the intergenerational redistributions associated with such a reform – even if one knows the pattern of reform-induced asset price changes.

Efficiency Gains

Most – but not all – observers believe that the implementation of a broad-based consumption tax like the flat tax or NRST would result in efficiency gains that would act to offset any reform-induced individual windfall losses; there is, however, considerable controversy regarding the magnitude of such gains.[33] There are several potential sources of such

[32] For a recent review, see Johnson, Diamond, and Zodrow (1997).
[33] For example, see the contrasting viewpoints offered by Gravelle in Chapter 2 and Jorgenson and Wilcoxen in Chapter 3 in this volume. See also Triest (1996), Randolph and Rogers (1995), Engen, Gravelle, and Smetters (1997), and Engen and Skinner (1996).

efficiency gains. Most important, a consumption tax would reduce the distortion of saving and investment decisions inherent in an income tax and thus improve the allocation of resources across present and future consumption. In addition, labor supply decisions would be distorted less if a consumption tax reform were accompanied by a reduction in marginal tax rates on labor income.[34]

A large number of other distortions would be eliminated under a consumption tax as well. For example, uniform treatment of all forms of business investment and saving would eliminate the interasset and interindustry distortions that characterize the current income tax. Although greatly reduced under the Tax Reform Act of 1986, distortions still remain.[35] In addition, the allocation of investment is distorted across depreciable assets and capital expenditures that receive expensing under current law, such as advertising and research and development expenditures. More important, the current tax system seriously distorts the allocation of investment across owner-occupied housing and other forms of investment, and potentially large gains might be obtained from eliminating this distortion (if consumption taxation of housing is politically feasible).[36] Adoption of the flat tax or NRST would also eliminate the current tax distortion favoring noncorporate over corporate investment. Although most analyses suggest that this distortion is fairly small, Gravelle and Kotlikoff (1989) argue that these studies neglect the very large efficiency costs of substituting away from corporate to noncorporate production of similar goods.[37]

Models that neglect any of these considerations would tend to understate the efficiency gains from a consumption-based reform, and thus tend to overstate any reform-induced windfall losses for the owners of existing capital. On the other hand, Fullerton and Rogers (1996) note that replacing an income tax with a consumption-based tax would tend to increase the relative prices of housing and of labor-intensive goods such as health care and medical services. Because these goods are consumed disproportionately by the elderly, increases in their relative prices would tend to reinforce the negative effects of reform attributable to any windfall tax imposed on elderly capital owners.

---

[34] Moreover, distortions in the allocation of leisure across periods would also be reduced, which would tend to lead to increases in labor supply; see Gravelle (Chapter 2 in this volume).

[35] For example, see Gravelle (1995).

[36] For example, see Jorgenson (1996c) and Jorgenson and Wilcoxen (Chapter 3 in this volume).

[37] A consumption tax would also eliminate current distortions of financial decisions (debt vs. equity) and capital gains realizations decisions, but the efficiency gains associated with these changes are difficult to estimate.

Simulation Studies of the Net Effects of a Flat Tax or NRST

This analysis suggests that implementation of either the flat tax or NRST would tend to result in a onetime capital levy that would be borne disproportionately by elderly capital owners but that a wide variety of other factors might act to offset this windfall loss. Although it is impossible to predict accurately such asset price changes and net intergenerational redistributions, some insight can be obtained with simulations of life-cycle models of the economic effects of a consumption tax reform.

The most widely cited study is by Auerbach (1996) who examines the effects of a wide variety of consumption tax reforms, including the Flat Tax and NRST. He uses the Auerbach-Kotlikoff (1987) single-good, representative individual, perfect foresight, dynamic overlapping generations model, modified in a somewhat ad hoc way to account for several of the factors described earlier, especially the consumption-tax-type features of the current tax system. In particular, Auerbach (1) accounts for the negative effects on asset values of accelerated depreciation under current law, (2) accounts for the existence of pension plans and other tax-deferred assets, and (3) tests the sensitivity of his results to introducing costs of adjusting the capital stock.

Several factors, however, are not considered in the Auerbach model. For example, he assumes the validity of the traditional view of dividend taxation and thus ignores any capitalization of future dividend taxes in asset values under the current income tax. In addition, his model assumes perfect certainty and competitive markets, and thus ignores the issue of the similarity of the taxation of inframarginal returns to capital under income and consumption taxation that are stressed by Hubbard (Chapter 4 in this volume). Interest rates are endogenous in the model, and, in most cases, Auerbach assumes a closed economy. Interest rates in the model initially tend to increase or decrease slightly and then move toward a long-run reduction of 1.2–1.4 percentage points. Both labor supply and savings are variable in the model, so the model captures the efficiency gains from smaller distortions of these decisions. However, because it is characterized by a single good and a single production sector, the model does not capture any efficiency gains from improved capital allocation or from elimination of distortions of the business choice of organizational form. There are no bequests in the model, all markets are competitive and there is no uncertainty.

The Auerbach model predicts that consumption tax reforms would have significant effects on the economy. Under a true flat-rate NRST with no demogrant or tax rebates and no adjustment costs (or transition rules), labor supply and investment increase sufficiently that output per capita initially increases by nearly 7 percent and by nearly 10 percent in the long run. The effects of reform on output are more modest with adjustment costs, as these increases decline to 4.5 and 8.9 percent. Under two versions of the flat tax (Hall-Rabushka and Armey-Shelby) with no adjustment costs or transition rules, output increases are more modest in the short run (4.7 and 2.7 percent) and in the long run (8.4 and 6.1 percent) but still quite significant.[38] With adjustment costs, the reform-induced changes in output per capita under the two versions of the flat tax are 2.9 and 1.0 percent in the short run and 7.6 and 5.3 percent in the long run.[39]

With respect to the capital levy issue, asset values decline initially in all the simulations without adjustment costs. Under the flat-rate NRST, this decline initially is 3.6 percent. Under the Hall-Rabushka and Armey-Shelby versions of the flat tax, asset values decline initially by 5.7 and 8.9 percent. As suggested by the discussion presented earlier, however, the introduction of adjustment costs in the model has a dramatic effect on these asset value changes. Asset values initially increase by 6.1 percent in the case of implementation of the NRST and by 3.0 percent under the Hall-Rabushka flat tax, and fall by only 0.3 percent under the Armey-Shelby flat tax. The net effects of reform on the welfare levels of elderly generations are fairly modest in Auerbach's simulations. With no adjustment costs, the elderly are slight gainers under the pure flat-rate NRST (as are all generations) and slight losers under the two versions of the flat tax (although all other generations are gainers). By comparison, with adjustment costs, the elderly gain under all reforms except the Armey-Shelby flat tax, where they suffer a slight loss. However, the introduction of adjustment costs slows down the attainment of the efficiency gains of reform, so that younger generations (who do not benefit from the reduction in the reform-induced capital levy) benefit considerably less from reform. Indeed, under the Hall-Rabushka version of the flat tax, individuals who are age twenty at the time of reform are slight net losers.

Zodrow and Williams (1998) obtain similar results. Transitional problems in general would be expected to be greater in their simulations, as theirs are the only simulation exercises that examine the replacement of both the income tax and the social security tax with an NRST. Their model is also based on the Auerbach-Kotlikoff model modified, as in Goulder and Summers (1989) and Keuschnigg (1990), to allow

---

[38] The Armey-Shelby proposal is characterized by larger personal exemptions and standard deductions and thus a higher tax rate than the Hall-Rabushka plan; see Auerbach (1996, pp. 54–55).

[39] Auerbach assumes a moderate level of adjustment costs, in between the early high estimates of Summers (1981b) and the more recent and much lower estimates of Cummins, Hassett, and Hubbard (1994).

for explicit calculation of firm values in the presence of adjustment costs. The model also includes a simple target bequest, following Fullerton and Rogers (1993); the assumed bequest behavior (a fixed nominal target bequest) implies that the elderly shift some of any reform-induced windfall loss to their heirs. The model also allows explicitly for saving in tax-deferred assets; however, it is characterized by fixed labor supply.

With fixed labor supply, output increases in the Zodrow-Williams model are initially very modest and increase very gradually (with the speed of adjustment declining with increases in adjustment costs) to a long-run increase of roughly 7.5 percent. In terms of asset price effects, with moderate adjustment costs, real asset values in the model decline by about 4 percent after the enactment of an NRST; this decline increases to about 7 percent with low adjustment costs, while asset prices increase slightly with high adjustment costs. In these simulations, the elderly are gainers from reform with moderate adjustment costs. However, as in the Auerbach simulations, the existence of adjustment costs implies that the efficiency gains from reform are delayed, so that most young and middle-aged generations are losers from reform, even though the long-run welfare gain in the model is significant (4.6 percent of lifetime income). By comparison, with low adjustment costs, the net welfare gains experienced by elderly generations are reduced significantly, with more than half of retired generations suffering welfare losses, and individuals near retirement suffering larger losses; however, reform-induced welfare gains to younger and future generations are attained earlier.

Finally, Altig et al. (1997) extend the Auerbach and Kotlikoff (1987) model to allow for twelve different income groups in each generation; they also model the existing tax system, including Social Security and Medicare, more carefully than in earlier versions of the Auerbach-Kotlikoff model, and extend the model to include bequests. Although Altig et al. perform a large number of simulations, their results for the implementation of the flat tax, with and without adjustment costs, are most relevant for this discussion.[40] Without adjustment costs, asset values decline by nearly 10 percent with the implementation of the flat tax. By comparison, with adjustment costs, this decline is only 3.6 percent. Without adjustment costs, very old generations are generally losers from reform, whereas middle-aged and younger generations are generally slight gainers or slight losers. In contrast, with adjustment costs, all elderly generations are gainers from reform, whereas middle-income young generations are net losers (due primarily to higher tax rates) and high- and low-income young generations are net gainers (the former due

---

[40] Altig et al. do not consider the implementation of an NRST.

primarily to lower tax rates and the latter due primarily to increased wages attributable to greater capital intensity).

Given the many problems associated with the use of such general-equilibrium life-cycle models to predict the effects of reform,[41] these results are by no means definitive. Nevertheless, they do suggest that once some of the additional factors described here – especially adjustment costs and the existence of tax-deferred assets – are taken into account, the capital levy and the welfare losses suffered by the elderly due to the implementation of a consumption tax may be significantly reduced or even eliminated. At a minimum, the results suggest that the case for special transition rules to prevent elderly capital owners from suffering large reform-induced welfare losses is not obvious, as any negative effects of reform on asset prices and on the welfare of the elderly may be partially or even fully offset by other reform-induced changes.[42]

ECONOMIC, LEGAL, AND POLITICAL PERSPECTIVES ON TAX TRANSITIONS

The implicit assumption in the analysis thus far has been that a reform-induced capital levy would be an unwelcome by-product of a change in tax regimes, and that some type of transitional relief might be appropriate to mitigate its effects, as well as the effects of other reform-induced redistributions of income and wealth.

Economic Perspectives

Many economists view tax-induced redistributions of income and wealth as fundamentally inequitable and are thus strong supporters of transitional provisions that reduce such redistributions. In particular, Feldstein (1976a,b) argues that reform-induced redistributions are objectionable on horizontal equity grounds. He stresses that whenever a tax system is changed unexpectedly – for example, when preferential tax treatment of a particular investment activity is eliminated – individuals who have made different types of investments based on the assumption of a continuation of the existing tax system will be treated very differently under the new tax law. Moreover, in most cases, a reform will not simply reverse the effects of a previous tax change because assets will have changed hands in the intervening period. Accordingly, Feldstein argues that

---

[41] For example, see Gravelle (Chapter 2 in this volume).

[42] As noted earlier, the case for transition rules is weakened if onetime reform-induced capital levies are concentrated among the very wealthy who are the biggest net gainers from reform.

reform-induced redistributions are typically arbitrary and thus undesirable from a social perspective.

More specifically, Feldstein (1976b, p. 95) suggests that the appropriate principle of horizontal equity for evaluating the effects of tax reform is that "if two individuals would have the same utility level if the tax remained unchanged, they should also have the same utility level if the tax is changed." (Note that it is the net effects of all reform-induced changes on individual welfare that Feldstein finds objectionable, rather than gains or losses on individual assets.) In addition, he argues that in evaluating the social costs associated with reform-induced redistributions, large losses are particularly undesirable; that is, he contends that large losses should have a significantly disproportionately negative impact on social welfare, relative to losses that are smaller in magnitude and thus, in his view, much less objectionable. Feldstein also stresses that the same logic should be applied to reform-induced windfall gains. That is, such gains should result in a smaller increase in social welfare than would an ordinary income increase of the same magnitude, and large gains should result in a disproportionately smaller increase in social welfare than small gains. Finally, Feldstein proposes that the relative desirability of alternative reform proposals (including any transition rules) should be gauged in terms of their effects on social welfare, calculated as an aggregation of reform-induced gains and losses, weighted as described earlier.

The general implication of Feldstein's approach is that transitional relief of some form is desirable in those cases in which individuals suffer reform-induced windfall losses – and that compensatory taxation is called for in those cases in which individuals enjoy reform-induced windfall gains. The most common method of transitional relief is "grandfathering" old assets, or providing them with the tax treatment specified under the prereform tax regime. In addition to grandfathering, other reform implementation tools include phasing in, delaying, or partially enacting reforms, and offsetting windfall gains and losses with compensating taxes. Analyses of "optimal tax reform" – the best way to implement tax reforms – include Feldstein (1976a,b), Bradford (1998), Diewert (1978), Howitt and Sinn (1989), and Zodrow (1981, 1985, 1988, 1992).

In marked contrast, Kotlikoff (1995, 1996a) – at least within the context of consumption tax reform – has argued that the capital levy or windfall tax element of implementing a consumption-based tax reform is one of its most essential features, and one that should not be eliminated with transitional relief. He notes that such a capital levy would provide a nondistortionary source of revenue to the government, which would in turn allow lower long-run tax rates and larger efficiency gains under the consumption tax. Moreover, Kotlikoff argues that the intergenerational distributional effects of such a capital levy are desirable, in that losses would be concentrated among relatively elderly generations. These losses would help reverse the redistribution from current young and unborn generations toward elderly generations associated with recent expansions of Medicare and Social Security, stressed by Auerbach, Gokhale, and Kotlikoff (1994). Thus, according to this view, a consumption tax reform that would impose windfall losses on the elderly would result in redistributions that are not arbitrary and capricious, but rather redistributions that can be justified as offsetting the undesirable effects of other redistributive government policies. The merits of this argument, as well as its political relevance, are clearly open to debate. However, the fact that recent redistributions toward the elderly have occurred as a result of explicit public policies suggests that the enactment of any reform that would impose a sizable windfall loss on this politically powerful group is unlikely. In addition, many observers have noted that a switch to a flat tax or NRST would tend to redistribute income from middle-income groups to the rich;[43] a capital levy would also tend to offset this redistribution and thus could be viewed as quite desirable on equity grounds.

Accordingly, in marked contrast to the "optimal tax reform" school, this point of view implies that transitional relief is undesirable, at least in the case of a consumption tax reform. More generally, this view would seem to imply that taxes that are assessed as a result of irrevocable decisions made in the past are in fact desirable in the sense that they are an efficient source of revenue. In addition, this view suggests that the desirability of reform-induced windfalls depends to some extent on who experiences them – that is, on their distribution across generations and across income classes, and whether those distributive effects are perceived to be desirable. By comparison, Feldstein explicitly disavows distributional considerations in his formulation, arguing that it is the arbitrary nature of reform-induced windfalls that is objectionable from a social viewpoint, independent of the income or wealth levels of the individuals who experience them.

Legal Perspectives

Opinion regarding the desirability of transition relief is similarly divided among legal scholars. Shaviro (2000) describes three stages in the evolution of legal thought on tax transitions. The first represents the "old view" that transitional relief, typically in the form of grandfathering,

---

[43] See Mieszkowski and Palumbo (Chapter 6 in this volume) for a review of these studies.

should in general be provided. Two rationales support this argument. The first, and more commonly cited, is the "reliance" argument, which holds that it is unfair to change tax rules affecting specific investments when taxpayers made those investments in response to incentives in the tax code – that is, when taxpayer behavior was induced by the tax code due to investor reliance on continuation of the tax incentive. The second rationale is that transitional relief is desirable because it is efficient in the sense that the promise of such relief reduces the extent to which taxpayers must engage in costly precautionary behavior protecting themselves from the effects of tax changes. Both of these arguments stress the importance of stability of the tax code.

The second stage cited by Shaviro is the development of the "new view" of transitional relief, which holds that the government should not be overly concerned about reform-induced redistributions and should in general avoid special transitional provisions. Both equity and efficiency arguments are made in support of this position. For example, in terms of equity, Graetz (1977) argues that many government policies induce redistributions of income but do not give rise to special attempts to compensate the losers or penalize the gainers. He argues that there is no particular reason to single out tax reform-induced redistributions as requiring special consideration in the form of transition rules. Furthermore, Shaviro (2000) notes that, given the large number of tax changes that have occurred in recent years, reliance arguments are inherently suspect, as investors should reasonably anticipate changes in the tax treatment of various investments. In terms of efficiency, Kaplow (1986, 1992) argues that the expectation of transition rules, encouraged by their pervasive use, reduces the incentives individuals and firms would otherwise face to diversify away the risk of unexpected tax reforms. He notes that if transition rules were avoided as a matter of public policy, individuals and firms would be much more likely to attempt to diversify away the risk of reform-induced redistributions. Such diversification would in turn greatly reduce their social cost.[44] In addition, such a policy would facilitate the enactment of desirable tax changes by making enactment of such provisions less costly; that is, proponents of this view would argue that flexibility in the tax system is more important than the stability criterion noted earlier.

Interestingly, the third and most recent stage in this evolution has reflected a return to the old view. In particular, there has been renewed support for transitional relief in the case of elimination of preferences

---

[44] Note, however, that it would be difficult to diversify away the risk of a broadly based windfall loss, such as the potential consumption-tax-induced reduction in the value of all preenactment capital described earlier.

under the income tax for certain types of investment activities. For example, Pearlman (1996) argues that reliance is a reasonable claim unless Congress explicitly signals that a tax provision is temporary, either by adopting a sunset clause or cautioning against reliance in the legislative history of the provision. Similarly, Logue (1996) argues that tax incentives should be viewed as an implicit contract and that the government should commit to providing full transition relief in order to avoid paying a risk premium on tax subsidies that extend over multiple years.[45]

Interestingly, three of the most prominent legal scholars who have looked explicitly at transitional issues related to the implementation of a consumption tax reform argue that "old view" reliance claims are insufficient to justify transitional relief, but nevertheless ultimately support transitional relief, although for different reasons. Specifically, as noted, Shaviro (2000) concludes that, given the many tax changes that have occurred in recent years, reliance claims based on an assumption of an unchanging tax structure are inherently suspect. More generally, he takes a very forward-looking perspective, arguing that in principle transition rules should be designed to encourage future good tax policy making (which he defines as a movement toward broad-based taxation, without specifying whether the broad base should be income or consumption). In particular, Shaviro argues that in principle transitional relief should not be provided when a tax preference is curtailed.[46] This has the effect of reducing the cost of a desirable reform and reducing the extent to which taxpayer behavior is modified by the original "undesirable" incentive (because it is subject to removal without transitional relief). He realizes, however, that such a policy is impractical, as politicians are unlikely to structure transition rules on the assumption that a policy they are enacting is a bad one. Accordingly, Shaviro concludes that as a general rule no transition rules should be provided for "policy changes."

In the case of a consumption tax, however, he argues that the windfall tax on old capital is not an essential part of the policy change of a movement to consumption taxation but an ancillary "accounting change" that could be reversed (by an offsetting accounting change) without altering the essence of the new policy.[47] That is, rather than

---

[45] See also Ramseyer and Nakazato (1989) and Goldberg (1994).

[46] By analogy, Shaviro argues that transitional relief should be provided when a tax preference is expanded.

[47] The discussion suggests that this interpretation is open to question in the sense that the taxation of existing capital could be viewed as an essential element of a consumption tax; without it, a consumption tax approximates a tax on wages.

reflecting the essential nature of a desirable or an undesirable policy change, accounting changes are simply an undesirable "by-product" of reform. Shaviro concludes that transition relief is appropriate for such accounting changes because it reduces reform-induced windfalls without creating any expectations about the relative desirability of future policy changes. In particular, he stresses that taxpayers should be allowed continued deductions for depreciation under a consumption tax. Shaviro also emphasizes that (1) it is the net effect of reform on an individual that should be of primary concern in thinking about the desirability of transition rules, rather than the effects of a single provision, and (2) the political bias toward providing transition relief for windfall losses without taxing windfall gains suggests that transition relief should in general be avoided.

Similarly, Kaplow (1995) – although in general an opponent of transition relief – also supports allowing some form of basis recovery in the case of the implementation of a consumption tax. His rationale is also a forward-looking one. Specifically, Kaplow argues that the capital levy that would occur in the absence of transition relief is undesirable because of its negative incentive effects on saving and investment – both to the extent that it is anticipated and to the extent that the imposition of a capital levy creates expectations that future capital levies will be enacted.

Finally, Pearlman (1996) also rejects the reliance claim for transition relief for existing capital in the case of implementation of a consumption tax. He argues that reliance claims are appropriate only when specific provisions in the tax code (e.g., tax incentives) were enacted to induce specific taxpayer behavior (e.g., investment in the tax-favored asset), and such is not the case for the elimination of deductions for tax basis under a consumption tax reform. He also stresses that decisions on providing transitional relief should examine the overall effect of reform on individual wealth, rather than the effects of a single change, and notes the political bias toward providing relief for windfall losses but ignoring windfall gains. Nevertheless, Pearlman ultimately concludes, largely on political grounds, that some form of transition relief would be essential under a consumption tax like the flat tax that explicitly denied deductions for existing basis. On the other hand, he notes that even though the same economic effects would occur under an NRST, the absence of deductions for basis under that tax would make the case for transitional relief much weaker.[48]

---

[48] McIntyre (1976) also notes that transition relief for existing assets under a new sales tax is unlikely.

Political Perspectives

Pearlman (1996, p. 416) notes that, from a political perspective, "We should expect near unanimity that it will be necessary to provide some form of transitional relief" for those cases – such as the flat tax – in which deductions for existing basis are denied. More generally, Pearlman (1996, pp. 397–98) notes that "Congress has been very willing to provide transition relief when tax provisions that favored taxpayers are narrowed or repealed." The large number of special transition rules that have accompanied recent major tax reforms in the United States is consistent with this viewpoint.

Nevertheless, it is interesting to note that the nature of these transition provisions appears to have changed in recent years. Specifically, general transition provisions have to some extent given way to hundreds of highly specific "rifle shot" transition rules, designed to protect a small number (sometimes one) of individuals or firms from reform-induced windfall losses. Such provisions raise some interesting economic and political questions. Highly specific transition rules often simply reflect raw political power. In particular, from a social perspective, they are commonly viewed as reflecting situations in which large firms or wealthy individuals with well-heeled lobbyists can avoid incurring reform-induced losses, while smaller firms or less wealthy individuals who cannot afford such high-priced advocates suffer such losses – even if in the aggregate the reform-induced losses that would be incurred in the absence of transition rules by the two groups are of comparable magnitude. For these reasons, highly specific transition rules are generally perceived to be extremely inequitable. For example, Pearlman (1996, p. 396) argues that they "may intensify public distrust of the [tax legislative] process and disdain for the tax system."

Despite this conventional wisdom, a clear advantage of tightly drawn transition rules is that they are less costly than generally applicable ones, in terms of both revenue and efficiency gains forgone. Moreover, such rules may even be equitable if political effort to obtain special transition rules is exerted primarily to avoid large losses; such a viewpoint is consistent with Feldstein's argument that large losses are disproportionately more costly from a social perspective than smaller ones (although Feldstein's argument is couched in terms of individual rather than firm losses). Thus, the social desirability of "rifle shot" transition rules is open to debate.

Finally, recent experience suggests there may be less political concern about the social costs of reform-induced redistributions than in previous years. In particular, a wide variety of provisions passed as part of the Tax Reform Act of 1986 presumably induced significant windfall losses but were accompanied by few if any transition rules (although some of these losses were reduced or eliminated by the rifle shot transition rules described earlier). These provisions include the elimination of preferential rates for capital gains, the elimination of the investment tax credit, the enactment of limitations on the deductibility of investment interest and passive losses, and the expansion of the alternative minimum tax.

To sum up, although all of the counterarguments to the conventional wisdom that reform-induced redistributions should be avoided through the use of transition rules have some merit, it nevertheless seems very likely that the transitional issues raised by the replacement of the income tax with the flat tax or NRST would be of great concern. Indeed, if these transitional issues were simply ignored, concerns about reform-induced redistributions could easily be sufficiently great to preclude the enactment of such a reform.

Potential Transition Rules to Reduce the Capital Levy

The Flat Tax

If deemed desirable, the introduction of transition relief would be straightforward under the flat tax. Many observers have noted that full protection would require allowing immediate expensing of all remaining basis on existing capital assets.[49] Because the revenue losses associated with immediate implementation of such a provision would be huge, these deductions would presumably be distributed over time. To maintain their real value, unused deductions would have to be carried forward with interest – such treatment could be termed "present value expensing" for existing assets.[50] As noted by Gravelle (1995), such full transition relief would, to a first approximation, eliminate the windfall tax on existing capital and convert the consumption tax to a wage tax.

A less generous approach would be to allow firms to continue taking the deductions for depreciation scheduled under current law. This

---

[49] For example, see Aaron and Galper (1985) and Bradford (1996a). Note that this assumes that market and book values are the same. If not, immediate expensing of the asset's market value would be required for existing assets to get the same tax treatment as new assets. Because deductions that are not equal to (especially if they were in excess of) current tax basis seem extremely unlikely, the discussion ignores this possibility.

[50] Aaron and Galper (1985) develop such a proposal. See also Bradford (1998), who discusses an alternative system that would allow continued deduction of depreciation allowances coupled with an annual tax credit equal to the product of the nominal interest rate and the undepreciated capital stock. This approach is equivalent in present value terms to immediate expensing of remaining tax basis, distributes the revenue cost of transitional relief over time, and has the added advantage of being neutral with respect to investment incentives in the presence of changes in tax rates over time.

approach has the advantage of being consistent with the notion of "reliance" – that is, that taxpayers should receive the tax treatment they expected under current law – and is the method that has been analyzed in several simulation studies of the effects of providing transition relief. However, it should be noted that the effects across the holders of existing assets of allowing deductions using existing depreciation schedules would be quite varied. For example, holders of rapidly depreciating assets that were purchased a considerable amount of time before the enactment of reform would be almost completely insulated from any windfall tax, while relatively little protection would be provided to holders of recently purchased slowly depreciating assets. Accordingly, alternative methods of providing transitional relief should be considered. For example, allowing immediate expensing (in present value terms if deemed desirable) of some fraction of remaining basis would result in a more uniform distribution of reform-induced losses.

The NRST

Mechanisms for transitional relief under the NRST are somewhat less obvious. For retail firms, deductions of remaining basis such as those described earlier, especially for inventories, would be straightforward to implement. Such deductions for other firms would, however, involve refunds, which would be politically unpopular and potentially subject to abuse.[51] Note that under the full price adjustment scenario, the real values of all assets decline, so that a partial adjustment – for example, only for inventories held by retailers – is undesirable in that it fully protects a single class of asset holder while providing no transitional relief for all other asset holders.

Estimates of the Effects of Transition Rules under the Flat Tax

The studies by Auerbach (1996) and by Altig et al. (1997) also include simulations in which transition relief is provided in the form of allowing firms to continue to receive the deductions for depreciation scheduled under current law. These simulations are performed only for the flat tax.

As expected, the provision of transition relief has a significant effect on the reform-induced change in asset prices. In the absence of transition relief, asset values fall initially by 5.7 and 8.9 percent under the two versions of the flat tax analyzed by Auerbach; with transition relief, asset

---

[51] If most nonretail businesses were subject to the NRST in the sense of filing claims for refunds for sales tax paid on dual-use goods (as recommended in the AFT proposal), transitional refunds could be added to the refunds issued under normal operation of the tax.

prices fall by 1.7 and 3.5 percent in these two cases.[52] Moreover, note that neither of these two cases allows for adjustment costs; the introduction of such costs would also tend to increase the value of existing assets. The introduction of transitional relief benefits the elderly, in both cases converting some reform-induced losses into gains. However, because transitional relief implies higher tax rates in the short and long runs, it harms young and future generations. In particular, long-run per capita output levels are roughly 2–3 percentage points lower than in the absence of transition relief, and long-run efficiency gains from reform are reduced by 0.6–1.0 percent of lifetime resources (including the value of leisure).

Similar results for the flat tax are obtained by Altig et al. Asset prices fall initially by 5 percent, as compared with 10 percent in the absence of transition relief. In the absence of transitional provisions, many older generations, at all income levels other than the lowest, are losers from reform; with transitional relief, virtually all the elderly are net gainers from reform. Transitional relief particularly helps avoid losses among the elderly in the middle of the income distribution. Again, transitional relief harms younger and future generations, relative to the case with no such provisions. Indeed, virtually all younger and future generations, other than those at the bottom and top of the lifetime income distribution, are net losers from reform with transitional relief.

OTHER ISSUES

A wide variety of other transitional issues would be raised by a move toward either a flat tax or NRST.

Short-Run Economic Dislocations

Implementing a tax reform as significant as a movement from income to consumption-based taxation would cause a number of short-run economic dislocations. With the exception of several studies that have considered the costs of adjusting the capital stock, these problems are not considered in the simulation models described here, although they could easily represent a significant cost of tax reform.

In particular, the models cited earlier assume that labor can be re-allocated instantaneously and costlessly, that reform-induced increases in labor supply can be accommodated without causing any short-run dis-locations, and that all prices adjust to their equilibrium instantaneously.

---

[52] Recall that Auerbach simulates the effects of both the Hall-Rabushka and Armey-Shelby versions of the flat tax.

These assumptions are obviously problematical. In particular, there would be considerable reallocation of labor from the production of consumption goods to the production of investment goods, and from the production of housing and other goods that are tax-favored under the existing income tax system into the production of other goods. Similarly, relative prices of goods facing producers and consumers would change. In addition, in the case of an NRST with full price adjustment, there would have to be a onetime increase in the prices of all consumption commodities.[53]

All of these changes would be likely to result in some short-run unemployment, although the magnitude is unclear. Gravelle (Chapter 2 in this volume) notes that in a recent study compiled by the Joint Committee on Taxation (1997), large negative effects – short-run contractions on the order of 1–2 percent of output – were obtained in simulations of consumption tax reforms utilizing several large-scale macroeconomic models characterized by sticky prices and wages. Moreover, one of these studies indicated that short-run adjustment costs were significantly larger for a VAT with full price adjustment than for a flat tax, which did not require such price accommodation.[54] Although the validity of these results is open to question – especially because increasing prices in response to an economy-wide reform-induced general price increase may be easier for retail firms than suggested by the models[55] – the prospect of incurring serious short-run employment and output losses could serve as a critical political impediment to the enactment of a consumption tax reform, as stressed by Gravelle and by Bull and Lindsey (1996).

Finally, note that implementation of the flat tax or NRST could cause potentially large transitional problems during the period between the time the policy is announced (or perceived to be a likely reform) and the time of enactment. In particular, the expectation of future enactment of an NRST would create huge incentives to draw down assets, accelerate consumption, and delay investment prior to the enactment of reform. These would presumably be mitigated to some extent by market forces, as the prices of consumption goods would increase while the prices of investment goods would decline. Note also that the opposite effects – a

---

[53] In the no price adjustment scenario, producer prices and wages would have to decline; see Bull and Lindsey (1996).

[54] See the discussion by Brinner of the DRI/McGraw-Hill model in Joint Committee on Taxation (1997, chap. 6). Gravelle (Chapter 2 in this volume) notes, however, that the adjustment to an NRST could be less costly than the adjustment to a VAT, because only retail prices must increase under the former tax, whereas both producer and consumer prices must increase under the latter.

[55] See the discussion by Reifschneider in Joint Committee on Taxation (1997, chap. 6).

temporary decline in consumption, coupled with an increase in investment – would be expected after the enactment of either the flat tax or NRST, as consumers adjusted their consumption and savings patterns to reflect the relatively favorable treatment of saving under the new consumption tax regime.[56] Nevertheless, these phenomena also clearly pose a risk for substantial economic dislocations.

Effects on Housing Values

Considerable concern has also been expressed about the effect of consumption tax reforms on housing prices. Under current law in the United States, housing is treated very generously, as the imputed rent earned on investment in owner-occupied housing is untaxed, while mortgage interest and property taxes are deductible. Under most consumption tax proposals, the consumption of the housing services provided by new homes would be either directly or indirectly subject to tax. Under the NRST, sales of new homes would be included in the tax base, which implies, given the full price adjustment scenario described earlier, that housing prices would increase by the amount of the tax. (Because the price of housing reflects the present value of future housing services, taxation at the time of purchase of a home is equivalent to future taxation of the housing services provided by the home.) By comparison, under the flat tax the tax on the consumption of housing services would – like other future consumption financed by current saving – be prepaid in the sense that homeowners would not get a deduction for investment in owner-occupied housing at the time of purchase.[57]

The generous treatment of owner-occupied housing under current law implies that, in contrast to the case of existing business assets described earlier, the implementation of a consumption tax would not tend to impose a onetime windfall loss on owners of existing homes. (Note that sales of existing owner-occupied homes would not be included in the tax base, so deduction of tax basis is not an issue.) Under an NRST, nominal house prices would increase, keeping real house prices constant. Under the flat tax, the treatment of housing – no deduction and no taxation of imputed returns – would be identical to that under current law, so that (nominal and real) housing prices would remain constant, despite the

---

[56] Note that under the flat tax, the deleterious preenactment effects on investment could be mitigated by specifying a preenactment effective date for allowing expensing for investment.

[57] However, in the unlikely event that the movement to a consumption-based system included the taxation of imputed rents on existing housing, the owners of existing homes would tend to suffer a onetime capital loss similar to that discussed in the case of non-housing capital.

tendency for the prices of other capital assets to decline. Thus, any real housing price declines would arise only from the changes in relative demands and elimination of deductions for home mortgage interest and/or property taxes. It is the effects of these changes on housing prices that have been the focus of concern.

The reform-induced decline in the demand for owner-occupied housing would result in a decline in house prices that potentially could be quite sizable. For example, Capozza, Green, and Hendershott (1996) analyze the effects of a flat tax, including elimination of deductions for home mortgage interest and property taxes, using a model in which all the effects of tax reform are capitalized into housing prices (i.e., there are no reform-induced quantity adjustments). Their analysis suggests that implementation of a flat tax would reduce house values by an average of 20 percent, with considerable fluctuations around this average across geographical areas.

These results are clearly at the high end of potential outcomes, because they essentially assume a completely inelastic supply of owner-occupied housing. Bruce and Holtz-Eakin (1997) argue that the supply of owner-occupied housing is highly elastic in the long run and also stress that the introduction of taxation of new housing under a flat tax or NRST would tend to increase the values of existing (untaxed) homes. In their model, the long-run effects of implementing a flat tax are minimal and even the short-run effects are quite modest. As stressed by Gravelle (1996a), a number of other factors would also tend to mitigate any reform-induced decline in the values of owner-occupied homes. The supply of owner-occupied homes would contract through the conversion of such homes into rental housing, especially because investment in rental housing, like all investment, would be treated so favorably under a consumption-based tax. Over the longer run, declines in new home construction and depreciation of the existing stock would also limit capital losses on existing houses.[58] Finally, reductions in marginal tax rates would stimulate demand, especially for first-time home-buyers who are cash-constrained, and any reform-induced reduction in interest rates would be reflected in higher housing demand and higher land prices. These countervailing effects are important enough that R. Hall (1995, p. 15) concludes that implementation of a consumption tax reform would have only "a modest negative effect on housing prices and demand." Similarly, Gravelle (1996a, p. 35) concludes that the effects of a consumption tax reform on housing prices "are likely to be limited even in the

---

[58] Gravelle also notes that because most homes are not on the market at any given point in time, declines in new home construction and depreciation of the existing stock may have a significant effect on the total supply of housing.

short run and quite small in the long run." This is clearly one area in which a thorough general equilibrium analysis, using a model that accounts explicitly for the costs of adjustment in the housing market and the potential for substitution between owner-occupied housing and rental housing, and between housing and other goods, could shed additional light on the effects of a consumption tax reform.[59]

Some Special Issues

The implementation of either the flat tax or NRST would raise a number of special issues related to changes in the tax treatment of capital income. Without attempting to be comprehensive, this section considers the most important of these issues, as well as some potential transition provisions.[60]

Interest on Existing Debt

Perhaps the most troublesome issue would be the treatment of preexisting debt, which was negotiated on the assumptions that interest expense would be deductible and interest income would be taxable. If interest rates fell sufficiently, much of this debt might be renegotiated. However, it is likely that demands for transition relief would be overwhelming in any case. Hall and Rabushka ([1985] 1995) note that any relief should be symmetric – deductibility of interest on old loans for borrowers should be accompanied by taxation of such interest for lenders (if they are taxable entities) – which would limit the revenue cost of such provisions.[61] In addition, grandfather rules for the interest on old loans could expire several years after reform, thus limiting but not eliminating the windfall losses attributable to reform. Alternatively, individuals and firms could be allowed special deductions, spread out over time, based on their level of interest payments in the year (or an average of several years) prior to the enactment of reform. It would be fairly straightforward to incorporate such treatment of existing debt under the flat tax. However, any attempt to grandfather interest income and expense would add considerable complexity to the NRST, as it would require tax filings by both nonretail firms and by individuals.

---

[59] See Diamond and Zodrow (1999) for a discussion of how changes in housing prices would affect the intergenerational and intragenerational redistributions associated with a consumption tax reform.

[60] For further discussion, see Sarkar and Zodrow (1993) and Pearlman (1996).

[61] Indeed, Hall and Rabushka suggest that interest expense could be only partially – say 90 percent – deductible whereas the associated interest income would be fully taxed, thus providing borrowers and lenders with an incentive to renegotiate the loan on a tax-free basis.

Capital Gains

Under the flat tax, capital gains accrued on existing assets would be exempt from tax. Such treatment would also help to alleviate any reform-induced windfall loss on existing capital owners. If such treatment were deemed too generous, it would be possible but extremely difficult to capture this windfall gain. Ideally, gains accrued prior to enactment would be calculated (which would involve a onetime evaluation of all assets) and then taxed in such a way as to replicate the expected tax burden under the income tax, taking into account the complex provisions of current law, including deferral, exemption at death, a lack of inflation indexing and preferential rates. An alternative approach, discussed by the U.S. Treasury (1977), would be to include in the tax base capital gains on assets purchased prior to the enactment of reform, and to phase out this provision over time.[62] Under the NRST, capital gains would be taxed when consumed. Such treatment would presumably extend deferral in some cases, but would also capture some gains that would have been exempt entirely when transferred at death.

Retained Earnings

Dividends paid from retained earnings accumulated prior to the enactment of reform would also escape tax at the individual level under the flat tax. Under the "new view" of dividend taxation described earlier, the elimination of individual-level dividend taxation would result in a windfall gain to owners of corporate shares, which would act to offset any reform-induced losses imposed on the owners of existing capital. If deemed desirable, however, this effect could be offset with a transition rule. For example, Bradford (1986) recommends an add-on tax on net corporate distributions. Alternatives would include special firm-level taxes based on retained earnings at the time of enactment, or individual-level taxes based on a formulation that would attempt to identify the fraction of distributed earnings attributable to prereform retained earnings. Such provisions would not be necessary under the NRST, because the increase in asset value due to the elimination of taxation of dividends at the individual level would be offset by the taxation of distributed earnings when consumed.

Changes in Relative Asset Values

Implementation of (pure versions of) either the flat tax or NRST would provide for uniform tax treatment of investment. Because the current

---

[62] The U.S. Treasury (1977) proposal included a final "recognition date" at which point all accumulated gains would be taxed (with provisions for spreading the tax payment over multiple years). Such treatment would be quite harsh, given the existence of unlimited deferral and exemption of gains transferred at death under current law.

tax system provides for preferential treatment of certain types of investments (e.g., investments in assets with relatively accelerated depreciation or investments that yield tax-exempt interest such as municipal bonds), reform would result in windfall gains and losses attributable to changes in relative asset prices. Such changes could be mitigated by extending tax-favored treatment for such assets to the new tax regime through the various methods mentioned earlier – grandfathering, phasing-in, partial or delayed enactment. Again, it would be simpler to effect such provisions under the flat tax than under an NRST.

Finally, as noted by Pearlman (1996), the enactment of a consumption-based tax reform would affect asset values through changes in the treatment of items such as net operating losses, foreign tax credits, alternative minimum taxes, and suspended passive activity loss credits. Such items would also be candidates for transitional relief in the form of grandfathering provisions.

CONCLUSION

Many observers have commented on the possibility that the implementation of a consumption-based tax like the flat tax or NRST would cause a huge transitional problem in the form of a onetime reduction in the real value of capital assets. Given conventional assumptions about the reactions of the monetary authorities to the imposition of these reforms – full price adjustment with the NRST and no price adjustment with the flat tax – such a windfall loss would be distributed uniformly across all capital owners in the case of the NRST but concentrated on equity owners in the case of the flat tax. If it were to occur, such a capital levy would cause an intergenerational redistribution of wealth from elderly capital owners to young and future generations and would pose a significant obstacle to the enactment of either of these consumption tax reforms.

However, a wide variety of other factors would act to offset partially or even fully this windfall loss, even in the absence of any special transition rules. Several simulations of the effects of consumption tax reforms suggest that, once such factors are taken into account, declines in reform-induced reductions in asset prices are reduced or reversed, and the elderly tend to be net gainers or only modest losers from reform.

Moreover, the discussion of the various perspectives on the use of transition rules presented here suggests that some transitional relief – at least under the flat tax, which is more amenable to such rules – is virtually inevitable. Moreover, it is in a sense fortuitous that transition rules are relatively more likely under the flat tax: relative to the NRST, losses under the flat tax are more concentrated because equity owners bear the full burden of any reform-induced capital levy. However, it would be possible to add transitional provisions to the NRST, especially if the tax took a form under which most firms, rather than only retailers, were in the system in any event. In both cases, such transitional provisions would further reduce any windfall losses associated with the implementation of a consumption tax reform.[63]

This discussion, of course, does not prove that the transitional effects of implementing the flat tax or NRST are not large enough to be of concern or, indeed, even to preclude such a reform.[64] However, it does suggest that it is certainly feasible that the enactment of these reforms would not, at least in the aggregate, impose huge generation-specific losses; in particular, the elderly might not experience large windfall losses – and, indeed, could even be net gainers – with the implementation of the flat tax or NRST. It is thus far from obvious that the transitional inter-generational redistributions associated with the flat tax or NRST make them infeasible policy options.

On the other hand, the aggregate simulation results described in this chapter neglect the very important transitional problems that arise when individual taxpayers in special circumstances are affected very negatively by a tax reform. For example, firms with a disproportionately large level of heavily debt-financed investment in newly purchased long-lived assets would be very negatively affected by the implementation of the flat tax. The challenge in this instance is to design transition rules so that they are well targeted toward providing relief only to taxpayers who are

---

[63] In addition, if windfall losses were concentrated among the elderly, they could in a very rough way be offset with increases in Social Security benefits. Such an approach, however, is obviously not very well targeted.

[64] In particular, skeptics would argue that such studies tend to overstate the behavioral responses and the associated efficiency gains that could be obtained from a consumption tax reform. See, for example, Gravelle (1991; Chapter 2 in this volume), Engen and Gale (1996) who argue that models that incorporate a precautionary saving motive have much smaller saving responses, and Bernheim (1997) who notes that alternative "psychological" models of saving behavior also imply smaller savings responses. Of course, smaller efficiency gains necessarily imply large reform-induced welfare losses and thus more severe transitional problems. In addition, such skeptics would argue that a large part of the gains in administrative and compliance simplicity that might be obtained with a consumption tax could also be obtained with a simplified income tax structure; for example, see Slemrod (1996). On the other hand, proponents of consumption taxes would argue that the models discussed here are (1) insufficiently detailed to capture many of the more subtle efficiency gains that might be obtained with a consumption tax reform, (2) ignore the potentially large reductions in administrative and compliance costs that might accompany such a reform, and (3) overstate the losses that would be experienced by the owners of existing capital to the extent that the "new view" of dividend taxation is valid and corporate share prices would increase under a consumption tax reform to reflect the elimination of the capitalization of the effects of dividend taxation at the individual level.

suffering large net losses as a result of reform. Well-designed grandfather rules that selectively reduce reform-induced losses without significantly reducing the efficiency gains from reform or causing large revenue losses are the preferable approach.[65] At the same time, such situation-specific problems always arise in the context of major tax reforms, and it is not clear that such problems would be significantly worse with a flat tax or an NRST reform than they would be, say, under a significant move toward comprehensive income taxation or than they were under the Tax Reform Act of 1986. Proponents of consumption-based taxes should not in principle be held to a higher standard regarding the minimization of windfall losses than supporters of earlier reforms of the income tax.

Finally, it is important to note that the factors that tend to reduce any reform-induced windfall losses experienced by the elderly also tend to delay the efficiency gains associated with reform. Indeed, the various simulations reported here suggest that middle-aged and young generations tend to be smaller gainers or net losers when adjustment costs are important and/or when transition rules are introduced, even though very young and future generations benefit – to a smaller extent – from the enactment of reform. Such a pattern of reform-induced intergenerational redistributions, under which most of the gainers from reform are either young or unborn and the gains they experience are not as large as suggested by analyses that ignore the factors stressed in this chapter, raises some provocative questions about the political feasibility of a realistic version of either the flat tax or the NRST.

[65] See Zodrow (1992).

Chapter 10

Historical and Contemporary Debate on Consumption Taxes

Malcolm Gillis

Recent debate over fundamental tax reform has centered on consumption taxes. Proposals for thoroughgoing tax reform involving mending of the income tax have been much less in evidence. For example, the U.S. Treasury's proposal for a "Comprehensive Business Income Tax" (see Hubbard, Chapter 4 in this volume) has not generated much interest. Discussion of the relative merits of competing consumption tax proposals has centered on four alternatives: a national retail sales tax, the flat tax, the Unlimited Savings Allowance tax (USA Tax), and the value-added tax. Former chairman of the House Ways and Means Committee Bill Archer has expressed a desire to "tear out the income tax by its roots," replacing it with a national retail sales tax (a tax on all final sales to consumers). The organization Americans for Fair Taxation (AFT) is the staunchest supporter of a broad-based single-stage national retail sales tax to replace personal and corporate income taxes and Social Security taxes. House Majority Leader Dick Armey is as ardent a supporter of the Hall-Rubushka flat tax as can be found anywhere.[1] The Nunn-Domenici tax on consumption (USA Tax) is the only live proposal for a direct cash flow tax on consumption, but support for the proposal has been largely confined to academic economists. This alternative, along with the AFT proposal for a national retail sales tax, completely defers tax on all income saved, and could allow consumption taxes on low-income households to go to virtually zero.

Finally, there is the value-added tax (VAT), more specifically the European Union tax credit type of VAT, in which all businesses are subject to tax but may deduct taxes paid on purchases against taxes due on sales (see Cnossen, Chapter 8 in this volume). The base of this type

---

[1] The flat tax proposal favored by Representative Armey would subject gross wages of individuals to tax, while imposing a subtraction method value-added tax on the production of goods and services by firms.

of VAT is total consumption in the economy. Unaccountably, the once vociferous proponents of a federal VAT for the United States have been relatively silent during the past decade.

The purposes of this chapter are modest: first, to provide some historical perspective on the long debate over the relative merits of consumption versus income as a tax base and, second, to identify some of the difficulties confronting competing proposals for heavier reliance on one or another form of consumption tax. Not least of these difficulties is the recent growth of electronic commerce, a problem not yet widely recognized in current discussions on consumption tax alternatives facing the United States.

HISTORY OF CONSUMPTION TAX ADVOCACY: A THUMBNAIL SKETCH

The debate over the relative merits of consumption versus income as a tax base is, of course, not new. And, contrary to impressions of many, the constituency for consumption-based taxation has not been confined to market-oriented economists or politicians.

The modern history of advocacy for consumption-based taxation began in Scotland nearly 250 years ago, with philosopher David Hume's (1779) publication of *Essays and Treatises on Several Subjects*. Hume, an opponent of both "high" taxes as well as a multiplicity of taxes, was an ardent proponent of consumption-based taxation.[2] His fiscal writings reflect the notion that equity in taxation requires that taxpayers' fiscal contributions be based on what they take out of society (their consumption) rather than what they put into it (as measured by their income). Neither Hume nor his followers saw fit to formalize his views regarding personal consumption as a resource-depleting activity. However, early in the twentieth century the idea that income constitutes a measure of one's contribution to society resonated well with the tenets of the marginal productivity theory of income distribution, which (under competition) requires, as a condition for efficiency in production, that labor be paid according to its marginal product.

After Hume, the paper trail of consumption tax testimonials goes cold for nearly 200 years, apart from scattered references. For the better part of the twentieth century, income taxation gained ascendancy, both in the writings of economists, and in the central government tax systems in the Western world. Moreover, throughout much of the postwar period, the superiority of income as a tax base was little

---

[2] According to Hume, "The best taxes are such as levied on consumptions" (Hume, [1752] 1985, pt. II, Essay VIII: para. 5). See also Hume (1779), Letter to Turgot, late September 1766.

questioned in economics and public finance textbooks, or in Ph.D. programs in economics.

The initial burden of resurrecting the arguments for consumption-based taxation fell primarily to a fervent socialist, the British economist Nicolas Kaldor, much admired by the leaders of postindependence India, Sri Lanka, and Guyana. During the early 1950s, these governments called on him to devise tax structures to promote savings and redistribute income from rich to poor, while at the same time garnering sufficient tax revenues to finance ambitious new development plans.

Kaldor was nothing if not consistent. In Sri Lanka, then India, and finally in Guyana, he produced full-blown proposals for national tax systems relying on consumption as a tax base, but with the consumption tax interlocked with a system of wealth and income taxes. The consumption tax proposals of Kaldor bear more than just a faint resemblance to the Nunn-Domenici USA Tax. Both the Kaldor version and the USA Tax call for direct taxes on consumption, wherein the tax base for individual taxpayers is essentially the difference between reported annual income and reported net savings. Kaldor's tax reform package was actually adopted in India but was repealed after a few months because it required information well beyond the capacities of the Indian tax administration, then and now.

It was not until publication of four landmark government studies in the late 1970s that comprehensive proposals for switching from income- to consumption-based taxes appeared in the United States, Britain, Sweden, and Australia. David Bradford's *Blueprints for Basic Tax Reform* (U.S. Treasury, 1977) was well received by economists but ignored by almost everyone else when first published in 1977 by the U.S. Treasury. At about the same time, the Meade Committee Report (Institute for Fiscal Studies, 1978) also endorsed consumption as the preferred tax base for Britain. Lodin (1978) came to similar conclusions for Sweden, as did the Matthews Committee (1975) in Australia. All four studies stressed the superiority of consumption taxes in fostering capital formation: whereas a direct consumption tax is neutral toward the choice between consumption and savings, the income tax penalizes savings.

CONSUMPTION TAXES IN PRACTICE IN
THE TWENTIETH CENTURY

U.S. proponents of consumption-based taxation enjoyed their first major victories at the subnational level, beginning early in the 1900s, when successive state governments began enacting broad-based, initially low-rate taxes on retail sales, initially in the form of business gross receipts taxes.

By 1960, over forty states were collecting retail taxes. That number now stands at forty-five.

Europe turned to more refined indirect tax mechanisms after World War II.[3] There, country after country replaced outmoded multiple-stage cascade taxes with the sleeker and much superior invoice-credit type of value-added tax, now required of all nations of the European Union. It is instructive to note that whereas in the public mind in the United States indirect consumption taxes tend to be associated with market-oriented economists and politicians, the flowering of the value-added tax in Europe was earliest in countries with left or left of center governments in Sweden, Denmark, and France. Surprising to some, the heaviest reliance on (and the highest rates of) value-added tax has tended to be in northern European nations, including all the Scandinavian countries usually perceived as bastions for cradle-to-grave welfare systems, rather than partisans of efficiency in taxation. In both Denmark and Sweden, the VAT rate has been as high as 25 percent. Moreover, the Swedish VAT was originally enacted in 1969 as a means of sharply reducing that nation's reliance on income taxes. Notably, the Swedes opted for a VAT over the retail sales tax because of the perceived superiority of the VAT in terms of economic growth and efficiency, owing to the more effective exemption of producer goods from taxation.

Other factors help explain Scandinavian readiness to rely heavily on the VAT. First, throughout virtually all of these nations, mechanisms have long been in place on the expenditure side of the budget to assist a broad spectrum of low-income families. In such circumstances, the impact of the VAT on income distribution, though not entirely beside the point, has not been a contentious issue. Second, Scandinavian policy makers have long recognized that sales taxes do not have to be inherently regressive, even when imposed at uniform rates, and with food taxable. The Scandinavians were not alone: as long ago as 1981, a widely cited OECD survey concluded that the VAT and general sales taxes in seven European nations "are, in practice probably proportional, or mildly progressive in their effects" (OECD, 1981), particularly when income-elastic services are included in the tax base.

In the years since 1965, the VAT has been by far the favored instrument of tax reform among developing nations as well. Brazil pioneered the VAT at the state level in 1967. During the next three decades, more than forty developing nations, including twenty in Africa, adopted this tax in one or another of its guises, ranging from the manufacturers' level VAT in Indonesia to the retail version in Chile and several other Latin

---

[3] See Cnossen (Chapter 8 in this volume) for a discussion of the relative merits of the VAT and the retail sales tax.

American nations.[4] Notably, except for the United States, virtually every nation that has implemented major tax reform over the past quarter century has adopted a value-added tax.

The reasons for the rapid spread of the VAT across developing nations are fairly straightforward. While the VAT can take many forms, one has proved superior in virtually all circumstances: a uniform-rate VAT extending through the retail stages, collected by the European Union–style tax credit mechanism (wherein all firm sales are taxable, but taxes paid on firm purchases are credited against taxes due on firm sales). This form of VAT has a number of advantages over its closest competitor, the single-stage retail sales tax. Taken singly, none of these advantages are overwhelming, but all together they make for a strong case for the VAT, especially in developing countries with inadequate tax administration and a high degree of dependence on foreign trade.

Another reason why the VAT has become the predominant form of sales tax worldwide has been a widespread perception that a properly designed VAT can raise more revenue with lower administrative and economic costs than other broad-based consumption taxes, and can do so in neutral fashion. This perception has proved to be essentially correct. The VAT possesses other advantages as well. It is clearly superior in its treatment of international trade: only under a VAT is it, in practice, possible to free all exports from tax. In addition, the VAT is well suited for implementing one of the basic aims for switching to consumption taxation: the encouragement of capital formation, a trait particularly important in the developing-country context. This advantage rests on two features of the VAT. The first is the marked superiority of the VAT in freeing capital (producer) goods and exports from indirect tax burden. Second, the VAT also encourages capital formation in a fashion that some might view as paradoxical: the high revenue productivity of the tax encourages capital formation by helping to contain inflationary pressures in nations previously plagued by persistently high budgetary deficits (see Gillis, 2001).

On the other hand, the VAT has had a fitful history in the United States. Michigan experimented with a somewhat bizarre form of VAT in the years after World War II. To little avail, a comprehensible and comprehensive case for the VAT in the United States was made in volume 3 of the report commonly known as Treasury I (U.S. Treasury, 1984c) produced by the Reagan administration Treasury Department in 1984. Since then, VAT proponents have, unaccountably, been relatively quiet.

---

[4] See Gillis et al. (1996, table 13-5); Gillis (2001).

THE OUTLOOK FOR FUNDAMENTAL TAX REFORM

Support for continued heavy reliance on income taxation waned notably in the United States after 1970. In that year, the income tax was the least detested tax, as measured by surveys of the Advisory Commission on Intergovernmental Relations (ACIR). But by 1983 public perceptions had changed, to the point that 35 percent of respondents in ACIR surveys cited the income tax as the worst tax. In fact, twice as many 1983 respondents (52 percent) favored enactment of a new federal sales tax over increased individual income taxes as the preferred source of new tax revenues (see Gillis, 1986, p. 129). More recently, public support for income taxation may have been weakened by growing societal concerns over violations of civil liberties by the Internal Revenue Service (see Gillis, Mieszkowski, and Zodrow, 1996, p. 727). Perhaps the last gasp for serious efforts toward comprehensive income tax reform came with the Reagan-era tax reform of 1986. Enacted with high expectations, this base-broadening, rate-compressing reform proved to be no less vulnerable to erosion from political exigencies than any other postwar income tax reform effort.

For these and other reasons, consumption tax proponents tended to dominate the national debate on fundamental tax reform during the 1990s. One outgrowth has been an explosion of research – mostly quite good research – on consumption as a tax base, much of it conducted under the auspices of the National Bureau of Economic Research. This work has done a great deal to narrow the zones of ignorance – for economists and policy makers alike – over the implications of a shift to consumption taxes for efficiency, the interests of the young versus older citizens, impact on income distribution, risk taking, interest rates as well as international effects; Gravelle (Chapter 2 in this volume) provides a review of these efforts. Moreover, for perhaps the first time in history, tax analysts have produced pioneering new empirical and theoretical studies on central issues of tax administration and taxpayer compliance, as well as transitional questions involved in any shift from income to consumption taxes. (See Gale and Holtzblatt, Chapter 7 in this volume; Zodrow, Chapter 9 in this volume.) Some of these focus on economic behavior, whereas others deal with administrative and taxpayer responses to tax law.

It might have been expected that the recent blossoming of research on consumption-based taxes would have, by the close of the century, led to a greater degree of consensus about the most favored direction for consumption tax reform. However, none of the major reform alternatives has yet gained the upper hand in the United States, although the flat tax and the national retail sales tax seem to have more vocal and numerous supporters than the other two options. In turn, advocates for a national value-added tax do seem to outnumber supporters of direct cash flow consumption taxes, but not by very much.

It is worth pondering why there has been a lack of strong coalescing around any single tax reform alternative. I can provide no answers to that question, only speculations.

The first has to do with verbal shrapnel from rhetorical combat. After having savaged much of the case for income taxes, proponents of the four main consumption tax options then began to turn their cannons on one another. Flat tax advocates attack the retail sales tax with the largely unsupported claim that *any* sales tax will inevitably become a complex, pervasive, multirate value-added tax – notwithstanding the fact that most versions of the flat tax proposal would apply a subtraction method VAT on firms. Proponents of a national retail sales tax (NRST) have tended to focus upon the *differences* between a flat-rate retail sales tax and a value-added tax levied at the same rate. In fact, they are essentially identical in terms of economic and income distribution effects and, as noted earlier in this chapter and elsewhere in this volume, the tax credit type of VAT has some advantages over the NRST, both in terms of ease of administration and enforcement. (See also Zodrow, 1999a, for a discussion of this matter.) Finally, advocates of direct cash flow consumption taxes have erred in the other direction, by failing to *stress* the differences – and many of the economic and administrative advantages – of this option. Indeed, supporters of this option are about the only group that can plausibly argue that their alternative could come close to matching or even improving upon the income distribution consequences of the present progressive-rate income tax. (It should, however, be noted that the income tax has not proved to be a very effective instrument of income redistribution, certainly relative to such fiscal tools available on the expenditure side of the budget as support of primary and secondary education, public health outlays, and the like; see Gillis, 1986, p. 128.)

Even so, the public seems to be suspicious of any tax reform proposal that skips too lightly over income distribution issues. It is not so much that more income redistribution is expected; it is that credible tax reform programs need to be very clear about their implications for income distribution. Of the four main consumption tax alternatives, only the USA Tax and Americans for Fair Taxation proposals come at all close to meeting this test. Indeed, one of the most prominent features of the AFT proposal is a tax rebate to compensate families for sales tax on food and other income-inelastic items, with size of rebate dependent upon family size. Mieszkowski and Palumbo (Chapter 6 in this volume) provide a discussion of the distributional effects of fundamental tax reform.

In any case, each of the alternatives on the table has its drawbacks, both real and perceived. If pressed to name the most significant problem now facing each of the four variants of consumption tax reform, I would answer as follows.

Flat tax proponents have tended to claim much too much for their program, relative to competing proposals for consumption tax reform. At times, advocates seem to be saying that the flat tax will resolve virtually all the fiscal and most of the economic problems facing society. As a result, this meritorious idea has been oversold, especially with regard to inflated claims of simplicity and ease of administration.

Advocates of the national retail sales tax, such as the AFT, can marshal many strong arguments on behalf of this option, but still have not responded definitively to questions about its political feasibility. AFT cites the widespread U.S. experience with state-level retail sales taxes as an advantage for a national RST. Nevertheless, the fact that forty-five states *already* operate retail sales taxes is clearly a very major problem for a national retail sales tax because states have in the past viewed the threat of an NRST as a "fiscal infringement" on their most reliable source of revenue. This issue is increasing in importance, as twenty-six states increased their sales tax rates between 1987 and 1991 (see Gillis et al., 1996, p. 752). Another problem is that roughly 40 percent of the bases of the state retail taxes consist of business purchases, so that many producer goods are also taxed (see Ring, 1999).

Certainly, a high rate of national retail sales tax on top of existing state rates could jeopardize the base of the state taxes, as some states already utilize tax-exclusive rates of 7–8 percent. If combined with federal rates of indirect taxes three or four times higher, serious administrative and compliance problems could be expected. In understanding this point, it is important to note that in the United States rates of indirect taxes have always been expressed on a tax-exclusive basis. However, the basic AFT proposal called for a tax-inclusive rate of 23 percent to replace all federal revenues. On a tax-exclusive basis, this would require a national retail sales tax rate of 30 percent, and a combined national-state tax rate of upward of 36 to 38 percent (tax exclusive). Even Danish and Norwegian value-added taxes have avoided rates this high. Moreover, Gale and Holtzblatt (Chapter 7 in this volume) argue that the required tax-exclusive rate would be considerably higher: between 50 and 100 percent, if government revenues are held constant and depending on the assumed impact of high rates on erosion of the tax base. The high rate of retail sales tax required to replace income and Social Security taxes is perhaps the biggest obstacle facing the "fair tax" proposal, as well as the retail VAT (see Gale, 1999, p. 443).

The principal failing of the direct consumption tax camp has been its inability to turn to its advantage the very notable differences between its concept and the indirect tax options, and its inability to capitalize on the strong arguments for replacing income taxes with direct consumption taxes presented in the four landmark studies of the mid-1970s.[5]

However, debate over the relative merits of different forms of consumption taxes is about to enter a new phase. Experience over the past five years has furnished advocates of direct consumption taxes with a potentially significant argument in support of their position: the rise of electronic commerce (e-commerce). Failure to adequately tax e-commerce could mean the eventual demise of virtually all forms of general sales taxation, including the RST and VAT.

As long as the overwhelming majority of e-commerce transactions were business to business, the threat to traditional forms of consumption taxation was not obvious. But with a steadily growing share of e-commerce taking the form of transactions between businesses and consumers, sales taxes of all kinds generally, and state retail taxes in particular, could conceivably become obsolete fiscal instruments within a decade or so. The future revenue productivity of existing state-level retail sales taxes would be seriously undermined should exclusions for Internet transactions be extended much beyond the current temporary moratorium, enacted by Congress in 1998. If the moratorium were to be expanded to all Internet sales and also made permanent, this would soon render obsolete state retail sales taxes and, in the U.S. context, weaken the case for a national level retail sales tax or VAT (see Weidenbaum, 2000).

Finally, proponents of value-added taxation in the United States have proved unable to dispel a notion commonly held by many lawmakers who have long believed that the VAT is more of "a money machine" than a flat tax or a single-stage retail sales tax. The reputation of the tax as a money machine has in fact turned out to be a significant argument against its adoption in some quarters.[6]

---

[5] An inefficient tax system is, however, a relatively costly means of limiting the growth of government.

[6] The fear that the VAT will in fact result in large revenue increases may account for the reluctance of many otherwise market-oriented politicians and even economists to endorse the tax (see Gillis, 1986). Liberals, on the other hand, fear the VAT will be regressive. A recent article by Becker and Mulligan (1998) agrees that a flat-rate VAT is in fact the most efficient way to raise revenue. The authors go on to argue that this is not an unalloyed advantage of VAT. Becker and Mulligan's analysis indicates that countries utilizing "more efficient" broad-based taxes such as a flat-rate VAT tend to have a larger

Should we expect fundamental tax reform in the form of broad-based federal taxes on consumption anytime soon? The near-term prospects for any of the four alternatives are doubtful as long as partisans for consumption-based taxation continue to be split into four competing camps. The outlook for a national RST or VAT is especially dim should any significant share of business-to-consumer e-commerce be excluded from the tax base. However, the rise of the Internet may well impel economists and policy makers alike again to consider seriously the possibility of direct taxes on consumption in the United States, if not Europe.

role for government in the economy. Indeed, the authors argue that less efficient tax systems can improve taxpayer welfare because the system creates additional political pressure for suppressing the growth of government.

Chapter 11

The Politics and Ideology of Fundamental Tax Reform

Joe Barnes

The recent public saliency of fundamental tax reform – specifically a shift to a single-rate consumption-based form of federal taxation – reflects the confluence of three important contemporary trends. The first is the ideological ascendancy of conservatism, with its long-standing suspicion of activist government. The second is the political rise of the national Republican Party, fully competitive with the Democrats on both the congressional and presidential levels. The third is a growing body of theoretical and empirical research critical of the income tax and supportive of consumption-based taxation.

At first glance, this confluence would appear to put fundamental tax reform within reach. But while the climate for reform may have improved markedly, serious and perhaps insurmountable obstacles remain. At the ideological level, fundamental tax reform risks fracturing the coalition between economic and social conservatives that has created the right's current dominance. As reform moves from vague campaign promise to comprehensive legislative proposal, moreover, it may place the Republican Party in conflict with some of its most important constituencies. Finally, the economic literature on fundamental tax reform – though extensive, sophisticated and suggestive – remains inconclusive on a number of key issues.

Fundamental tax reform entails significant political and ideological risks for those promoting it. Given the expectations raised by the measures currently under discussion, the potential costs of failure are high. Prospects for reform are, on balance, poor. Markedly absent from the heated debate over the disposition of the anticipated federal budget surplus, for instance, has been any serious discussion of using part of it to cover transition costs associated with fundamental tax reform.

BACKGROUND

If fundamental tax reform has not yet risen to the top of the American domestic policy agenda – a position held, for the moment at least, by the future of the Social Security system – it is nonetheless the subject of interest to experts and laymen alike. Advocates of fundamental reform include respected economists, powerful politicians, influential think tanks, and well-financed lobbying groups. They promise a tax system that would be fairer, more efficient, and simpler – one that would bolster national savings and boost economic growth. If these advocates have their way, the next few years will witness a national debate on the issue.

It is important to recall the magnitude of the task that reformers are urging today. They seek far more than another overhaul of the current code like the one that was achieved in 1986 – an accomplishment hailed as heroic at the time and historic in the years that have followed.[1] Many advocates of fundamental tax reform would dismiss any similar attempt as mere "tinkering."[2] They see incremental change at best as a waste of time, at worst a tragic lost opportunity for long-overdue reform. Rather, reformers seek change that is fundamental in the truest sense of the word: the abolition of the eighty-five-year-old graduated-rate federal income tax and its replacement by a single-rate tax on consumption. The tax reform of 1986 – the result of a two-and-a-half-year bipartisan effort by executive and legislative branches that came near to collapse more than once – pales in comparison.

As discussed by Gillis (Chapter 10 in this volume), consumption-based taxation is not new. Indeed, excise taxes and customs duties were, with a brief exception during the Civil War, the dominant sources of federal revenue until the introduction of the income tax on a permanent basis early in this century.[3] Retail sales taxes remain a fixture of American state and local finance. As described by Cnossen (Chapter 8 in this volume), the value-added tax (VAT) has been used extensively around the world, most notably in western Europe, in conjunction with individual and corporate income taxes. But current American reform proposals would elevate consumption-based taxation to a unique status: they would shift the United States to exclusive reliance on consumption taxes – something never attempted by an industrialized country.[4]

---

[1] Birnbaum and Murray (1987) provide a lively account of the complex political wrangling leading to passage of the Tax Reform Act of 1986.

[2] See, for example, Representative Richard "Dick" Armey (R.-Texas), quoted in Sease and Herman (1996, p. 120).

[3] For a general history of the income tax, see Ratner (1942) and Paul (1954). Eisenstein (1961) provides an enlightening and often entertaining look at the interplay of taxation and ideology.

[4] Graetz (1997, p. 201).

Easily the best known of consumption tax proposals is the flat tax (FT).[5] Developed by Robert Hall and Alvin Rabushka, the FT has attained a status with policy makers and opinion shapers rare for scholarly work. Their book, *The Flat Tax*, has become something of a bible for proponents of fundamental tax reform.[6] The FT plan put forward by Steven Forbes in his failed 1996 bid for the Republican presidential nomination was explicitly based on the Hall-Rabushka proposal, as are plans that have been promoted by congressional Republicans.[7]

The FT would mark a clear break with the current tax code in several important areas. The first and most dramatic is its move to consumption as the tax base. For individuals, the FT would exempt interest income, dividends, and capital gains from taxation. For businesses, it would replace today's system of multiyear depreciation with full and immediate expensing of capital and intermediate goods. It is essentially equivalent to a subtraction-method VAT, except that wages are deductible for businesses and taxed at the individual level.[8] Second, the FT would mark a decisive step away from the graduated rates that have been a feature of the income tax since its first, if temporary, introduction in 1862.[9] The FT, as its name implies, would have a single rate applicable for individuals (above certain exempt amounts) and businesses alike. Third, the FT would eliminate almost all of the special treatment of various sources and uses of income embedded in today's income tax code. Employer-provided heath insurance, for instance, would be included in income; deductions for home mortgage interest, state and local taxes, and charitable contributions would be abolished.

A proposal for a national retail sales tax (NRST) – also promoted by congressional Republicans[10] – has gained somewhat surprising importance in the tax reform debate. This is due in part to an ambitious, $15 million-plus campaign on behalf of the idea of an NRST by a Houston-based group called Americans for Fair Taxation.[11] At a superficial level,

---

[5] See Aaron and Gale (1996, pp. 1–25) for a brief overview of the various types of consumption-based taxes, including the FT.

[6] Hall and Rabushka ([1985] 1995).

[7] See H.R. 2060 and S. 1050 (1995), introduced by Representative Dick Armey (R.-Texas) and Senator Richard Shelby (R.-Alabama), respectively.

[8] Graetz (1997, pp. 216–20). The treatment of exports and imports does differ under the FT and VAT (see Cnossen, Chapter 8 in this volume).

[9] The 1862 income tax had two rates (Graetz, 1997, p. 15). The income tax of 1894, over-turned a year later by the Supreme Court in the *Pollack* case, had a single rate. The income tax of 1913 featured no less than six. See Ratner (1942, pp. 168–93, 321–41); Paul (1954, pp. 32–40, 86–109).

[10] See H.R. 2001 (1997), sponsored by Dan Schaefer (R.-Colorado) and H.R. 2001 (1999) sponsored by Billy Tauzin (R.-Louisiana).

[11] See *Houston Chronicle*, 1998, and *New York Times*, 1998.

the NRST would appear to be quite different from the FT. The former would tax goods and services at the retail business level only, whereas the latter would be levied on individuals and businesses. But, like the FT, the NRST features a single rate and would represent a shift to consumption as a tax base.

There are other proposals for consumption-based taxation. They include a national VAT and the Unlimited Savings Allowance Tax (USA Tax), a cash flow consumption tax.[12] The latter is very much the ugly duckling of the tax reform debate. Its multiple-rate structure and complex transition provisions make it unappealing to many tax reform zealots and mainstream economists alike. Although both the VAT and the USA Tax continue to have their supporters, the current focus is clearly upon the FT and the NRST.

The public profile of these two proposals reflects in part the continuing disenchantment with the current income tax code, widely perceived as unfair in its burden, incomprehensible in its detail, and intrusive in its collection. Polling consistently reveals its unpopularity with the public.[13] Twenty-five years after presidential candidate Jimmy Carter called the tax code "a disgrace to the human race," it remains, in the minds of many, precisely that. Many of the achievements of 1986, moreover, have proved distressingly transitory. The number of marginal rates has increased; the top rate has risen. New complexities have been grafted onto a system already too complicated for even well-trained accountants to understand.

But more appears to be at work than mere weariness with the many inadequacies of the current tax system. There is no shortage, for instance, of proposals to reform the income tax.[14] None, however, has acquired the public profile or impassioned advocacy of consumption-based tax

[12] The USA tax proposal is found in S. 772 (1995), introduced by Senator Pete Domenici (R.-New Mexico). As noted by Gillis (Chapter 10 in this volume), the USA tax bears more than a passing resemblance to a similar cash flow consumption tax proposed by Nicholas Kaldor in the 1950s.

[13] See for, instance, a Yankelovich poll conducted in March 1997, showing that 54 percent of respondents consider the federal tax system as either "not too fair" or "not fair at all" versus 45 percent who believe it to be either "very fair" or "moderately fair." This close result is, however, a little misleading, in that those who consider the federal tax system "not fair at all" outnumber those who believe it "very fair" by 23 to 3 percent. These and other polling data on taxation are available from Public Opinion Online, Roper Center (2001).

[14] See Pechman (1990) for perhaps the best-known scholarly proposal for income tax reform. Other proposals include H.R. 3620 (1998) introduced by Representative Dick Gephardt (D.-Missouri) and, for the business tax portion of the income tax, the Comprehensive Business Income Tax concept developed by the Department of the Treasury (1992). The last proposal is discussed in Hubbard (Chapter 4 in this volume).

proposals. The reasons for the rising calls for fundamental tax reform lie, at least in part, elsewhere.

IDEOLOGICAL UNDERPINNINGS

One such area is ideology – something that no discussion of taxation can long escape. Taxation, after all, goes to the heart of fundamental questions about the role of the state, the nature of the individual, and the relationship between the two – questions that continue to divide reasonable individuals and defy definitive answers. To ask about a tax system "Is it just?" is immediately, if often implicitly, to introduce into the discussion personal values as deeply held as they are often irreconcilable.[15] Fairness, like beauty, lies in the eye of the beholder.

Ideology has colored the debate on income taxation for at least a century, with the left, broadly defined, supporting income taxation and the right generally in opposition. Even to describe this ideological division is to reveal one's own biases. Is it a conflict between the poor and the rich? Between exploiters of resentment and defenders of merit? Between the collectivist impulse and individualism? Between egalitarianism and privilege? For the purposes of this essay, it does not matter. What *does* matter is, first, that ideology has long played a role in the debate on taxation and, second, that it has shaped and continues to shape that debate in consistent ways.

While it is easy to overdraw historical parallels, a cursory examination of earlier debates on taxation certainly prompts an uncanny sense of déjà vu. The graduated income tax, even at rates only a fraction of those in effect today, has been consistently assailed as an impediment to hard work and thrift – precisely the disincentives to labor and saving still described and decried today.[16] It was also condemned as inquisitorial and leading to fraud – arguments still current today.[17] Most important of all, earlier debates became most contentious precisely when they touched upon a concept, ability to pay, which continues to agitate discussion of taxation today: the idea that richer taxpayers can and should pay a high proportion of their income in taxes.[18]

---

[15] These conflicts occur not just between broader value systems but within them. See, for instance, Okun (1975, pp. 1–31) for a classic delineation of the conflict between two quintessentially American values – equality and efficiency.
[16] Eisenstein (1961, pp. 57–88).
[17] Ratner (1942, pp. 121–37).
[18] Hall and Rabushka ([1985] 1995, pp. 27–28) put the origins of the concept at around 1930. But those origins surely reach further back. Paul (1954, p. 12) notes that ability to pay was an element in debates on American income taxation as early as the Civil War. In Europe, it was a subject of considerable dispute at least as early as 1848. That year, John Stuart Mill ([1849] 1970, pp. 159–60) criticized arguments for a graduated income

The NRST and FT enter this debate forthrightly. Either would mark a step away from the progressivity of marginal tax rates that has been part of our income tax system from its very beginnings. Although the distributional effects of the FT and NRST, over a given period or lifetime, are the subject of some controversy, there is little doubt that their introduction will sharply reduce the tax burden of the very wealthy.[19] Hall and Rabushka, for their part, make it very clear that their proposal is premised on a rejection of the concept of ability to pay.[20] So, implicitly, is the NRST.

When it comes to taxation, a century has made surprisingly little difference, at least where rhetoric is concerned. The comparison with the debates of 1894 is particularly revealing. Then, as now, supporters of the income tax accused their opponents of serving the interests of the wealthy. William Jennings Bryan saw the graduated income tax as a "by far the most effective weapon against the Plutocratic policy."[21] Today, critics decry consumption-based taxation as an ill-disguised ploy to benefit the rich.[22] Then, as now, supporters of consumption-based taxation accused *their* opponents of fomenting class division. Senator John Sherman described the income tax as an "attempt to array the rich against the poor and the poor against the rich" – a sentiment echoed today by supporters of the FT.[23]

Concerns over increasing inequality drove much of the populist agitation for an income tax a century ago when census data showed a growing concentration of wealth; they continue to motivate defenders of a progressive income tax today. Worries over infringement of personal freedom colored opposition to the income tax a century ago; they still do so. Such sentiments, it must be noted, are not limited to politicians. William Gale, for instance, argues that tax reform proposals should be viewed in part against the backdrop of growing inequality.[24] Hall and Rabushka, for their part, assert that high tax rates threaten individual freedom.[25] Ideology – those often unarticulated but ever-present

---

tax and Karl Marx and Friedrich Engels ([1848] 1965, p. 94) called for its institution. Paul (1954, pp. 715–18) traces an even lengthier history of progressive taxation – one reaching back to the Middle Ages and, indeed, the ancient world.

[19] Feenberg, Mitrusi, and Poterba (1997); Cronin, Nunns, and Toder (1996); Mieszkowski and Palumbo (Chapter 6 in this volume).

[20] Hall and Rabushka ([1985] 1995, p. 28).   [21] Quoted in Ratner (1942, p. 172).

[22] See McIntyre (1998).

[23] Sherman is quoted in Ratner (1942, p. 186). His attack ends with his famous description of the income tax as "socialism, communism, devilism." Representative Dick Armey (1996, p. 114) has excoriated opponents of the FT as fomenters of class warfare.

[24] See Gale in Sease and Herman (1996, p. 131).

[25] Hall and Rabushka ([1985] 1995, p. 28).

assumptions about man, the state, and society that we bring to any issue – remains an important element in how we view taxation and therefore tax reform.

Ideology is thus still very much with us. One of the most remarked upon developments of the past thirty years has been the resurgence of the right on the American scene. Contemporary American conservatism reflects two major ideological strains. They may, at risk of oversimplification, be called the libertarian and the traditional; their adherents are the economic and social conservatives, who have become a staple of analysis of contemporary American politics.[26] While dominant among Republicans, these ideological positions also find adherents among Independents and even Democrats. It is conservatism's ability to unite these two strains into one movement that has given it the ascendancy it enjoys over liberalism today. There has been an intense effort within the conservative movement since the 1950s to find common intellectual ground between these factions. General opposition to activist government has proved by far the most fruitful. For economic conservatives, economic intervention represents both a direct infringement of individual liberty and a broader distortion of the free-market system they see as guaranteeing it; for traditionalists, social intervention represents the imposition of alien values at odds with their religious beliefs and moral codes. Over the course of recent decades, libertarians and traditionalists have found agreement on a broad range of issues from opposition to civil rights legislation in the early 1960s to support for school vouchers today. Antigovernment rhetoric remains a rallying cry for conservatives of all stripes.

How fundamental tax reform will affect the relationship between economic and social conservatives and therefore broader conservative unity is ambiguous. Its appeal to libertarians on ideological grounds is obvious. Insofar as they reject the egalitarianism symbolized by a graduated income tax, many would welcome a flat rate. With their strong support for free markets, libertarians would find intellectually congenial the arguments for consumption-based taxation on efficiency grounds. Given their concerns over the intrusiveness of government libertarians would also presumably applaud reform proposals, notably the NRST, which promise to abolish federal direct taxation altogether.

To the extent that a focus on fundamental tax reform shifts debate away from issues that often divide social and economic conservatives – such as abortion, homosexuality, sex education, and creation science – it may serve as a unifying force. But fundamental tax reform risks alienat-

---

[26] See Dionne (1996, pp. 151–97) and Frum (1994, pp. 190–205), for an analysis of the American right from a liberal and conservative perspective, respectively.

ing social conservatives on two counts. First, if fundamental tax reform is perceived as rebounding disproportionately to the advantage of the rich, it risks a populist backlash among less-affluent social conservatives. Second, if fundamental tax reform is seen as being pursued to the detriment of issues close to the heart of social conservatives, they could take it as a sign of bad faith. More generally, many social conservatives remain highly suspicious of the motives of their libertarian brethren. To date, however, the restiveness of social conservatives has stopped short of outright revolt; the abject failure of Pat Buchanan's third party bid in 2000 is clear evidence of the enduring strength of the social conservative–libertarian ideological alliance.

In general, social conservatives have been strong supporters of tax cuts, particularly if couched in "pro-family" terms. Whether that support will encompass fundamental tax reform as the debate over it narrows to specific detail, however, is far from clear.

POLITICAL REALITIES

The ascendancy of conservatism and the rise of the Republican Party are intimately intertwined. The GOP's political success is attributable, at least in part, to a broad ideological turn away from liberalism – a response to the damage, real or perceived, done to America by the welfare state and social permissiveness. But the Republican Party has also helped advance the conservative cause, fostering the emergence of local activists and national leaders capable of promoting conservative principles, transforming those principles into effective campaign platforms, and translating those platforms, in turn, into effective public policy. Clearly the minority party a generation ago, the GOP is every bit the equal of the Democrats as a national political force.

Although some overhaul of the income tax code is conceivable under divided government, it is difficult to imagine large numbers of Democrats, long associated with the redistribution of income through a graduated income tax, embracing either the FT or NRST. The Clinton administration, for its part, consistently opposed consumption-based taxation; Lawrence Summers, then deputy secretary of the treasury, was particularly critical of the idea.[27] Republican control of both branches of government potentially alters this equation. Influential party leaders have long been powerful advocates of reform. The FT and NRST have also found at least tentative backing among the party rank and file. Support for flat versus graduated tax rates is higher among Republicans

---

[27] See Summers in Sease and Herman (1996, pp. 132–38). Summers's opposition is ironic, in light of his seminal work (Summers, 1981a) on the benefits of a move to consumption-based taxation.

(62 percent) than among Democrats (36 percent) or independents (42 percent).[28] As noted earlier, reform is attractive on ideological grounds to economic conservatives, a critical source of Republican electoral strength. If it is couched in terms of reducing the size of government, it may appeal to social conservatives as well. Moreover, in specific political terms, reform potentially appeals to important constituencies.

Among those constituencies are the very rich. Clear beneficiaries of either the FT or the NRST, the wealthy also have an obvious interest in the abolition of estate and gift taxes – unsurprisingly, part of the GOP's FT and NRST proposals. From the point of view of simple self-interest, the support of rich individuals for fundamental tax reform is neither surprising nor, it should be added, sinister. As a group, after all, they pay a higher percentage of their income in taxes than other Americans – and a lion's share of the total tax burden. While relatively small in number, moreover, the wealthy possess disproportionate political clout in an electoral system driven in large part by campaign finance.

The simplification promised by fundamental reform proposals also appeals to another important GOP constituency: the self-employed or small businessmen. The whole question of compliance costs is a complex one, with widely divergent estimates of those costs under both the current income tax system and alternatives to it.[29] But the burden of compliance almost certainly falls with particular harshness upon these two groups. Small businessmen, in particular, have long been vociferous in their criticism of the current tax code, playing a critical role in the House of Representatives 1998 vote to abolish the tax code by July 4, 2002.[30]

Fundamental reform proposals containing tax reductions based on implicit if unidentified expenditure cuts also appeal to middle-class voters in general, the swing group in most elections. Both major GOP reform proposals, for instance, reduce federal revenue, without itemizing offsetting reductions in spending.[31]

---

[28] These data come from a Gallup poll conducted in November 1997. They may be found at Public Opinion Online via Lexis/Nexis. Support for flat versus graduated tax rates is higher among conservatives (54 percent), than among liberals (41 percent) or moderates (40 percent). The higher the income, the greater the support for a flat rate.

[29] Slemrod (1996); Gale and Holtzblatt (Chapter 7 in this volume).

[30] See *Los Angeles Times*, 1998. The bill, which carried the House by a nearly party-line vote, failed in the Senate.

[31] According to the Department of the Treasury, the Armey-Shelby FT would have led in 1996 to a revenue loss of $138 billion; see Sease and Herman (1996, p. 138). The Tauzin-Schaefer NRST, though technically revenue neutral, taxes purchases of goods and services by the federal government without allowing an increase in overall Federal revenues – effectively lowering the general tax rate by reducing the size of government; see Gale et al. (1998), and Gale and Holtzblatt (Chapter 7 in this volume).

Fundamental tax reform also taps into public sentiment against the IRS. It is difficult to disentangle that sentiment from a general dislike of the federal tax burden. But there is a group of voters – passionately committed and increasingly vocal – whose detestation of the IRS is very specific. This animus may reflect unfortunate personal experience at the hands of that agency, a principled stand against its intrusiveness in the lives of citizens, or, for that matter, both. It is also clearly related to the broader antigovernment posture of contemporary conservatism. Nothing, for the white middle-class American, embodies the federal government in a palpable and unpleasant way like the IRS. The NRST in particular, with its promise to abolish the IRS lock, stock, and barrel, draws on this powerful sentiment.

In theory, then, fundamental tax reform offers real political advantages for the GOP. Whether those advantages will lead to actual tax reform is, however, another question altogether. An ideal system always looks more attractive than actual legislation. Both the GOP's FT and NRST plans, for instance, are extremely sketchy. It is safe to assume that any proposal will undergo dramatic elaboration during the protracted legislative process that will by necessity precede enactment.

The public, though clearly more aware of tax reform as an issue than ten years ago, can be expected to take a much closer look when and if reform moves to the top of the domestic policy agenda. Interest groups, armed with mailing lists, telephone banks, and highly paid lobbyists, will enter the fray with a vengeance. Political IOUs will be redeemed; publicity campaigns will blanket newspapers and television.

The fate of the Clinton health care proposal certainly represents a sobering warning to Republicans. Universal health care went in one year from a spectacularly successful campaign promise to a political fiasco of the first order. The result in part was a near catastrophe for the Democrats in the elections of 1994. Some observers believe that GOP leaders, even those associated with fundamental tax reform, have no current intention of running such a risk.[32] They see reform purely as a political issue, useful in mobilizing voters and raising money, but nothing more. After assuming control of the Congress in 1994, Republicans certainly showed little interest in at least one purported goal of fundamental tax reform: simplicity. Their efforts during this period actually increased the complexity of the tax code, creating 250 new sections and amending 800 others. The treatment of capital gains, in particular, became much more complicated.

Nor can Republicans take particular heart from success in another area of domestic policy: welfare reform. In sharp contrast with

[32] Birnbaum (1998).

legislation that, by definition, affected only the poor directly, fundamental tax reform will place Republicans in direct conflict with important
interest groups – and interest groups, more to the point, that the GOP
will be extremely hesitant to offend.

Under the FT, there will be immense pressure to maintain special tax
treatment for a variety of sources and uses of income. Homeowners, for
instance, will fight to maintain the mortgage interest deduction. As homeowners tend to be more affluent, they are likelier to vote Republican.
State and local governments – many now in Republican hands – will seek
to retain the deductibility of certain state and local taxes, as well as
special treatment of state and local bonds. Nonprofit groups will agitate
to maintain the deductibility of charitable contributions. These groups
include churches, many evangelical, whose members count themselves
among the GOP's staunchest supporters. Removal of special tax treatment of certain fringe benefits – notably employer-provided health
insurance – will also face sharp criticism from the millions of relatively
affluent workers who benefit from them. Under the NRST, there will be
similar and no less severe pressures to exempt a whole range of transactions – purchases of homes and purchases by charities chief among
them – from taxation.

Moreover, Republicans will face the intractable and perhaps insuper-
able problem of transition relief with either the FT or the NRST. The
sums involved are potentially immense; the issues are extraordinarily
complex.[33] A shift to consumption-based taxation without relief would
lead to significant economic losses by individuals, many elderly, who hold
savings that they would like to draw down, by businesses in possession
of significant inventories and undepreciated assets, and by indebted
enterprises and households currently enjoying special treatment of
interest payments. Many of those households are affluent. Many of
those enterprises are large. Each group represents a traditional source
of Republican support. The political pressure to accommodate them, at
least in part, may well prove irresistible.

There will, moreover, be pressure on Republicans to adopt rough
distributional neutrality between the old and new systems. This was the
approach taken in 1986; it was an important element in the development
of the USA Tax.[34] Any attempt to do so, however, will force Republicans
to move away from their single-rate structure. The advantages accruing
to the very wealthiest individuals under consumption-based taxation will
become the focus of public attention and partisan criticism. The salaried
worker who pays proportionately more of his or her income in annual
personal taxes under the FT than his or her wealthy employer, we can

---

[33] Pearlman (1996); Zodrow (Chapter 9 in this volume).
[34] McLure and Zodrow (1987); Penner (1996).

be confident, will rapidly become a feature of the debate. So will the middle-class family paying tax on medical care for their children under the NRST while the rich enjoy tax-free vacations abroad. Arguments based on lifetime taxation or the ultimate burden of the business tax – however cogent from an economic point of view – will likely carry little weight with many voters.

These pressures will place Republicans in a quandary. Efforts to maintain special treatment or grant transition relief will necessarily narrow the available tax base and require an increase in the single rate. They also increase the complexity of the resulting code. Both decrease the general political appeal of reform. Combined with a move away from a single-rate tax structure, such political accommodations would also diminish and perhaps eliminate any of the efficiency gains from the introduction of fundamental reform – a conclusion on which advocates and opponents of reform find themselves in rare agreement.

The existence of large projected federal budget surpluses – estimated in the trillions over the course of the next decade – would appear at first sight to make the task of reformers easier. Using part of these surpluses would permit a lower tax rate, generous transition relief, or a combination of both. But surpluses also raise an important question: from a political point of view, why should Republicans take on important interest groups – including those traditionally allied with their own party – when a simple tax cut is both so attractive and so possible? Indeed, it is such a tax cut – and not fundamental tax reform – that Republicans have put at the top of their economic agenda. In fact, fundamental tax reform has been most notable for its *absence* from the national debate on what to do with the expected budget surplus.[35] As long as projected budget surpluses exist, Republicans will be sorely tempted to make tax cuts and not fundamental tax reform their top priority. Tax cuts are popular and, more to the political point, *easy*.

ECONOMIC ANALYSES

Developments within the economics discipline have also helped shape the current debate on fundamental tax reform. Support for consumption taxation has a long and proud lineage within the economics profession (see Gillis, Chapter 10 in this volume). As early as the mid-nineteenth century, John Stuart Mill observed that an income tax, by reducing the return on savings, discouraged investment.[36] Twentieth-century economists who support the expenditure tax number among the most

[35] See Barnes (1999).
[36] Mill ([1849] 1970, pp. 165–66, 376–79) was a flat-taxer with a twist: he believed in a flat consumption tax above a certain minimal income level but also limits on the amounts individuals could inherit.

distinguished in the field of public finance: Irving Fisher, Nicholas Kaldor, and James Meade.[37]

Recent decades, moreover, have seen growing interest in consumption-based taxation. Part of this is due to developments within the profession itself – particularly the rising influence of neoclassical economics. Grounded in microeconomics – the theory of economic behavior of rational households and profit-maximizing firms – neoclassical economists have used sophisticated models and empirical techniques to identify, aggregate, and compare the effects of the current tax code and alternatives to it. A growing body of theoretical work on optimal taxation, in addition, has cast doubt on the ability of graduated rates to maximize social welfare.[38]

There is today a large and rich economic literature covering the full range of issues related to taxation – its effect on personal savings, economic growth, income distribution, asset valuation, and compliance costs. Administrative, transitional, and international questions raised by the possible introduction of consumption-based taxation have recently been the subject of an impressive and growing body of research, much of which is discussed in this volume.

Many economists have become more open to the potential advantages offered by a simplified, single-rate tax system based on consumption. The reasons are several. Most fundamentally, consumption-based taxation would remove the incentive given to consumption over savings under the current income tax system; insofar as those savings represent future consumption, the income tax penalizes individuals who prefer it to current consumption.[39] Consumption-based taxation also promises to increase savings and therefore investment and growth – perhaps the key economic argument on its behalf.[40] With their low flat rate and broadened base, the FT or the NRST could also reduce many of the economic distortions – between work and leisure and among various types of investment – induced by the current income tax code. In addition, the simplicity promised by reform plans could reduce the administrative and compliance costs associated with the current code.

---

[37] Kaldor (1955, pp. 11–12) depicts an even more impressive lineage, citing Pigou, Marshall, and even Keynes among those who saw the virtues of a consumption tax – at least in theory. Kaldor, Meade (Institute for Fiscal Studies, 1978), and Fisher and Fisher (1942) still make rewarding reading.

[38] Slemrod et al. (1994) review the optimal tax literature and present their own finding that social welfare can be maximized by a two-bracket income tax – one featuring a *lower* marginal rate on higher incomes.

[39] Mieszkowski (1980).

[40] Kotlikoff (1996b), for instance, cites the savings crisis as the chief reason to institute consumption-based taxation.

To say that economists are more open to the potential advantages of consumption-based taxation is one thing; to assert that there exists anything like unanimity of opinion about its specific effects or general advisability is, however, another. Some of the most important issues associated with fundamental tax reform – its effects on general economic performance, savings, labor supply, interest rates, and housing prices – remain subjects of considerable professional dispute.

As Gravelle points out (Chapter 2 in this volume), it is premature to speak of a consensus about the advisability of instituting fundamental tax reform.[41] For whatever reasons – incommensurate theoretical assumptions, alternative models with different results, paucity of data, different estimating techniques – we do not, at least today, have unambiguous answers to at least two key questions related to fundamental tax reform: (1) How will it affect the real growth of the American economy? (2) What will it do to the allocation of resources, among households and enterprises, within that economy? The future may well hold clearer answers. The flood of research currently underway certainly suggests as much. At the very least, the economics literature is cautionary: its very volume and complexity serve as reminder of the difficulty of the issues involved and the uncertainty necessarily attached to fundamental reform. But it leaves the lay reader with the uneasy sense that a plausible economic argument can be made for very nearly any position on fundamental tax reform – a view shared, it should be added, by economists as well.[42]

Politicians and ideologues have, of course, exploited this ambiguity. They will continue to do so. This may reflect a cynical attempt to gain a rhetorical edge. But the all-too-human tendency to select evidence and argument that support our existing beliefs is also plainly at work. Liberals tend to like low elasticities of behavioral responses to taxation; conservatives generally prefer higher ones.[43] And, given the current state of the literature on consumption-based taxation, they will have no trouble finding either. Individual economists and specific studies will be promoted, perhaps even financed, depending on the conformity of their findings to specific ideological presuppositions. Some scholarly findings will be cited and others simply ignored, on the basis of their political utility. Think tanks and advocacy groups can be expected to produce an endless series of analyses – often first rate – that support their specific agendas. This is not to suggest that further economic research on tax reform is an exercise in futility, much less that it must be irredeemably tainted with ideological or political bias. But in the absence of definitive economic

[41] Gravelle (Chapter 2 in this volume).   [42] McLure and Zodrow (1994).
[43] Rosen (1999, p. 398).

answers, politics and ideology, as confused as they too may be, could well provide those answers instead – and prove decisive as we determine whether to institute fundamental tax reform.

CONCLUSION

Fundamental tax reform represents a major gamble – economically, politically, and ideologically. The economic gamble is perhaps the most obvious: to introduce either the FT or the NRST, neither of which has been tested as a major source of revenue by any other country, holds clear risks. But the political and ideological stakes are also high. The comfortable idea, prevalent among tax reformers, that *any* federal system would be preferable to the current one is simply false. The property tax system Prime Minister Thatcher attempted to replace in the United Kingdom was much disliked; but the poll tax she put in its place was hated.[44] The tax on goods and services introduced by Prime Minister Mulroney in Canada was not only a political liability; it helped contribute to one of the most lop-sided defeats in modern parliamentary history.[45]

The comparison to 1986 is stark. The tax reform of that year was viewed as a success in large part because initial public expectations were so low. It was essentially the work of a small group of individuals behind closed doors; it was effectively removed, by implicit bipartisan agreement, from the political campaign of 1986. Fundamental tax reform, embodied by the FT or the NRST, represents a far more dramatic shift in policy; its promoters, in the political arena and among advocacy groups, have committed themselves thus far to a strategy of high public profile. The standard of success is much higher. Any failure to achieve it will be more obvious. And the cost of such failure will be all the more dear.

Success might even prove bittersweet, in light of the expectations that have been raised. Given the protracted and complex legislative process involved, the final form of fundamental reform may well resemble the little-loved USA Tax, in general character if not in specific detail: complicated, cumbersome, anything but "clean" – in short, a reform perhaps not so fundamental at all. It may mark an improvement over the current system; as such, it may be a laudable goal. But it will be a far cry indeed from the idealized systems that today so excite supporters of funda-

---

[44] Graetz (1997, p. 263).
[45] In 1993, Mulroney's Progressive Conservatives dropped from 154 to 2 seats in the Canadian parliament. He was no longer leader of the party at the time. After the introduction of the Goods and Services Tax, Mulroney's popularity rating never rose above 20 percent. See *Washington Post* (1993).

mental tax reform, whatever their ideological, political, or economic reasons.

Even so modest and unsatisfactory a reform, however, remains unlikely for the foreseeable future. Indeed, with the wave of interest in reform during the mid- and late 1990s we may already have seen, at least for the time being, the high-water mark of opposition to the income tax.[46] President George W. Bush has not placed any particular emphasis on fundamental tax reform. The striking lack of any significant proposals to use part of the expected federal budget surplus to ease the transition to consumption-based taxation suggests that the political will for reform is wanting. Such an opportunity, moreover, may not arise for years, perhaps decades to come. In the meanwhile, the current income tax – disliked by economists, derided by politicians, and detested by the general public – will likely remain, as it has for decades, the chief source of federal revenue.

---

[46] References to the flat tax in the Lexis/Nexis data base plummeted between 1996, when Steve Forbes made it a campaign issue, and 1999. In 2000, the references almost disappeared.

Bibliography

BILLS

U.S. House. 1995. *Freedom and Fairness Restoration Act of 1995.* 104th Cong., 1st sess., H.R. 2060 and S. 1050.
  1997. *Freedom and Fairness Restoration Act of 1997.* 105th Cong., 1st sess., H.R. 1040 and S. 1040.
  1997. *The National Retail Sales Tax Act of 1997.* June 23. 105th Cong., 1st sess., H.R. 2001.
  1999. *The National Retail Sales Tax Act of 1999.* 106th Cong., 1st sess., H.R. 2001.
  1998. *Gephardt 10 Percent Tax Act of 1998.* 105th Cong., 2d sess., H.R. 3620.
U.S. Senate. 1995. *USA Tax Act of 1995.* 104th Cong., 1st sess., S. 772.

SECONDARY SOURCES

Aaron, Henry J., and William G. Gale (eds.). 1996. *Economic Effects of Fundamental Tax Reform.* Washington, D.C.: Brookings Institution Press.
  1997. "Fundamental Tax Reform: Miracle or Mirage." In Robert D. Reischauer (ed.), *Setting National Priorities: Budget Choices for the Next Century*, pp. 235–62. Washington, D.C.: Brookings Institution Press.
Aaron, Henry J., and Harvey Galper. 1985. *Assessing Tax Reform.* Washington, D.C.: Brookings Institution.
Aaron, Henry J., Harvey Galper, and Joseph A. Pechman (eds.). 1988. *Uneasy Compromise: Problems of a Hybrid Income-Consumption Tax.* Washington, D.C.: Brookings Institution.
Adler, Michael, and Bernard Dumas. 1983. "International Portfolio Choice and Corporation Finance: A Synthesis." *Journal of Finance* 38.3 (June): 925–84.
Agha, Ali, and Jonathan Haughton. 1996. "Designing VAT Systems: Some Efficiency Considerations." *Review of Economics and Statistics* 78.2: 303–8.
Aiyagari, S. Rao. 1994. "Uninsured Idiosyncratic Risk and Aggregate Saving." *Quarterly Journal of Economics* 109.3 (August): 659–84.
Alliance USA. 1995. "Description and Explanation of the Unlimited Savings Allowance Income Tax System." *Tax Notes* 66 (March 10): 1485–575.

Alm, James, Betty R. Jackson, and Michael McKee. 1992. "Estimating the Determinants of Taxpayer Compliance with Experimental Data." *National Tax Journal* 45.1 (March): 107–14.

Altig, David, Alan J. Auerbach, Laurence J. Kotlikoff, Kent A. Smetters, and Jan Walliser. 1997. "Simulating U.S. Tax Reform." NBER Working Paper no. W6248, October. Cambridge, Mass.

Altonji, Joseph G., Fumio Hayashi, and Laurence J. Kotlikoff. 1992. "Is the Extended Family Altruistically Linked? Direct Tests Using Micro Data." *American Economic Review* 82.5 (December): 1177–98.

Altshuler, Rosanne, and R. Glenn Hubbard. 2000. "The Effect of the Tax Reform Act of 1986 on the Location of Assets in Financial Services Firms." NBER Working Paper no. W7903, September. Cambridge, Mass.

Altshuler, Rosanne, and Jack M. Mintz. 1995. "U.S. Interest-Allocation Rules: Effects and Policy." *International Tax and Public Finance* 2.1 (May): 7–35.

Altshuler, Rosanne, and T. Scott Newlon. 1993. "The Effects of U.S. Tax Policy on the Income Repatriation Patterns of U.S. Multinational Corporations." In Alberto Giovannini, R. Glenn Hubbard, and Joel Slemrod (eds.), *Studies in International Taxation*, pp. 77–115. Chicago: University of Chicago Press.

Altshuler, Rosanne, T. Scott Newlon, and William C. Randolph. 1995. "Do Repatriation Taxes Matter? Evidence from the Tax Returns of U.S. Multinationals." In Martin Feldstein, James R. Hines Jr., and R. Glenn Hubbard (eds.), *The Effects of Taxation on Multinational Corporations*, pp. 253–72. Chicago: University of Chicago Press.

American Law Institute. 1993. *Federal Income Tax Project, Integration of the Individual and Corporate Income Taxes*. Philadelphia: American Law Institute.

Americans for Fair Taxation. 1997. *The National Retail Sales Tax, Tax Evasion and the Underground Economy* <http://www.fairtax.org/impact/nationalretail.htm>.

Andreoni, James, Brian Erard, and Jonathan Feinstein. 1998. "Tax Compliance." *Journal of Economic Literature* 36.2 (June): 818–60.

Andrews, William D. 1974. "A Consumption-Type or Cash Flow Personal Income Tax." *Harvard Law Review* 87 (April): 1113–88.

Armey, Richard. 1995. "Caveat Emptor: The Case against the National Sales Tax." *Policy Review* 73 (Summer): 31–35.

——— 1996. *The Flat Tax: A Citizen's Guide to the Facts on What It Will Do for You, Your Country, and Your Pocketbook*. New York: Fawcett Columbine.

Armington, Paul S. 1969. "The Geographic Pattern of Trade and the Effects of Price Changes." *IMF Staff Papers* 16.2 (July): 179–201.

Arthur D. Little Inc. 1988. *Development of Methodology for Estimating the Taxpayer Paperwork Burden*. Final Report to the Department of the Treasury, June. Washington, D.C.: Internal Revenue Service.

Asprey Committee, Taxation Review Committee. 1975. *Full Report: 31 January 1975*. Canberra: Australian Government Printing Service.

Atkeson, Andrew, and Masao Ogaki. 1996. "Wealth-Varying Intertemporal Elasticities of Substitution: Evidence from Panel and Aggregate Data." *Journal of Monetary Economics* 38.3 (December): 507–34.

Attanasio, Orazio P., and Martin Browning. 1995. "Consumption over the Life Cycle and over the Business Cycle." *American Economic Review* 85.5 (December): 1118–37.

Auerbach, Alan J. 1983. "Corporate Taxation in the United States." *Brookings Papers on Economic Activity* 2: 451–513.

———. 1996. "Tax Reform, Capital Allocation, Efficiency, and Growth." In Henry J. Aaron and William G. Gale (eds.), *Economic Effects of Fundamental Tax Reform*, pp. 29–73. Washington, D.C.: Brookings Institution Press.

———. 1997. "The Future of Fundamental Tax Reform." *American Economic Review* 87 (May 2): 143–46.

Auerbach, Alan J., Jagadeesh Gokhale, and Laurence J. Kotlikoff. 1994. "Generational Accounting: A Meaningful Way to Evaluate Fiscal Policy." *Journal of Economic Perspectives* 8.1 (Winter): 73–94.

Auerbach, Alan J., and Kevin Hassett. 1993. "Taxation and Foreign Direct Investment in the United States: A Reconsideration of the Evidence." In Alberto Giovannini, R. Glenn Hubbard, and Joel Slemrod (eds.), *Studies in International Taxation*, pp. 119–44. Chicago: University of Chicago Press.

Auerbach, Alan J., and Laurence J. Kotlikoff. 1983. "National Savings, Economic Welfare, and the Structure of Taxation." In Martin Feldstein (ed.), *Behavioral Simulation Methods in Tax Policy Analysis*, pp. 459–93. Chicago: University of Chicago Press.

———. 1987. *Dynamic Fiscal Policy*. Cambridge: Cambridge University Press.

———. 1995. *Macroeconomics: An Integrated Approach*. Cincinnati: International Thomson, South-Western College.

Auerbach, Alan J., Laurence J. Kotlikoff, and Jonathan Skinner. 1983. "The Efficiency Gains from Dynamic Tax Reform." *International Economic Review* 24.1: 81–100.

Auerbach, Alan J., Laurence J. Kotlikoff, Kent Smetters, and Jan Walliser. 1997. "Fundamental Tax Reform and Macroeconomic Performance." In *Joint Committee on Taxation Tax Modeling Project and 1997 Tax Symposium Papers*, pp. 83–100. Washington, D.C.: U.S. Government Printing Office.

Australian Government. 1985. *Reform of the Australian Tax System: Draft White Paper*. Canberra: Australian Government Printing Service.

Ballard, Charles L. 1990. "On the Specification of Simulation Models for Evaluating Income and Consumption Taxes." In Manfred Rose (ed.), *Heidelberg Congress on Taxing Consumption*, pp. 147–88. Berlin: Springer-Verlag.

———. 1997. "Taxation and Saving." In John G. Head and Richard Krever (eds.), *Taxation towards 2000*, pp. 267–92. Melbourne: Australian Tax Research Foundation.

———. 1999a. "International Aspects of Fundamental Tax Reform." Working Paper, March 12. Michigan State University.

———. 1999b. "How Many Hours Are in a Simulated Day? The Effects of Time Endowment on the Results of Tax-Policy Simulation Models." Working Paper, October 22. Michigan State University.

Ballard, Charles L., Don Fullerton, John B. Shoven, and John Whalley. 1985. *A General Equilibrium Model for Tax Policy Evaluation*. Chicago: University of Chicago Press.

Ballard, Charles L., and Larry H. Goulder. 1985. "Consumption Taxes, Foresight, and Welfare: A Computable General Equilibrium Analysis." In John Piggott and John Whalley (eds.), *New Developments in Applied General Equilibrium Analysis*, pp. 253–82. Cambridge: Cambridge University Press.

Barnes, Joe. 1999. "Surplus Offers a One-Time Only Chance for Tax Reform." *Houston Chronicle*, September 29, p. 29A.

Bartlett, Bruce. 1995. "Replacing Federal Taxes with a Sales Tax." *Tax Notes* 68 (August 21): 997–1003.

Becker, Gary S., and Casey B. Mulligan. 1998. "Deadweight Costs and the Size of Government." NBER Working Paper no. W6789, November. Cambridge, Mass.

Becker, Gary S., and Nigel Tomes. 1986. "Human Capital and the Rise and Fall of Families." *Journal of Labor Economics* 4.3, pt. 2 (July): S1–39.

Bernheim, B. Douglas. 1997. "Rethinking Saving Incentives." In Alan J. Auerbach (ed.), *Fiscal Policy: Lessons from Economic Research*, pp. 259–311. Cambridge, Mass.: MIT Press.

Besley, Timothy J., and Harvey S. Rosen. 1999. "Sales Taxes and Prices: An Empirical Analysis." *National Tax Journal* 52.2 (June): 157–78.

Bird, Richard M., and Pierre Pascal Gendron. 1998. "Dual VATs and Cross-Border Trade: Two Problems, One Solution?" *International Tax and Public Finance* 5.3 (July): 429–42.

Birnbaum, Jeffrey H. 1998. "Fundamental Tax Reform: Public Perception and Political Rhetoric." *National Tax Journal* 51.3 (September): 565–67.

Birnbaum, Jeffrey H., and Alan S. Murray. 1987. *Showdown at Gucci Gulch: Lawmakers, Lobbyists, and the Unlikely Triumph of Tax Reform*. New York: Random House.

Blumenthal, Marsha, and Joel Slemrod. 1992. "The Compliance Cost of the U.S. Individual Income Tax System: A Second Look after Tax Reform." *National Tax Journal* 45.2 (June): 185–202.

1995. "The Compliance Cost of Taxing Foreign-Source Income: Its Magnitude, Determinants, and Policy Implications." *International Tax and Public Finance* 2.1 (May): 37–53.

Boskin, Michael J. (ed.). 1996. *Frontiers of Tax Reform*. Stanford: Hoover Institution Press.

Boskin, Michael J., and William G. Gale. 1987. "New Results on the Effects of Tax Policy on the International Location of Investment." In Martin Feldstein (ed.), *The Effects of Taxation on Capital Accumulation*, pp. 201–19. Chicago: University of Chicago Press.

Bradford, David F. 1986. *Untangling the Income Tax*. Cambridge, Mass.: Harvard University Press.

1996a. "Consumption Taxes: Some Fundamental Transition Issues." In Michael J. Boskin (ed.), *Frontiers of Tax Reform*, pp. 123–50. Stanford: Hoover Institution Press.

1996b. "Treatment of Financial Services under Income and Consumption Taxes." In Henry J. Aaron and William G. Gale (eds.), *Economic Effects of*

Fundamental Tax Reform, pp. 437–60. Washington, D.C.: Brookings Institution Press.

1998. "Transition to and Tax Rate Flexibility in a Cash-Flow Type Tax." NBER Working Paper no. W6465, March. Cambridge, Mass.

Brady, Nicholas F. 1992. Remarks Presented at the Graduate School of Business, Columbia University, December 10.

Brashares, Edith, Janet Furman Speyrer, and George N. Carlson. 1988. "Distributional Aspects of a Federal Value-Added Tax." *National Tax Journal* 41.2 (June): 155–74.

Break, George F., and Joseph A. Pechman. 1975. *Federal Tax Reform: The Impossible Dream?* Washington, D.C.: Brookings Institution.

Brinner, Roger E. (DRI/McGraw-Hill). 1997. "Modeling the Macroeconomic Consequences of Tax Policy." In *Joint Committee on Taxation Tax Modeling Project and 1997 Tax Symposium Papers*, pp. 212–42. Washington, D.C.: U.S. Government Printing Office.

Brown, Edgar Cary. 1948. "Business-Income Taxation and Investment Incentives." In Lloyd A. Metzler et al. (eds.), *Income, Employment and Public Policy: Essays in Honor of Alvin H. Hansen*, pp. 300–16. New York: W. W. Norton.

Browning, Edgar K. 1978. "The Burden of Taxation." *Journal of Political Economy* 86.4 (August): 649–71.

1995. "Tax Incidence Analysis for Policy Makers." In David F. Bradford (ed.), *Distributional Analysis of Tax Policy*, pp. 164–80. Washington, D.C.: American Enterprise Institute Press.

Browning, Edgar K., and William R. Johnson. 1979. *The Distribution of the Tax Burden*. Washington, D.C.: American Enterprises Institute.

Bruce, Donald, and Douglas Holtz-Eakin. 1997. "Apocalypse Now? Fundamental Tax Reform and Residential Housing Values." NBER Working Paper no. W6282, November. Cambridge, Mass.

Bull, Nicholas, and Lawrence B. Lindsey. 1996. "Monetary Implications of Tax Reforms." *National Tax Journal* 49.3 (September): 359–79.

Bulow, Jeremy I., and Lawrence H. Summers. 1984. "The Taxation of Risky Assets." *Journal of Political Economy* 92.1 (February): 20–39.

Bureau of Economic Analysis. 1994. *Survey of Current Business*. July. Washington, D.C.: U.S. Government Printing Office.

Bureau of Labor Statistics. 1998. "Major Sector Productivity and Costs Index." Series ID: PRS84006092 <http://146.142.4.24/cgi-bin/surveymost>.

Burton, David, and Dan Mastromarco. 1997. "Emancipating America from the Income Tax: How a National Sales Tax Would Work." *Policy Analysis*, no. 272, April 15. Washington, D.C.: Cato Institute.

Calegari, Michael. 1998. "Flat Taxes and Effective Tax Planning." *National Tax Journal* 51.4 (December): 689–713.

Capozza, Dennis R., Richard K. Green, and Patric H. Hendershott. 1996. "Taxes, Mortgage Borrowing, and Residential Land Prices." In Henry J. Aaron and William G. Gale (eds.), *Economic Effects of Fundamental Tax Reform*, pp. 171–98. Washington, D.C.: Brookings Institution Press.

Carroll, Christopher D. 1998. "Why Do the Rich Save So Much?" Johns Hopkins University, June 23. Mimeograph.

Carroll, Robert, Douglas Holtz-Eakin, Mark Rider, and Harvey S. Rosen. 1998. "Entrepreneurs, Income Taxes, and Investment." NBER Working Paper no. W6374, January. Cambridge, Mass.

Casanegra de Jantscher, Milka. 1987. "Problems in Administering a Consumption Tax." In Charles E. Walker and Mark A. Bloomfield (eds.), *The Consumption Tax: A Better Alternative?*, pp. 300–5. Cambridge, Mass.: Harper and Row, Ballinger.

Caspersen, Erik, and Gilbert E. Metcalf. 1994. "Is a Value Added Tax Regressive? Annual versus Lifetime Incidence Measures." *National Tax Journal* 47.4 (December): 731–46.

Chamley, Christophe. 1981. "The Welfare Cost of Capital Income Taxation in a Growing Economy." *Journal of Political Economy* 89.3 (June): 468–96.

Chernick, Howard, and Andrew Reschovsky. 1997. "Who Pays the Gasoline Tax?" *National Tax Journal* 50.2 (June): 233–59.

Clotfelter, Charles T. 1983. "Tax Evasion and Tax Rates: An Analysis of Individual Returns." *Review of Economics and Statistics* 65.3 (August): 363–73.

Clotfelter, Charles T., and Richard L. Schmalbeck. 1996. "The Impact of Fundamental Tax Reform on Nonprofit Organizations." In Henry J. Aaron and William G. Gale (eds.), *Economic Effects of Fundamental Tax Reform*, pp. 211–43. Washington, D.C.: Brookings Institution Press.

Cnossen, Sijbren. 1987. "VAT and RST: A Comparison." *Canadian Tax Journal* 35.3 (May–June): 559–615.

1994. "Administrative and Compliance Costs of the VAT: A Review of the Evidence." *Tax Notes International* 8.25 (June 20): 1649–68.

1996. "VAT Treatment of Immovable Property." In Victor Thuronyi (ed.), *Tax Law Design and Drafting*, pp. 231–45. Washington, D.C.: International Monetary Fund.

1998. "Global Trends and Issues in Value Added Taxation." *International Tax and Public Finance* 5.3 (July): 399–428.

1999a. "VAT Treatment of Financial Services." In Gustaf Lindencrona, Sven-Olof Lodin, and Bertil Wiman (eds.), *International Studies in Taxation: Law and Economics – Liber Amicorum Leif Mutén*, pp. 92–103. Deventer: Kluwer.

1999b. "What Rate Structure for Australia's GST? The OECD Experience." *Tax Notes International* 18.21 (May 10): 2137–50.

1999c. "Fundamental Tax Reform in the United States." *De Economist* 147.2 (June): 229–37.

Cnossen, Sijbren, and Carl S. Shoup. 1987. "Coordination of Value-Added Taxes." In Sijbren Cnossen (ed.), *Tax Coordination in the European Community*, 7: 59–84. London: Kluwer Law and Taxation.

Cohen, Darrel, Kevin A. Hassett, and R. Glenn Hubbard. 1999. "Inflation and the User Cost of Capital: Does Inflation Still Matter?" In Martin Feldstein (ed.), *The Costs and Benefits of Price Stability*, pp. 199–233. Chicago: University of Chicago Press.

Commission on Taxation. 1984. *Third Report: Indirect Taxation.* Dublin: Stationery Office.

Committee on Ways and Means. 1996. *Hearings on Replacing the Federal Income Tax.* U.S. House of Representatives, 104th Cong., 1st sess.

Congressional Budget Office (CBO). 1993. *Effects of Adopting a Value-Added Tax.* Washington, D.C.: U.S. Government Printing Office.

    1997a. *Comparing Income and Consumption Tax Bases.* Washington, D.C.: U.S. Government Printing Office, June.

    1997b. *The Economic Effects of Comprehensive Tax Reform.* Washington, D.C.: U.S. Government Printing Office, July.

Cronin, Julie Anne, James Nunns, and Eric J. Toder. 1996. "Distributional Effects of Recent Tax Reform Proposals." Paper presented at the James A. Baker III Institute for Public Policy, Rice University, Second Annual Conference, November 12–13.

Cummins, Jason G., Kevin A. Hassett, and R. Glenn Hubbard. 1994. "A Reconsideration of Investment Behavior Using Tax Reforms as Natural Experiments." *Brookings Papers on Economic Activity*, no. 2: 1–59.

Davies, James B., France St. Hilaire, and John Whalley. 1984. "Some Calculations of Lifetime Tax Incidence." *American Economic Review* 74.4 (September): 633–49.

Deaton, Angus. 1991. "Saving and Liquidity Constraints." *Econometrica* 59.5 (September): 1221–48.

Desai, Mihir A., and James R. Hines Jr. 1999. "'Basket Cases': Tax Incentives and International Joint Venture Participation by American Multinational Firms." *Journal of Public Economics* 71.3 (March): 379–402.

Diamond, John, and George R. Zodrow. 1999. "Housing and Intergenerational and Intragenerational Redistributions under a Consumption Tax Reform." *1998 Proceedings of the Ninety-First Annual Conference on Taxation*, pp. 25–31. Washington, D.C.: National Tax Association.

Diamond, Peter A., and James A. Mirrlees. 1971. "Optimal Taxation and Public Production: I – Production Efficiency." *American Economic Review* 61.1 (March): 8–27.

Diewert, W. Erwin. 1978. "Optimal Tax Perturbations." *Journal of Public Economics* 10.2 (October): 139–77.

Dionne, E. J., Jr. 1996. *They Only Look Dead: Why Progressives Will Dominate the Next Political Era.* New York: Simon and Schuster.

Downs, Thomas W., and Cuneyt Demirgures. 1992. "The Asset Price Theory of Shareholder Re-Evaluations: Tests with the Tax Reforms of the 1980s." *Financial Review* 27.2 (May): 151–84.

DRI/McGraw-Hill. 1995. "Residential Real Estate Impacts of Flat Tax Legislation." Summary prepared for the National Association of Realtors, May.

    1996. "The Impact of the Flat Tax on Mortgage Foreclosures and Losses." Summary prepared for the National Association of Realtors, January.

Due, John F. 1997. "The Swiss Value-Added Tax." *Canadian Tax Journal* 45.2: 260–68.

Due, John F., and Ulla Brems. 1986. "The Controversial Norwegian Value Added Tax." University of Illinois at Urbana-Champaign Bureau of Economic and Business Research Faculty Paper no. 1245, April 28.

Due, John F., and John L. Mikesell. 1995. *Sales Taxation: State and Local Structure and Administration.* 2d ed. Washington, D.C.: Urban Institute Press.

Dunbar, Amy, and Thomas Pogue. 1998. "Estimating Flat Tax Incidence and Yield: A Sensitivity Analysis." *National Tax Journal* 51.2 (June): 303–24.

Duverne, Denis. 1990. "Coordinate Audits of Income Tax and VAT." Paris. Manuscript.

Dynan, Karen E. 1994. "Relative Wage Changes and Estimates of the Rate of Time Preference." Board of Governors of the Federal Reserve System. Mimeograph.

Dynan, Karen E., Jonathan Skinner, and Stephen P. Zeldes. 1998. "Do the Rich Save More?" Board of Governors of the Federal Reserve System. Mimeograph. Available as NBER Working Paper no. W7906, September 2000. Cambridge, Mass.

Eisenstein, Louis. 1961. *The Ideologies of Taxation.* New York: Ronald Press.

Engen, Eric M. 1994. "Precautionary Saving and the Structure of Taxation." Board of Governors of the Federal Reserve System. Mimeograph.

Engen, Eric M., and William G. Gale. 1996. "The Effects of Fundamental Tax Reform on Saving." In Henry J. Aaron and William G. Gale (eds.), *Economic Effects of Fundamental Tax Reform*, pp. 83–112. Washington, D.C.: Brookings Institution Press.

———. 1997. "Macroeconomic Effects of Fundamental Tax Reform: Simulations with a Stochastic Life-Cycle, Overlapping Generations, General Equilibrium Model." In *Joint Committee on Taxation Tax Modeling Project and 1997 Tax Symposium Papers*, pp. 101–29. Washington, D.C.: U.S. Government Printing Office.

Engen, Eric M., Jane Gravelle, and Kent Smetters. 1997. "Dynamic Tax Models: Why They Do the Things They Do." *National Tax Journal* 50.3 (September): 657–82.

Engen, Eric M., and Jonathan Skinner. 1996. "Taxation and Economic Growth." *National Tax Journal* 49.4 (December): 617–42.

European Commission. 1996. *Directorate XXI, the Sixth VAT Directive.* Brussels.

Evans, David S., and Boyan Jovanovic. 1989. "An Estimated Model of Entrepreneurial Choice under Liquidity Constraints." *Journal of Political Economy* 97.4 (August): 808–27.

Evans, Owen J. 1983. "Tax Policy, the Interest Elasticity of Saving, and Capital Accumulation: Numerical Analysis of Theoretical Models." *American Economic Review* 73.3 (June): 398–410.

Fazzari, Steven M., Robert Glenn Hubbard, and Bruce C. Petersen. 1988. "Financing Constraints and Corporate Investment." *Brookings Papers on Economic Activity*, no. 1: 141–95.

Federal Reserve Board, Survey of Consumer Finances. 1983–89. Panel Survey <http://www.federalreserve.gov/pubs/oss/oss2/scfindex.html>.

Feenberg, Daniel R., Andrew W. Mitrusi, and James M. Poterba. 1997. "Distributional Effects of Adopting a National Retail Sales Tax." In James M.

Poterba (ed.), *Tax Policy and the Economy*, 11:49–89. Cambridge, Mass.: MIT Press.

Feinstein, Jonathan S. 1991. "An Econometric Analysis of Income Tax Evasion and Its Detection." *Rand Journal of Economics* 22.1 (Spring): 14–35.

Feld, Alan L. 1995. "Living with the Flat Tax." *National Tax Journal* 48.4 (December): 603–17.

Feldstein, Martin. 1976a. "Compensation in Tax Reform." *National Tax Journal* 29.2 (June): 123–30.

———. 1976b. "On the Theory of Tax Reform." *Journal of Public Economics* 6.1–2 (July–August): 77–104.

———. 1978. "The Welfare Cost of Capital Income Taxation." *Journal of Political Economy* 86.2, pt. 2 (April): S21–51.

———. 1988. "Imputing Corporate Tax Liabilities to Individual Taxpayers." *National Tax Journal* 41.1 (March): 37–59.

———. 1994. "Tax Policy and International Capital Flows." *Weltwirtschaftliches Archiv* 130.4: 675–97.

———. 1995a. "The Effect of Marginal Tax Rates on Taxable Income: A Panel Study of the 1986 Tax Reform Act." *Journal of Political Economy* 103.3 (June): 551–72.

———. 1995b. "The Effect of a Consumption Tax on the Rate of Interest." NBER Working Paper no. W5397, December. Cambridge, Mass.

Feldstein, Martin, and Phillipe Bacchetta. 1991. "National Saving and International Investment." In B. Douglas Bernheim and John B. Shoven (eds.), *National Saving and Economic Performance*, pp. 201–20. Chicago: University of Chicago Press.

Feldstein, Martin, and Charles Horioka. 1980. "Domestic Savings and International Capital Flows." *Economic Journal* 90.358 (June): 314–29.

Fisher, Irving, and Herbert W. Fisher. 1942. *Constructive Income Taxation, a Proposal for Reform*. New York: Harper.

Foster, J. D. 1996. "The Flat Tax and Housing Values." *Tax Notes* 71 (June 24): 1795–803.

Fox, William F. (ed.). 1992. *Sales Taxation: Critical Issues in Policy and Administration*. Westport, Conn.: Greenwood, Praeger.

Frankel, Jeffrey A. 1991. "Quantifying International Capital Mobility in the 1980s." In B. Douglas Bernheim and John B. Shoven (eds.), *National Saving and Economic Performance*, pp. 227–60. Chicago: University of Chicago Press.

French, Kenneth R., and James M. Poterba. 1991. "Investor Diversification and International Equity Markets." *American Economic Review* 81.2 (May): 222–26.

Frisch, Daniel J. 1983. "Issues in the Taxation of Foreign Source Income." In Martin Feldstein (ed.), *Behavioral Simulation Methods in Tax Policy Analysis*, pp. 289–330. Chicago: University of Chicago Press.

Froot, Kenneth A., and James R. Hines Jr. 1995. "Interest Allocation Rules, Financing Patterns, and the Operations of U.S. Multinationals." In Martin Feldstein, James R. Hines Jr., and R. Glenn Hubbard (eds.), *The Effects of*

Taxation on Multinational Corporations, pp. 277–307. Chicago: University of Chicago Press.

Frum, David. 1994. *Dead Right*. New York: Basic Books.

Fullerton, Don, A. Thomas King, John B. Shoven, and John Whalley. 1981. "Corporate Tax Integration in the United States: A General Equilibrium Approach." *American Economic Review* 71.4 (September): 677–91.

Fullerton, Don, and Diane Lim Rogers. 1993. *Who Bears the Lifetime Tax Burden?* Washington, D.C.: Brookings Institution Press.

1996. "Lifetime Effects of Fundamental Tax Reform." In Henry J. Aaron and William G. Gale (eds.), *Economic Effects of Fundamental Tax Reform*, pp. 321–47. Washington, D.C.: Brookings Institution Press.

Fullerton, Don, John B. Shoven, and John Whalley. 1983. "Replacing the U.S. Income Tax with a Progressive Consumption Tax: A Sequenced General Equilibrium Approach." *Journal of Public Economics* 20.1 (February): 3–23.

Gale, William G. 1997. "Tax Reform Is Dead, Long Live Tax Reform." Brookings Policy Brief no. 12, February. Washington, D.C.

1998a. "An Evaluation of a National Retail Sales Tax." Washington, D.C. Manuscript.

1998b. "Don't Buy the Sales Tax." Brookings Policy Brief no. 31, March. Washington, D.C.

1998c. "Let's Revamp the Tax Code – But How?" *Wall Street Journal*, April 15, p. A22.

1999. "The Required Tax Rate in a National Retail Sales Tax." *National Tax Journal* 52.3 (September): 443–57.

Gale, William G., and Kevin A. Hassett. 1998. "A Framework for Evaluating the Flat Tax." Brookings Institution and the American Enterprise Institute, Washington, D.C. Mimeograph.

Gale, William G., and Janet Holtzblatt. 1997. "On the Possibility of a No-Return Tax System." *National Tax Journal* 50.3 (September): 475–85.

Gale, William G., Scott Houser, and John Karl Scholz. 1996. "Distributional Effects of Fundamental Tax Reform." In Henry J. Aaron and William G. Gale (eds.), *Economic Effects of Fundamental Tax Reform*, pp. 281–315. Washington, D.C.: Brookings Institution Press.

Gale, William G., Evan F. Koenig, Diane Lim Rogers, and John Sabelhaus. 1998. "Taxing Government in a National Retail Sales Tax." *Tax Notes* 81 (October 5): 97–109.

General Accounting Office (GAO). 1993. *Value-Added Tax: Administrative Costs Vary with Complexity and Number of Businesses*. Washington, D.C.: U.S. Government Printing Office.

1996. *Tax Administration: Alternative Filing Systems*, GAO/GGD-97-6, October. Washington, D.C.

1998. *Tax Administration: Potential Impact of Alternative Taxes on Taxpayers and Administrators*, GGD-98-37. Washington, D.C.

1999. *Tax Administration: Allegations of IRS Employee Misconduct*, GAO/GGD-99-82, May. Washington, D.C.

Genser, Bernd, Andreas Haufler, and Peter Birch Sorensen. 1995. "Indirect Taxation in an Integrated Europe: Is There a Way of Avoiding Trade Distortions without Sacrificing National Tax Autonomy?" *Journal of Economic Integration* 10.2 (June): 178–205.

Gentry, William M., and R. Glenn Hubbard. 1997a. "Distributional Implications of Introducing a Broad-Based Consumption Tax." In James M. Poterba (ed.), *Tax Policy and the Economy*, 11:1–47. Cambridge, Mass.: MIT Press.

1997b. *Fundamental Tax Reform and Corporate Finance*. Washington, D.C.: American Enterprise Institute Press.

1998a. "Fundamental Tax Reform and Corporate Financial Policy." In James M. Poterba (ed.), *Tax Policy and the Economy*, 12:191–227. Cambridge, Mass.: MIT Press.

1998b. "Entrepreneurship and Household Saving." Columbia University. Mimeograph. Available as NBER Working Paper no. W7894, September 2000. Cambridge, Mass.

2000. "Tax Policy and Entrepreneurial Entry." Columbia University, August 29. Mimeograph. Abridged version in *American Economic Review* 90 (May 2000): 283–87.

Gerardi, Geraldine, Michael J. Graetz, and Harvey S. Rosen. 1990. "Corporate Integration Puzzles." *National Tax Journal* 43.3 (September): 307–14.

Gertler, Mark, and Simon Gilchrist. 1994. "Monetary Policy, Business Cycles, and the Behavior of Small Manufacturing Firms." *Quarterly Journal of Economics* 109.2 (May): 309–40.

Gillis, Malcolm. 1986. "Worldwide Experience in Sales Taxation: Lessons for North America." *Policy Sciences* 19.2 (September): 125–42.

2001. "Tax Policy and Capital Formation: African Experience with the Value-Added Tax." *Policy Sciences*.

Gillis, Malcolm, Peter Mieszkowski, and George R. Zodrow. 1996. "Indirect Consumption Taxes: Common Issues and Differences among the Alternative Approaches." *Tax Law Review* 51 (Summer): 725–74.

Gillis, Malcom, Dwight H. Perkins, Michael Roemer, and Donald Snodgrass. 1996. *Economics of Development*. 4th ed. New York: W. W. Norton.

Goldberg, Daniel S. 1994. "Tax Subsidies: One-Time vs. Periodic. An Economic Analysis of the Tax Policy Alternatives." *Tax Law Review* 49 (Winter): 305–47.

Golob, John E. 1995. "How Would Tax Reform Affect Financial Markets?" *Federal Reserve Bank of Kansas City Economic Review* 80: 19–39.

Goodspeed, Timothy, and Ann Witte. 2000. "International Taxation." In Boudewijn Bouckaert and Gerrit De Geest (eds.), *Encyclopedia of Law and Economics*, pp. 256–300. London: Edward Elgar.

Gordon, Roger H. 1985. "Taxation of Corporate Capital Income: Tax Revenues versus Tax Distortions." *Quarterly Journal of Economics* 10.1 (February): 1–27.

Gordon, Roger H., and A. Lans Bovenberg. 1996. "Why Is Capital So Immobile Internationally? Possible Explanations and Implications for Capital Income Taxation." *American Economic Review* 86.5 (December): 1057–75.

Goulder, Lawrence H., John B. Shoven, and John Whalley. 1983. "Domestic Tax Policy and the Foreign Sector: The Importance of Alternative Foreign Sector Formulations to Results from a General Equilibrium Tax Analysis Model."

In Martin Feldstein (ed.), *Behavioral Simulation Methods in Tax Policy Analysis*, pp. 333–64. Chicago: University of Chicago Press.

Goulder, Lawrence H., and Lawrence H. Summers. 1989. "Tax Policy, Asset Prices, and Growth: A General Equilibrium Analysis." *Journal of Public Economics* 38.3 (April): 265–96.

Graetz, Michael J. 1977. "Legal Transitions: The Case of Retroactivity in Income Tax Revision." *University of Pennsylvania Law Review* 126: 47–87.

1997. *The Decline (and Fall?) of the Income Tax.* New York: W. W. Norton.

Gravelle, Jane G. 1991. "Income, Consumption, and Wage Taxation in a Life-Cycle Model: Separating Efficiency from Redistribution." *American Economic Review* 81.4 (September): 985–95.

1994. *The Economic Effects of Taxing Capital Income.* Cambridge, Mass.: MIT Press.

1995. "The Flat Tax and Other Proposals: Who Will Bear the Tax Burden?" Congressional Research Service Report for Congress no. 95-1141E, November 29. Washington, D.C.: U.S. Library of Congress.

1996a. "The Flat Tax and Other Proposals: Effects on Housing." Congressional Research Service Report for Congress no. 96-379E, April 29. Washington, D.C.: U.S. Library of Congress.

1996b. "The Distributional Effects of Fundamental Tax Revisions." Congressional Research Service, June. Published in *San Diego Law Review* 33 (Fall): 1419–57.

1997. "Simulations of Economic Effects for Flat Rate Income and Consumption Tax Proposals." In *Joint Committee on Taxation Tax Modeling Project and 1997 Tax Symposium Papers*, pp. 243–69. Washington, D.C.: U.S. Government Printing Office.

Gravelle, Jane G., and Laurence J. Kotlikoff. 1989. "The Incidence and Efficiency Costs of Corporate Taxation When Corporate and Noncorporate Firms Produce the Same Good." *Journal of Political Economy* 97.4 (August): 749–80.

Gravelle, Jane G., and Kent Smetters. 1998. "Who Bears the Burden of the Corporate Tax (and Why)? The Open Economy Case." Technical Paper 1998-1, Congressional Budget Office, August. Washington, D.C.

Gravelle, Jane G., and G. Thomas Woodward. 1998. "Short-Run Macroeconomic Effects of Fundamental Tax Reform." Congressional Research Service Report for Congress no. 90-901E, October 30. Washington, D.C.: U.S. Library of Congress.

Gruber, Jonathan, and James Poterba. 1996. "Fundamental Tax Reform and Employer-Provided Health Insurance." In Henry J. Aaron and William G. Gale (eds.), *Economic Effects of Fundamental Tax Reform*, pp. 125–62. Washington, D.C.: Brookings Institution Press.

Grubert, Harry, Timothy Goodspeed, and Deborah Swenson. 1993. "Explaining the Low Taxable Income of Foreign-Controlled Companies in the United States." In Alberto Giovannini, R. Glenn Hubbard, and Joel Slemrod (eds.), *Studies in International Taxation*, pp. 237–70. Chicago: University of Chicago Press.

Grubert, Harry, and John Mutti. 1991. "Taxes, Tariffs and Transfer Pricing in Multinational Corporate Decision Making." *Review of Economics and Statistics* 73.2 (May): 285–93.

Grubert, Harry, and T. Scott Newlon. 1995. "The International Implications of Consumption Tax Proposals." *National Tax Journal* 48.4 (December): 619–47.

Hall, Arthur. 1995. "Compliance Costs of Alternative Tax Systems." Testimony before House Ways and Means Committee, June 6.

1996. "Compliance Costs of Alternative Tax Systems II." Testimony before House Ways and Means Committee, March 20.

Hall, Robert E. 1995. "The International Consequences of the Leading Consumption Tax Proposals." Paper presented at a conference on Fundamental Tax Reform, Stanford University, December 1.

1996a. "The Effects of Tax Reform on Prices and Asset Values." In James M. Poterba (ed.), *Tax Policy and the Economy*, 10:71–88. Cambridge, Mass.: MIT Press.

1996b. "Transition Issues in Moving to a Consumption Tax: A Tax Lawyer's Perspective: Comment." In Henry J. Aaron and William G. Gale (eds.), *Economic Effects of Fundamental Tax Reform*, pp. 427–34. Washington, D.C.: Brookings Institution Press.

1997. "Potential Disruption from the Move to a Consumption Tax." *American Economic Review* 87.2 (May): 147–50.

Hall, Robert E., and Alvin Rabushka. 1983. *Low Tax, Simple Tax, Flat Tax.* New York: McGraw-Hill.

[1985] 1995. *The Flat Tax.* 2 ed. Stanford: Hoover Institution Press.

1996. "The Flat Tax: A Simple, Progressive Consumption Tax." In Michael J. Boskin (ed.), *Frontiers of Tax Reform*, pp. 27–53. Stanford: Hoover Institution Press.

Hamilton, Amy. 1998. "The Tax Gap and Inklings of a Focus on Noncompliance." *Tax Notes* 79 (May 25): 933–36.

Harberger, Arnold C. 1962. "The Incidence of the Corporation Income Tax." *Journal of Political Economy* 70.3 (June): 215–40.

1990. "The Uniform-Tax Controversy." In Vito Tanzi (ed.), *Public finance, Trade, and Development: Proceedings of the 44th Congress of the International Institute of Public Finance, Istanbul, 1988*, pp. 3–17. Detroit: Wayne State University Press.

1995. "The ABCs of Corporate Tax Incidence: Insights into the Open-Economy Case." In American Council for Capital Formation (ed.), *Tax Policy and Economic Growth*, pp. 51–71. Washington, D.C.: ACCF Center for Policy Research.

Harris, David, Randall Morck, Joel Slemrod, and Bernard Yeung. 1993. "Income Shifting in U.S. Multinational Corporations." In Alberto Giovannini, R. Glenn Hubbard, and Joel Slemrod (eds.), *Studies in International Taxation*, pp. 277–302. Chicago: University of Chicago Press.

Hartman, David G. 1984. "Tax Policy and Foreign Direct Investment in the United States." *National Tax Journal* 37.4 (December): 475–87.

1985. "Tax Policy and Foreign Direct Investment." *Journal of Public Economics* 26.1 (February): 107–21.

Hassett, Kevin A., and R. Glenn Hubbard. 1997. "Tax Policy and Investment." In Alan J. Auerbach (ed.), *Fiscal Policy: Lessons from Economic Research*, pp. 339–85. Cambridge, Mass.: MIT Press.

He, Xuming, and Pin Ng. 1999. "COBS: Qualitatively Constrained Smoothing via Linear Programming." *Computational Statistics* 14.3: 315–37.

Heckman, James J. 1993. "What Has Been Learned about Labor Supply in the Past Twenty Years?" *American Economic Review* 83.2 (May): 116–21.

Hellerstein, Walter. 1988. "Florida's Sales Tax on Services." *National Tax Journal* 41.1 (March): 1–18.

Hemming, Richard, and John A. Kay. 1981. "The United Kingdom." In Henry J. Aaron (ed.), *The Value-Added Tax: Lessons from Europe*, pp. 75–90. Washington, D.C.: Brookings Institution.

Hines, James R., Jr. 1988. "Taxation and U.S. Multinational Investment." In Lawrence H. Summers (ed.), *Tax Policy and the Economy*, 2:33–61. Cambridge, Mass.: National Bureau of Economic Research.

1993. "On the Sensitivity of R&D to Delicate Tax Changes: The Behavior of U.S. Multinationals in the 1980s." In Alberto Giovannini, R. Glenn Hubbard, and Joel Slemrod (eds.), *Studies in International Taxation*, pp. 149–87. Chicago: University of Chicago Press.

1994. "No Place like Home: Tax Incentives and the Location of R&D by American Multinationals." In James M. Poterba (ed.), *Tax Policy and the Economy*, 8:65–104. Cambridge, Mass.: MIT Press.

1995. "Taxes, Technology Transfer, and the R&D Activities of Multinational Firms." In Martin Feldstein, James R. Hines Jr., and R. Glenn Hubbard (eds.), *The Effects of Taxation on Multinational Corporations*, pp. 225–48. Chicago: University of Chicago Press.

1996. "Fundamental Tax Reform in an International Setting." In Henry J. Aaron and William G. Gale (eds.), *Economic Effects of Fundamental Tax Reform*, pp. 465–93. Washington, D.C.: Brookings Institution Press.

1997. "Tax Policy and the Activities of Multinational Corporations." In Alan J. Auerbach (ed.), *Fiscal Policy: Lessons from Economic Research*, pp. 401–45. Cambridge, Mass.: MIT Press.

1999a. "Lessons from Behavioral Responses to International Taxation." *National Tax Journal* 52.2 (June): 305–22.

1999b. "The Case against Deferral: A Deferential Reconsideration." *National Tax Journal* 53.3 (September): 385–404.

Hines, James R., Jr., and R. Glenn Hubbard. 1990. "Coming Home to America: Dividend Repatriations by U.S. Multinationals." In Assaf Razin and Joel Slemrod (eds.), *Taxation in the Global Economy*, pp. 161–200. Chicago: University of Chicago Press.

Hines, James R., Jr., and Eric M. Rice. 1994. "Fiscal Paradise: Foreign Tax Havens and American Business." *Quarterly Journal of Economics* 109.1 (February): 149–82.

Ho, Mun S., and Dale W. Jorgenson. 1994. "Trade Policy and U.S. Economic Growth." *Journal of Policy Modeling* 16.2 (April): 119–46.

Holtz-Eakin, Douglas, David Joulfaian, and Harvey S. Rosen. 1994. "Entrepreneurial Decisions and Liquidity Constraints." *Rand Journal of Economics* 25.2 (Summer): 334–47.

Houston Chronicle. 1998. "Local Trio's Plan for Tax on Sales, Not Income, Gains Support." April 6, pp. 1A and 8A.

Howard Government's Plan. 1998. *Tax Reform: Not a New Tax – a New Tax System*. Canberra: Australian Government Printing Service.

Howitt, Peter, and Hans Werner Sinn. 1989. "Gradual Reforms of Capital Income Taxation." *American Economic Review* 79.1 (March): 106–24.

Hubbard, R. Glenn. 1989. "Tax Corporate Cash Flow, Not Income." *Wall Street Journal*, February 16, p. A14.

      1995. "Distributional Tables and Tax Policy." In David F. Bradford (ed.), *Distributional Analysis of Tax Policy*, pp. 81–95. Washington, D.C.: American Enterprise Institute Press.

      1997. "How Different Are Income and Consumption Taxes?" *American Economic Review* 87.2 (May): 138–42.

      1998. "Capital-Market Imperfections and Investment." *Journal of Economic Literature* 36.1 (March): 193–225.

Hubbard, R. Glenn and Kenneth L. Judd. 1986. "Liquidity Constraints, Fiscal Policy, and Consumption." *Brookings Papers on Economic Activity*, no. 1:1–50.

      1987. "Social Security and Individual Welfare: Precautionary Saving, Borrowing Constraints, and the Payroll Tax." *American Economic Review* 77.4 (September): 630–46.

Hubbard, R. Glenn, Jonathan Skinner, and Stephen P. Zeldes. 1994. "The Importance of Precautionary Motives in Explaining Individual and Aggregate Saving." *Carnegie Rochester Conference Series on Public Policy* 40 (June): 59–125.

      1995. "Precautionary Saving and Social Insurance." *Journal of Political Economy* 103.2 (April): 360–99.

Huggett, Mark. 1996. "Wealth Distribution in Life-Cycle Economies." *Journal of Monetary Economics* 38.3 (December): 469–94.

Hume, David. [1752] 1985. *Essays: Moral, Political and Literary*. Ed. Eugene F. Miller. Indianapolis: Liberty Fund.

      1779. *Essays and Treatises on Several Subjects*. Edinburgh: J. Williams.

Hurd, Michael, Daniel McFadden, and Angela Merrill. 1998. "Healthy, Wealthy, and Wise? Socio-Economic Status, Morbidity, and Mortality among the Elderly." Rand Corporation, July. Mimeograph.

Institute for Fiscal Studies (Meade Commission). 1978. *The Structure and Reform of Direct Taxation*. London: George Allen & Unwin.

Internal Revenue Service (IRS). 1993. *A Study of Administrative Issues in Implementing a Federal Value Added Tax*. Washington, D.C.

      1996. *Federal Tax Compliance Research: Individual Income Tax Gap Estimates for 1985, 1988, and 1992*. Internal Revenue Service Publication 1415, Revision 4-96. Washington, D.C.

      1997. *Statistics of Income Bulletin* (Summer). Washington, D.C.

Johansen, Leif. 1960. *A Multi-Sectoral Study of Economic Growth*. Amsterdam: North-Holland.

Johnson, Craig E., John Diamond, and George R. Zodrow. 1997. "Bequests, Saving, and Taxation." In *1996 Proceedings of the Eighty-Ninth Annual Conference on Taxation of the National Tax Association at Boston, Massachusetts, November 10–12*, pp. 37–45. Washington, D.C.: National Tax Association.

Joint Committee on Taxation (JCT). 1993. *Methodology and Issues in Measuring Changes in the Distribution of Tax Burdens.* Washington, D.C.: U.S. Government Printing Office.

1997. *Joint Committee on Taxation Tax Modeling Project and 1997 Tax Symposium Papers.* Washington, D.C.: U.S. Government Printing Office.

Jorgenson, Dale W. 1986. "Econometric Methods for Modeling Producer Behavior." In Zvi Griliches and Michael D. Intriligator (eds.), *Handbook of Econometrics*, 3:1841–915. Amsterdam: North-Holland.

1990. "Productivity and Economic Growth." In Ernst R. Berndt and Jack E. Triplett (eds.), *Fifty Years of Economic Measurement: The Jubilee of the Conference on Research in Income and Wealth*, pp. 19–118. Chicago: University of Chicago Press.

1995. *Productivity*. Vol. 2, *International Comparisons of Economic Growth.* Cambridge, Mass.: MIT Press.

1996a. "Empirical Studies of Depreciation." *Economic Inquiry* 34.1 (January): 24–42.

1996b. *Investment*. Vol. 2, *Tax Policy and the Cost of Capital.* Cambridge, Mass.: MIT Press.

1996c. "The Economic Impact of Fundamental Tax Reform." In Michael J. Boskin (ed.), *Frontiers of Tax Reform*, pp. 181–95. Stanford: Hoover Institution Press.

1997. *Welfare*. Vol. 2, *Measuring Social Welfare.* Cambridge, Mass.: MIT Press.

1998. *Growth*. Vol. 2, *Energy, the Environment, and Economic Growth.* Cambridge, Mass.: MIT Press.

Jorgenson, Dale W., and Ralph Landau (eds.). 1993. *Tax Reform and the Cost of Capital: An International Comparison.* Washington, D.C.: Brookings Institution Press.

Jorgenson, Dale W., Daniel T. Slesnick, and Peter J. Wilcoxen. 1992. "Carbon Taxes and Economic Welfare." *Brookings Papers on Economic Activity: Microeconomics 1992*: 393–431.

Jorgenson, Dale W., and Peter J. Wilcoxen. 1990a. "Environmental Regulation and U.S. Economic Growth." *Rand Journal of Economics* 21.2 (Summer): 314–40.

1990b. "Intertemporal General Equilibrium Modeling of U.S. Environmental Regulation." *Journal of Policy Modeling* 12.4 (Winter): 715–44.

1993. "Energy, the Environment, and Economic Growth." In Allen V. Kneese and James L. Sweeney (eds.), *Handbook of Natural Resource and Energy Economics*, 3:1267–349. Amsterdam: North Holland.

1997. "The Effects of Fundamental Tax Reform and the Feasibility of Dynamic Revenue Estimation." In *Joint Committee on Taxation Tax Modeling Project and 1997 Tax Symposium Papers*, pp. 130–51. Washington, D.C.: U.S. Government Printing Office.

Jorgenson, Dale W., and Kun Young Yun. 1990. "Tax Reform and U.S. Economic Growth." *Journal of Political Economy* 98.5, pt. 2 (October): S151–93.

1991a. "The Excess Burden of Taxation in the U.S." *Journal of Accounting, Auditing, and Finance* 6.4 (Fall): 487–509.

1991b. *Tax Reform and the Cost of Capital.* Oxford: Oxford University Press.

Jun, Joosung. 1990. "U.S. Tax Policy and Direct Investment Abroad." In Assaf Razin and Joel Slemrod (eds.), *Taxation in the Global Economy*, pp. 55–74. Chicago: University of Chicago Press.

Kaldor, Nicholas. 1955. *An Expenditure Tax.* London: George Allen and Unwin.

Kaplow, Louis. 1986. "An Economic Analysis of Legal Transitions." *Harvard Law Review* 99 (January): 509–617.

1992. "Government Relief for Risk Associated with Government Action." *Scandinavian Journal of Economics* 94.4: 525–41.

1994. "Taxation and Risk Taking: A General Equilibrium Perspective." *National Tax Journal* 47.4 (December): 789–98.

1995. "Recovery of Pre-Enactment Basis under a Consumption Tax: The USA Tax System." *Tax Notes* 68 (August 28): 1109–18.

Kasten, Richard A., and Eric J. Toder. 1995. "Distributional Analysis at the Congressional Budget Office." In David F. Bradford (ed.), *Distributional Analysis of Tax Policy*, pp. 120–27. Washington, D.C.: American Enterprise Institute Press.

Kay, John A., and Evan H. Davis. 1990. "The VAT and Services." In Malcolm Gillis, Carl S. Shoup, and Gerardo P. Sicat (eds.), *Value Added Taxation in Developing Countries: A World Bank Symposium*, pp. 70–82. Washington, D.C.: World Bank.

Kennickell, Arthur B., and Douglas McManus. 1994. "Multiple Imputation of the 1983 and 1989 Waves of the SCF." *American Statistical Association, 1994 Proceedings of the Section on Survey Research Methods*, 1:523–28. Alexandria, Va.: American Statistical Association.

Kennickell, Arthur B., and Martha Starr-McCluer. 1996. "Household Saving and Portfolio Change: Evidence From the 1983–89 SCF Panel." In Board of Governors of the Federal Reserve System (ed.), *Finance and Economics Discussion Series: 96/18* (April).

Keuschnigg, Christian. 1990. "Corporate Taxation and Growth: A Dynamic General Equilibrium Simulation Study." In Johann K. Brunner and Hans-Georg Petersen (eds.), *Simulation Models in Tax and Transfer Policy*, pp. 245–78. Frankfurt: Campus Verlag.

Kim, Taejoo. 2000. "The Effects of Taxes on Foreign Direct Investment in the U.S." Working Paper. Michigan State University.

King, Mervyn A. 1975. "Current Policy Problems in Business Taxation." In *Bedrifts Beskatning*, pp. 74–91. Bergen: Norwegian School of Economics.

Kotlikoff, Laurence J. 1995. "The Economic Argument for Consumption Taxation." Testimony before the Committee on Ways and Means, U.S. House of Representatives, June 6.

1996a. "Saving and Consumption Taxation: The Federal Retail Sales Tax Example." In Michael J. Boskin (ed.), *Frontiers of Tax Reform*, pp. 160–80. Stanford: Hoover Institution Press.

1996b. "The Economic Impact of Consumption Taxation." Paper presented at the James A. Baker III Institute for Public Policy, Rice University, Second Annual Conference, November 12–13.

1997. "Replacing the U.S. Federal Tax System with a Retail Sales Tax Macro-economic and Distributional Impacts." Report prepared for the National Tax Research Council. Houston, Tex.

KPMG. 1996. *Draft Report on the Treatment of Financial Services*. Washington, D.C.

KPMG Peat Marwick Policy Economics Group. 1989. *Study of Value-Added Taxation in the United States*. Washington, D.C.

Lawrance, Emily C. 1991. "Poverty and the Rate of Time Preference: Evidence from Panel Data." *Journal of Political Economy* 99.1 (February): 54–77.

Lexis/Nexis Online Database. 2000. <web.lexis-nexis.com/universe>.

Lodin, Sven-Olof. 1978. *Progressive Expenditure Tax – An Alternative?* Report of the 1972 Government Commission on Taxation. Stockholm: LiberForlag.

Logue, Kyle D. 1996. "Tax Transitions, Opportunistic Retroactivity, and the Benefits of Government Precommitment." *Michigan Law Review* 94.5 (March): 1129–96.

Los Angeles Times. 1998. "Tax Vote Shows Growing Clout of Small Business." June 19, pp. DI and D5.

Lyon, Andrew B. 1989a. "The Effect of the Investment Tax Credit on the Value of the Firm." *Journal of Public Economics* 38.2 (March): 227–47.

1989b. "Did ACRS Really Cause Stock Prices to Fall?" NBER Working Paper no. W2990. May. Washington, D.C.

Lyon, Andrew B., and Peter R. Merrill. 1999. "The Stock Market and Consumption Tax Reform." *1998 Proceedings of the Ninety First Annual Conference*, pp. 307–13. Washington, D.C.: National Tax Association.

Lyon, Andrew B., and Robert M. Schwab. 1995. "Consumption Taxes in a Life-Cycle Framework: Are Sin Taxes Regressive?" *Review of Economics and Statistics* 77.3 (August): 389–406.

Lyon, Andrew B., and Gerald Silverstein. 1995. "The Alternative Minimum Tax and the Behavior of Multinational Corporations." In Martin Feldstein, James R. Hines Jr., and R. Glenn Hubbard (eds.), *The Effects of Taxation on Multinational Corporations*, pp. 153–77. Chicago: University of Chicago Press.

Mansur, Ahsan Habib, and John Whalley. 1984. "Numerical Specification of Applied General Equilibrium Models: Estimation, Calibration, and Data." In Herbert E. Scarf and John B. Shoven (eds.), *Applied General Equilibrium Analysis*, pp. 69–127. Cambridge: Cambridge University Press.

Mark, Stephen T., Therese J. McGuire, and Leslie E. Papke. 2000. "The Influence of Taxes on Employment and Population Growth: Evidence from the Washington, D.C. Metropolitan Area." *National Tax Journal* 53.1 (March): 105–23.

Marx, Karl, and Friedrich Engels. [1848] 1965. *The Communist Manifesto*. New York: Washington Square.

Mastromarco, Dan. 1998. "The 'Fair Tax' and Tax Compliance: An Analytical Perspective." *Tax Notes* 78 (April 20): 379–87.

Matthews Committee. 1975. *Report of the Committee of Inquiry into Inflation and Taxation*. Canberra: Australian Government Printing Service.

McIntyre, Michael J. 1976. "Transition Rules: Learning to Live with Tax Reform." *Tax Notes* 4 (August 30): 7–13.

McIntyre, Robert S. 1998. "Why Not Tax Reform." *Nation*, April 27, p. 5.

McLure, Charles E., Jr. 1987. *The Value-Added Tax: Key to Deficit Reduction?* Washington, D.C.: American Enterprise Institute.

——— 1988. "The 1986 Act: Tax Reform's Finest Hour or Death Throes of the Income Tax?" *National Tax Journal* 41.3 (September): 303–15.

——— 1990. "Income Distribution and Tax Incidence under the VAT." In Malcolm Gillis, Carl S. Shoup, and Gerardo P. Sicat (eds.), *Value Added Taxation in Developing Countries: A World Bank Symposium*, pp. 32–40. Washington, D.C.: World Bank.

——— 1993. "Economic, Administrative, and Political Factors in Choosing a General Consumption Tax." *National Tax Journal* 46.3 (September): 345–58.

——— 1996. "The U.S. Debate on Consumption-Based Taxes: Implications for the Americas." Hoover Institution, Stanford University. Manuscript.

——— 1997. "Taxation of Electronic Commerce: Economic Objectives, Technological Constraints, and Tax Laws." *Tax Law Review* 52 (Spring): 269–424.

McLure, Charles E., Jr., Jack Mutti, Victor Thuronyi, and George R. Zodrow. 1990. *The Taxation of Income from Business and Capital in Colombia: Fiscal Reform in the Developing World*. Durham: Duke University Press.

McLure, Charles E., Jr., and George R. Zodrow. 1987. "Treasury I and the Tax Reform Act of 1986: The Economics and Politics of Tax Reform." *Journal of Economic Perspectives* 1.1 (Summer): 37–58.

——— 1990. "Administrative Advantages of the Individual Tax Prepayment Approach to the Direct Consumption of Taxation." In Manfred Rose (ed.), *Heidelberg Congress on Taxing Consumption*, pp. 335–81. Berlin: Springer-Verlag.

——— 1994. "The Study and Practice of Income Tax Policy." In John M. Quigley and Eugene Smolensky (eds.), *Modern Public Finance*, pp. 165–209. Cambridge, Mass.: Harvard University Press.

——— 1996a. "A Hybrid Approach to the Direct Taxation of Consumption." In Michael J. Boskin (ed.), *Frontiers of Tax Reform*, pp. 70–90. Stanford: Hoover Institution Press.

——— 1996b. "A Hybrid Consumption-Based Direct Tax Proposed for Bolivia." *International Tax and Public Finance* 3.1 (January): 97–112.

——— 1998. "The Economic Case for Foreign Tax Credits for Cash Flow Taxes." *National Tax Journal* 51.1 (March): 1–22.

Menchik, Paul L., and Martin David. 1982. "The Incidence of a Lifetime Consumption Tax." *National Tax Journal* 35.2 (June): 189–203.

Mendoza, Enrique G., and Linda L. Tesar. 1998. "The International Ramifications of Tax Reforms: Supply-Side Economics in a Global Economy." *American Economic Review* 88.1 (March): 226–45.

Metcalf, Gilbert E. 1994. "Life Cycles versus Annual Perspectives on the Incidence of a Value Added Tax." In James M. Poterba (ed.), *Tax Policy and the Economy*, 8:45–64. Cambridge, Mass.: MIT Press.

1997. "The National Sales Tax: Who Bears the Burden?" *Policy Analysis*, no. 289, December 8. Washington, D.C.: CATO Institute.

1999. "A Distributional Analysis of Green Tax Reforms." *National Tax Journal* 52.4 (December): 655–81.

Mieszkowski, Peter. 1980. "The Advisability and Feasibility of an Expenditure Tax System." In Henry J. Aaron and Michael J. Boskin (eds.), *The Economics of Taxation*, pp. 179–201. Washington, D.C.: Brookings Institution.

Mieszkowski, Peter, and Michael G. Palumbo. 1997. "The Distributive Effects of Adopting a Federal Retail Sales Tax." Rice University. Manuscript.

1998. "Is a National Retail Sales Tax Administrable? A Proposal for a Hybrid NRST." Rice University. Manuscript.

Mikesell, John L. 1997. "The American Retail Sales Tax: Considerations on Their Structure, Operations, and Potential as a Foundation for a Federal Sales Tax." *National Tax Journal* 50.1 (March): 149–65.

Mill, John Stuart. [1849] 1970. *Principles of Political Economy*. New York: Pelican.

Mishkin, Frederic S. 1984. "Are Real Interest Rates Equal across Countries? An Empirical Investigation of International Parity Conditions." *Journal of Finance* 39.5 (December): 1345–57.

Mulligan, Casey B. 1997. *Parental Priorities and Economic Inequality*. Chicago: University of Chicago Press.

Murray, Matthew N. 1997a. "Would Tax Evasion and Tax Avoidance Undermine a National Retail Sales Tax?" *National Tax Journal* 50.1 (March): 167–82.

1997b. "Administration and Compliance Aspects of a National Retail Sales Tax." University of Tennessee–Knoxville. Manuscript.

Musgrave, Richard A. 1959. *The Theory of Public Finance*. New York: McGraw-Hill.

Mutti, John. 1993. "Income Shifting in U.S. Multinational Corporations: Comment." In Alberto Giovannini, R. Glenn Hubbard, and Joel Slemrod (eds.), *Studies in International Taxation*, pp. 302–7. Chicago: University of Chicago Press.

Neumark Report. 1963. "Report of the Fiscal and Financial Committee." In *The EEC Reports on Tax Harmonization*, pp. 93–156. Amsterdam: International Bureau of Fiscal Documentation.

New York Times. 1998. "A New Form of Lobbying Puts Public Face on Private Interest." September 30, pp. A1 and A14.

New Zealand. 1985. *White Paper on Goods and Services Tax*. Wellington: Government Printer.

Newlon, T. Scott. 1987. "Tax Policy and the Multinational Firm's Financial Policy and Investment Decisions." Ph.D. dissertation, Princeton University.

Norland, Douglas L., and Kim Y. Ninassi. 1998. *Price It Right: Energy Pricing and Fundamental Tax Reform*. Washington, D.C.: Alliance to Save Energy.

Normann, Göran. 1981. "Sweden." In Henry J. Aaron (ed.), *The Value-Added Tax: Lessons from Europe*, pp. 61–73. Washington, D.C.: Brookings Institution.

Nutter, Sarah E. 1997. "Corporate Foreign Tax Credit, 1993: An Industry and Geographic Focus." Internal Revenue Service, *Statistics of Income Bulletin* (Fall): 97–143. Washington, D.C.

Obstfeld, Maurice. 1995. "International Capital Mobility in the 1990s." In Peter B. Kenen (ed.), *Understanding Interdependence: The Macroeconomics of the Open Economy*, pp. 201–61. Princeton: Princeton University Press.

OECD. 1988. *Taxing Consumption*. Paris.

1998. *Consumption Tax Trends*. Paris.

2000. *National Accounts of OECD Countries 1988/1998*. 2000 ed. <http://www.oecd.org/std/nahome.htm>.

OECD, Committee on Fiscal Affairs. 1981. *The Impact of Consumption Taxes at Different Income Levels*. Paris.

Office of Management and Budget (OMB). 1998. "Draft Report to Congress on the Costs and Benefits of Federal Regulations." *Federal Register* 63.158 (August 17): 44034–99.

Okun, Arthur M. 1975. *Equality and Efficiency, the Big Tradeoff*. Washington, D.C.: Brookings Institution.

Oldman, Oliver, and LaVerne Woods. 1983. "Would a Value-Added Tax System Relieve Tax Compliance Problems?" In *Income Tax Compliance: A Report of the ABA Section of Taxation Invitational Conference on Income Tax Compliance*, pp. 317–38. Reston, Va.: American Bar Association.

Palumbo, Michael G. 1999. "Uncertain Medical Expenses and Precautionary Saving Near the End of the Life Cycle." *Review of Economic Studies* 66.2: 395–421.

Park, Thae S. 1986. "Relationship between Personal Income and Adjusted Gross Income: Revised Estimates, 1947–83." *Survey of Current Business* 66.5 (May): 34–40.

Paul, Randolph E. 1954. *Taxation in the United States*. Boston: Little, Brown.

Payne, James L. 1993. *Costly Returns: The Burdens of the U.S. Income Tax System*. San Francisco: ICS Press.

Pearlman, Ronald A. 1996. "Transition Issues in Moving to a Consumption Tax: A Tax Lawyer's Perspective." In Henry J. Aaron and William G. Gale (eds.), *Economic Effects of Fundamental Tax Reform*, pp. 393–427. Washington, D.C.: Brookings Institution Press.

Peat Marwick Mitchell. 1982. "Report to the American Retail Federation on Costs to Retailers of Sales and Use Tax Compliance." Washington, D.C.: Mimeograph.

Pechman, Joseph A. 1985. *Who Paid the Taxes, 1966–85?* Washington, D.C.: Brookings Institution.

1990. "The Future of the Income Tax." *American Economic Review* 80.1 (March): 1–20.

Penner, Rudolph G. 1996. Remarks at the James A. Baker III Institute for Public Policy, Rice University, Second Annual Conference, November 12–13.

Poddar, Satya, and Morley English. 1997. "Taxation of Financial Services under a Value-Added Tax: Applying the Cash-Flow Approach." *National Tax Journal* 50.1 (March): 89–111.

Poterba, James M. 1989. "Lifetime Incidence and the Distributional Burden of Excise Taxes." *American Economic Review* 79.2 (May): 325–30.

———. 1991. "Is the Gasoline Tax Regressive?" In David F. Bradford (ed.), *Tax Policy and the Economy*, 5:145–64. Cambridge, Mass.: MIT Press.

———. 1993. "Taxation and Foreign Direct Investment in the United States: A Reconsideration of the Evidence: Comment." In Alberto Giovannini, R. Glenn Hubbard, and Joel Slemrod (eds.), *Studies in International Taxation*, pp. 145–47. Chicago: University of Chicago Press.

Poterba, James M., Julio J. Rotemberg, and Lawrence H. Summers. 1986. "A Tax-Based Test for Nominal Rigidities." *American Economic Review* 76.4 (September): 659–75.

Prakken, Joel L. (Macroeconomic Advisers). 1997. "Simulations of a Flat Tax with the Washington University Macro Model." In *Joint Committee on Taxation Tax Modeling Project and 1997 Tax Symposium Papers*, pp. 164–83. Washington, D.C.: U.S. Government Printing Office.

Public Opinion Online, Roper Center, University of Connecticut. 2001. <www.ropercenter.uconn.edu>.

Quadrini, Vincenzo. 2000. "Entrepreneurship, Saving, and Social Mobility." *Review of Economic Dynamics* 3.1 (January): 1–40.

Ramseyer, Mark, and Minoru Nakazato. 1989. "Tax Transitions and the Protection Racket: A Reply to Professors Graetz and Kaplow." *Virginia Law Review* 75 (September): 1155–75.

Randolph, William C., and Diane Lim Rogers. 1995. "The Implications for Tax Policy of Uncertainty about Labor-Supply and Savings Responses." *National Tax Journal* 48.3 September: 429–46.

Ratner, Sidney. 1942. *American Taxation, Its History as a Social Force in Democracy*. New York: W. W. Norton.

Reifenschneider, David. 1997. "Modeling the Macroeconomic Consequences of Tax Policy." In *Joint Committee on Taxation Tax Modeling Project and 1997 Tax Symposium Papers*, pp. 285–93. Washington, D.C.: U.S. Government Printing Office.

Ring, Raymond J., Jr. 1989. "The Proportion of Consumers' and Producers' Goods in the General Sales Tax." *National Tax Journal* 42.2 (June): 167–79.

———. 1999. "Consumers' Share and Producers' Share of the General Sales Tax." *National Tax Journal* 52.1 (March): 79–90.

Robbins, Gary, and Aldona Robbins. 1997. "Tax Reform Simulations Using the Fiscal Associates' General Equilibrium Model." In *Joint Committee on Taxation Tax Modeling Project and 1997 Tax Symposium Papers*, pp. 184–211. Washington, D.C.: U.S. Government Printing Office.

Rogers, Diane Lim. 1997. "Assessing the Effects of Fundamental Tax Reform with the Fullerton-Rogers General Equilibrium Model." In *Joint Committee on Taxation Tax Modeling Project and 1997 Tax Symposium Papers*, pp. 49–82. Washington, D.C.: U.S. Government Printing Office.

Rosen, Harvey S. 1999. *Public Finance*. 5th ed. New York: McGraw-Hill.

Sabelhaus, John. 1993. "What Is the Distributional Burden of Taxing Consumption?" *National Tax Journal* 46.3 (September): 331–44.

Samwick, Andrew A. 1998. "Tax Reform and Target Saving." *National Tax Journal* 51.3 (September): 621–35.

Sandford, Cedric, Michael Godwin, and Peter Hardwick. 1989. *Administrative and Compliance Costs of Taxation.* Bath: Fiscal Publications.

Sandford, Cedric, and John Hasseldine. 1992. *The Compliance Costs of Business Taxes in New Zealand.* Wellington: Victoria University.

Sarkar, Shounak, and George R. Zodrow. 1993. "Transitional Issues in Moving to a Direct Consumption Tax." *National Tax Journal* 46.3 (September): 359–76.

Sease, Douglas R., and Tom Herman (eds.). 1996. *The Flat Tax Primer: A Nonpartisan Guide to What It Means for the Economy, the Government – and You.* New York: Viking.

Seidman, Laurence S. 1997. *The USA Tax: A Progressive Consumption Tax.* Cambridge, Mass.: MIT Press.

Seltzer, David R. 1997. "Federal Income Tax Compliance Costs: A Case Study of Hewlett-Packard Company." *National Tax Journal* 50.3 (September): 487–93.

Senate Budget Committee. 1998. *Tax Expenditures: Compendium of Background Material on Individual Provisions.* Washington, D.C.: U.S. Government Printing Office.

Shaviro, Daniel. 2000. *When Rules Change: An Economic and Political Analysis of Transition Relief and Retroactivity.* Chicago: University of Chicago Press.

Shoup, Carl S. 1969. "Experience with the Value-Added Tax in Denmark, and Prospects in Sweden." *Finanzarchiv* 28.2 (March): 236–52.

Shoven, John B. 1976. "The Incidence and Efficiency Effects of Taxes on Income from Capital." *Journal of Political Economy* 84.6 (December): 1261–83.

Slemrod, Joel. 1984. "Optimal Tax Simplification: Toward a Framework for Analysis." *Proceedings of the Seventy-Sixth Annual Conference of the National Tax Association*, pp. 158–62. Columbus, Ohio: National Tax Association–Tax Institute of America.

1989a. "Complexity, Compliance Costs, and Tax Evasion." In Jeffrey A. Roth and John T. Scholz (eds.), *Taxpayer Compliance*, vol. 2, *Social Science Perspectives*, pp. 156–81. Philadelphia: University of Pennsylvania Press.

1989b. "The Return to Tax Simplification: An Econometric Analysis." *Public Finance Quarterly* 17.1 (January): 3–27.

1990a. "Tax Effects on Foreign Direct Investment in the United States: Evidence from a Cross-Country Comparison." In Assaf Razin and Joel Slemrod (eds.), *Taxation in the Global Economy*, pp. 79–117. Chicago: University of Chicago Press.

1990b. "The Impact of the Tax Reform Act of 1986 on Foreign Direct Investment to and from the United States." In Joel Slemrod (ed.), *Do Taxes Matter? The Impact of the Tax Reform Act of 1986*, pp. 168–97. Cambridge, Mass.: MIT Press.

1992. "Taxation and Inequality: A Time-Exposure Perspective." In James M. Poterba (ed.), *Tax Policy and the Economy*, 6:105–27. Cambridge, Mass.: MIT Press.

1996. "Which Is the Simplest Tax System of Them All?" In Henry J. Aaron and William G. Gale (eds.), *Economic Effects of Fundamental Tax Reform*, pp. 355–84. Washington, D.C.: Brookings Institution Press.

1997. "Deconstructing the Income Tax." *American Economic Review* 87.2 (May): 151–5.

Slemrod, Joel, and Jon Bakija. 1996. *Taxing Ourselves: A Citizen's Guide to the Great Debate over Tax Reform*. Cambridge, Mass.: MIT Press.

Slemrod, Joel, and Marsha Blumenthal. 1996. "The Income Tax Compliance Cost of Big Business." *Public Finance Quarterly* 24.4 (October): 411–38.

Slemrod, Joel, and Roger H. Gordon. 1988. "Do We Collect Any Revenue from Taxing Capital Income?" In Lawrence H. Summers (ed.), *Tax Policy and the Economy*, 2:89–130. Cambridge, Mass.: National Bureau of Economic Research.

Slemrod, Joel, and Nikki Sorum. 1984. "The Compliance Cost of the U.S. Individual Income Tax System." *National Tax Journal* 37.4 (December): 461–74.

Slemrod, Joel, and Shlomo Yitzhaki. 2000. "Tax Avoidance, Evasion, and Administration." NBER Working Paper no. W7473, January. Cambridge, Mass.

Slemrod, Joel, Shlomo Yitzhaki, Joram Mayshar, and Michael Lundholm. 1994. "The Optimal Two-Bracket Linear Income Tax." *Journal of Public Economics* 53.2 (February): 269–90.

Solow, Robert M. 1994. "Perspectives on Growth Theory." *Journal of Economic Perspectives* 8.1 (Winter): 45–54.

Steuerle, C. Eugene. 1997. "Paying Taxpayers to File Electronic Returns." *Tax Notes* 77 (October 27): 477–78.

Strauss, Robert P. 1996. "The Effects of a Flat Federal Consumption Tax on the States." In Robert D. Ebel (ed.), *1995 Proceedings of the Eighty-Eighth Annual Conference on Taxation*, pp. 10–23. Columbus: National Tax Association–Tax Institute of America.

Summers, Lawrence H. 1981a. "Capital Taxation and Accumulation in a Life Cycle Growth Model." *American Economic Review* 74.4 (September): 533–44.

1981b. "Taxation and Investment: A Q-Theory Approach." *Brookings Papers on Economic Activity* 1:67–140.

Swedish Ministry of Finance. 1983. *Skall Matmomsen Slopas?* Stockholm: SOU 54.

Tait, Alan. 1988. *Value Added Tax: International Practice and Problems*. Washington, D.C.: International Monetary Fund.

Tanzi, Vito. 1995. *Taxation in an Integrating World*. Washington, D.C.: Brookings Institution Press.

Thalmann, Philippe, Lawrence H. Goulder, and François Delorme. 1996. "Assessing the International Spillover Effects of Capital Income Taxation." *International Tax and Public Finance* 3.4 (October): 449–77.

Triest, Robert K. 1996. "Fundamental Tax Reform and Labor Supply." In Henry J. Aaron and William G. Gale (eds.), *Economic Effects of Fundamental Tax Reform*, pp. 247–71. Washington, D.C.: Brookings Institution Press.

Ulbrich, Holley H. 1985. "State and Local Taxation of Interstate Mail Order Sales." Washington, D.C.: Advisory Commission on Intergovernmental Relations. Preliminary Draft.

United Nations. 1993. *System of National Accounts, 1993*. New York.

U.S. Bureau of the Census. 1994. "Income, Poverty and Valuation of Non-Cash Benefits." 1993. Current Population Reports, series P60-188. Washington, D.C.: U.S. Government Printing Office.

U.S. Department of the Treasury. 1977. *Blueprints for Basic Tax Reform*. Washington, D.C.: U.S. Government Printing Office. Also available as David F. Bradford, and the U.S. Treasury Tax Policy Staff, *Blueprints for Basic Tax Reform* (Arlington: Tax Analysts, 1984).

1984a. *Tax Reform for Fairness, Simplicity, and Economic Growth*. Washington, D.C.: U.S. Government Printing Office.

1984b. *Tax Reform for Fairness, Simplicity, and Economic Growth*. Vol. 1, *Overview*. Washington, D.C.: U.S. Government Printing Office.

1984c. *Tax Reform for Fairness, Simplicity, and Economic Growth*. Vol. 3, *Value-Added Tax*. Washington, D.C.: U.S. Government Printing Office.

1992. *Integration of the Individual and Corporate Tax Systems: Taxing Business Income Once*. Washington, D.C.: U.S. Government Printing Office.

U. S. Department of the Treasury, Office of Tax Analysis. 1996. "New Armey-Shelby Flat Tax Would Still Lose Money, Treasury Finds." *Tax Notes* 70 (January 22): 451–61.

Vaillancourt, François. 1989. *The Administrative and Compliance Costs of the Personal Income Tax and Payroll Tax System in Canada, 1986*. Toronto: Canadian Tax Foundation.

Wall Street Journal. 1997. "Departure Tax." February 5, p. A18.

Washington Post. 1993. "Canada's Value-Added Tax: A Cautionary Tale for Clinton." April 16, p. A6.

Wasylenko, Michael. 1997. "Taxation and Economic Development: The State of the Economic Literature." *New England Economic Review* (March–April): 36–52.

Weidenbaum, Murray. 1996. "The Nunn-Domenici USA Tax: Analysis and Comparisons." In Michael J. Boskin (ed.), *Frontiers of Tax Reform*, pp. 54–69. Stanford: Hoover Institution Press.

2000. "A Tax System for an E-Commerce Economy." In Washington University, Center for the Study of American Business, *Policy Brief* 205, June. St. Louis, Mo.

Weisbach, David A. 1999. "Implementing the Flat Tax." University of Chicago Law School. Mimeograph.

Whalley, John. 1990. "Foreign Responses to U.S. Tax Reform." In Joel Slemrod (ed.), *Do Taxes Matter? The Impact of the Tax Reform Act of 1986*, pp. 286–314. Cambridge, Mass.: MIT Press.

Wilcoxen, Peter J. 1992. "An Introduction to Intertemporal Modeling." In Peter B. Dixon, Brian R. Parmenter, Alan A. Powell, and Peter J. Wilcoxen (eds.), *Notes and Problems in Applied General Equilibrium Economics*, pp. 277–84. Amsterdam: North-Holland.

Wilkins, John G. (Coopers & Lybrand). 1997. "Dynamic Revenue Estimating: Can It Work? Simulations of the Effects of Three Alternative Tax Systems." In *Joint Committee on Taxation Tax Modeling Project and 1997 Tax Symposium Papers*, pp. 270–84. Washington, D.C.: U.S. Government Printing Office.

Willis, Lynda D. 1997. "Taxpayer Compliance: Analyzing the Nature of the Income Tax Gap." Testimony before the National Commission on Restructuring the Internal Revenue Service, GAO/T-GGD-97-35, January 9.

Wolff, Edward N. 1995. *Top Heavy: A Study of the Increasing Inequality of Wealth in America*. New York: Twentieth Century Fund Press.

Zimmerman, Dennis. 1995. "Consumption Taxes and State-Local Tax Systems." Congressional Research Service Report for Congress no. 95-1150E, November 29. Washington, D.C.: Library of Congress.

Zodrow, George R. 1981. "Implementing Tax Reform." *National Tax Journal* 34.4 (December): 401–18.

1985. "Optimal Tax Reform in the Presence of Adjustment Costs." *Journal of Public Economics* 27.2 (July): 211–30.

1988. "The Windfall Recapture Tax: Issues of Theory and Design." *Public Finance Quarterly* 16.4 (October): 387–424.

1991. "On the 'Traditional' and 'New' Views of Dividend Taxation." *National Tax Journal* 44.4 (December): 497–509.

1992. "Grandfather Rules and the Theory of Optimal Tax Reform." *Journal of Public Economics* 49.2 (November): 163–90.

1995. "Taxation, Uncertainty and the Choice of a Consumption Tax Base." *Journal of Public Economics* 58.2 (October): 257–65.

1997a. "On the Transition to Indirect or Direct Consumption-Based Taxation." In Richard Krever (ed.), *Tax Conversations: A Guide to the Key Issues in the Tax Reform Debate. Essays in Honour of John G. Head*, pp. 27–59. London: Kluwer Law International.

1997b. "Reflections on the Consumption Tax Option." In John G. Head and Richard Krever (eds.), *Taxation Towards 2000*, pp. 45–79. Melbourne: Australian Tax Research Foundation.

1999a. "The Sales Tax, the VAT, and Taxes in between – Or, Is the Only Good NRST and 'VAT in Drag?'" *National Tax Journal* 53.3 (September): 429–42.

1999b. *State Sales and Income Taxes: An Economic Analysis*, no. 15. College Station: Texas A&M University Press.

Zodrow, George R., and Charles E. McLure Jr. 1991. "Implementing Direct Consumption Taxes in Developing Countries." *Tax Law Review* 46 (Summer): 407–87.

Zodrow, George R., and Michael F. Williams. 1998. "Intergenerational Transitional Issues in the Implementation of a National Retail Sales Tax." Rice University. Manuscript.

Index

337

multinational companies
  interest-allocation tax rules,
    117–19
  tax credits for foreign-source income,
    110–13, 115–17
  tax deferral, 113–15
  tax treatment of foreign-source income,
    113–19
  under territorial tax system, 120–1
  transfer pricing to avoid tax, 116–23
  under U.S. interest-allocation rules,
    117–19
Murray, Matthew N., 237
Mutti, John, 116

national retail sales tax (NRST)
  administration and compliance under,
    196–8, 235–42
  capital income tax treatment under, 93,
    258–9
  capital levy in implementation of, 251–3
  complexity of, 198–200
  costs of proposed hybrid system, 204–5
  differences from VAT, 216, 235, 242–3
  economic effects of, 216
  effect of implementation on price level,
    248–9
  effects of implementation of, 263–6
  estimated compliance cost of, 12–14
  estimates of tax rates under, 13–14
  exemptions under, 225–35, 243–4
  IRS would be abolished under, 303
  political feasibility of, 291
  potential for transition relief under, 274
  proponents of, 19
  proposal for, 2, 56, 119, 247
  Republican plan for, 303–4
  Schaefer-Tauzin, 197–8, 247
  simulation of economic impact of
    proposed, 70–88
  state-level administration of, 203
  taxation of foreign source income
    under, 8
  tax base compared to VAT base, 223–5
  tax burden distribution under, 216
  tax collection under, 70
  tax evasion under, 199–203
  uniform taxation under, 223–31
  See also retail sales tax (RST)
Neumark Committee (1963), 221
Ng Pin, 167
Nunn, Sam, 2, 119
Nunns, James, 156

Obstfeld, Maurice, 126
"old" capital, 62, 96, 101, 246, 261, 265–8
  See also capital stock; elderly people

Organisation for Economic Cooperation
  and Development (OECD), 204, 287
output
  in infinite-horizon models, 37
  in intertemporal models, 34
  in life-cycle models, 37
  in reduced-form models, 27–32, 34, 38,
    45–6
  with shift to consumption-based tax,
    26–8

Palumbo, Michael, 10–12, 204–5, 216, 227,
    237, 260
Payne, James L., 187–9
Pearlman, Ronald A., 209–10, 246, 248,
    270–2, 281
personal consumption tax (PCT), 147
Poddar, Satya, 230n24
Pogue, Thomas, 156n11
political debate, 17–21, 272–3, 294–308
Poterba, James, 52, 125, 129, 154, 157, 207,
    227
producer goods
  dual-use under NRST and VAT, 232–4
  in RST state-level tax base, 232

Quadrini, Vincenzo, 107

Rabushka, Alvin, 1, 119, 205, 211, 245, 248,
    255, 279, 296, 299
reduced-form models
  with full employment, 45–6
  with unemployment, 29–31
Republicans
  conservatism of, 300–1
  political advantage in fundamental tax
    reform, 303
  promotion of Hall-Rabushka flat tax
    proposal, 296–7
  promotion of NRST proposal, 296–7
  support for consumption-based
    taxation, 301–2
Reschovsky, Andrew, 154n9
retail sales tax (RST)
  Canada, 216, 218, 220, 222
  factors determining choice of, 221–3
  Group of Seven (G-7) experience with,
    217–21
  potential for national-level, 243
  state-level in United States, 29, 218–19,
    232, 291
return to capital
  burden of consumption tax on, 145–7
  taxation under consumption tax reform,
    97
  taxation under income tax reform, 97
  tax on inframarginal, 93–4